BORROWED TIME

BORROWED TIME
CALGARY 1976–2019

GEORGE WEBBER

FOREWORD BY WILL FERGUSON

RMB

Borrowed Time is dedicated to my mom, Del Webber.
This year marks the centenary of her birth on November 30, 1921.

Many thanks to Glenbow and especially to Manager of Collections Daryl Betenia
for the generous support and encouragement over many years.
All of the photographs in this book reside in Glenbow's collection.

Special thanks to Publisher Don Gorman and Art Director Chyla Cardinal of RMB.
This is the sixth book that we have done together.
Every one of them has been a blessing.

FOREWORD

When my oldest son moved to the West Coast, I took him for a farewell coffee and banana cream pie at Calgary's Blackfoot Diner. He doesn't like banana cream pie – no one does – but that's not the point. I wanted him to remember a different Calgary, one far from the curtain-of-glass skylines and suburban sprawl. Not a hidden Calgary, not exactly, because it has always been there in front of us, if we look.

George Webber has been looking, capturing and chronicling this Calgary for 45 years. It's a Calgary of faded storefronts and hotel rooms, of Legion halls and billiard balls, of shuttered storefronts in various stages of decay, of boarded-up bungalows awaiting the wrecking ball.

This remarkable collection runs from the punk-hair mohawks of the 1970s to the pale goth roller-girls of later years, as the black-and-white images give way to splashes of colour just as surely as Stampede Wrestling gives way to the Calgary Stampede: garish cotton-candy pinks and Tilt-a-Whirl rides, the gaping mouth of a plastic clown, a happy receptacle for our garbage. It is a credit to the singular talent of Webber that he makes such kitsch appear poignant and haunting.

He finds beauty in rust and weeds; the corroded hood of an abandoned car with wildflowers reaching out reads like a visual haiku. A still-life study of a ketchup bottle and five-dollar bills becomes a Rothko arrangement of red and blue, set against the metallic grey of unpolished silverware. Whether it's the darkening sky over a trailer park or the snow globe composition of a yellow taxi, luminous amid the storm, stabs of colour punctuate these photos. Pawnshops and bottle depots glow as though lit from within, suggesting a rich inner life, just as sunlight through the beer bottles on a tavern table creates accidental chandeliers.

In the world of George Webber, light both reveals and conceals details; it can create halos and ethereal haze, but can just as often be stark, sharp, sudden. It softens features, but also throws into relief the lines in a face.

Here are the bruised and the broken, the lost and the lonely: vignettes frozen in time, those in-between moments of weariness and doubt and quiet desperation. A priest sits lost in thought in front of a framed picture we cannot see; the glaring light has obliterated it – or perhaps the frame was empty all along.

The craggy face of an Old Testament prophet in a stained Santa beard stares out at us with misaligned eyes in front of a pair of dartboards, as though he himself were a human target.

An elderly man stands at a washbasin alongside an array of corner-curling Sunshine Girls, clipped and plastered on the tiled walls, the glamour shots to a most unglamourous backdrop. Here is that gap, so often explored by

Webber, between what is peddled and what is lived, with the airbrushed models juxtaposed against the grit of the here-and-now. "All that Glitters is Gold" proclaims the billboard above a scene that is neither glittering nor gold: a brick wall and a weathered fence with loose slats. But there is another elegy folded within that scene, for the billboard itself is now faded, an advertisement for Kodak film, long gone as well. A eulogy for an elegy.

Webber has the uncanny ability to capture entire stories in a single frame: a girl in camouflage kisses a shirtless man who, in turn, keeps a careful grip on the wallet in his back pocket. Their faces are turned away from the camera, but that moment contains multitudes.

In the visual clamour of the Ranchman's saloon, redolent of the sawdust and line dancers inside, an insidious glimpse of the Golden Arches pokes through, a reminder that the Ranchman's itself has been swallowed up by the developments along Macleod Trail. The Blackfoot Truck Stop where I said goodbye to my son appears as well, muted in the magic hour.

The devil is in the details, but so are angels, fallen and otherwise. A handwritten lament, at once intimate and public, proclaims "I Miss You Miranda." In the end, time is always borrowed, and this book is ultimately a lover's lament for a city that is shedding its past like slats in a fence. It is a message written in light across the years: I miss you.

—Will Ferguson
July 18, 2021

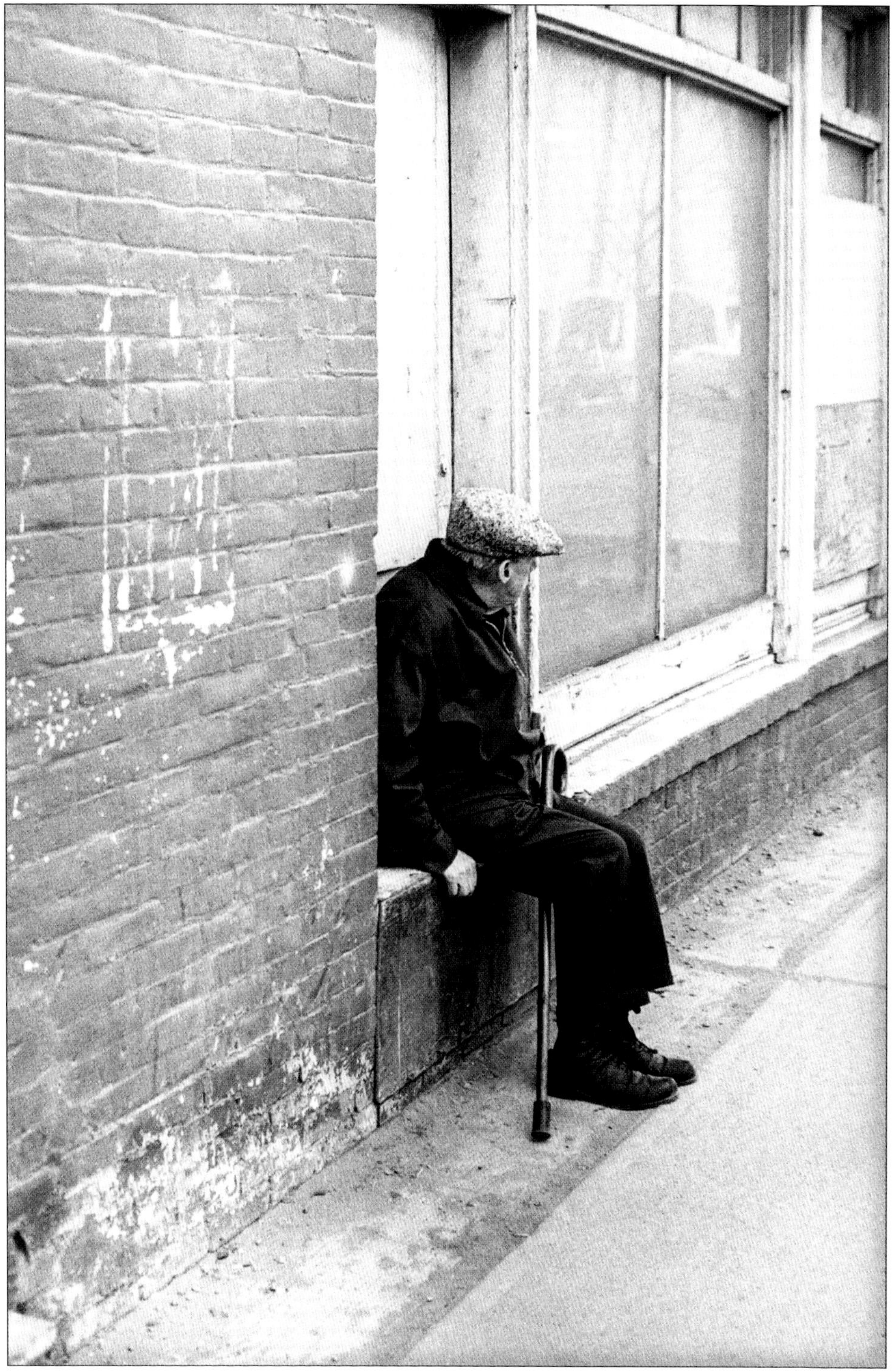

Man With Cane, 1976

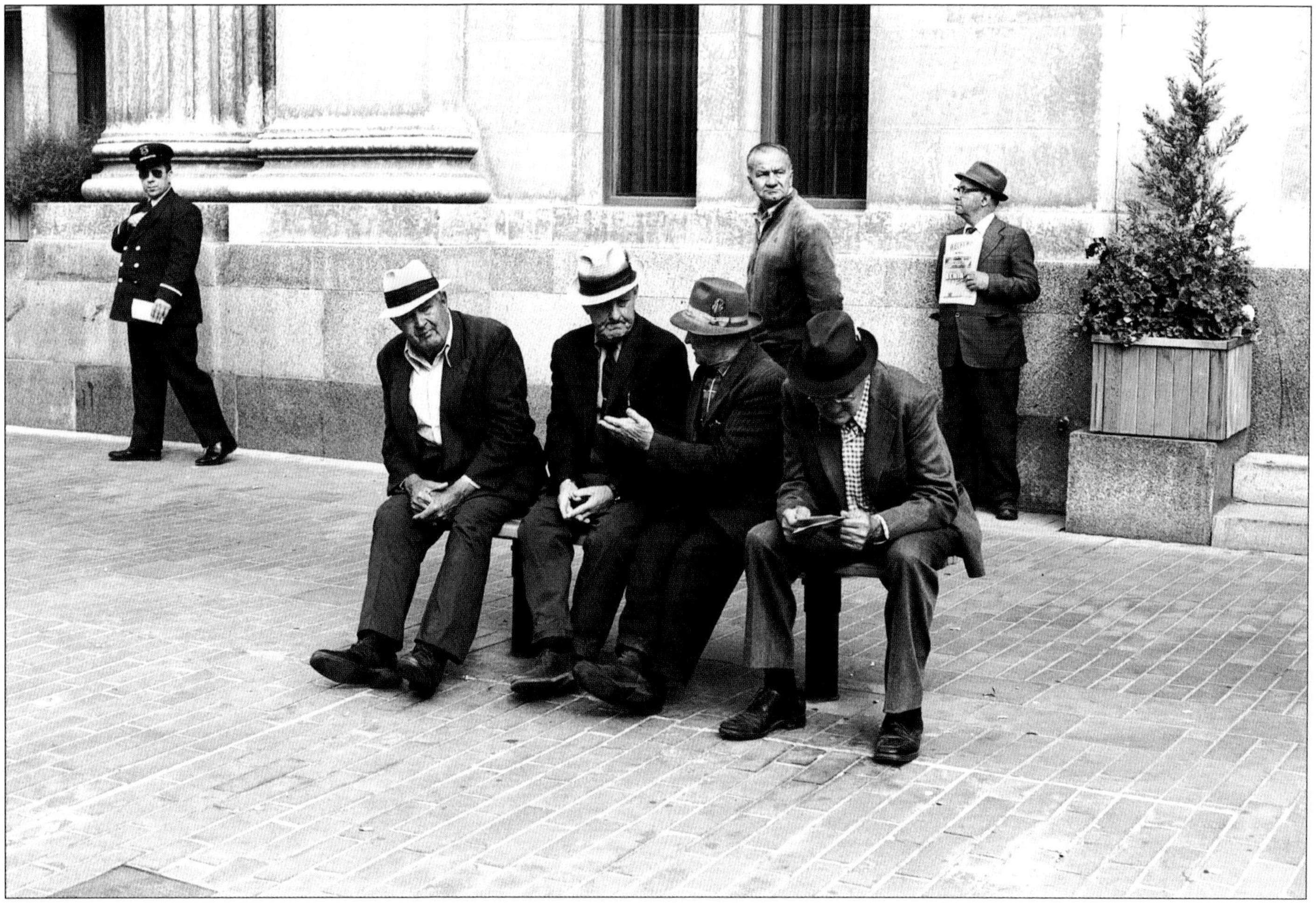

Men on Bench, 1976

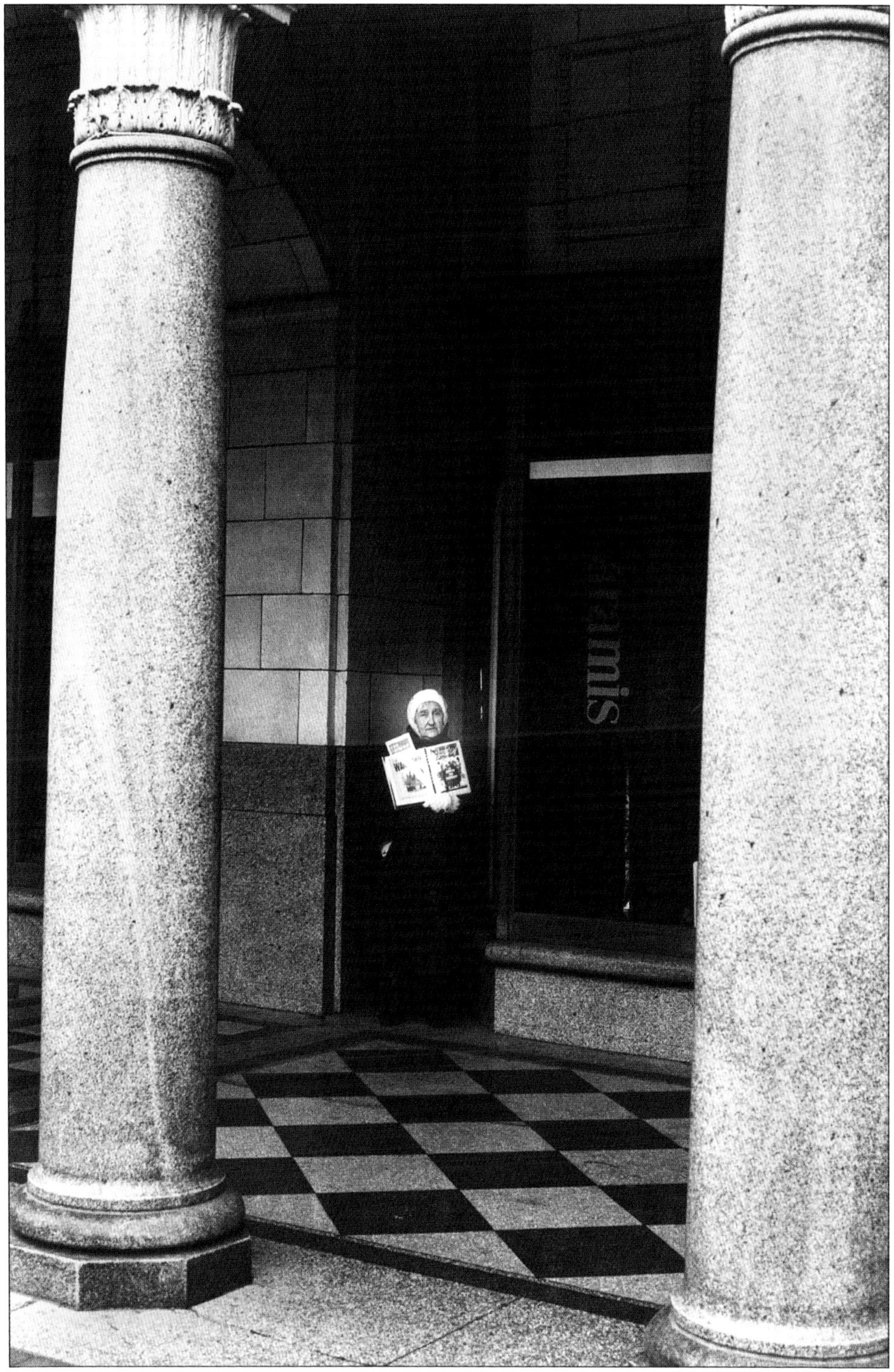

Watchtower woman, 1976

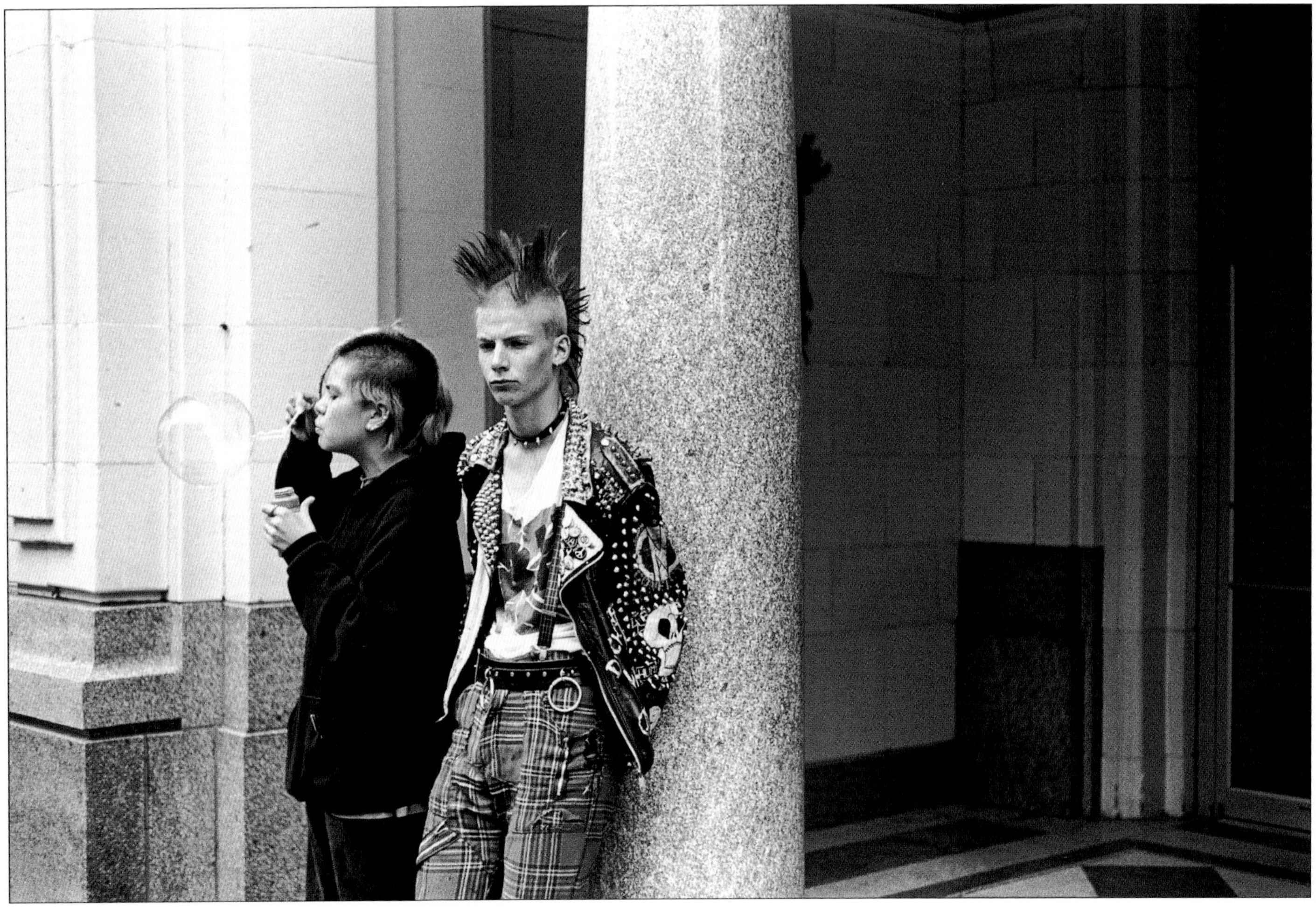

Scuzz and Alexis, 1992

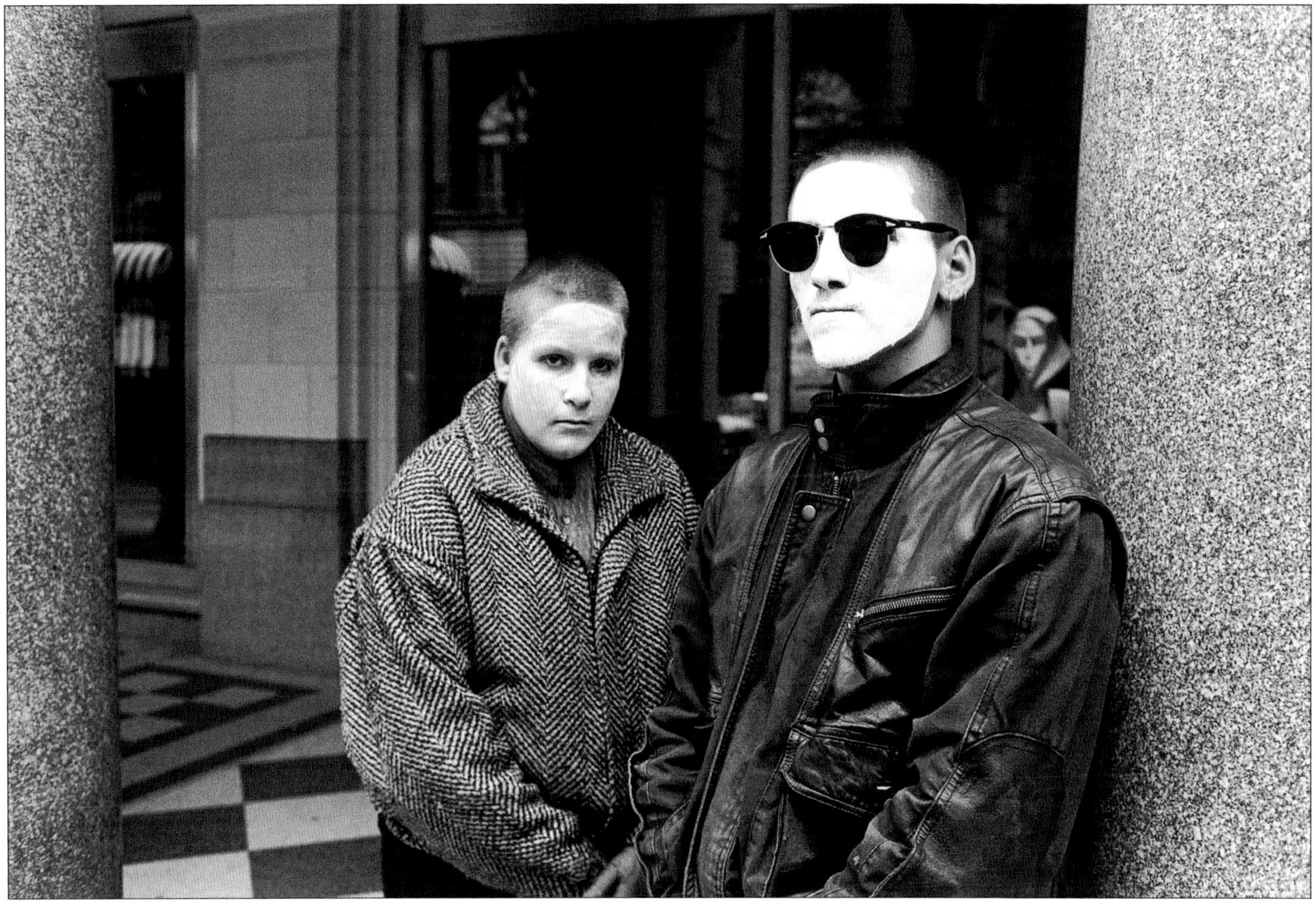

Two young men, 1991

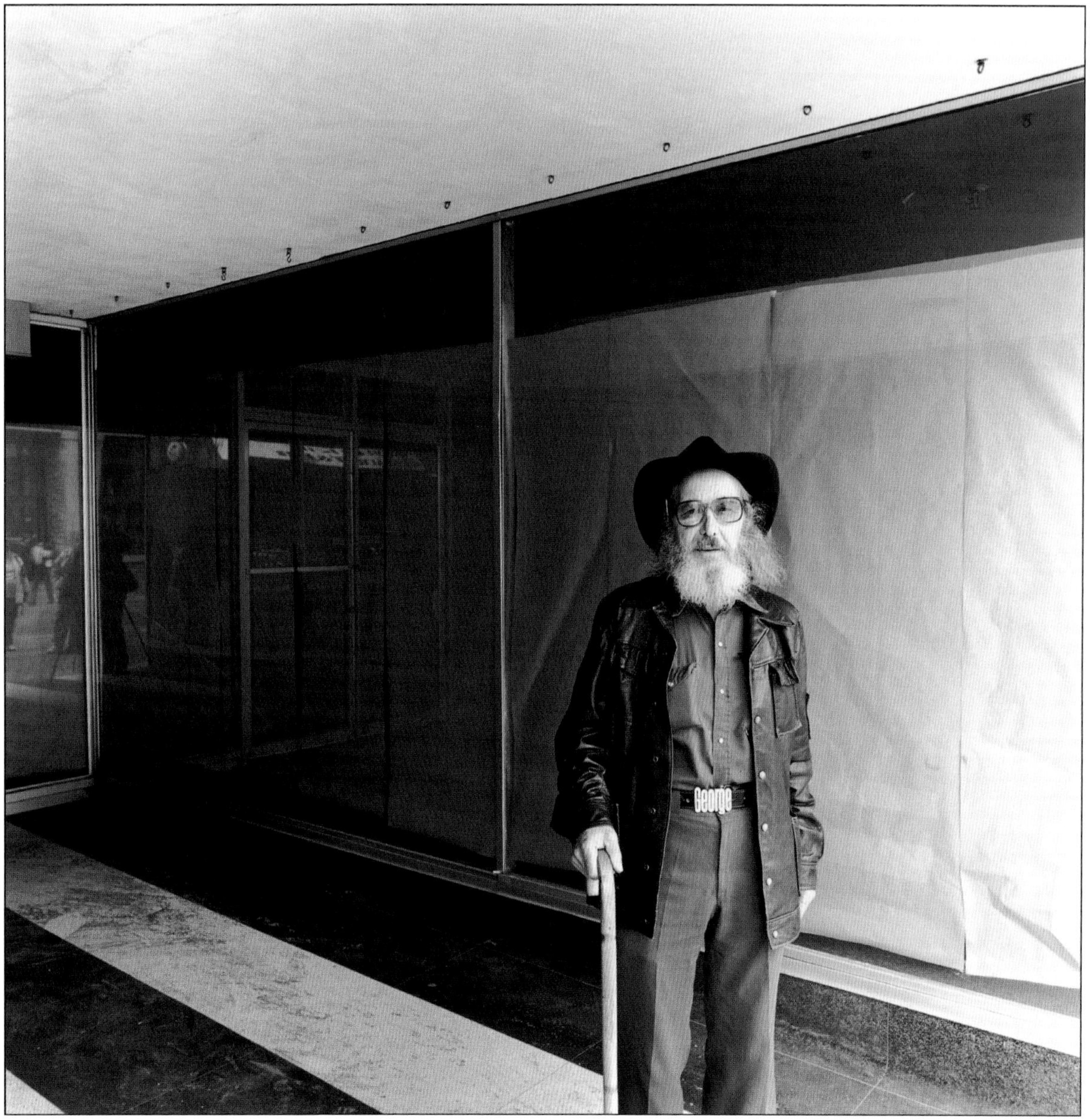

George Kiemele, 1994

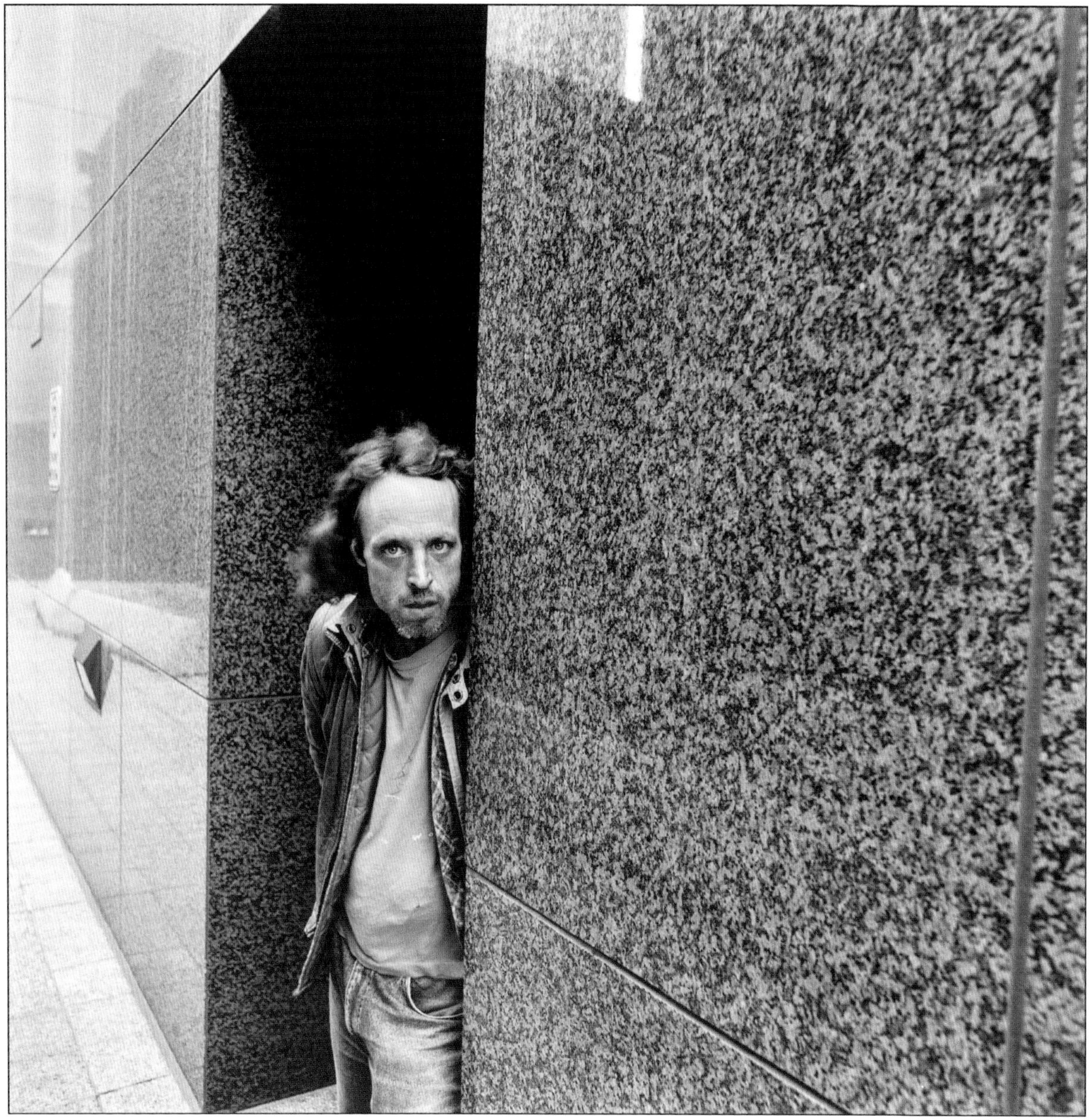

DV, 1994

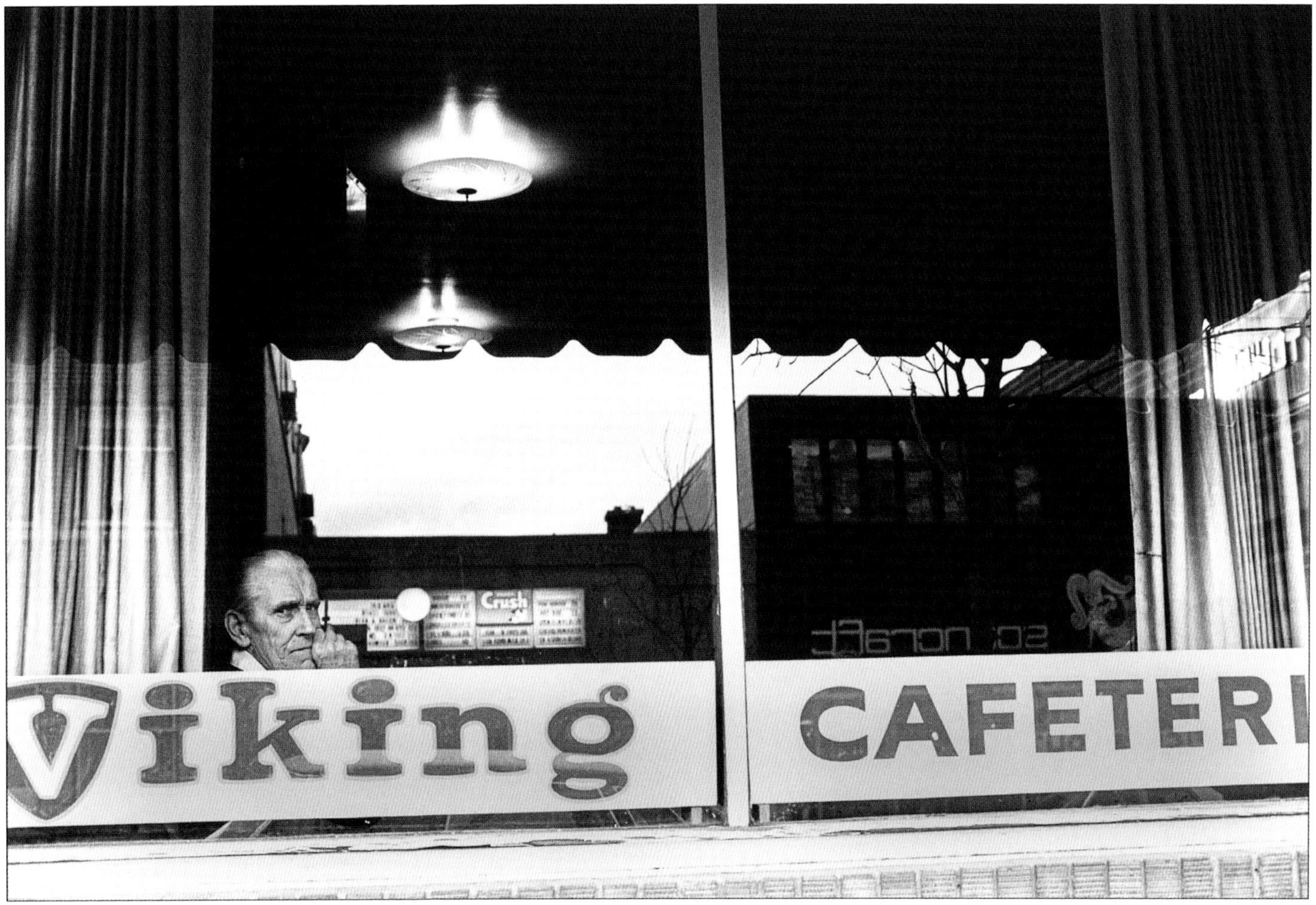

Viking Cafeteria, 1977

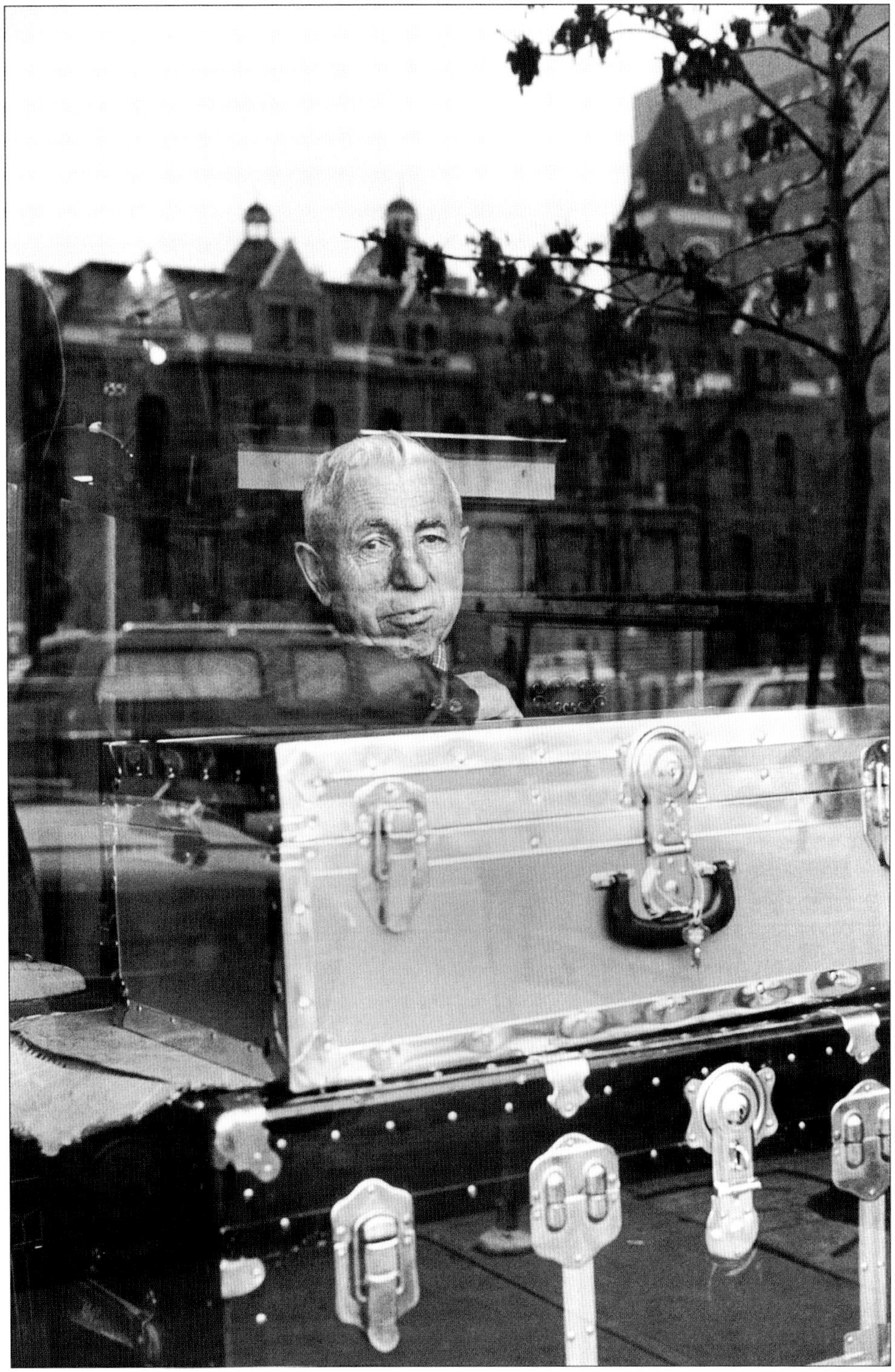

Mr. Aizanman, 1977

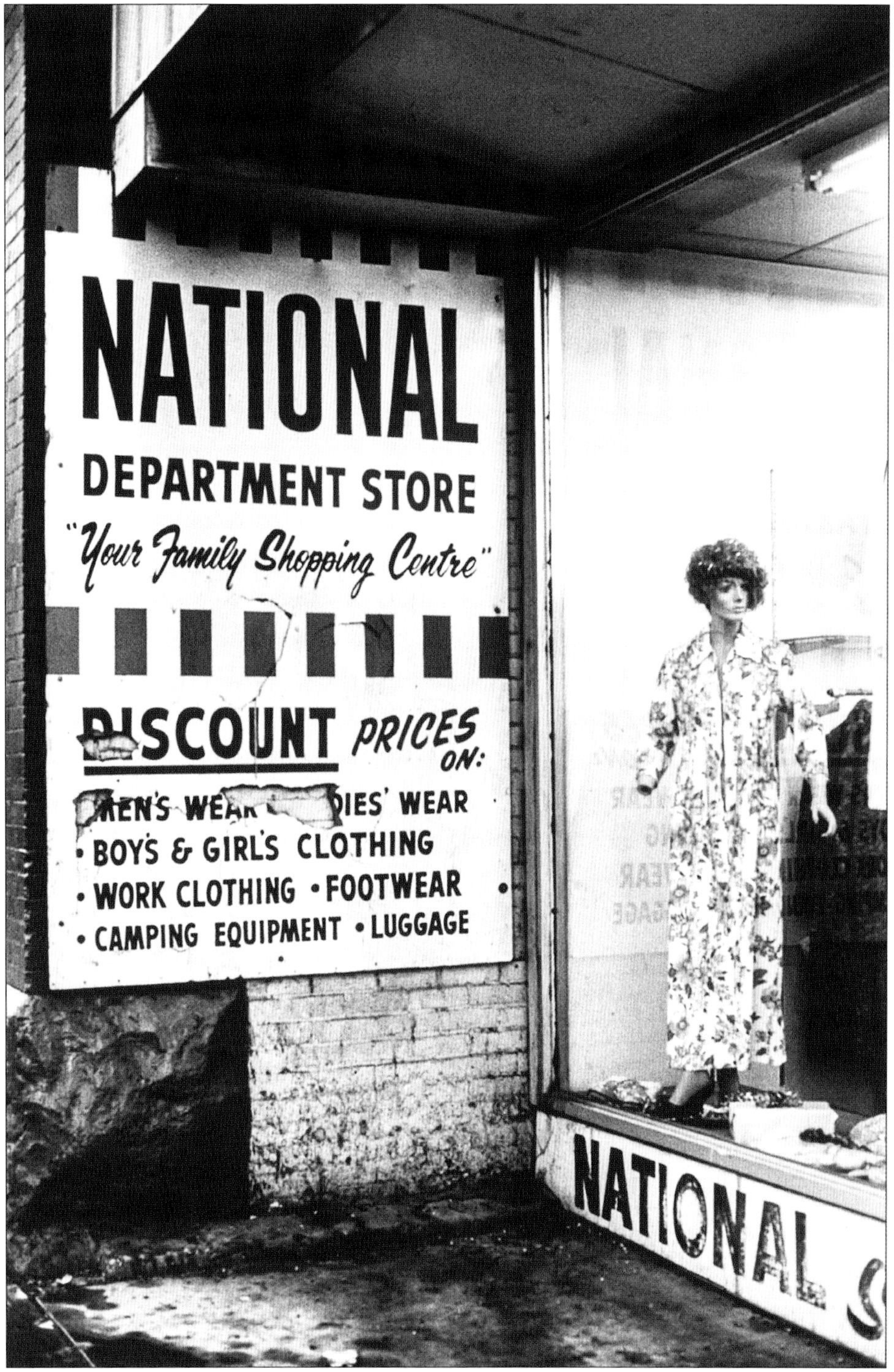

National Department Store, 1977

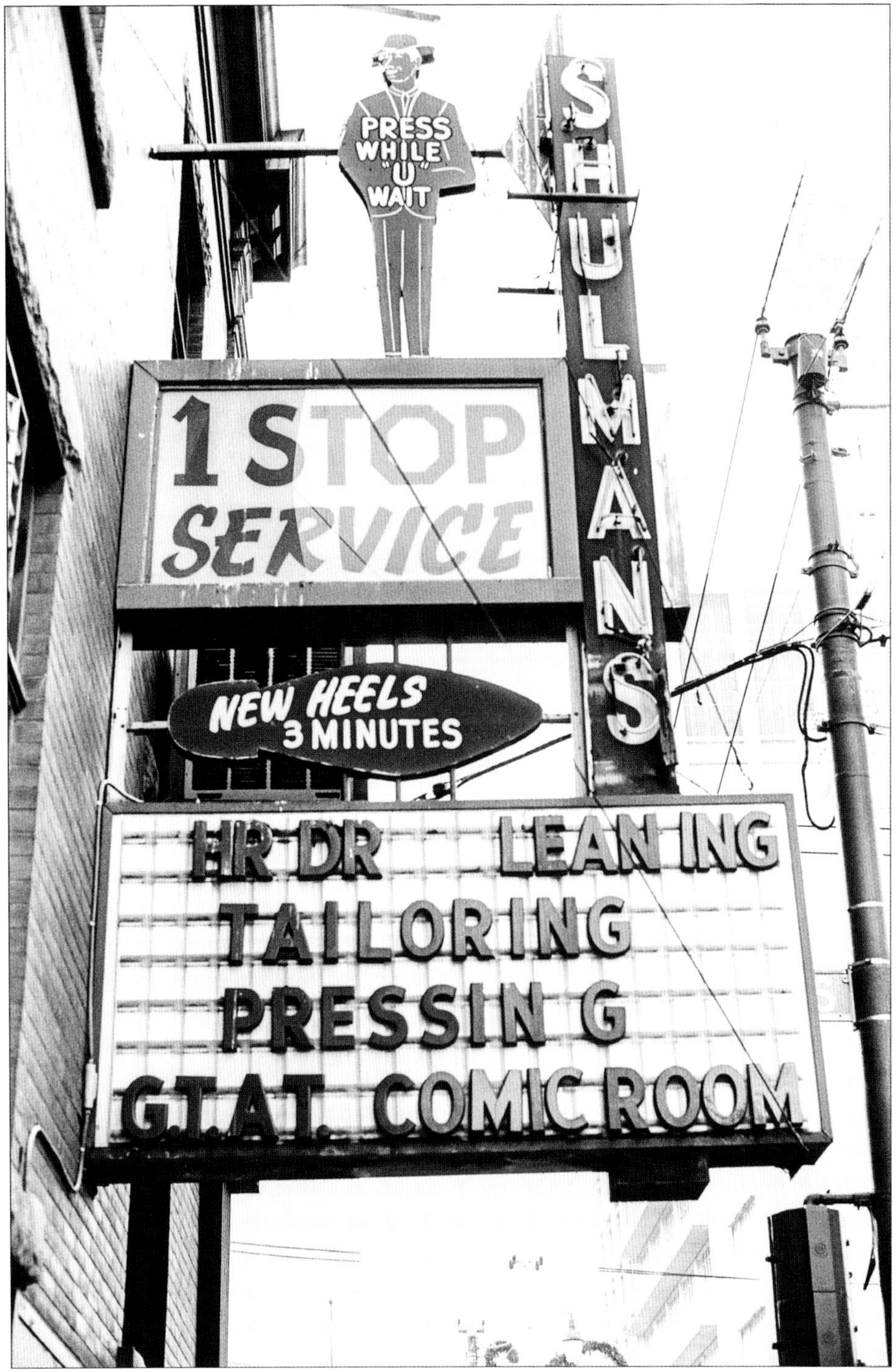

Shulman's, 1977

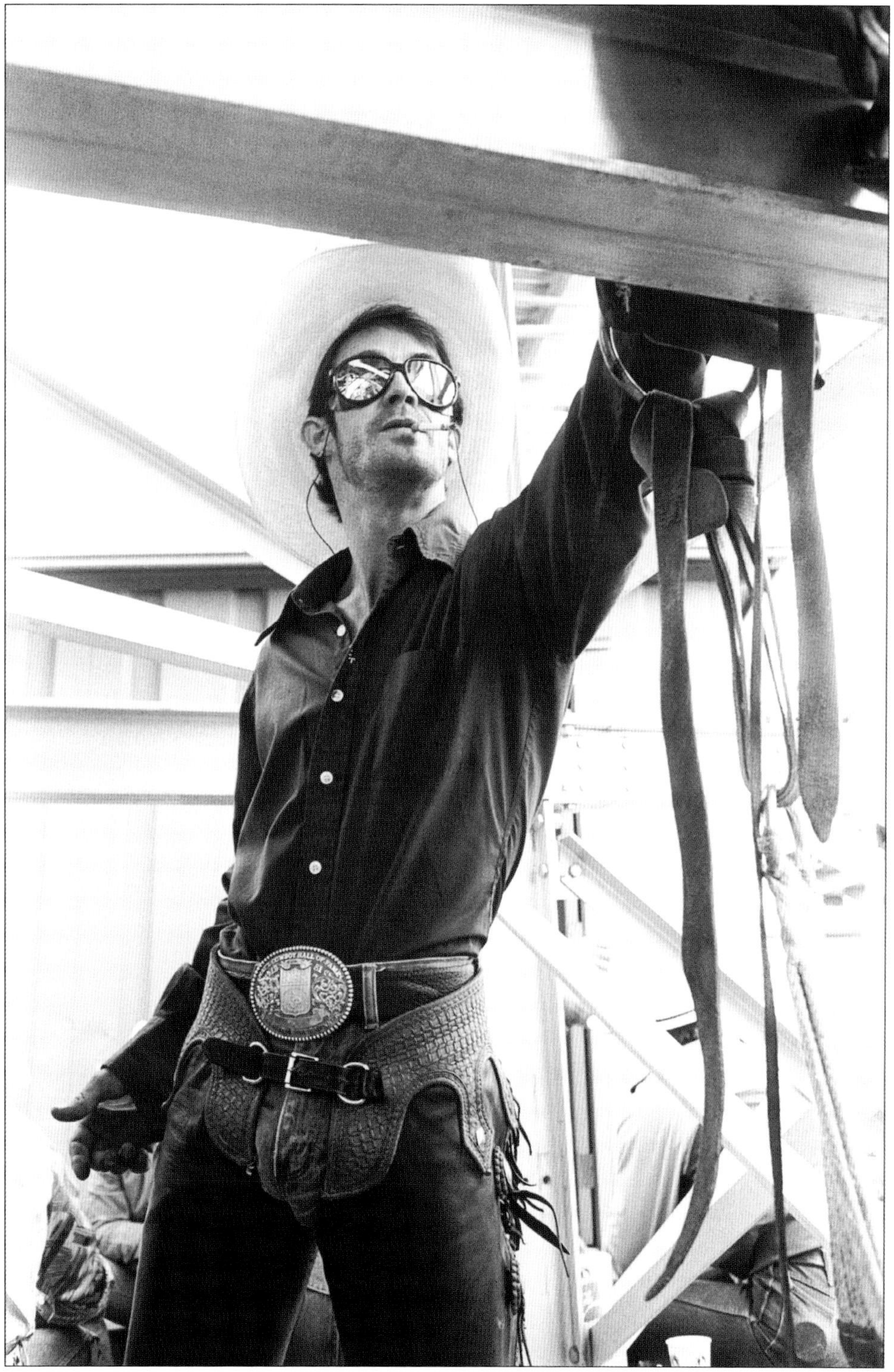

Stampede, 1982

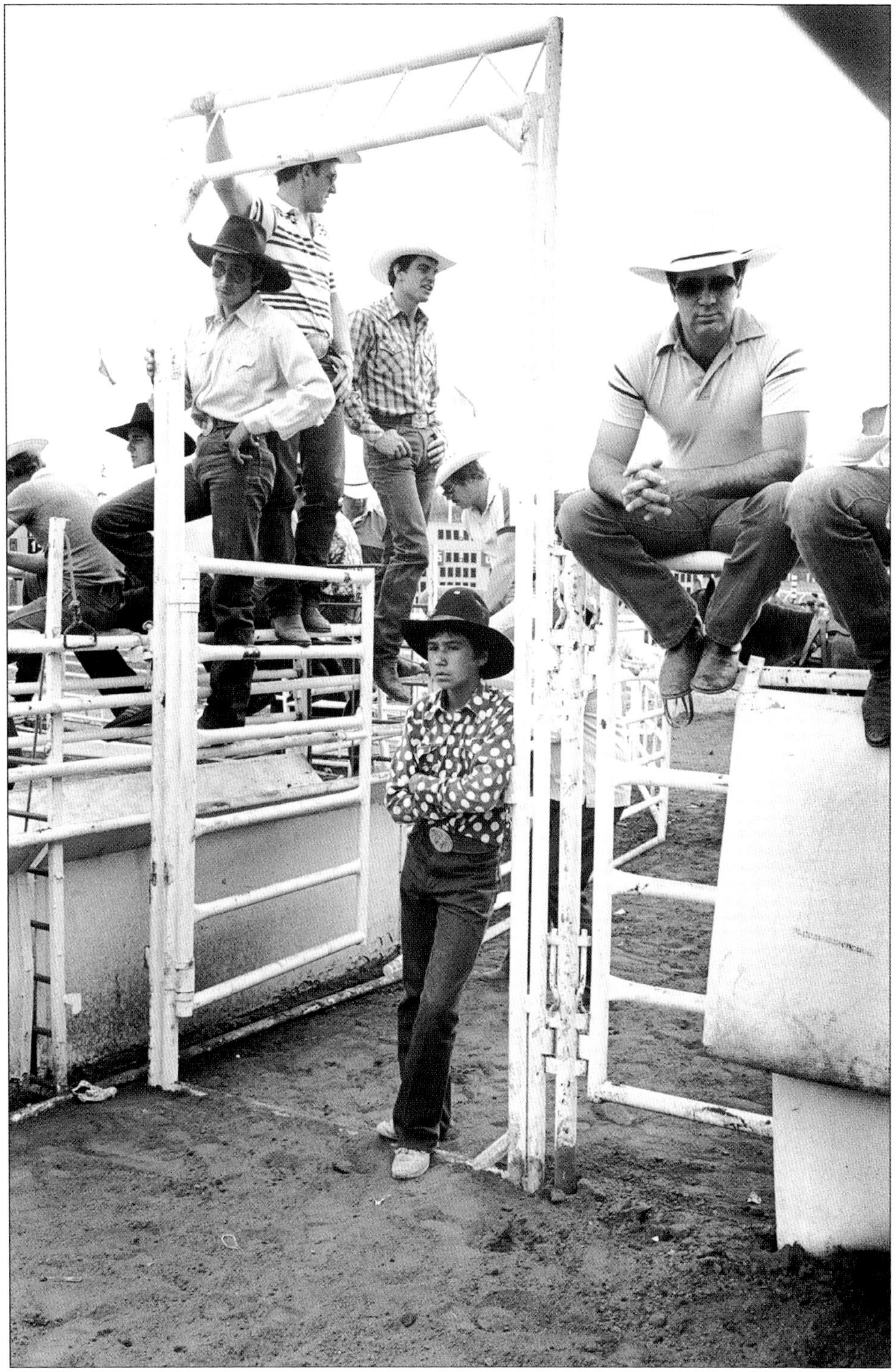

Stampede, 1982

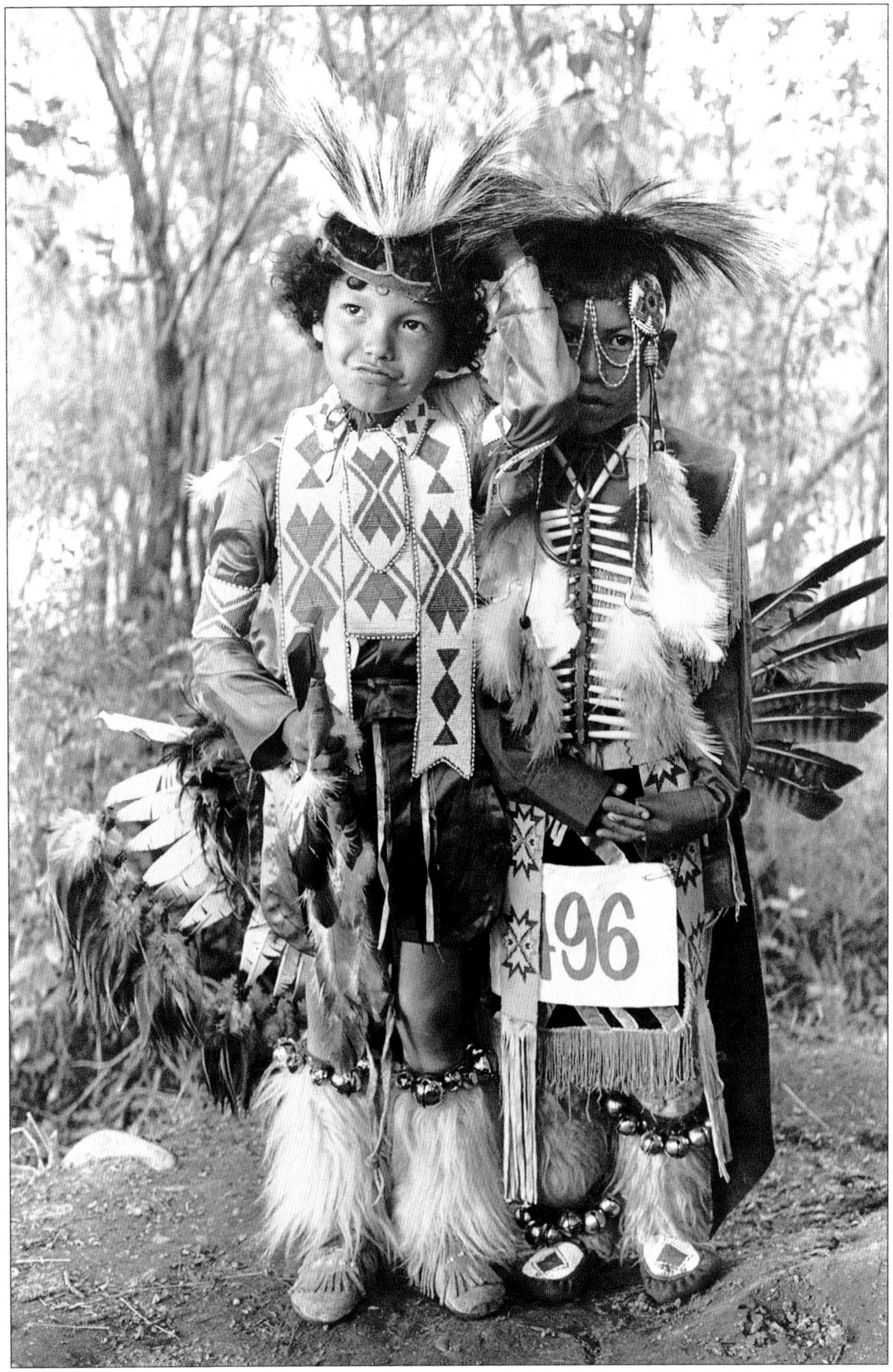

Stampede, 1982

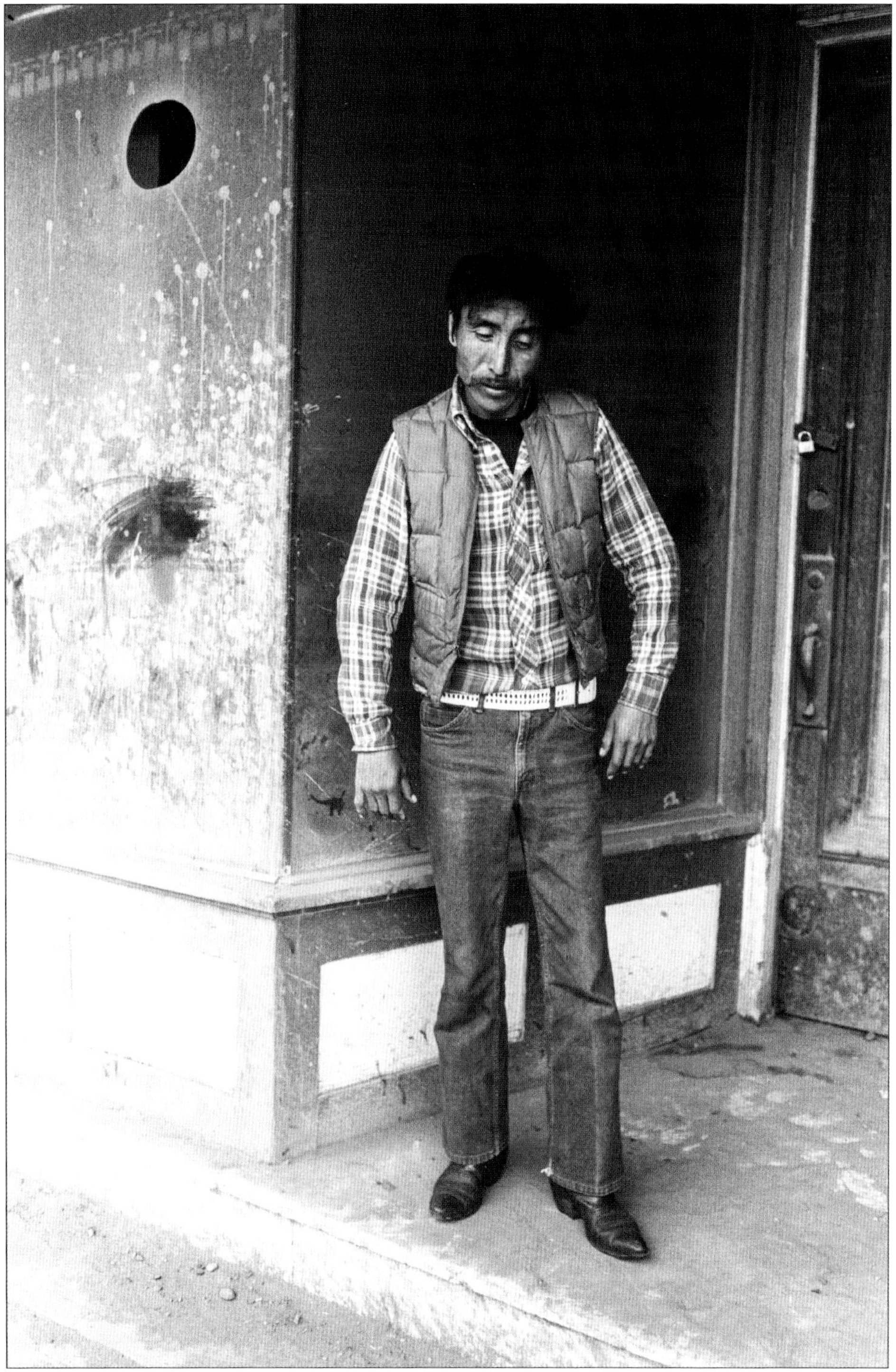

First Nations man, 1983

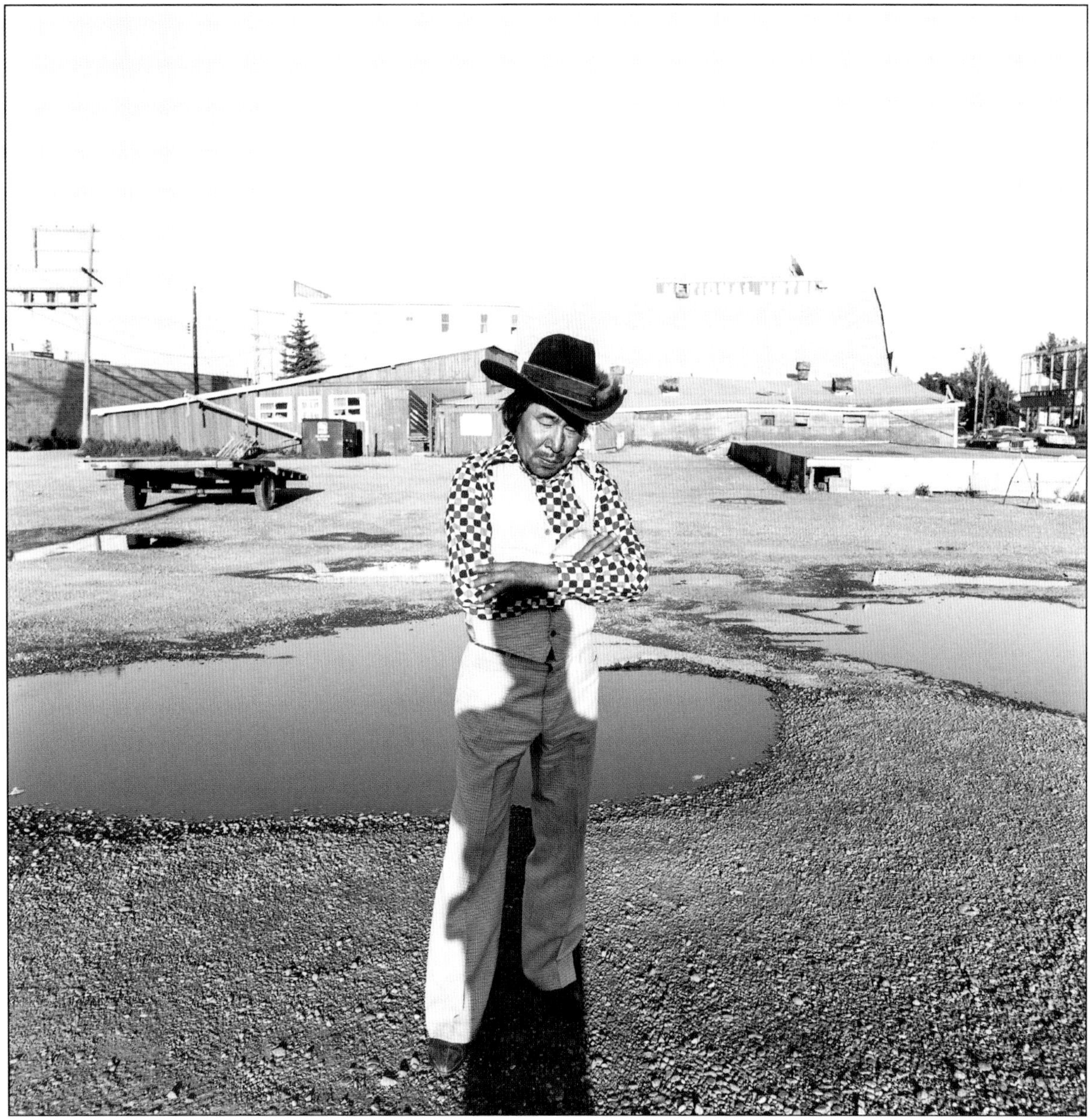

Danny Frazer, 1985

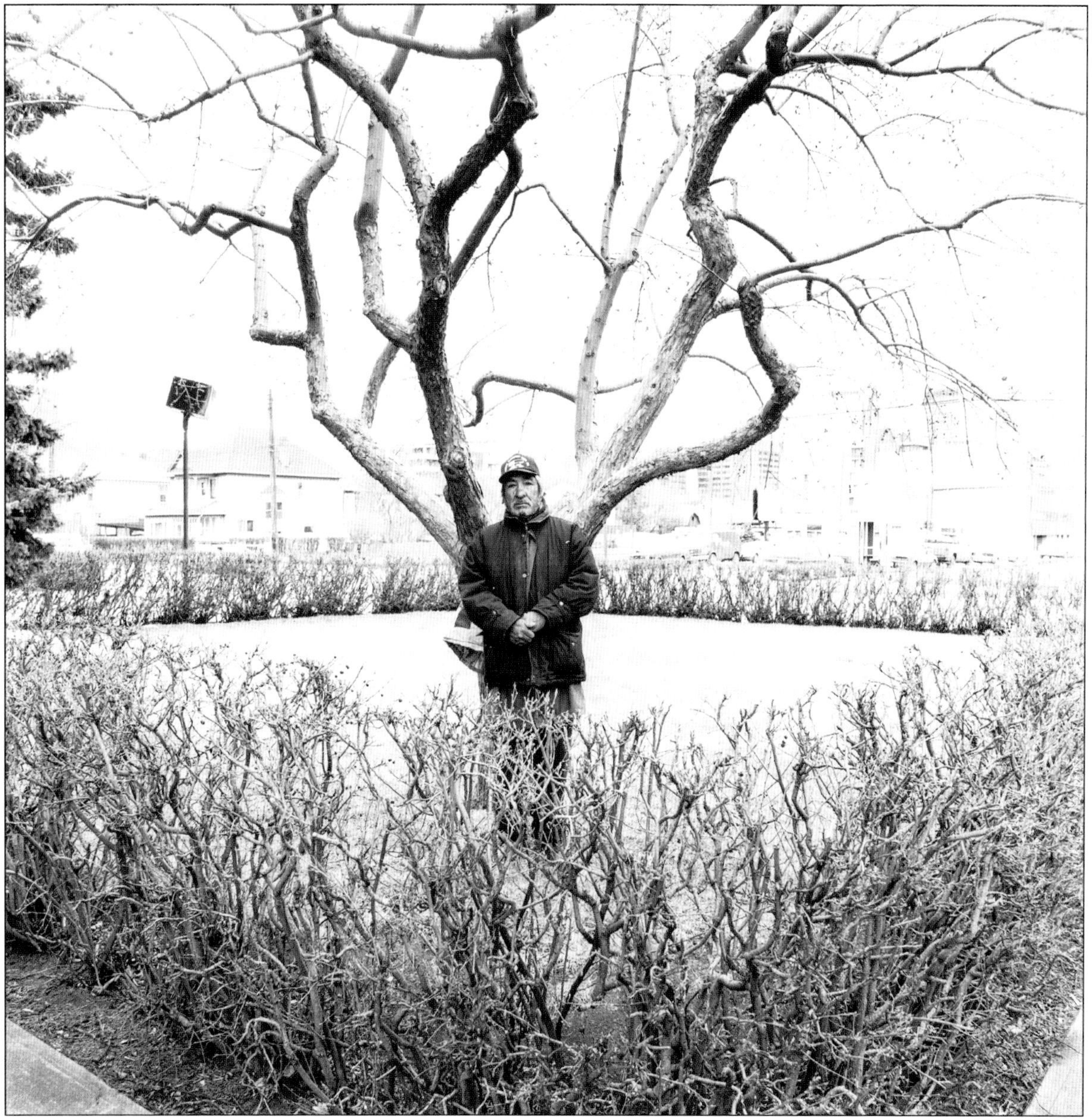

Solomon Many Shots, 1994

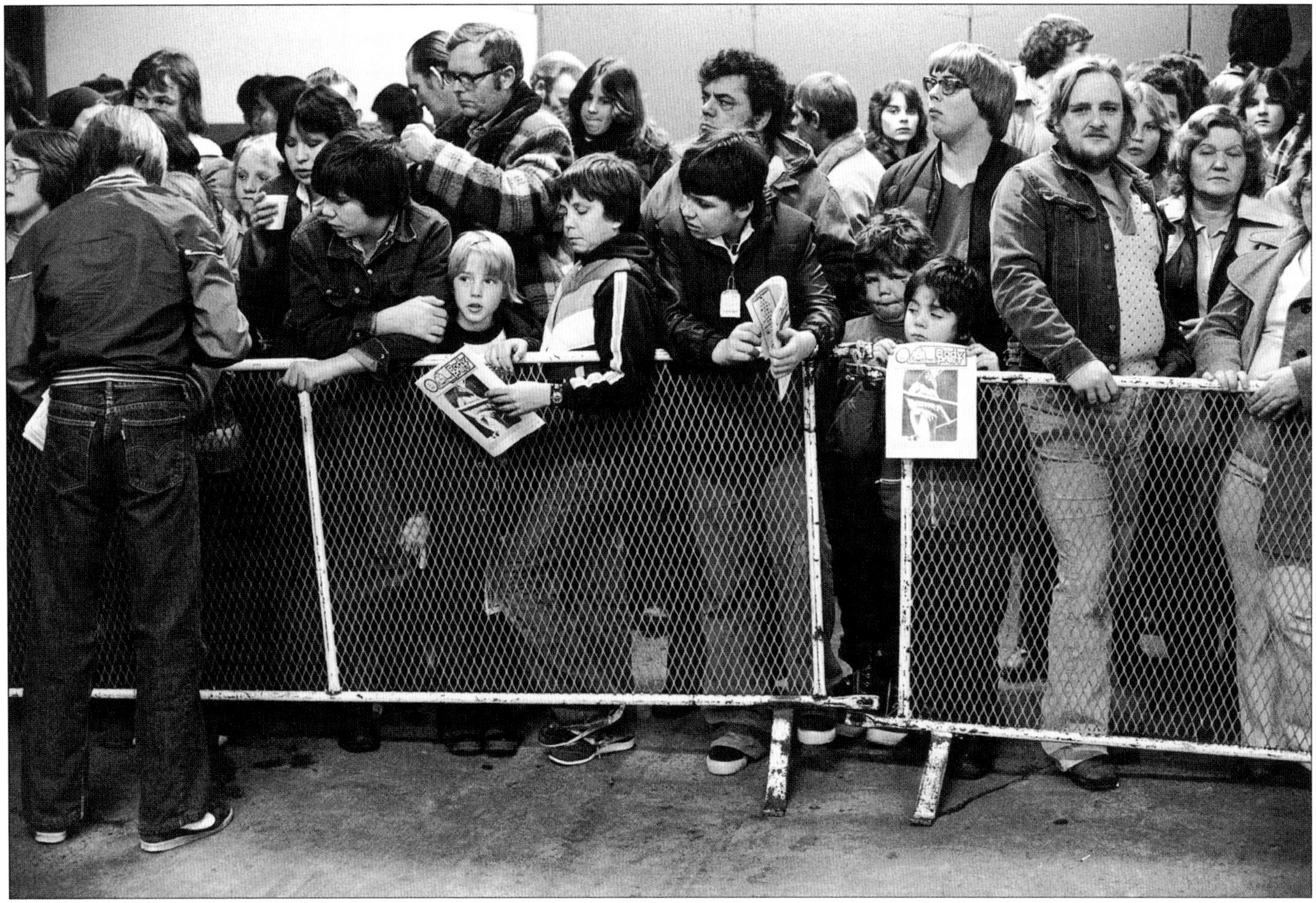

Victoria Pavilion, 1980

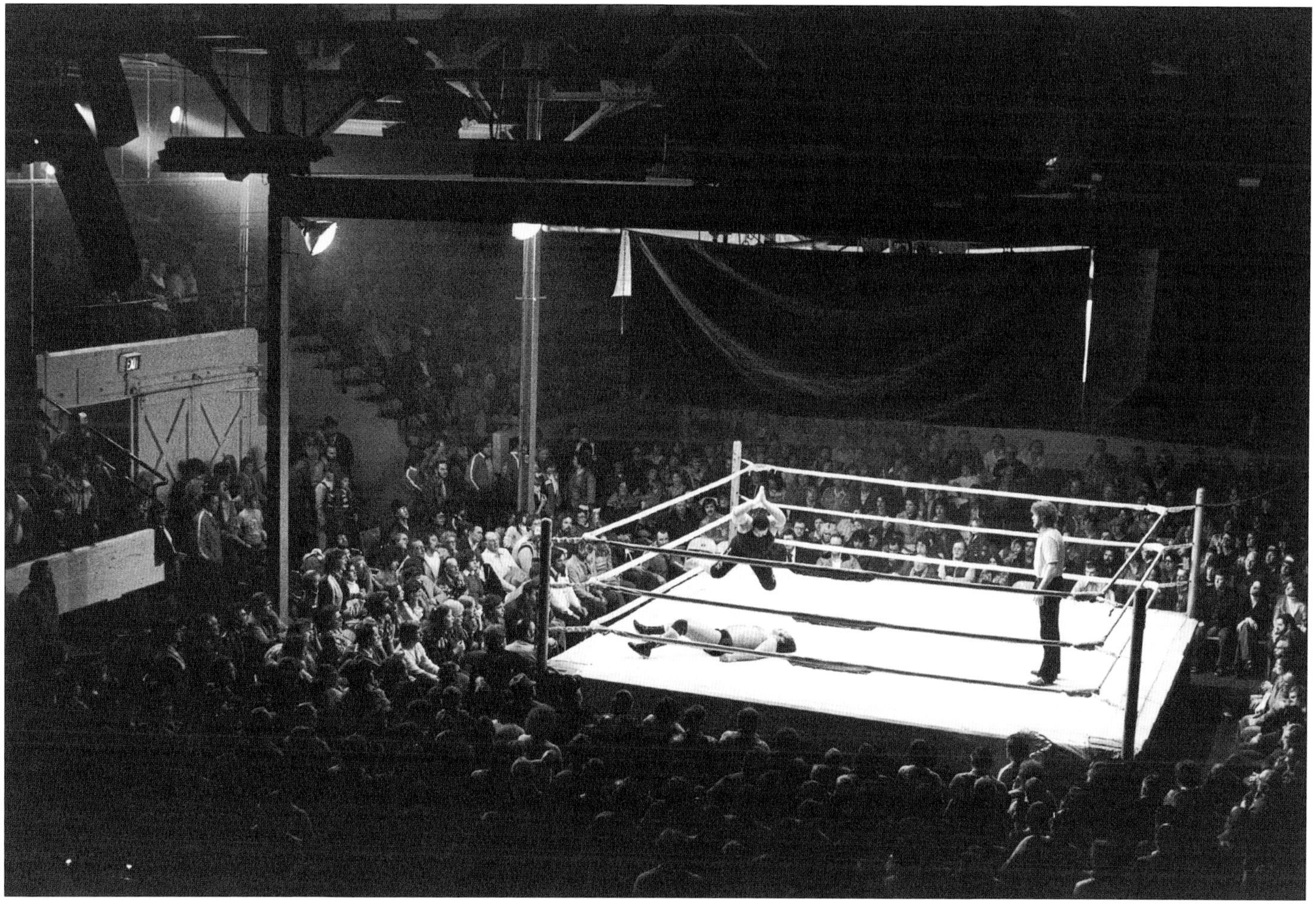

Victoria Pavilion, 1980

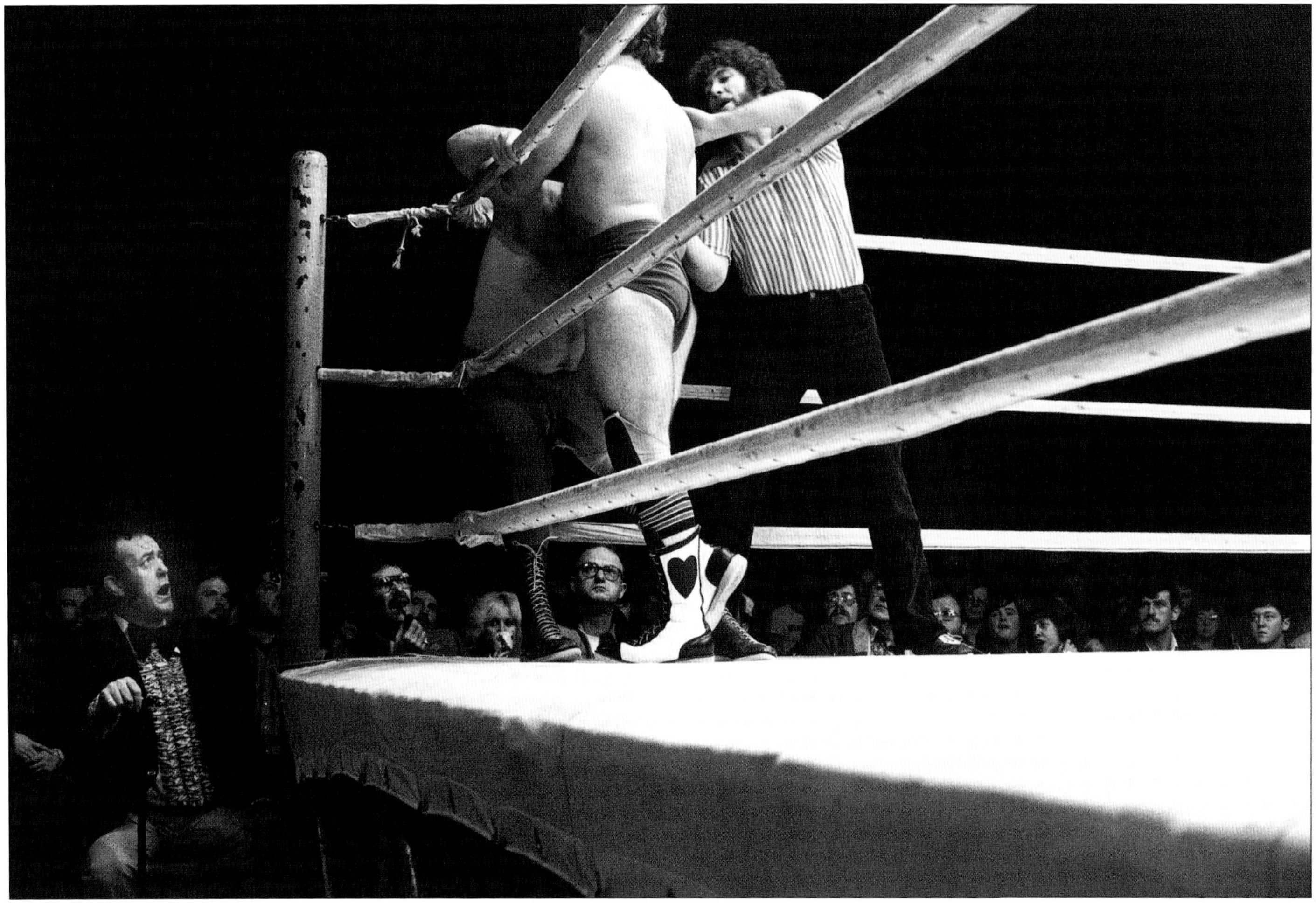

Victoria Pavilion, 1980

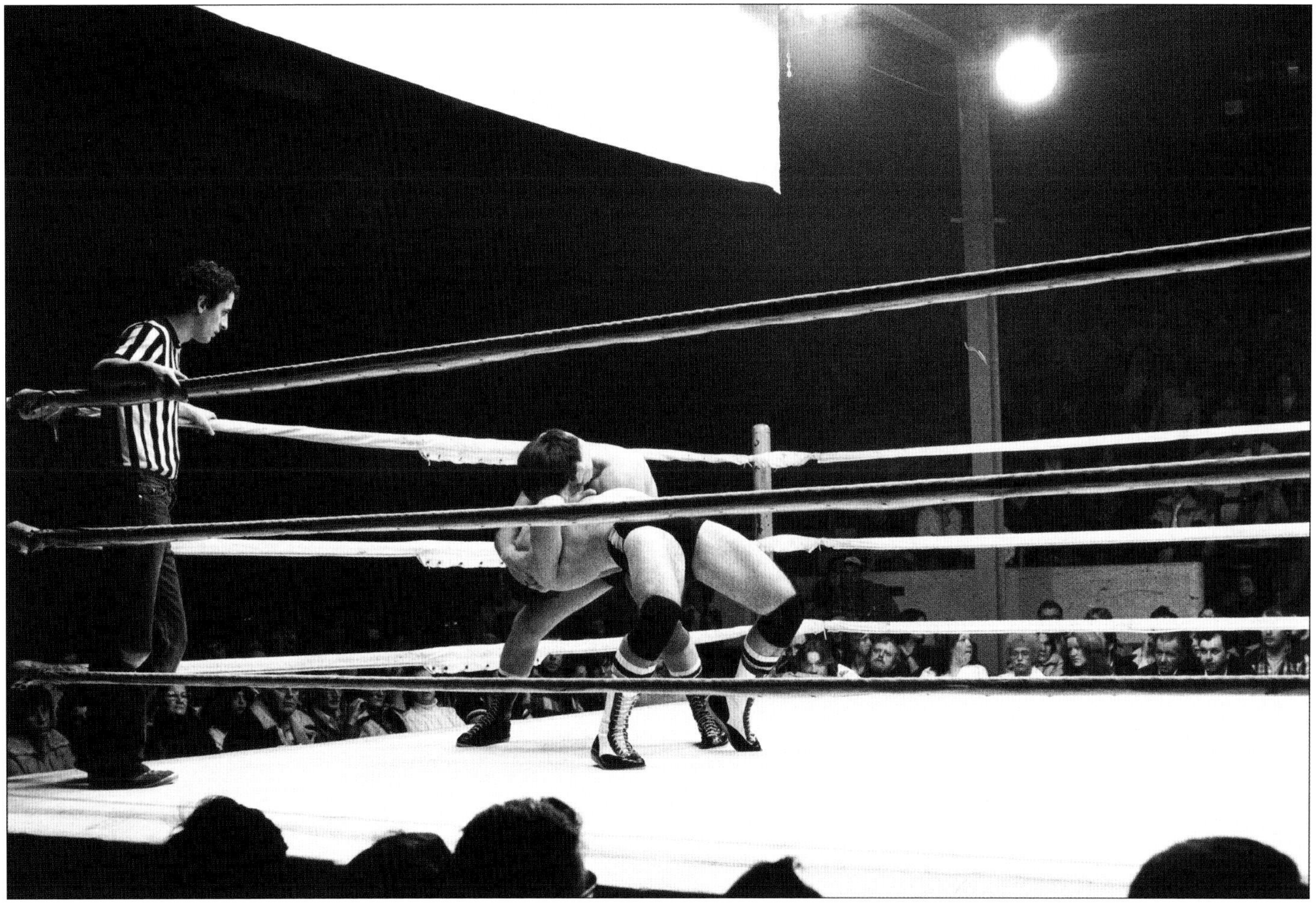

Victoria Pavilion, 1980

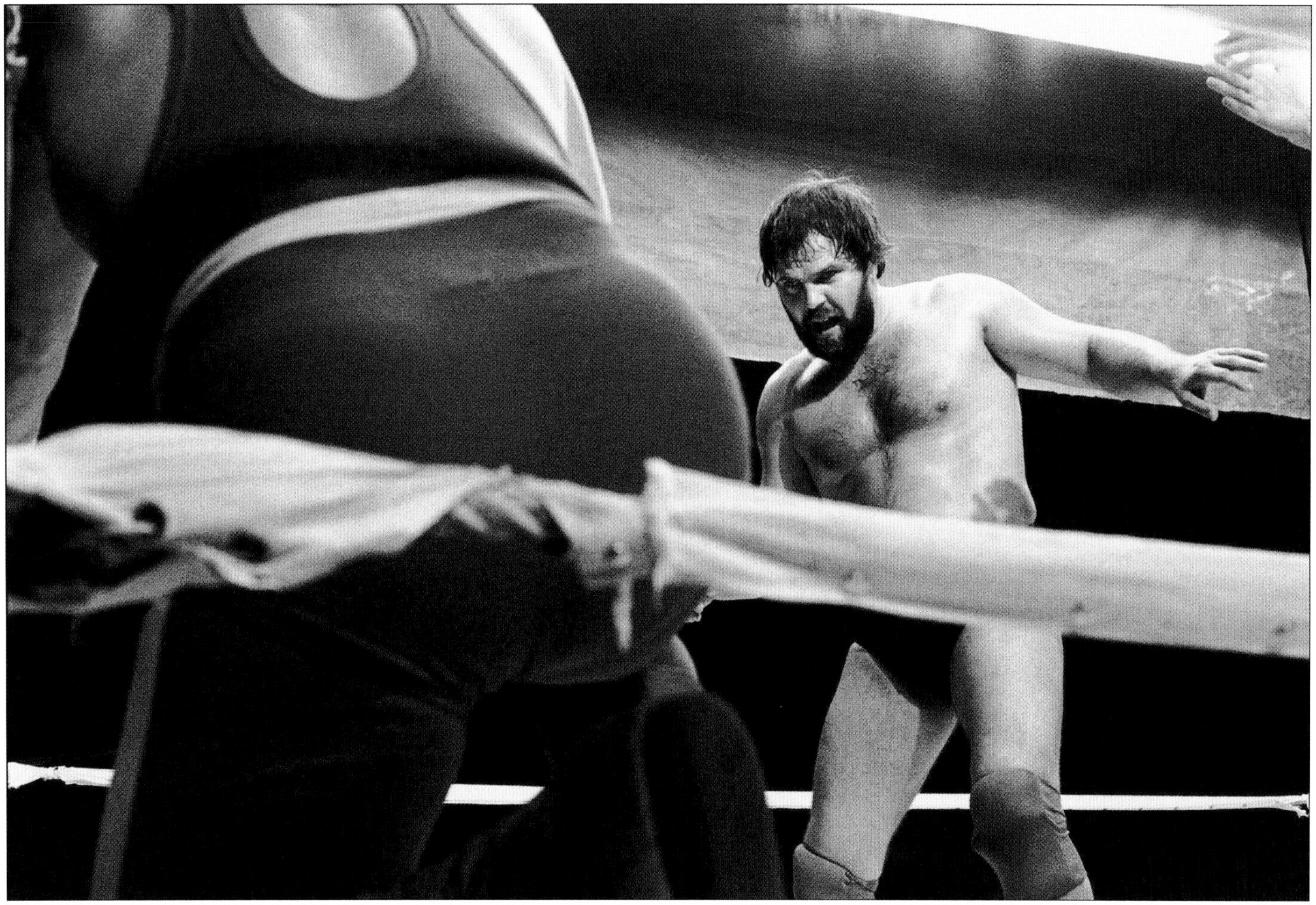

Victoria Pavilion, 1979

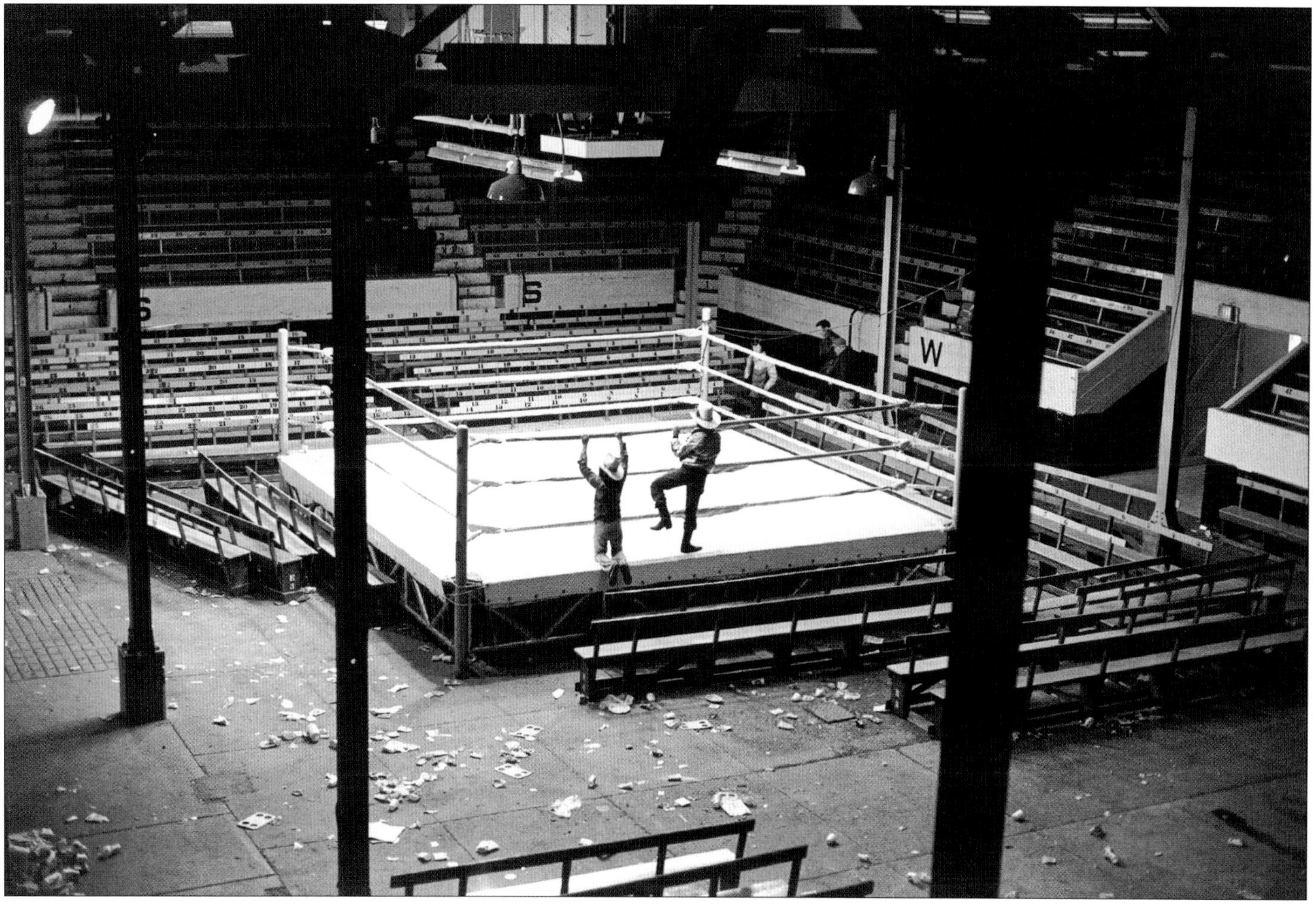

Victoria Pavilion, 1978

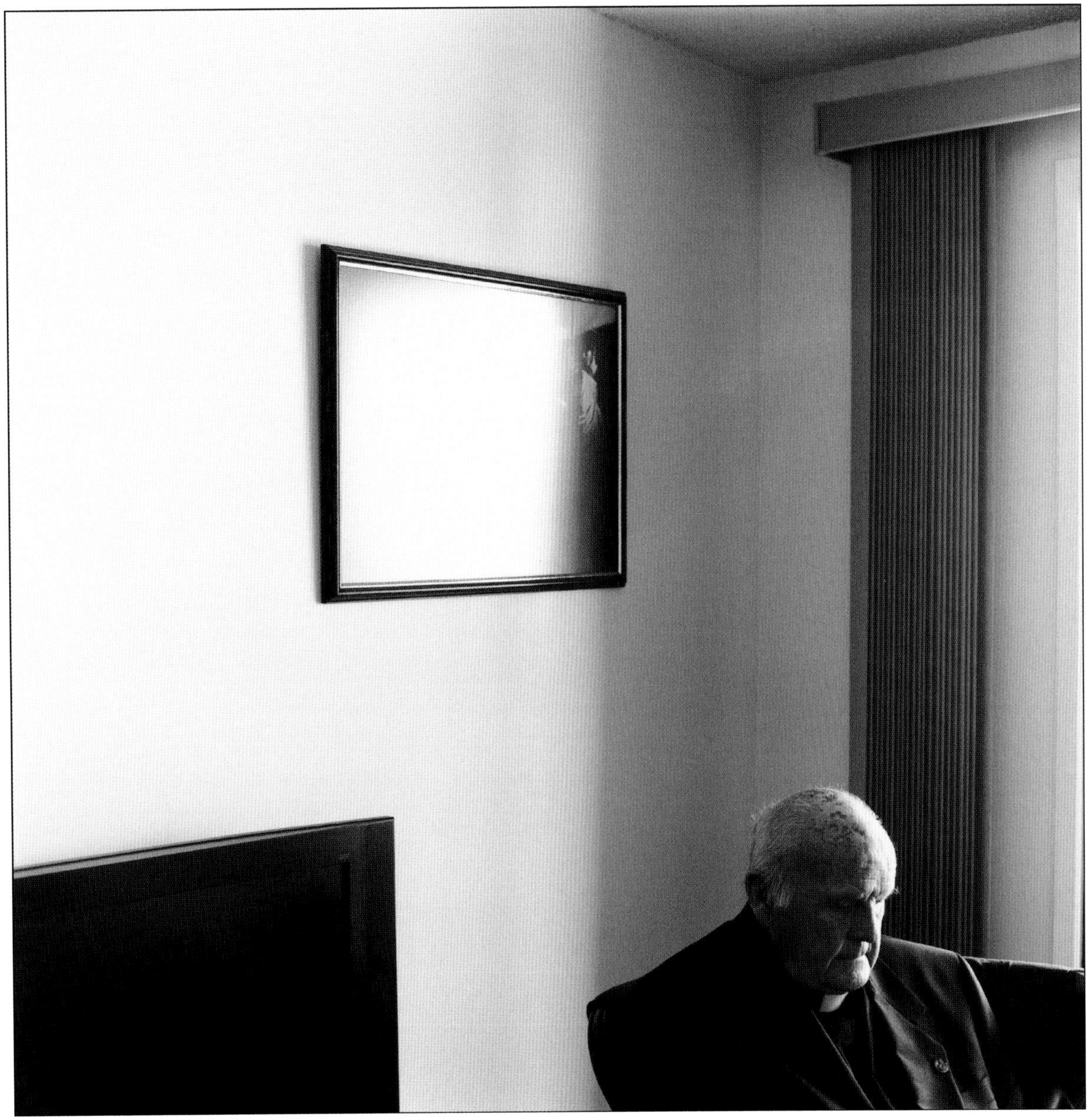

Reverend Denis Fleming, 2007

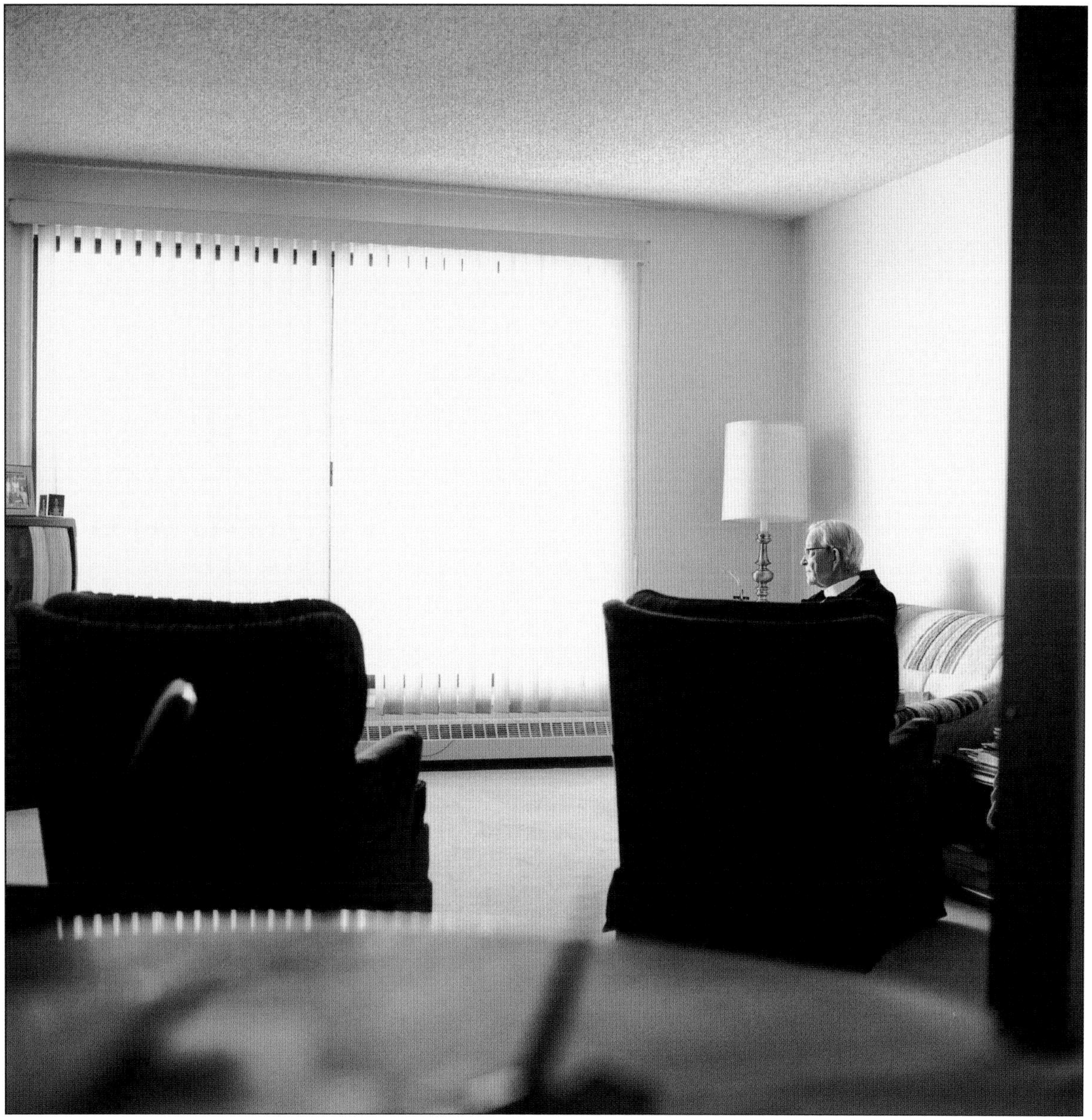

Reverend Patrick Cramer, 2007

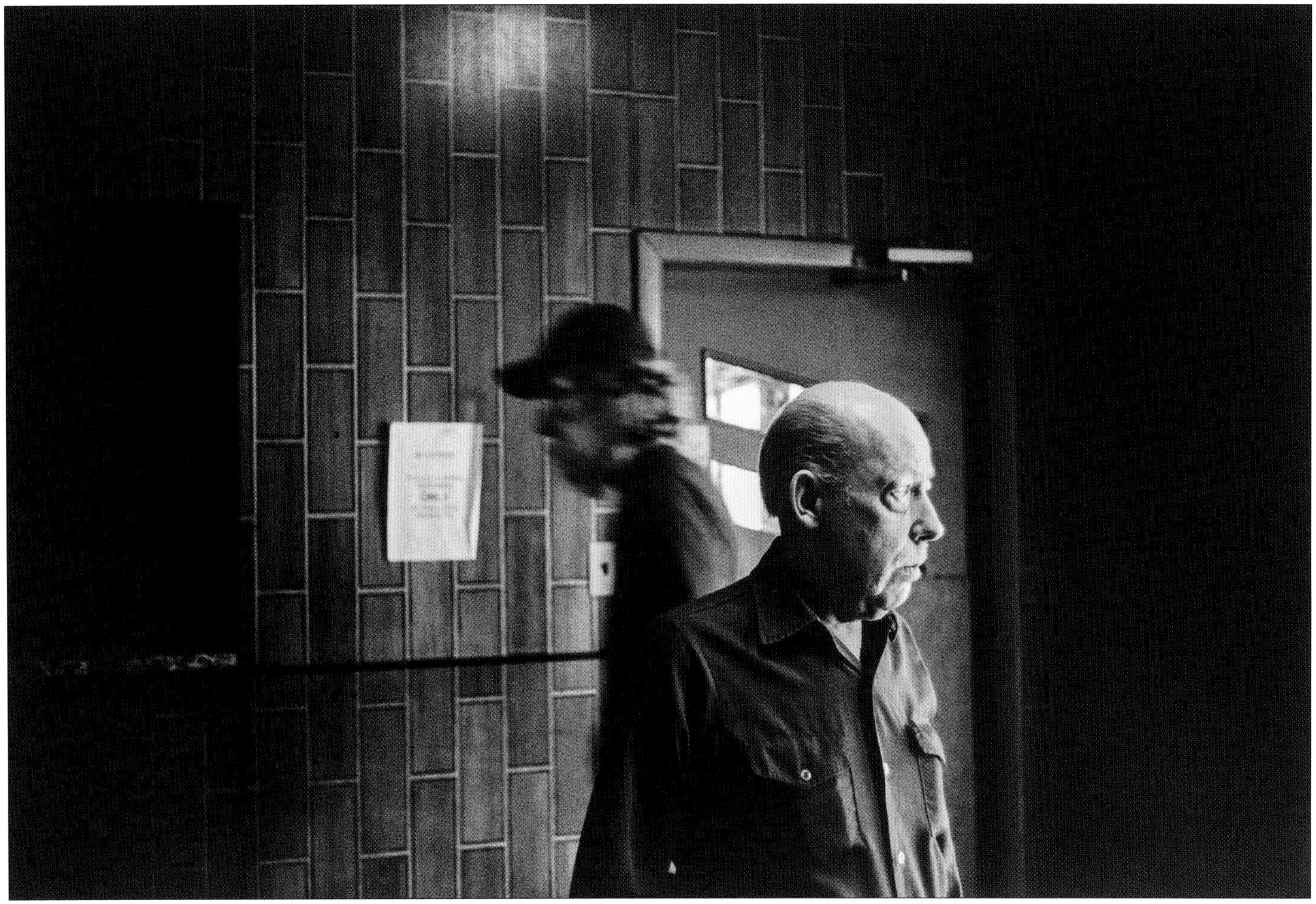

Pete Rosenvard, St Louis Hotel, 2006

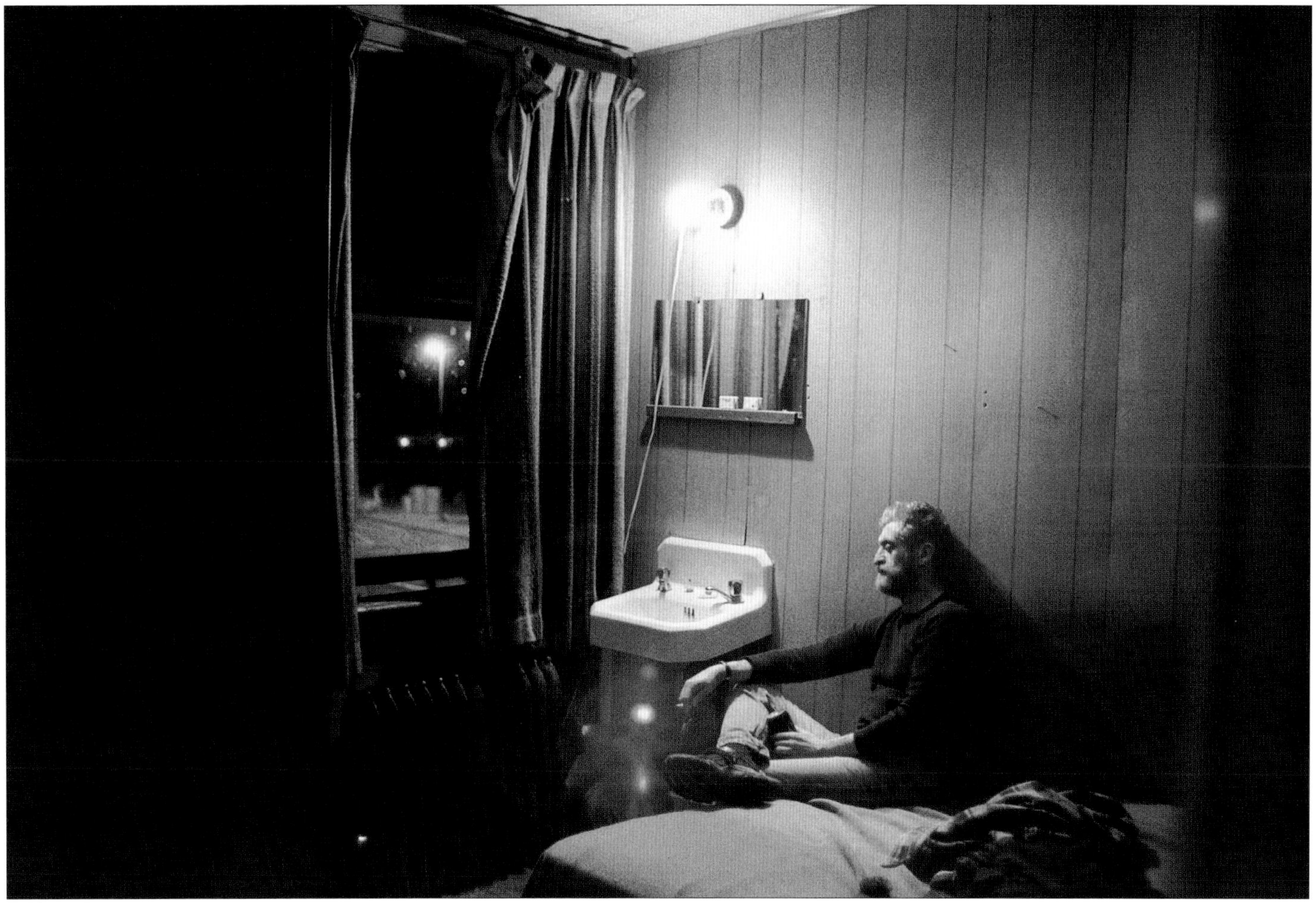

Man in his room, St Louis Hotel, 2006

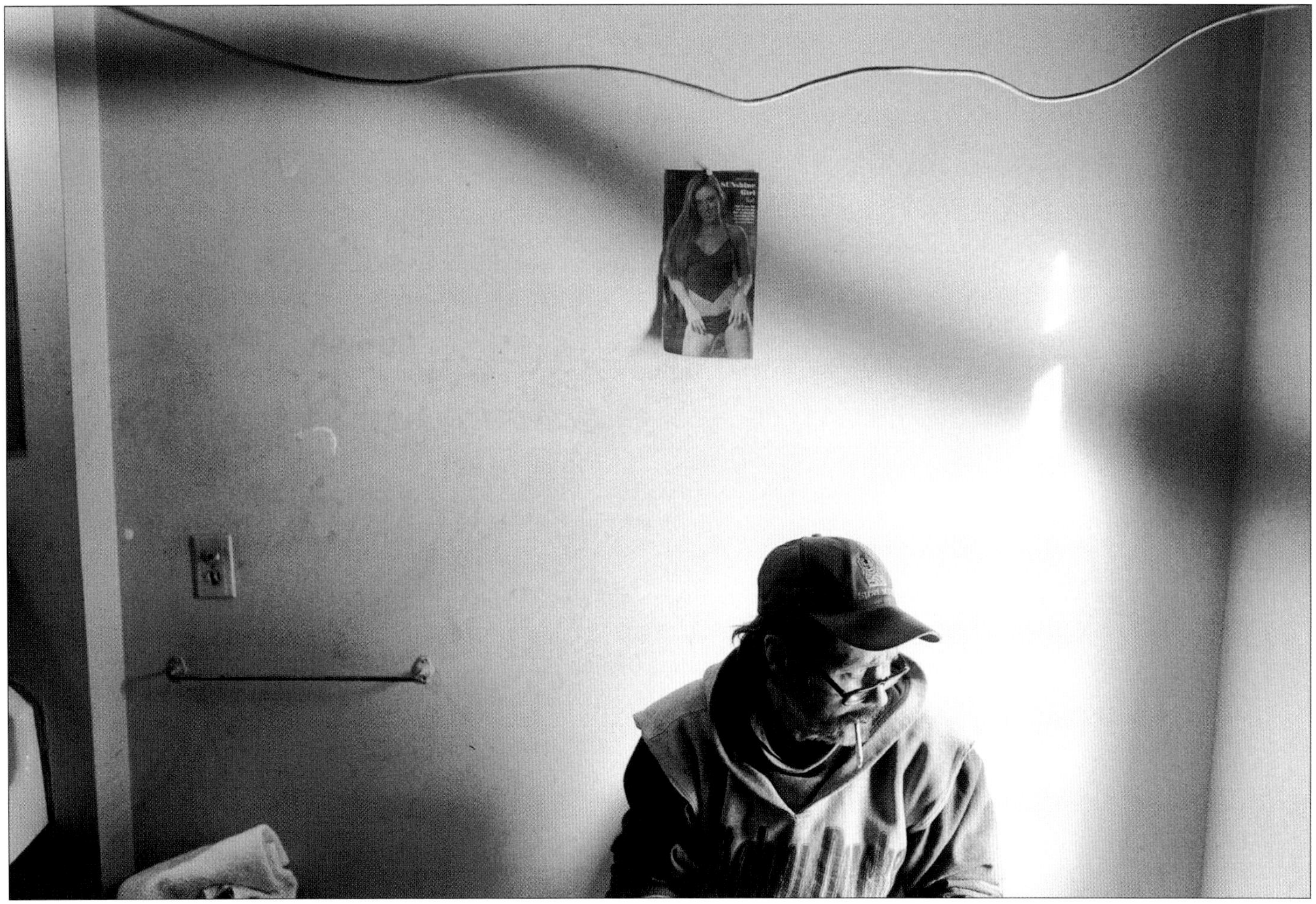

Reg Johnson, King Edward Hotel, 2004

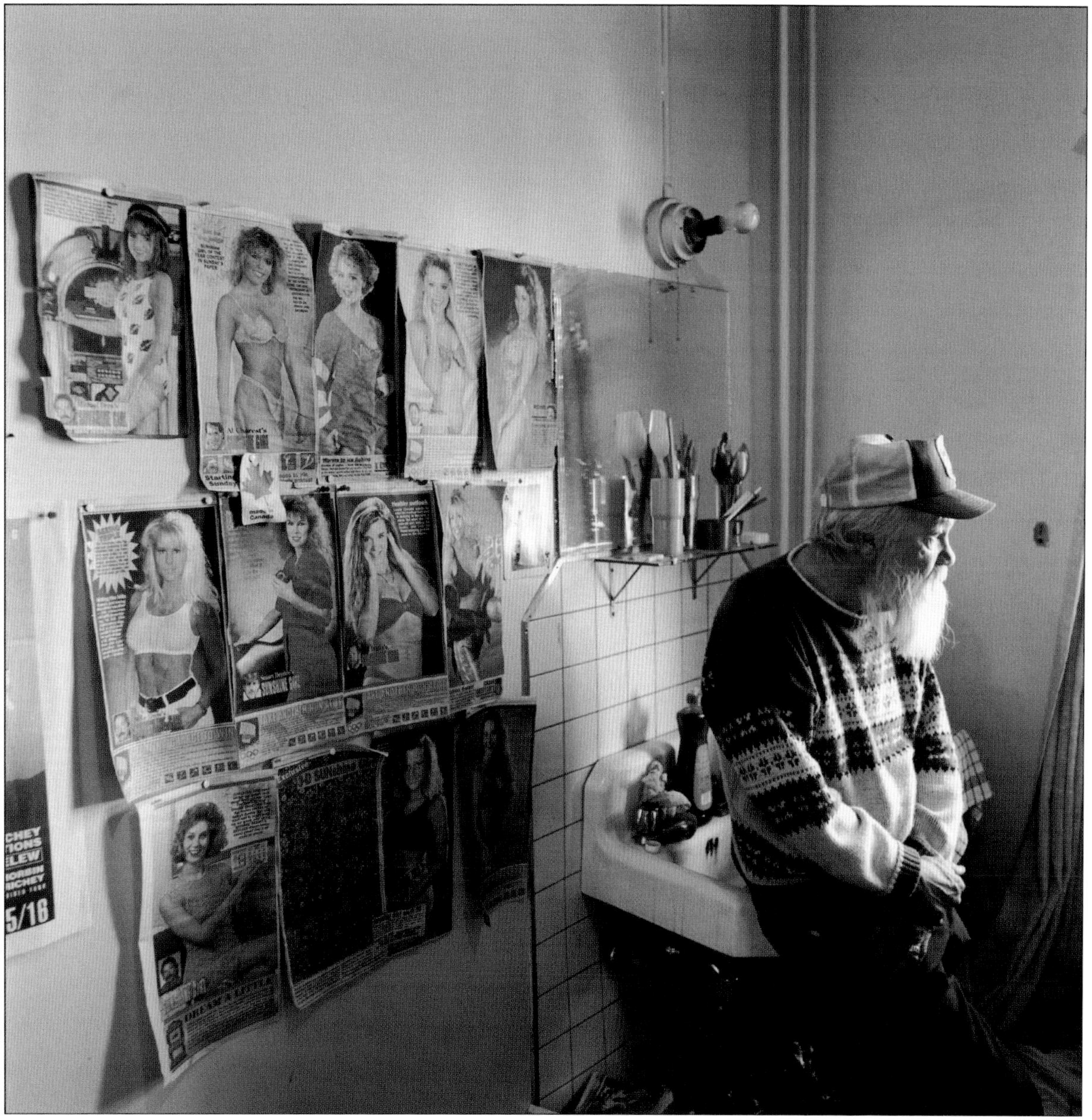

Ron Beards, National Hotel, 1994

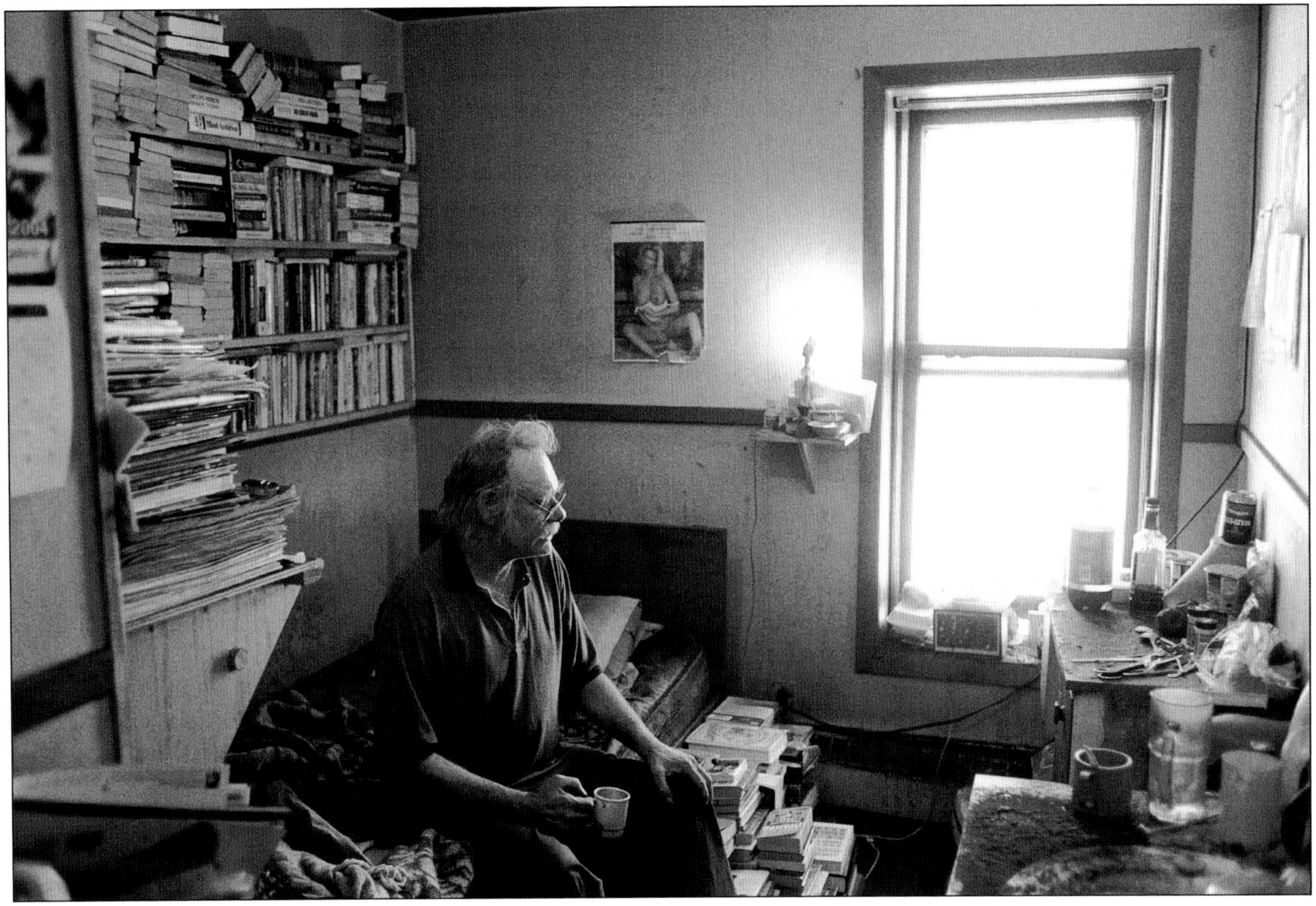

Robin Randell, King Edward Hotel, 2004

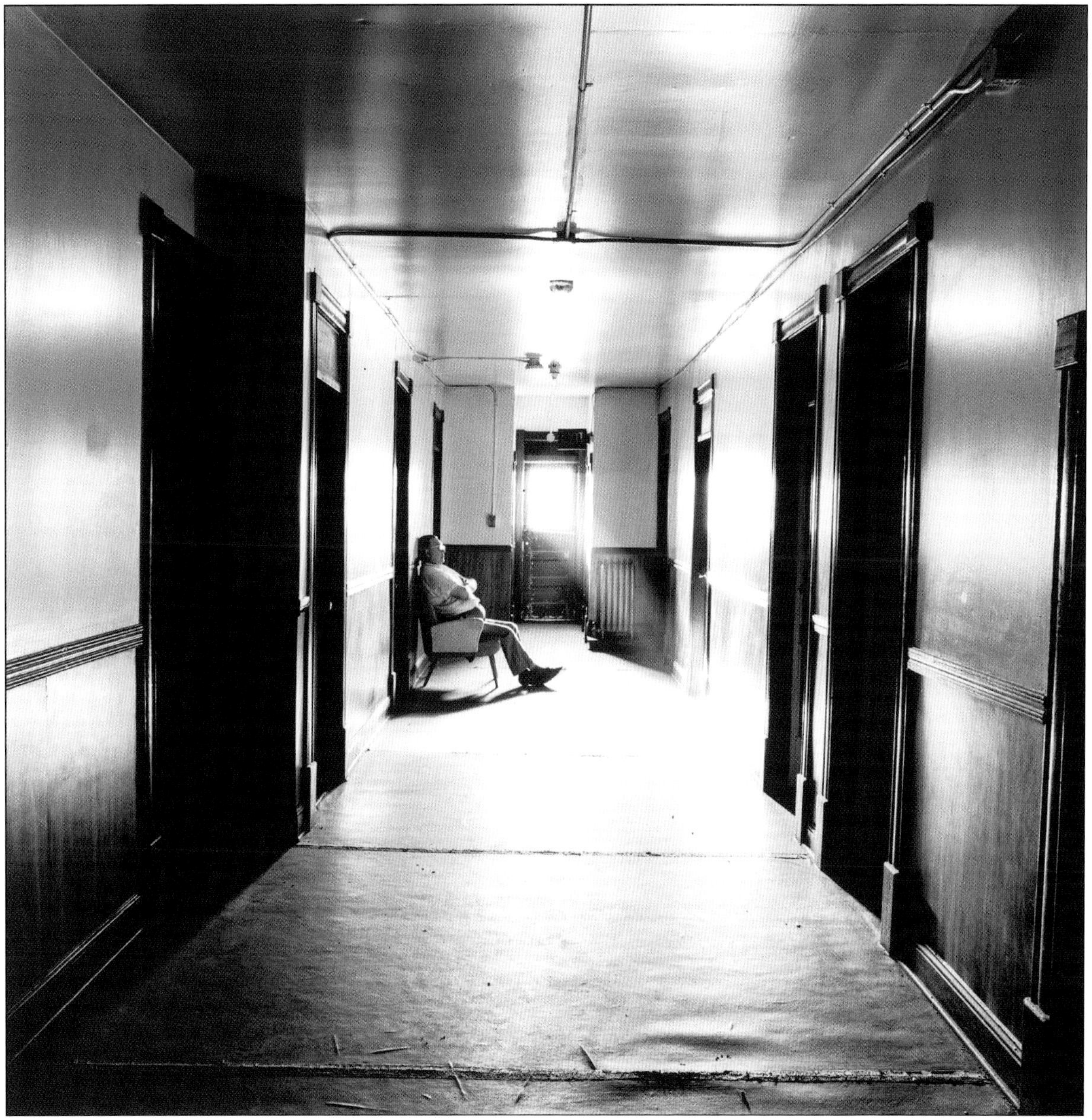

Bill Garstang, National Hotel, 1994

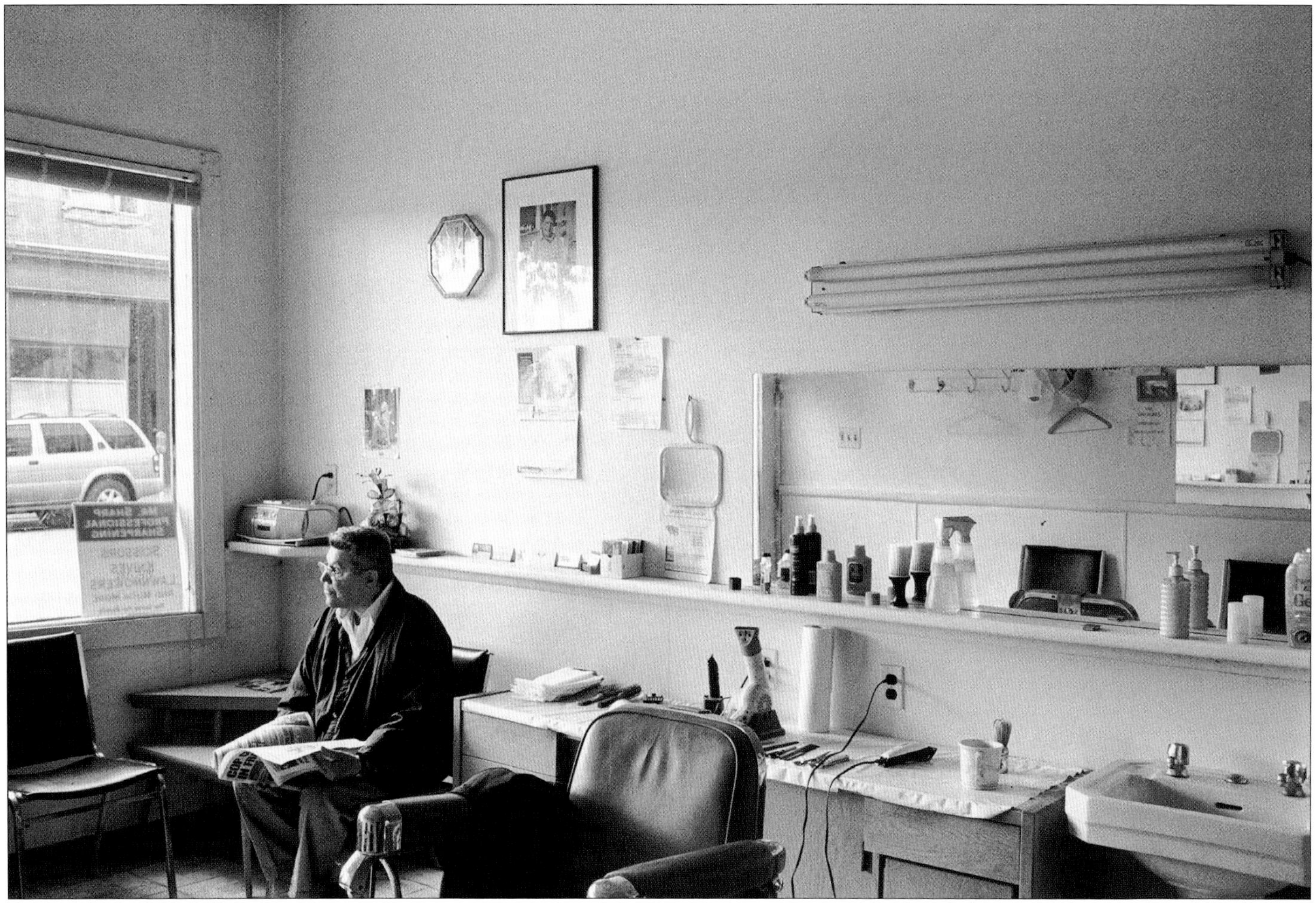

Sam Iovinelli, barber, 2006

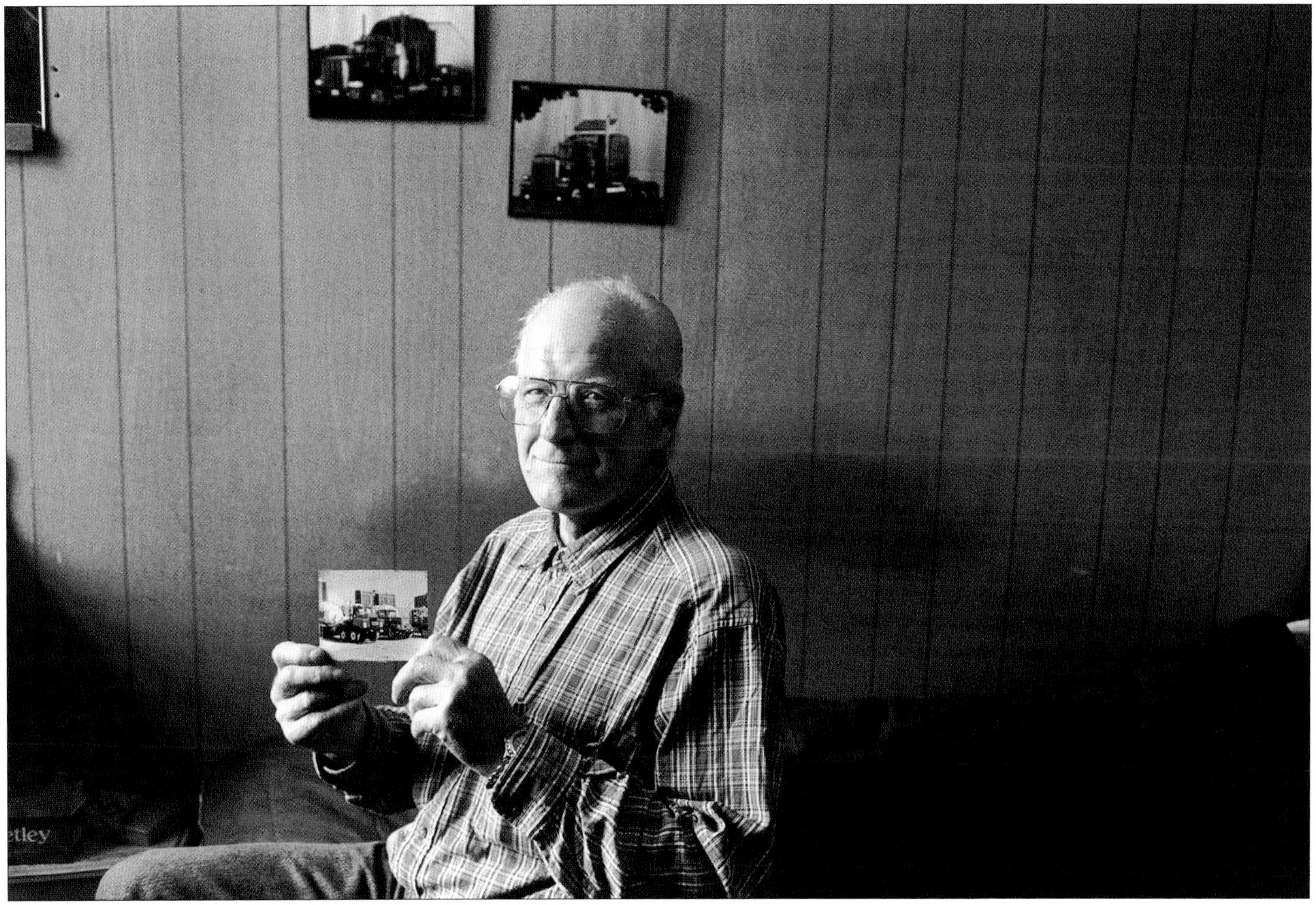

Ed Mielke, St Louis Hotel, 2006

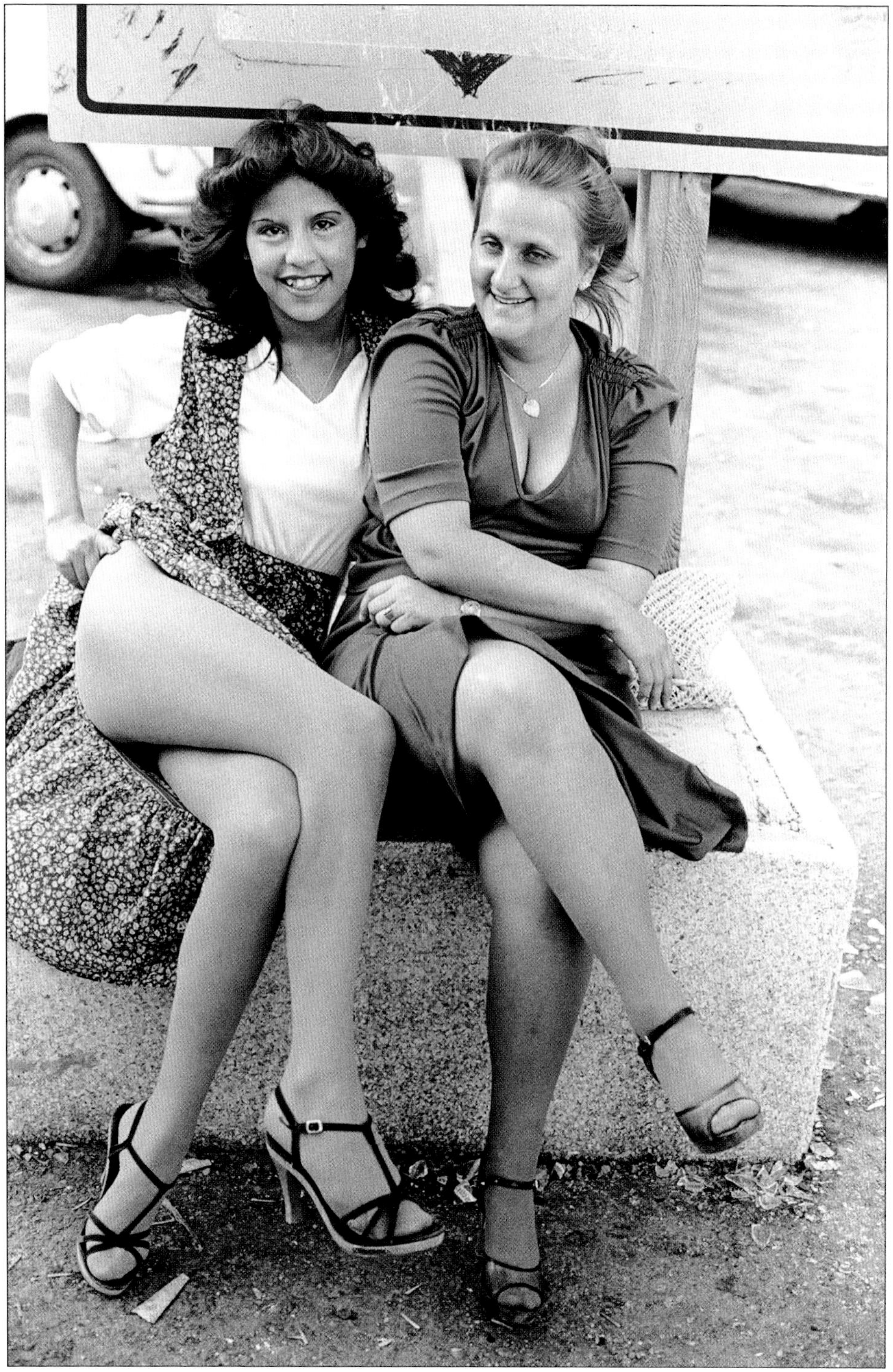

Two women, 1979

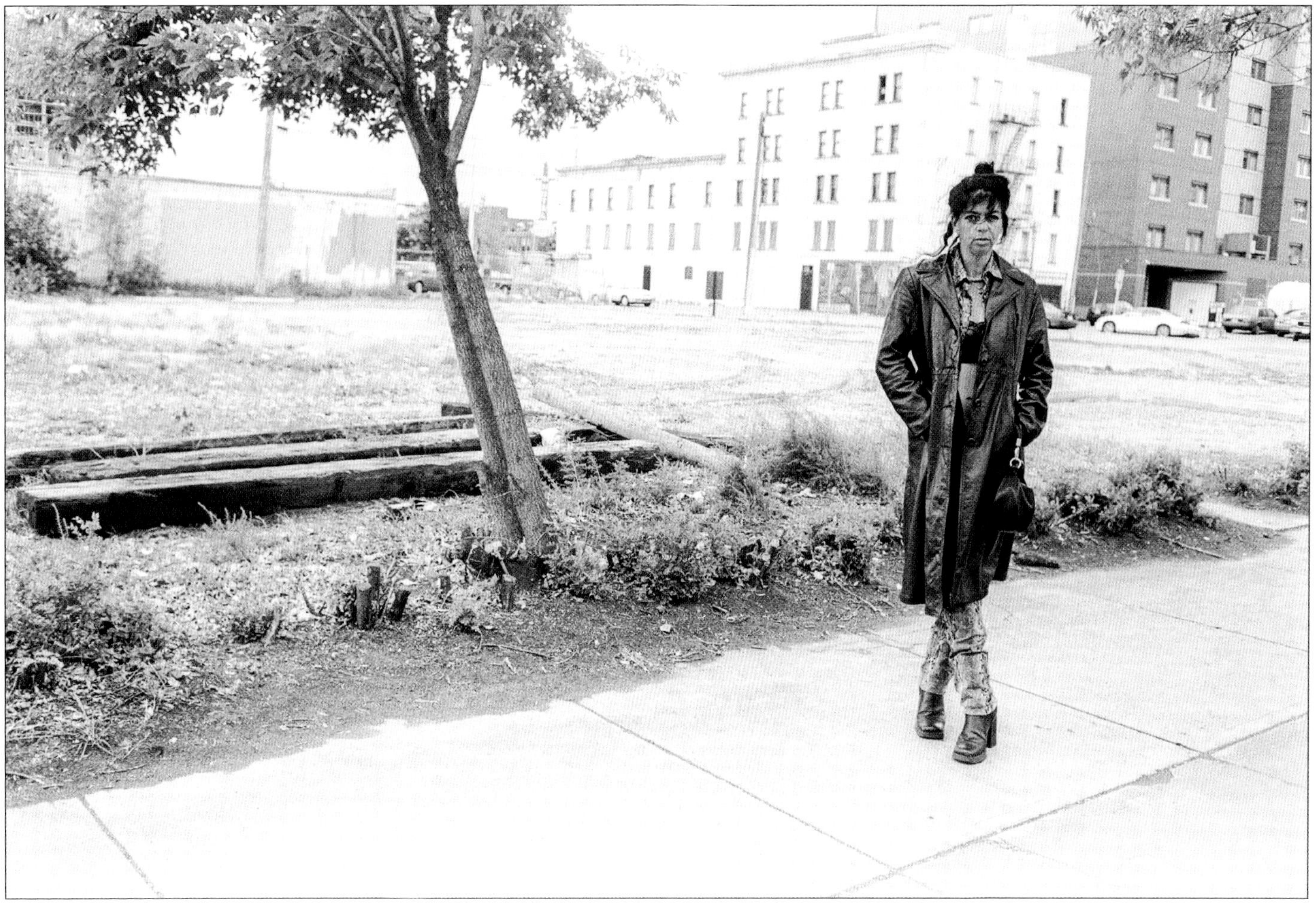

Kitalina Star Walker, 2006

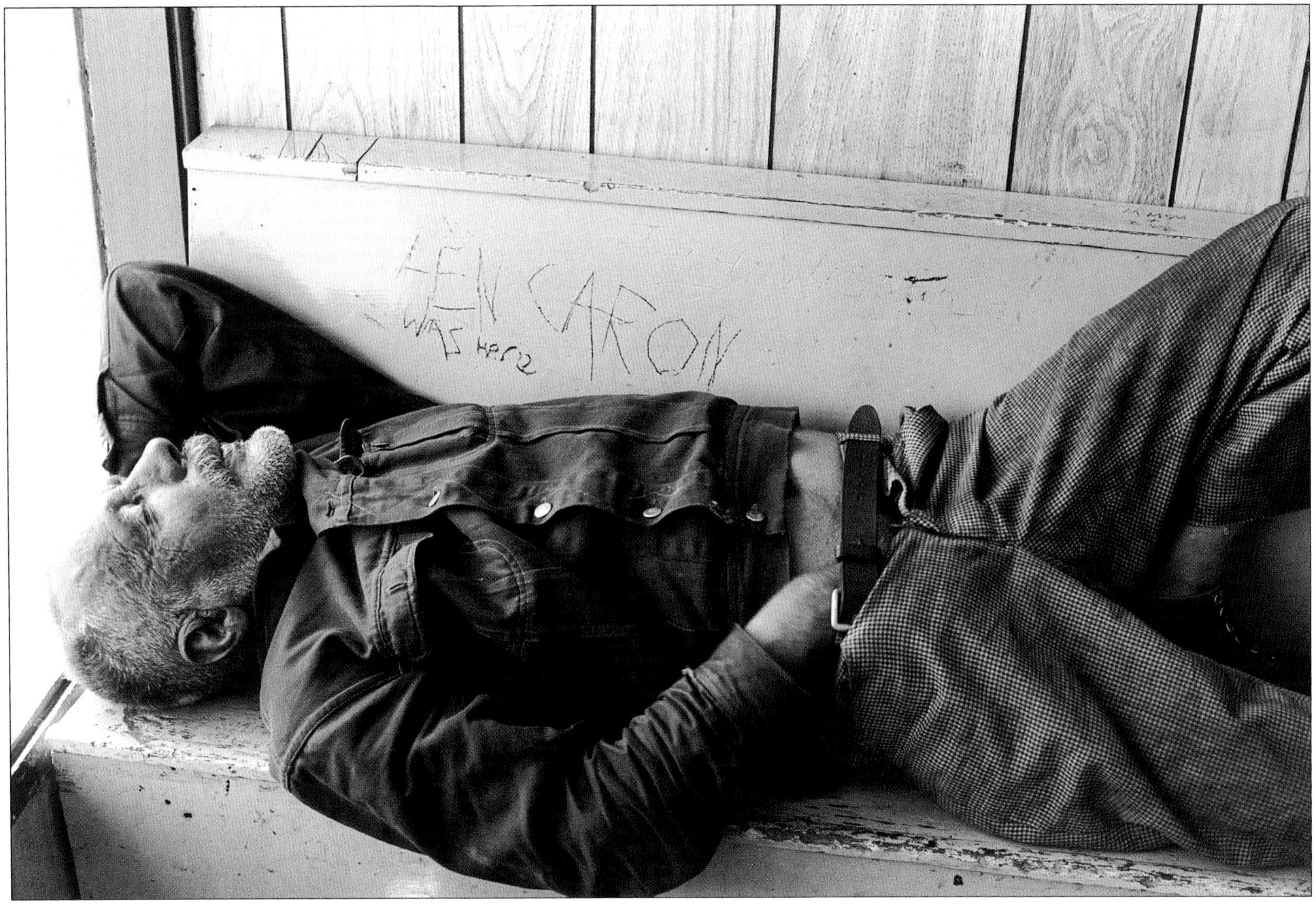

Sleeping man, 1977

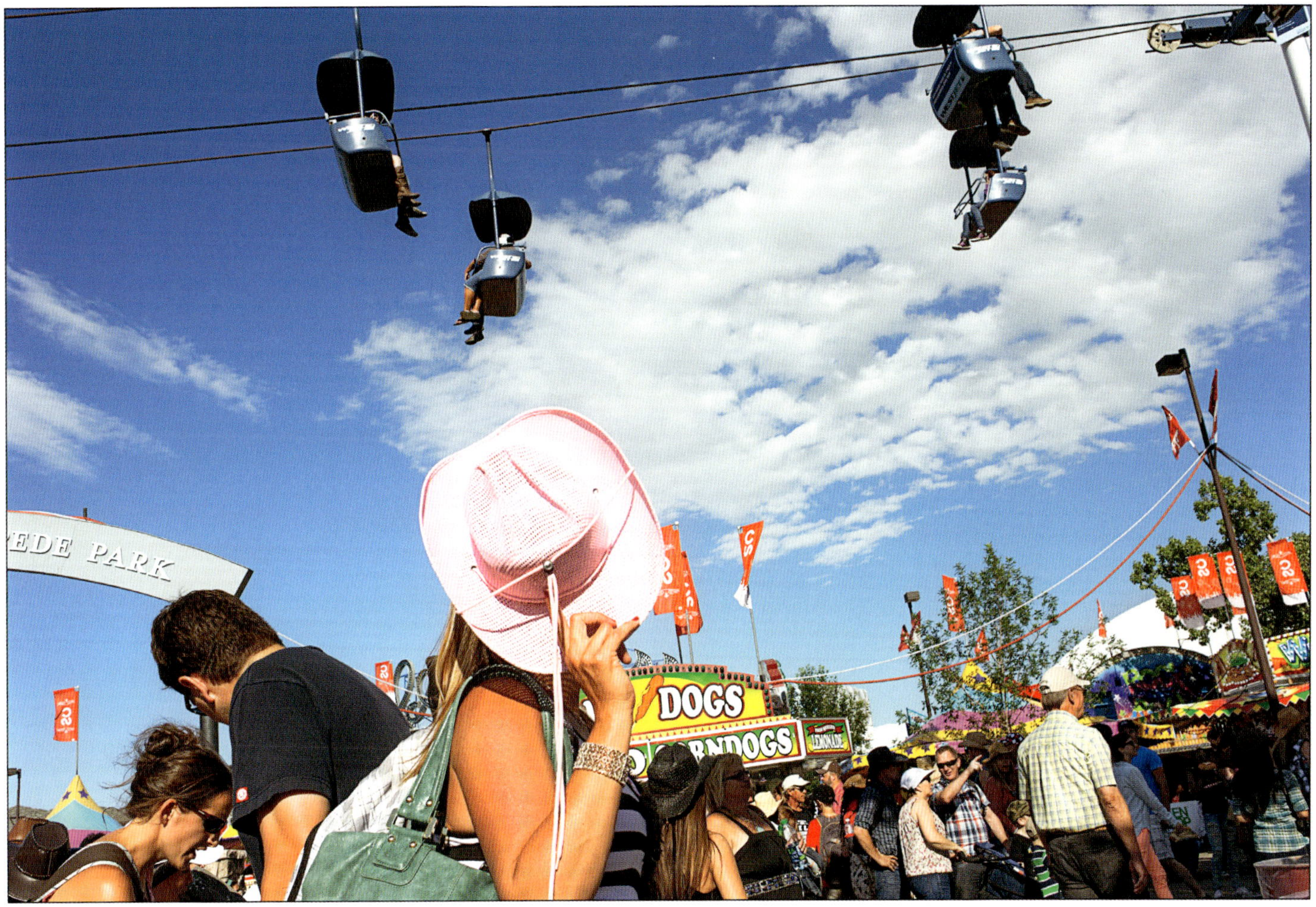

Stampede, 2013

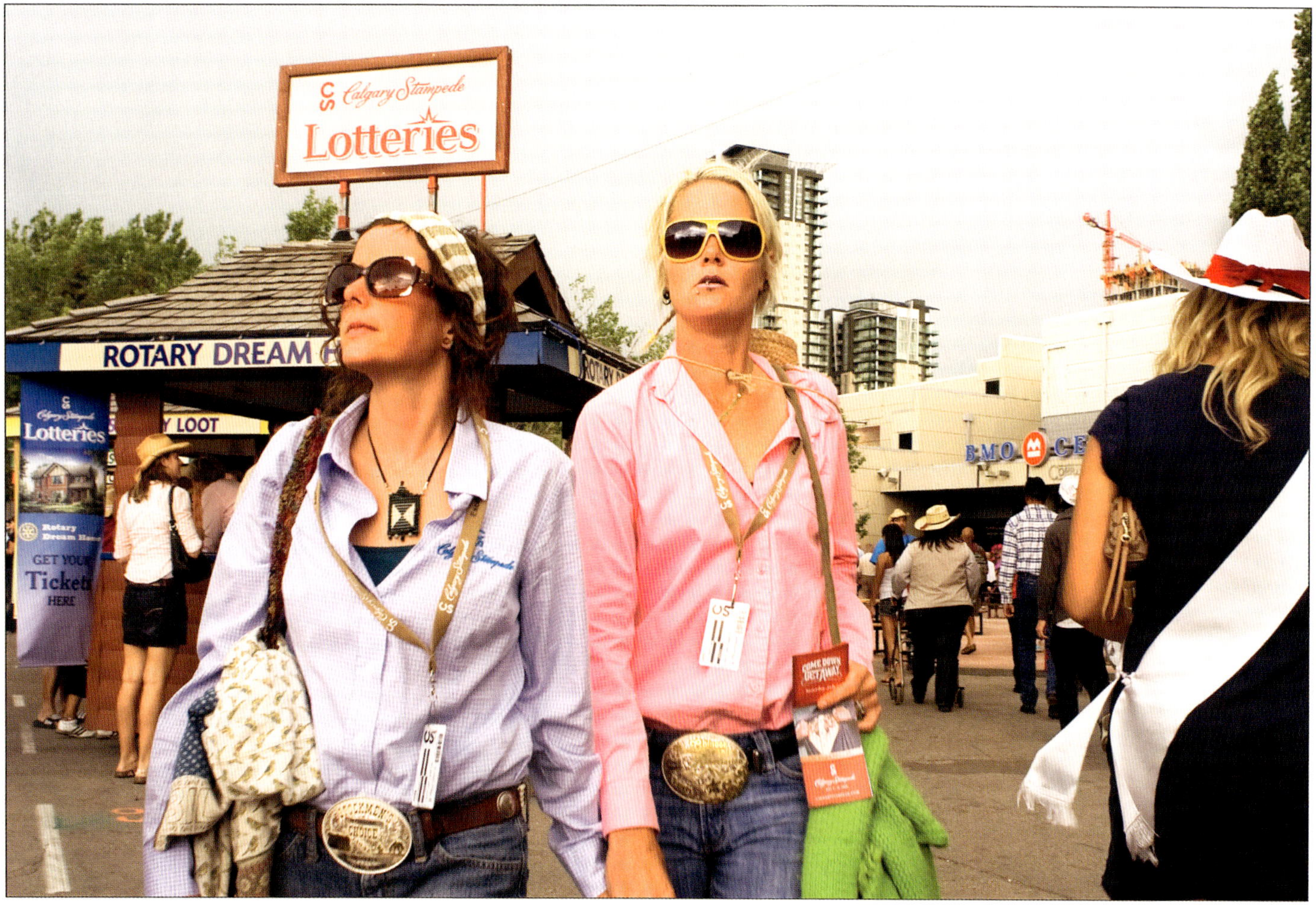

Stampede, 2009

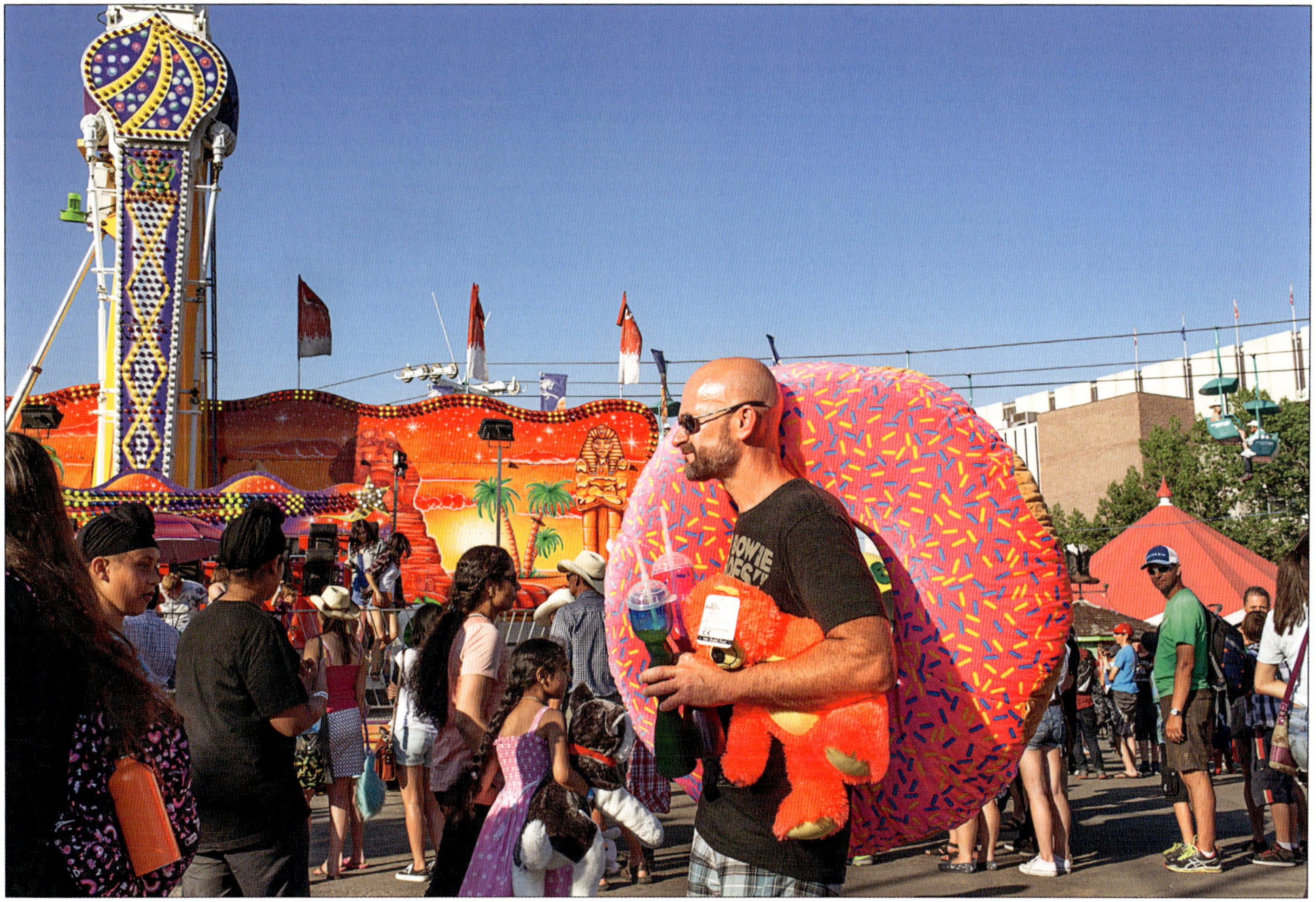

Stampede, 2014

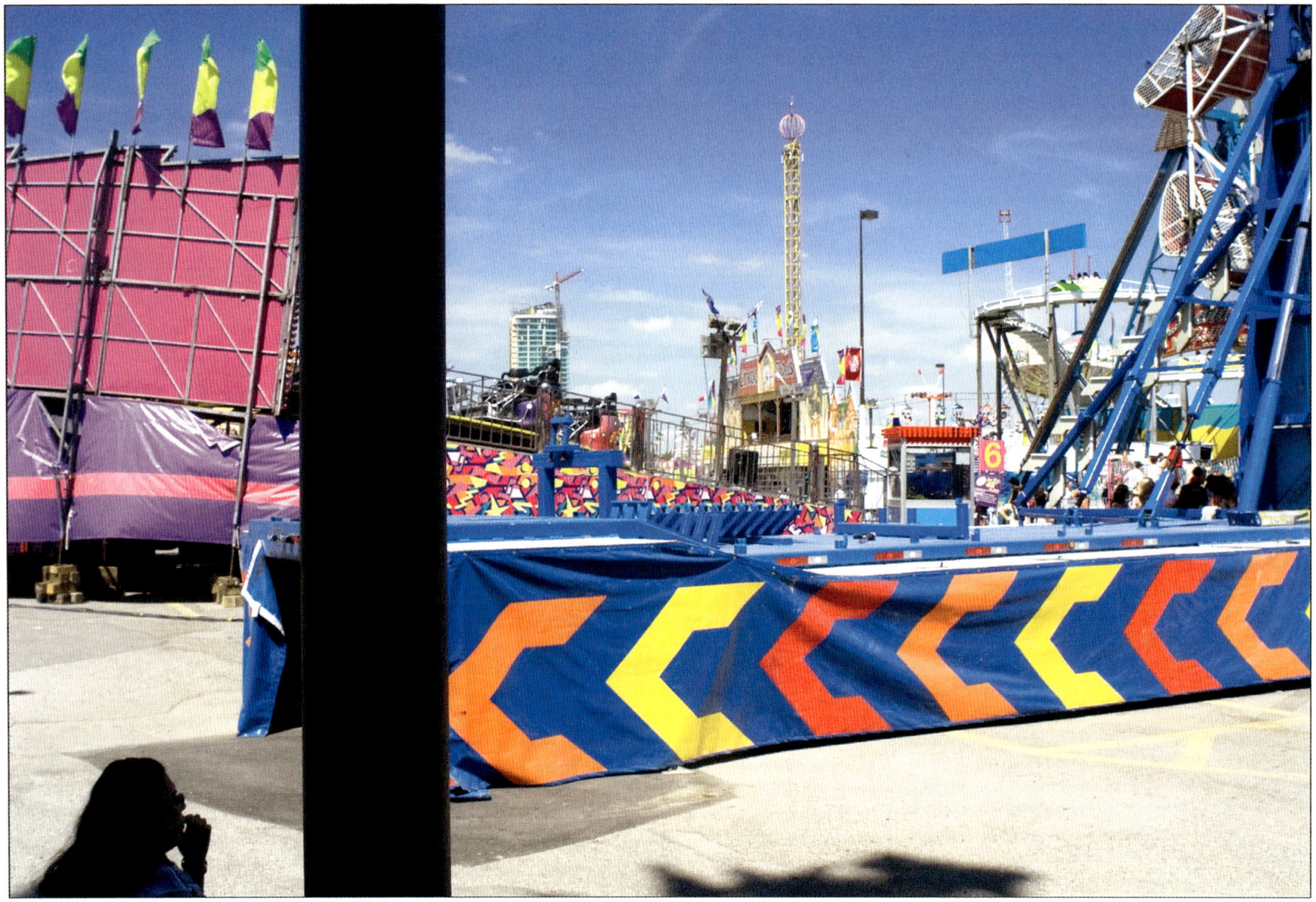

Stampede, 2007

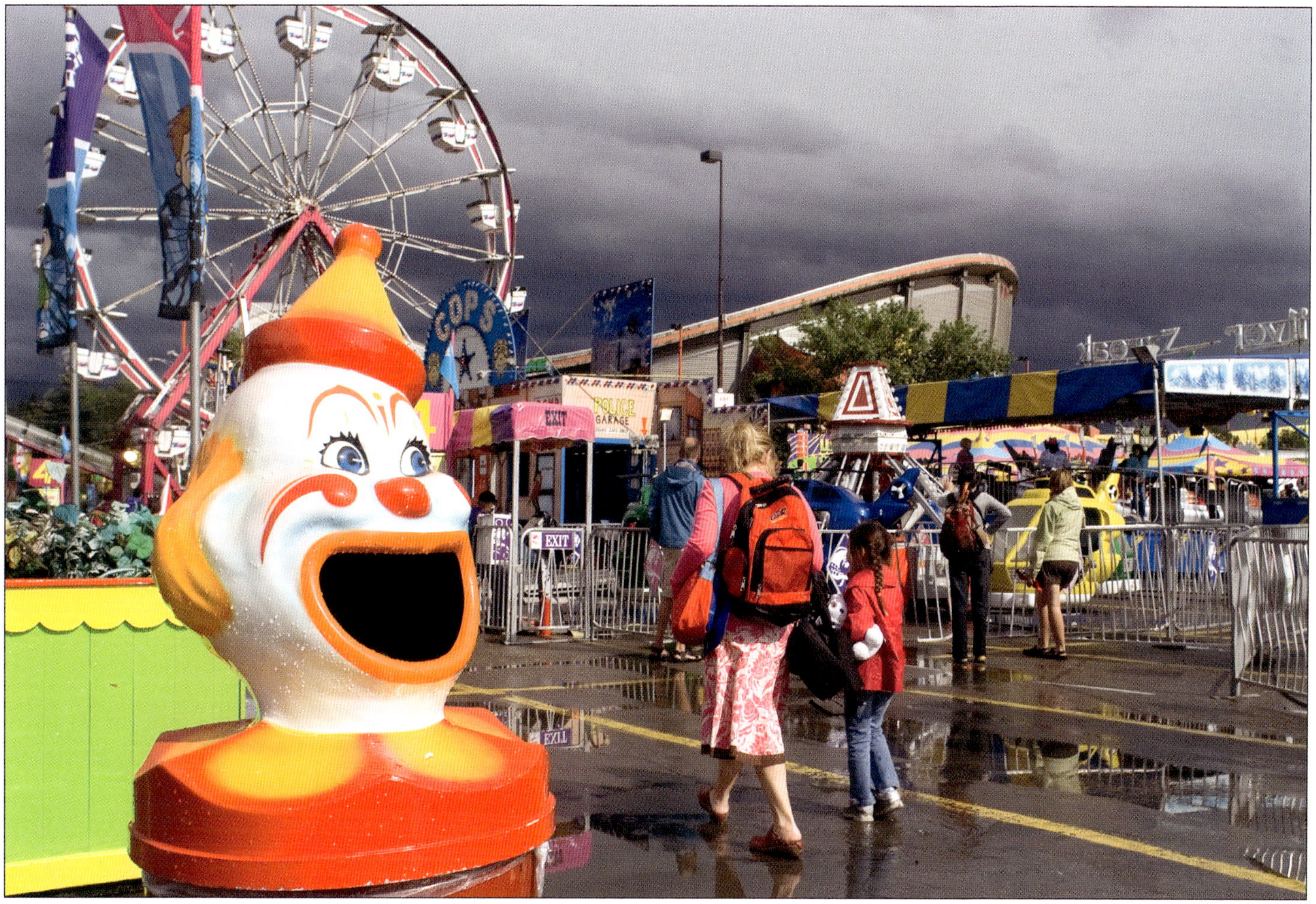

Stampede, 2009

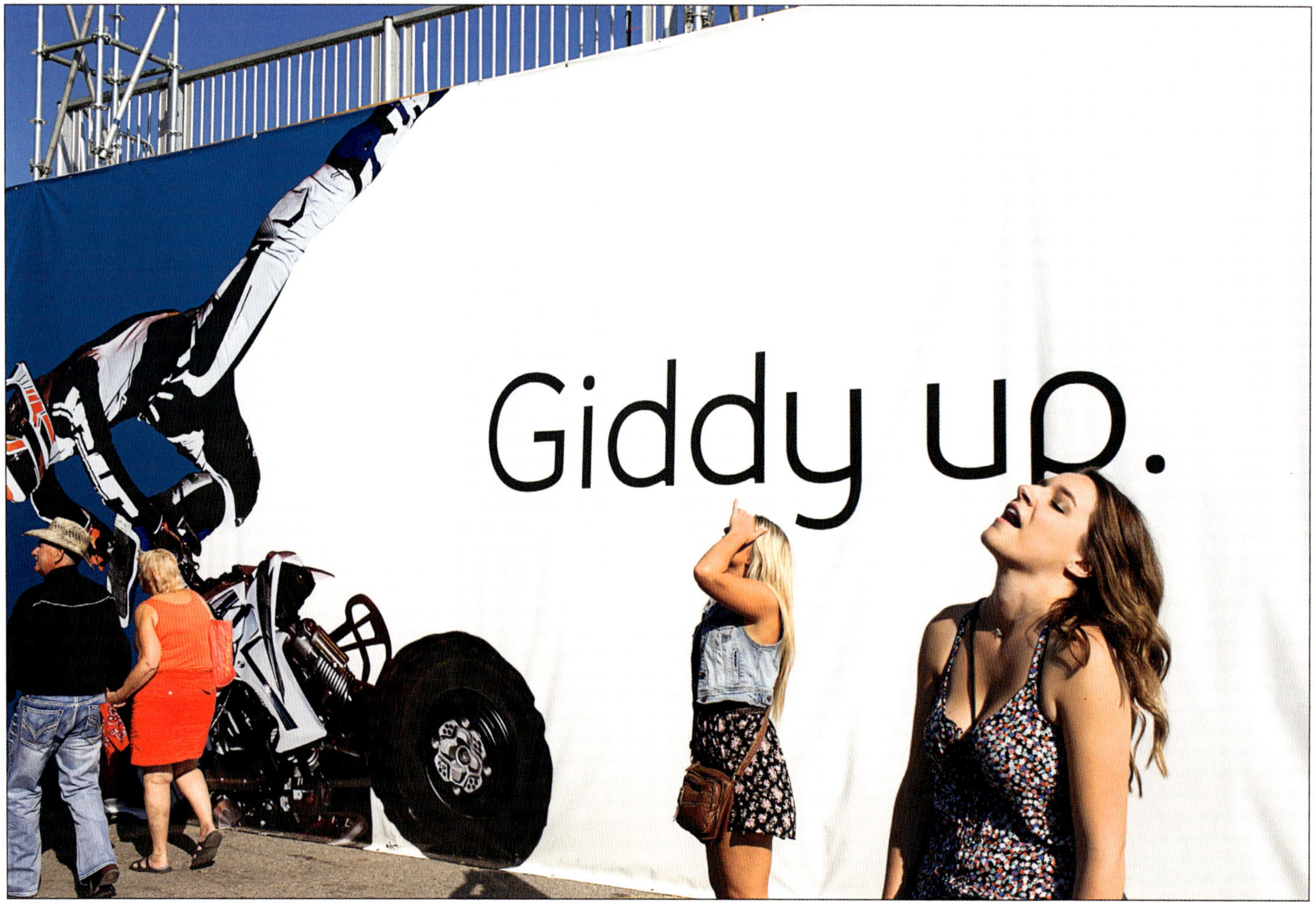

Stampede, 2014

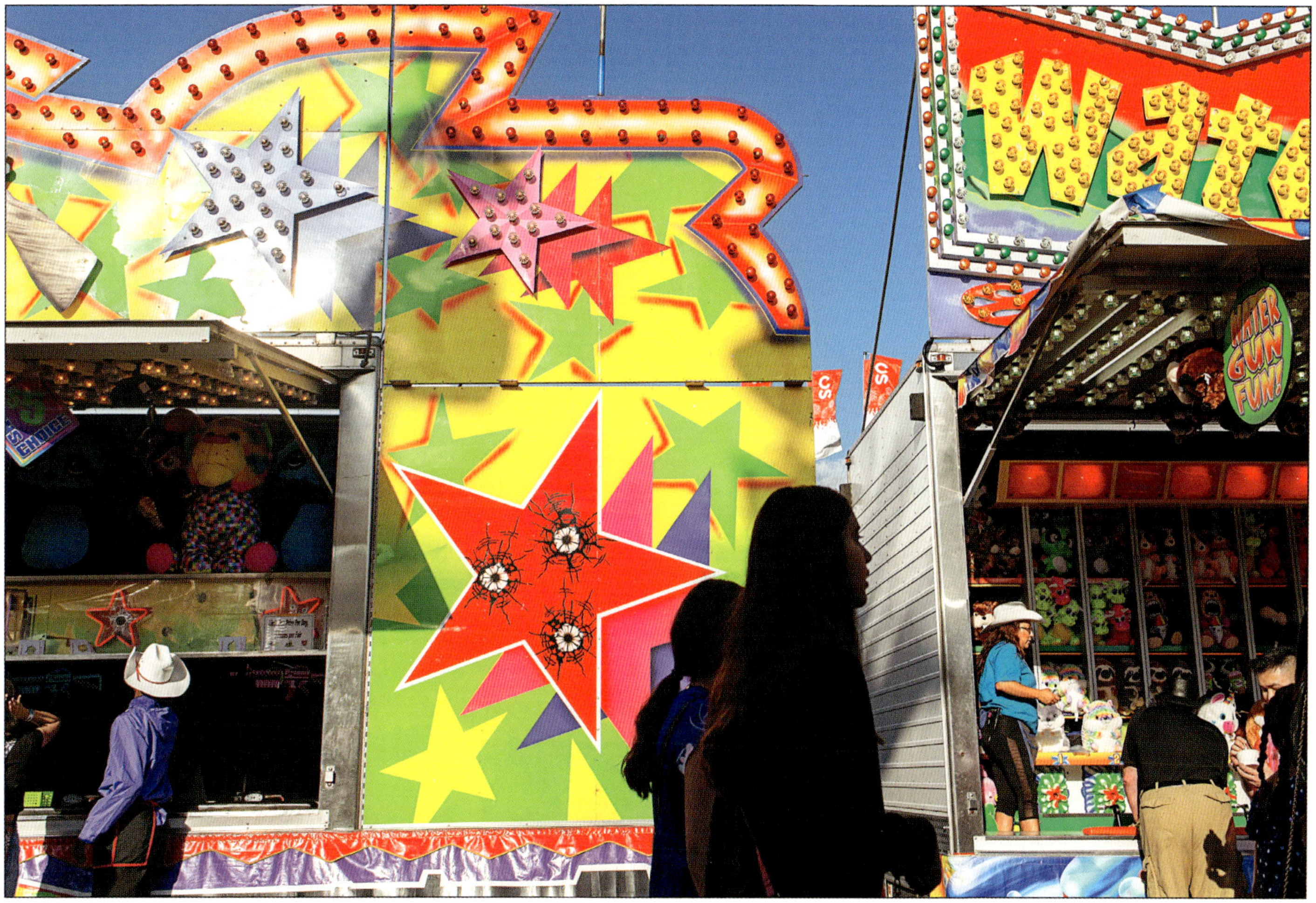

Stampede, 2019

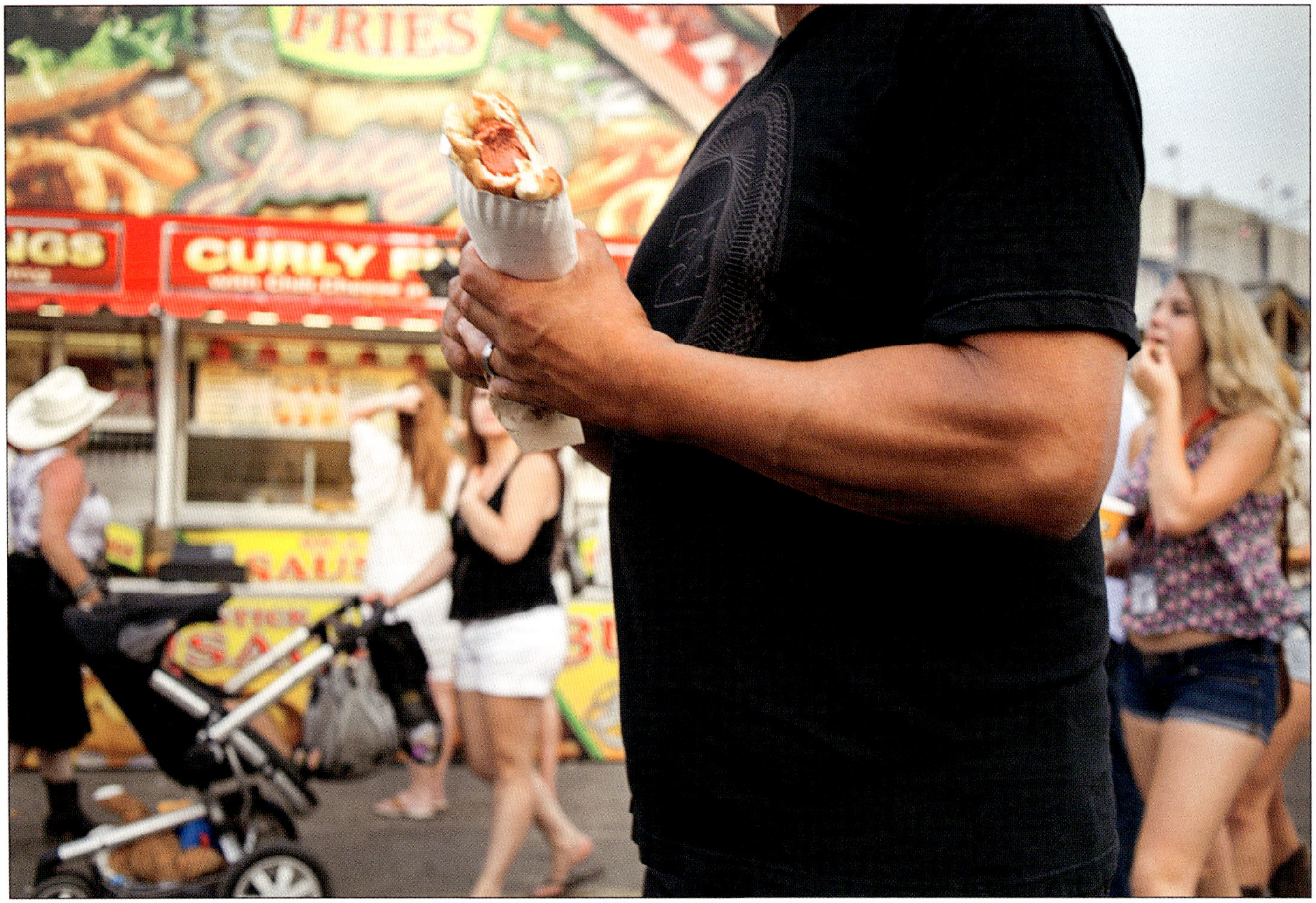

Stampede, 2015

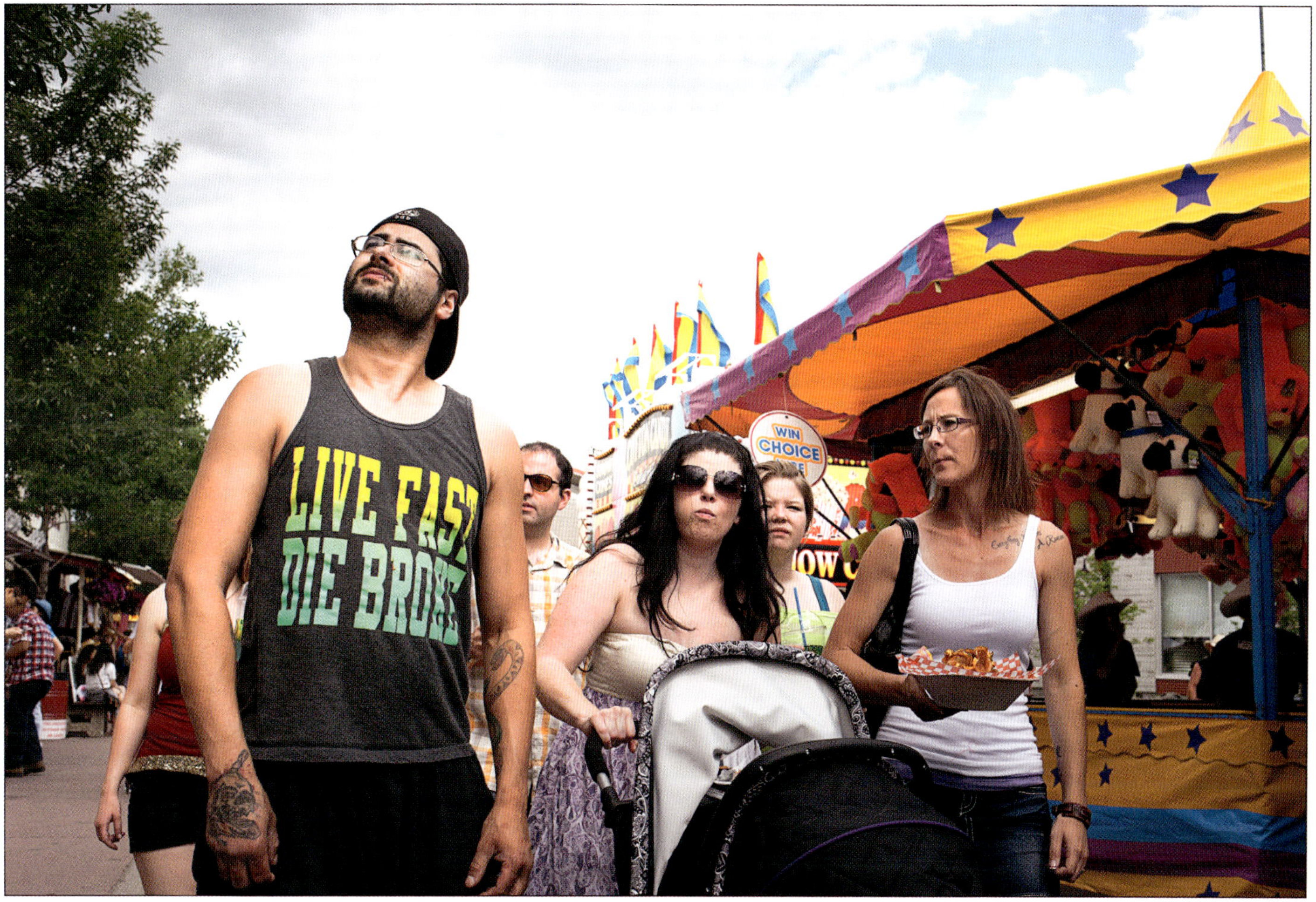

Stampede, 2015

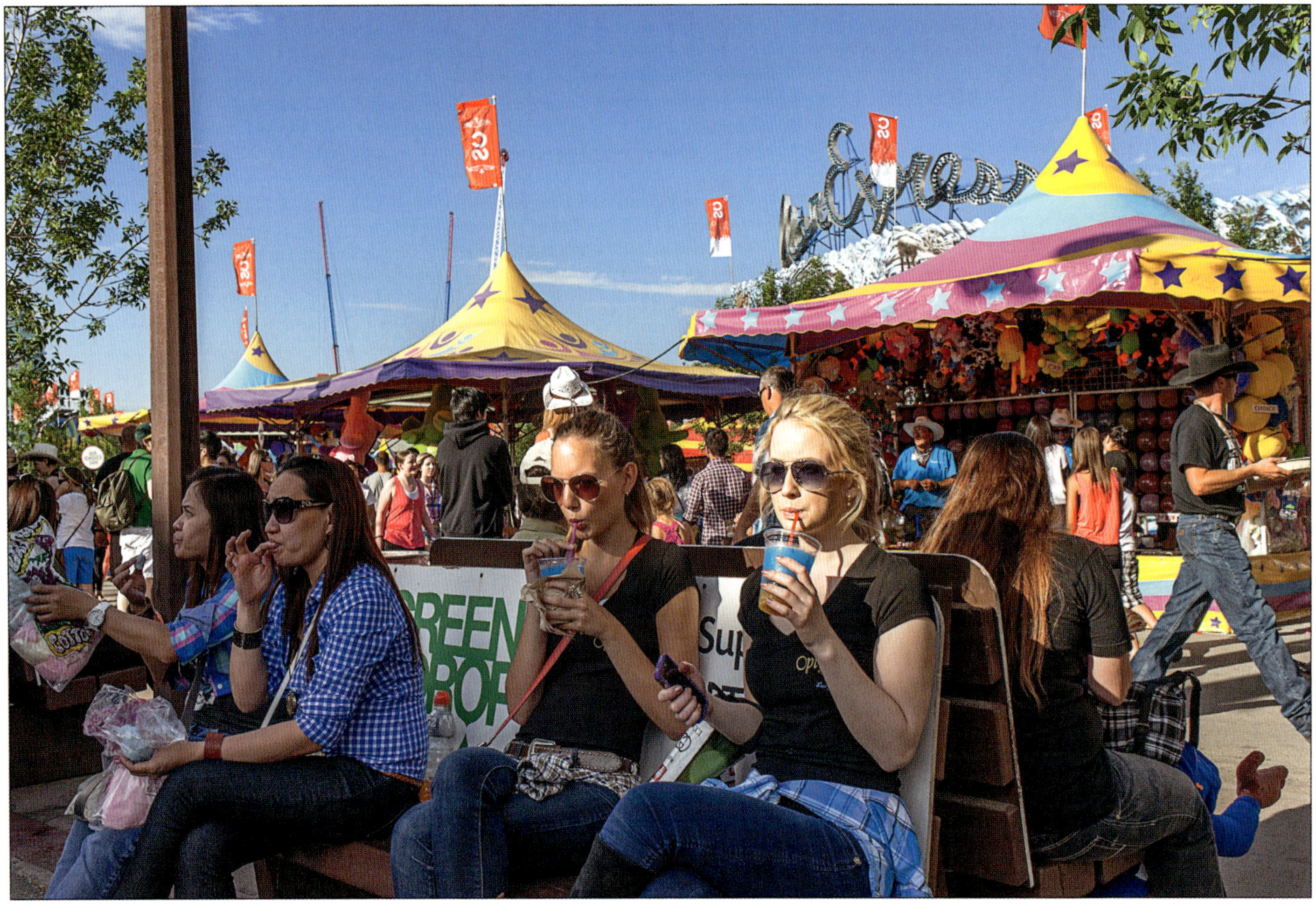

Stampede, 2013

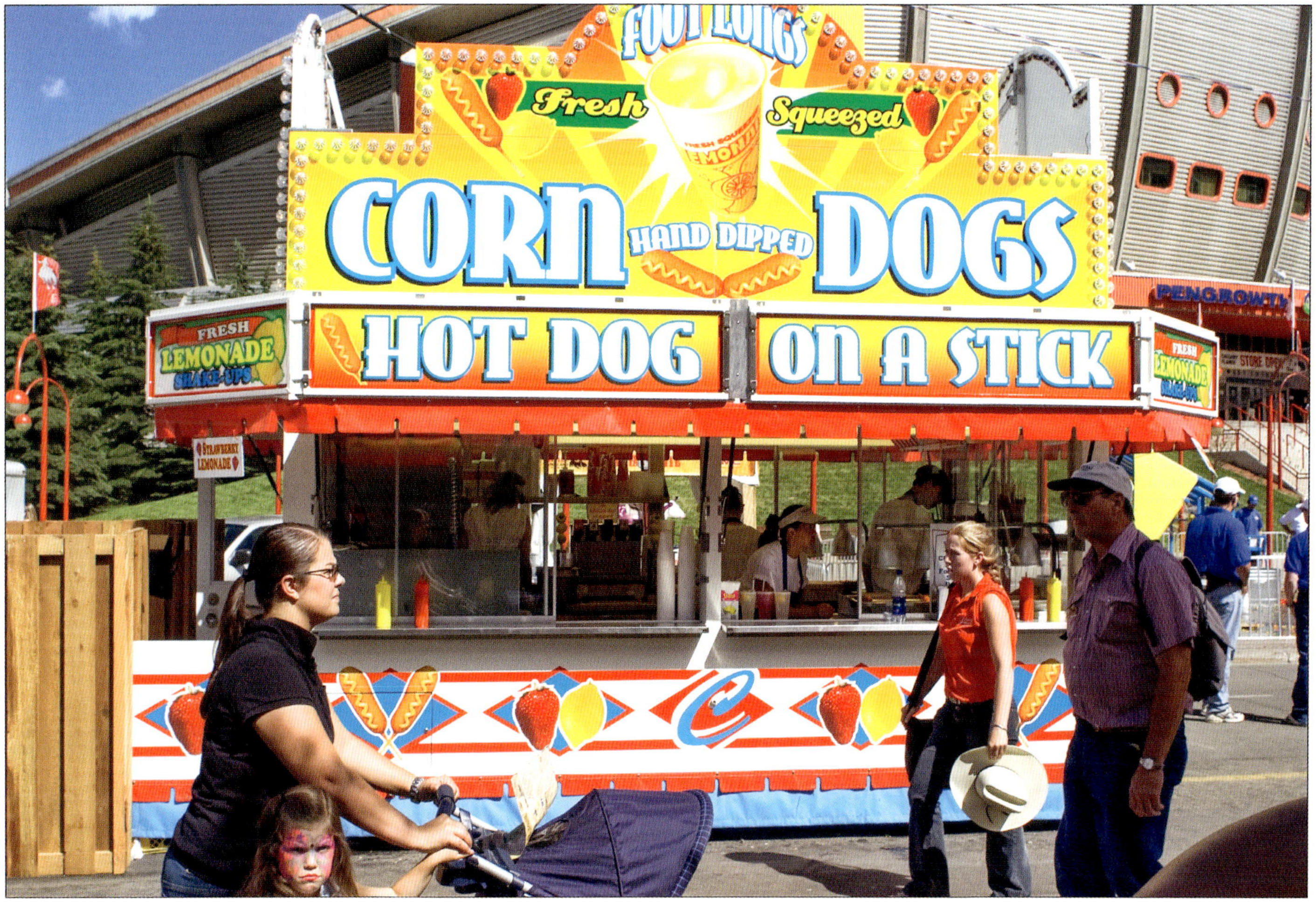

Stampede, 2005

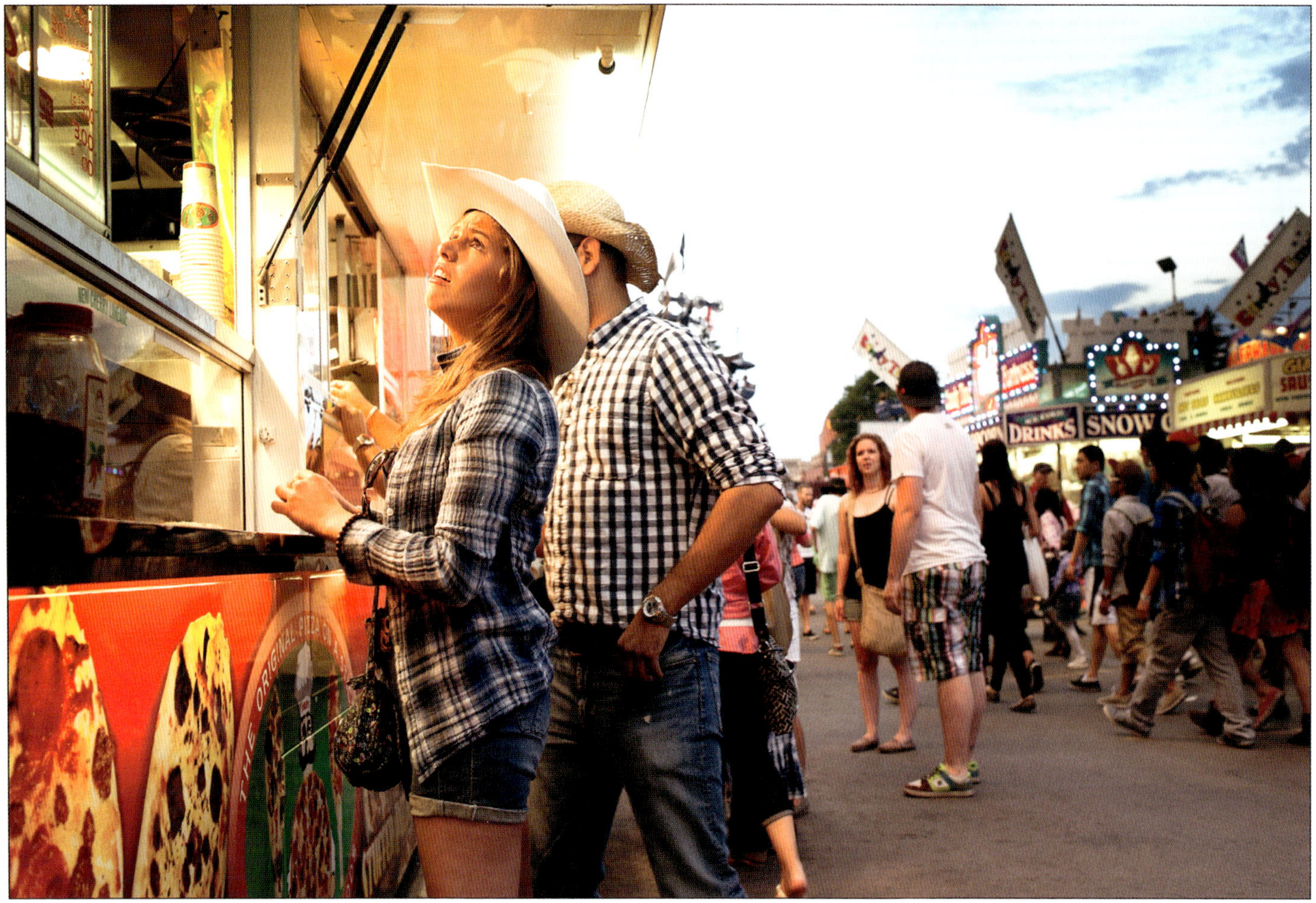

Stampede, 2012

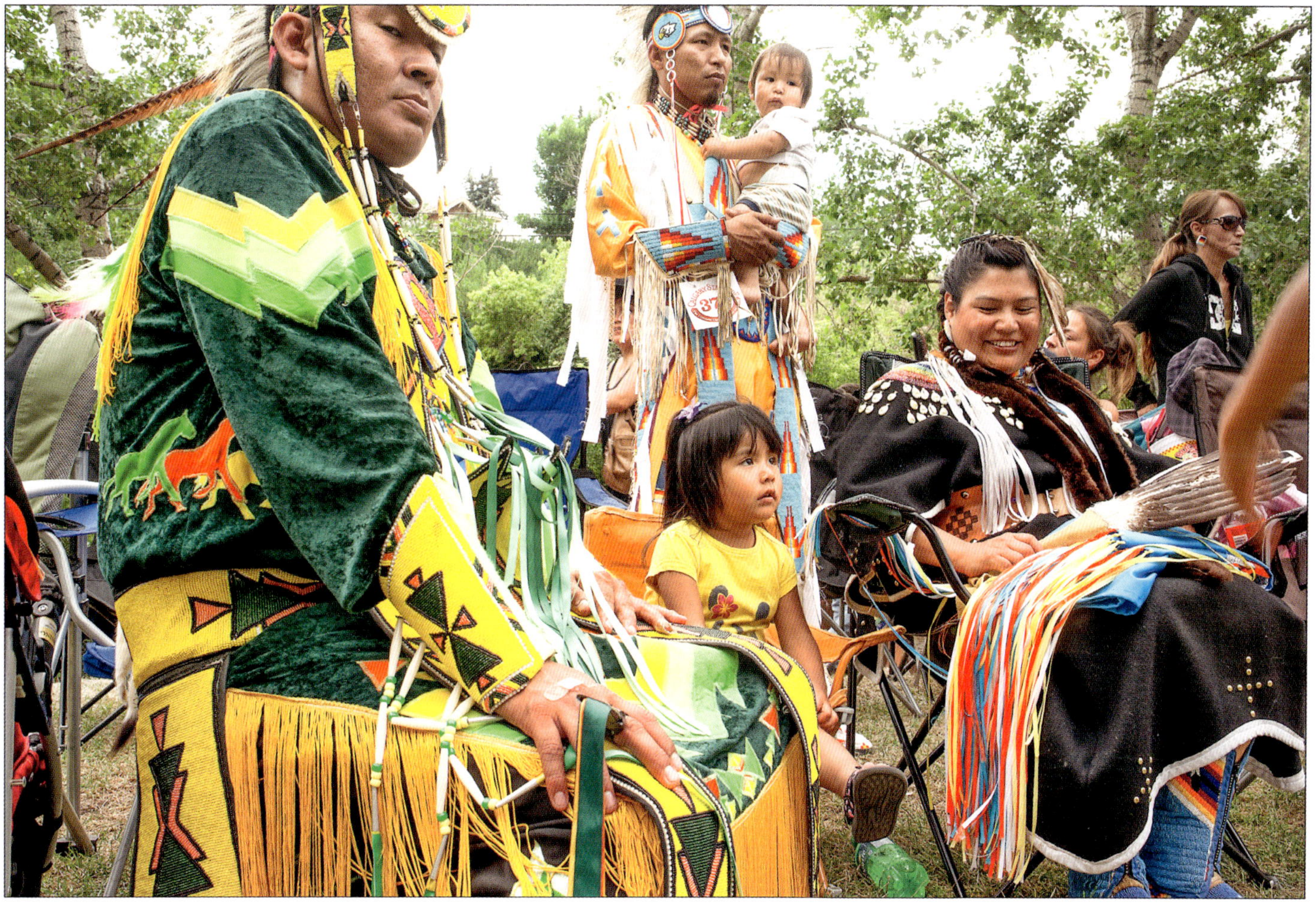

Stampede, 2012

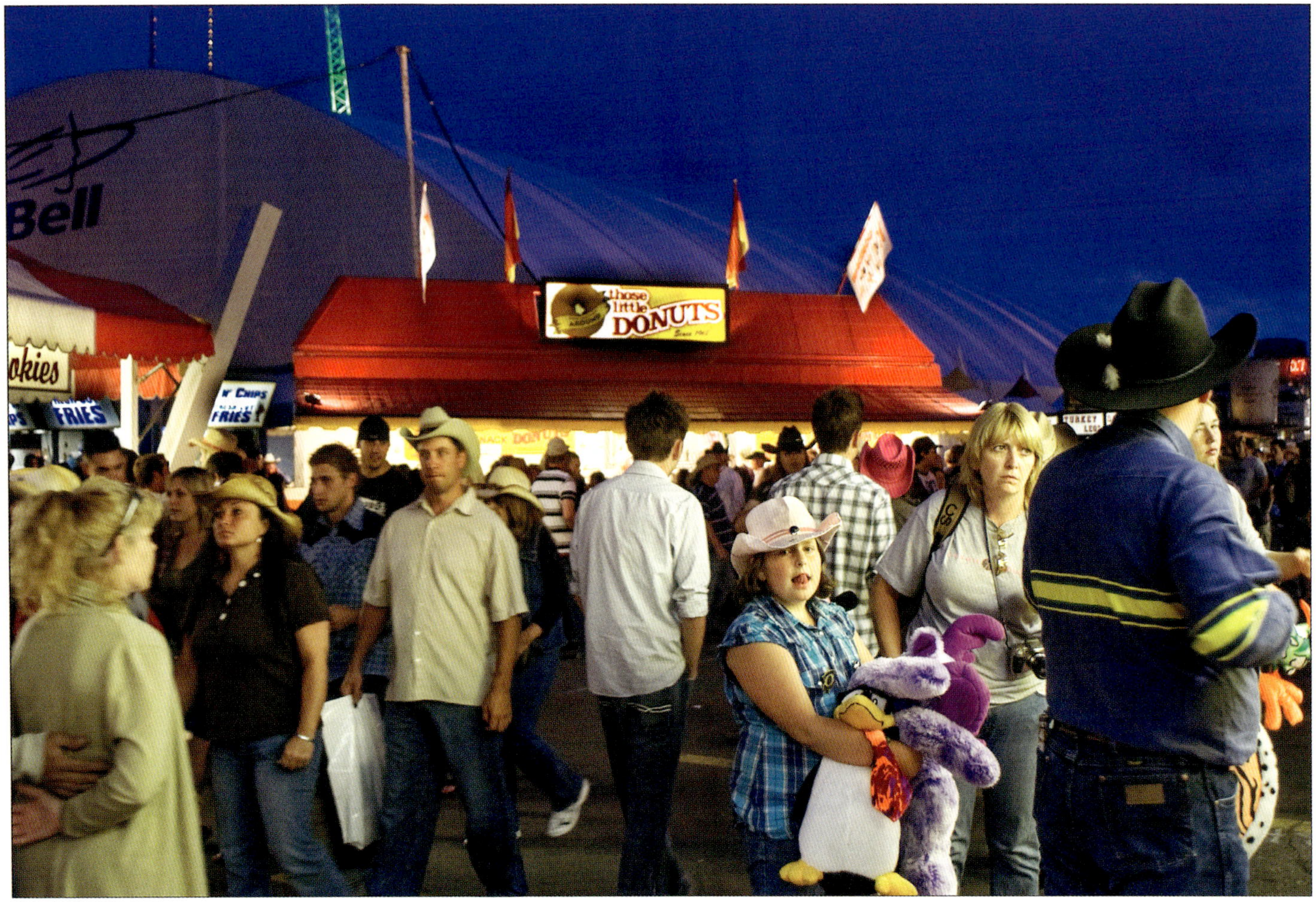

Stampede, 2007

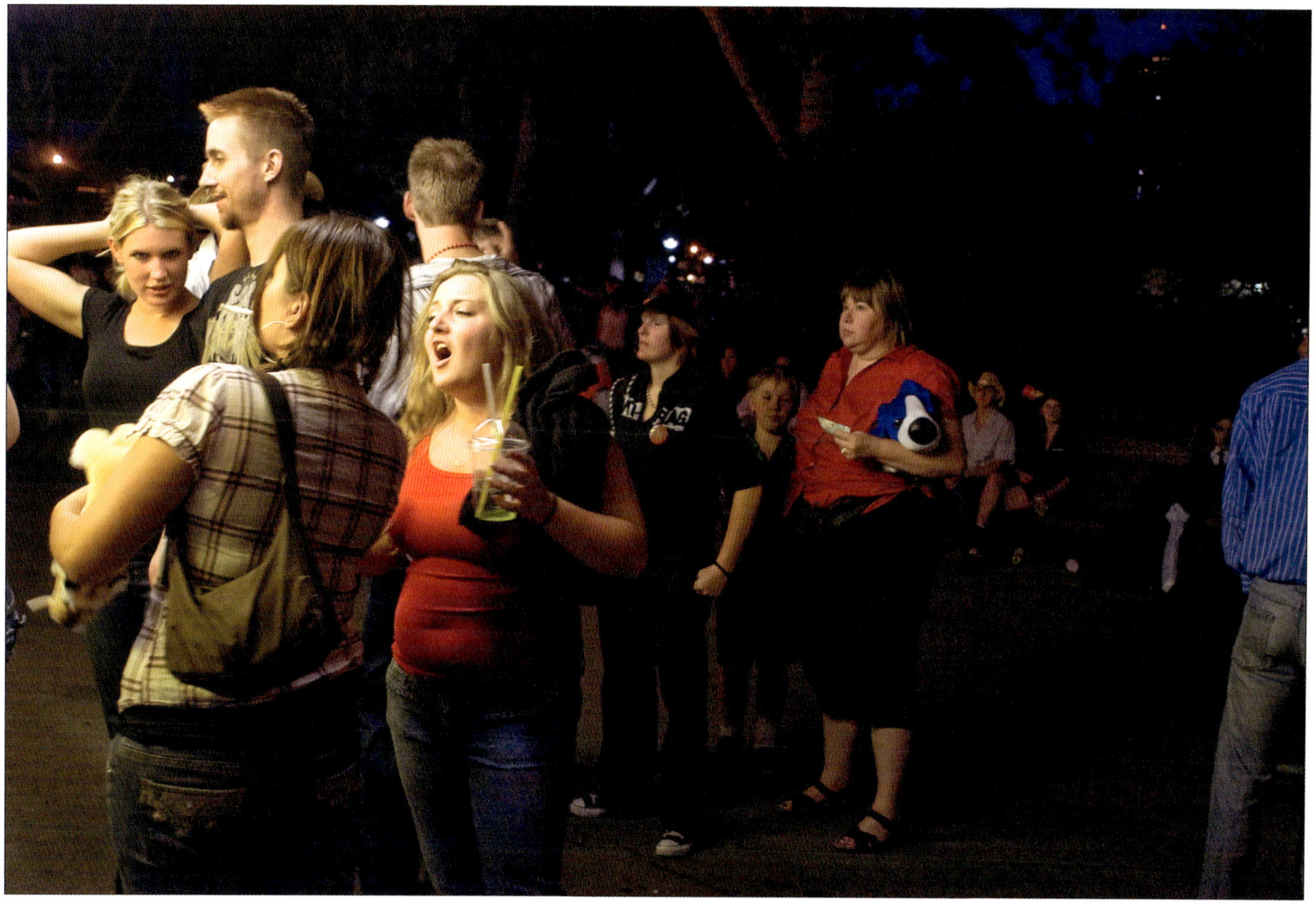

Stampede, 2007

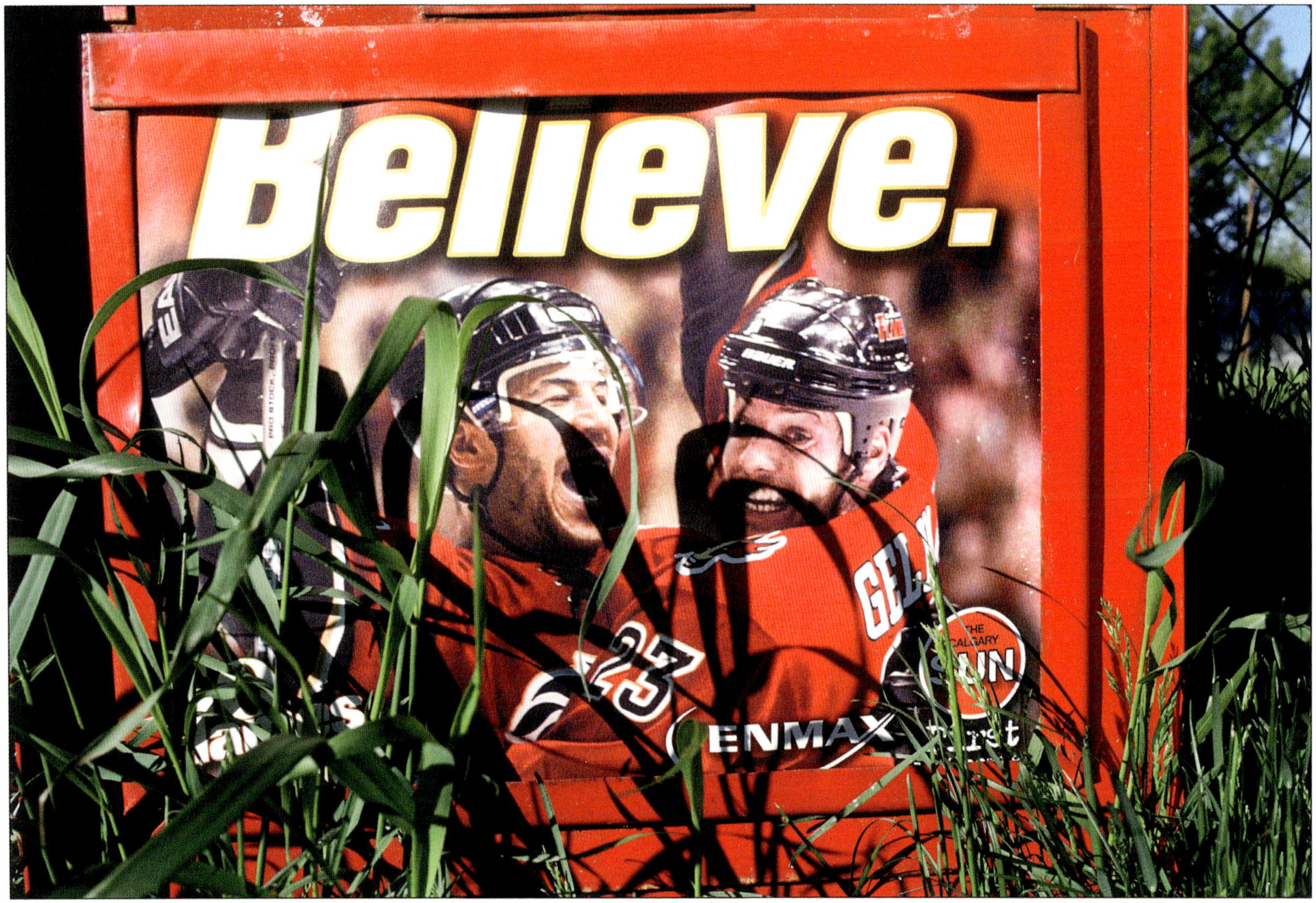

Sun box, 2004

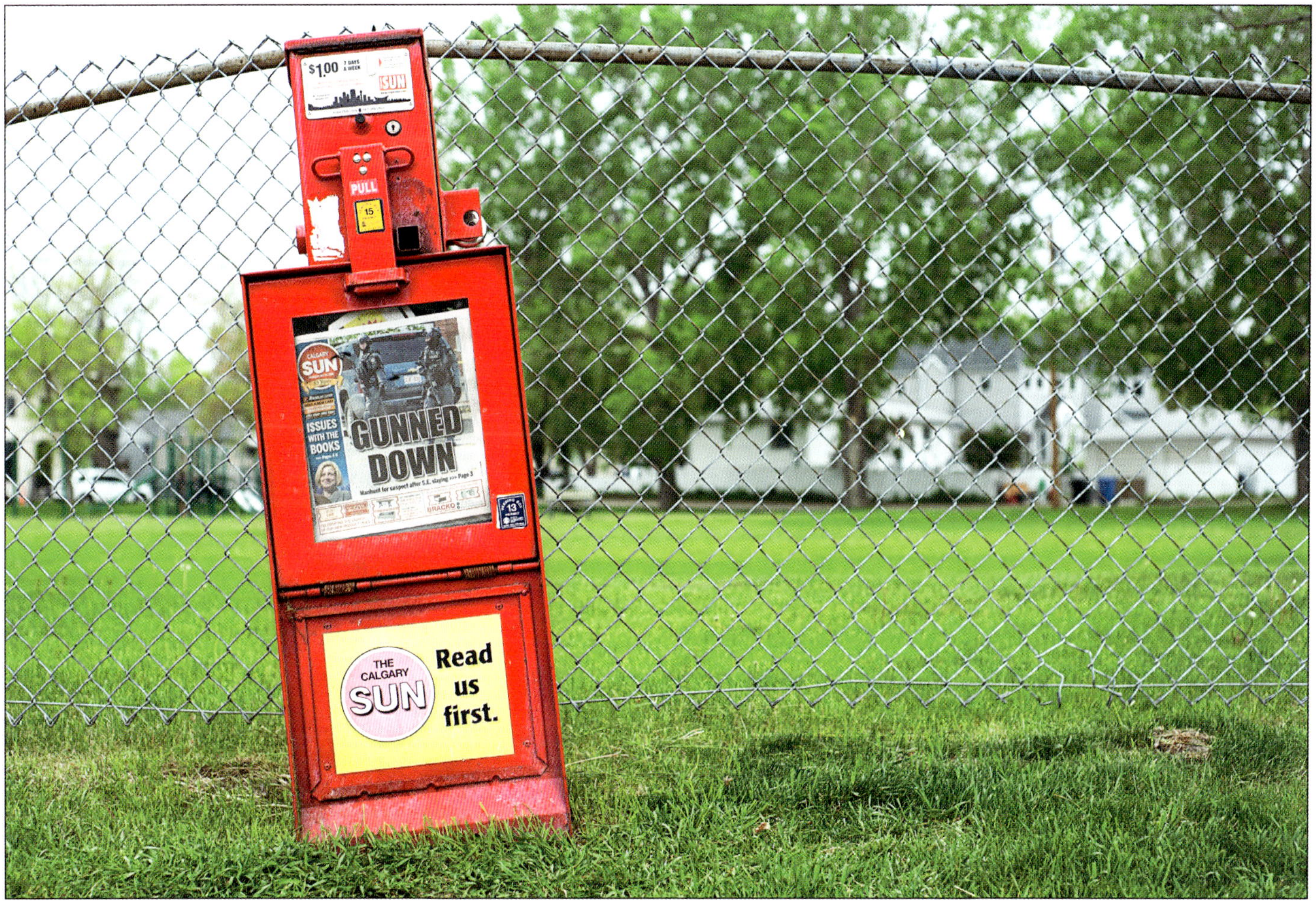
$1.00
SUN
PULL
SUN
ISSUES WITH THE BOOKS
GUNNED DOWN
THE CALGARY SUN
Read us first.

Sun box, 2015

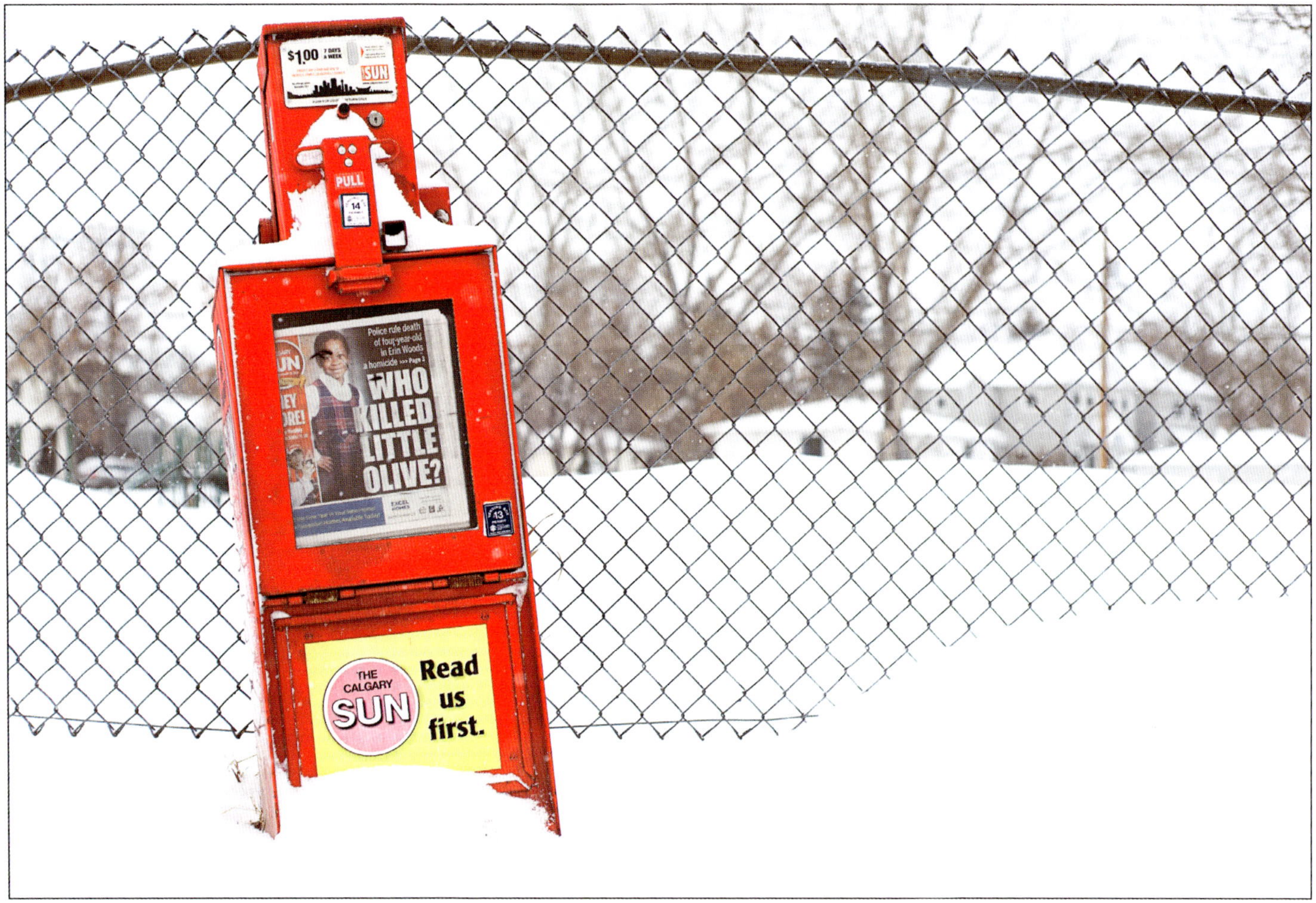
$1.00
SUN
PULL
Police rule death of four-year-old in Erin Woods a homicide
WHO KILLED LITTLE OLIVE?
THE CALGARY SUN
Read us first.

Sun box, 2015

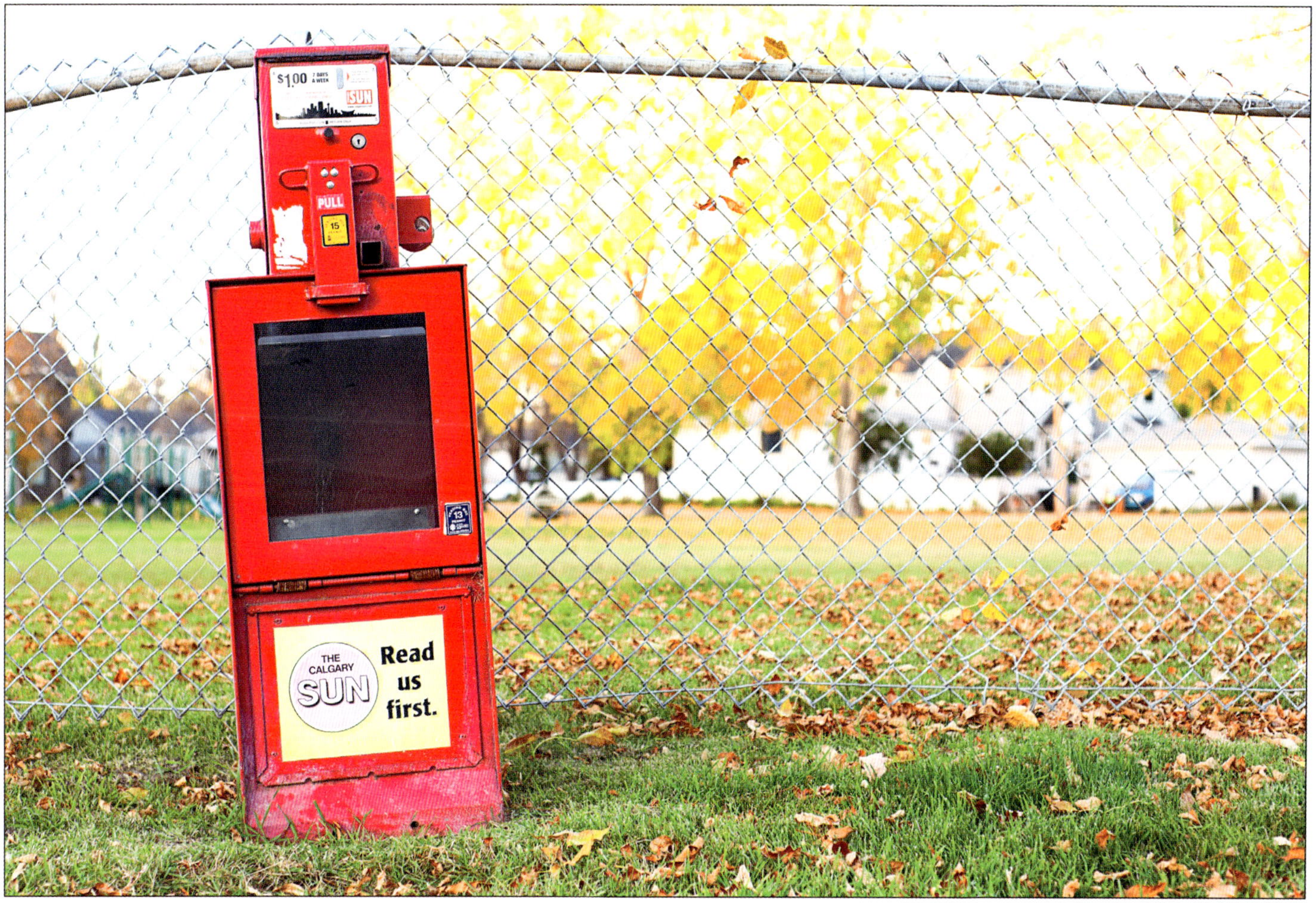

Sun box, 2015

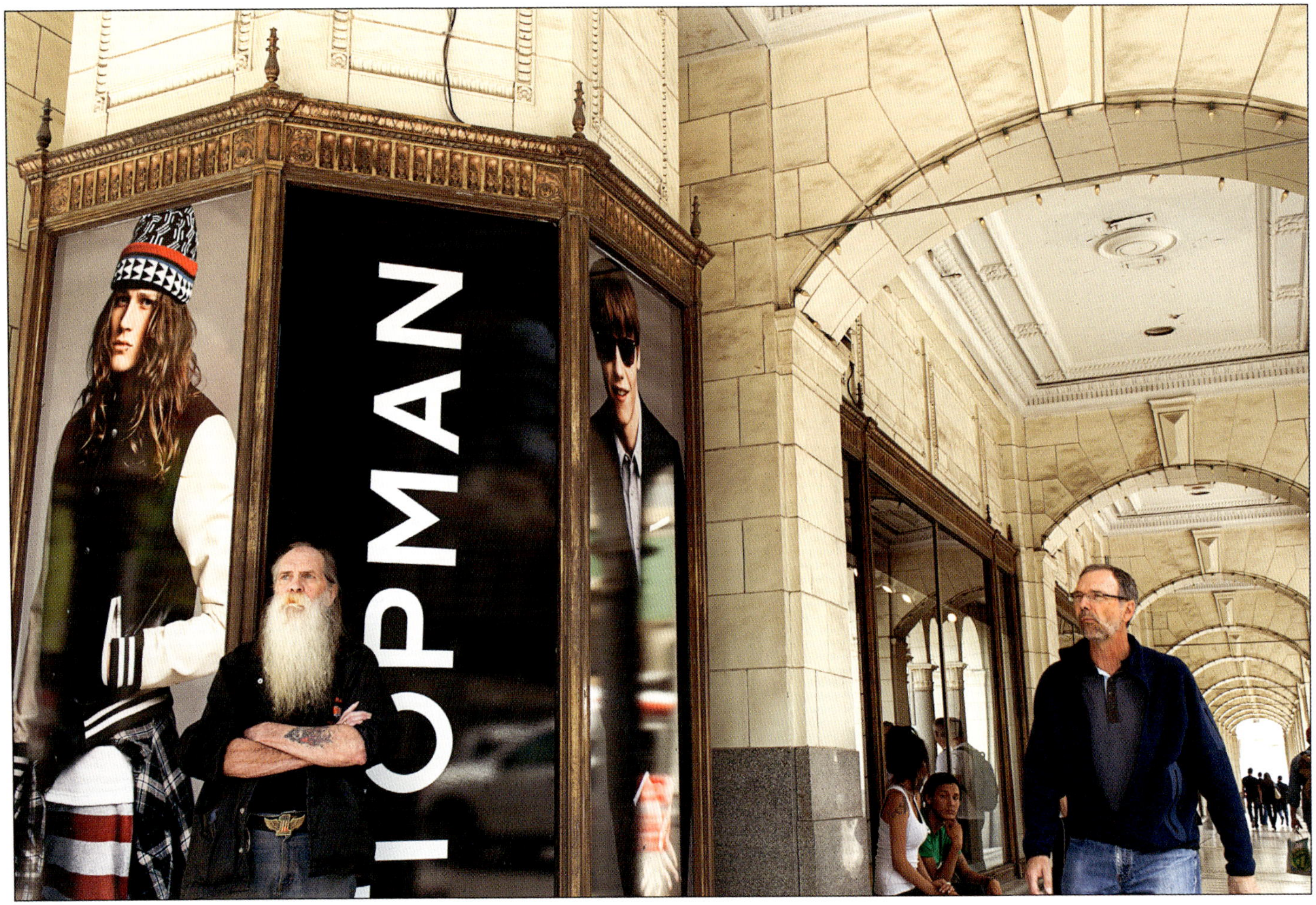

Hudson's Bay, 2013

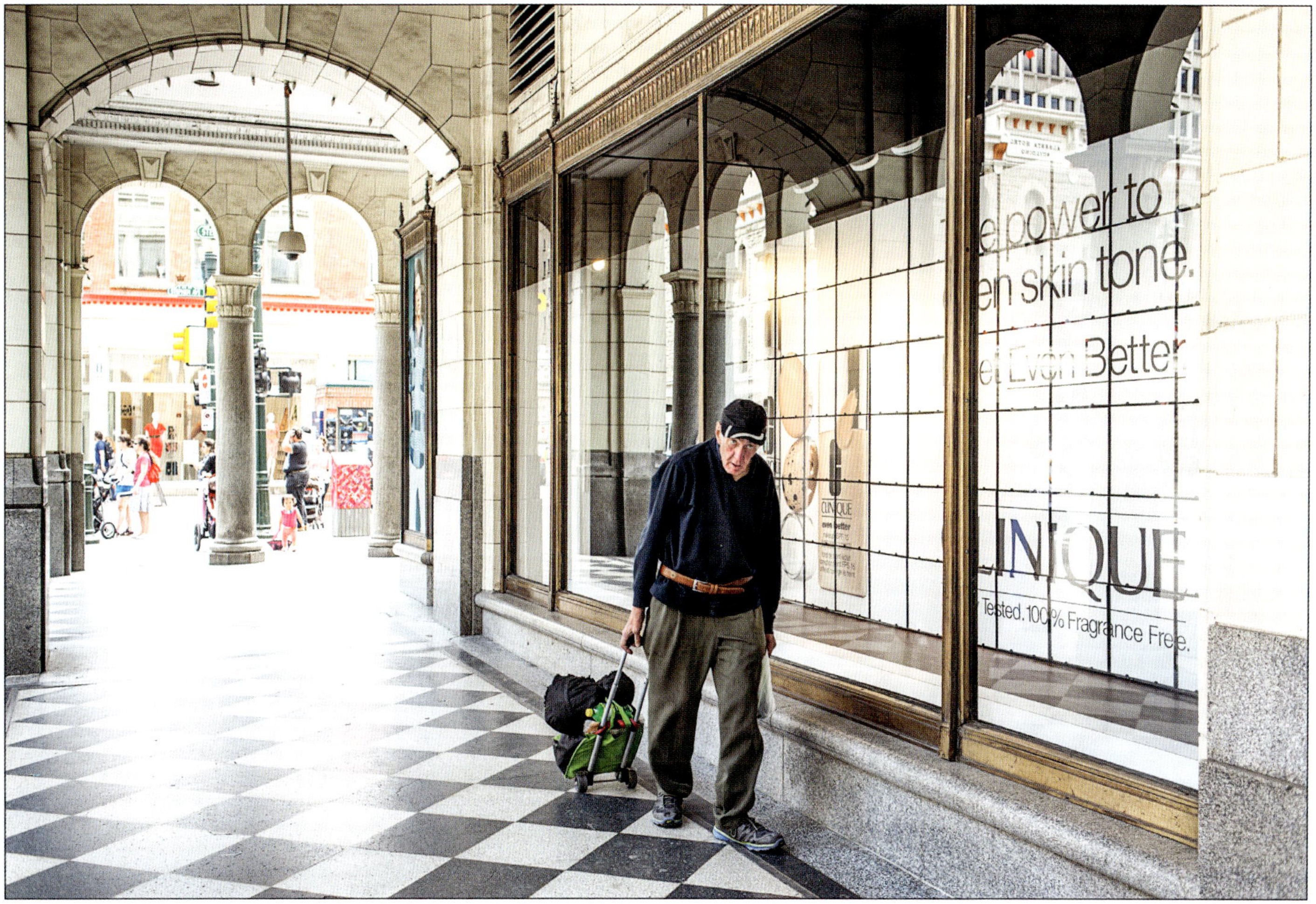

Hudson's Bay, 2014

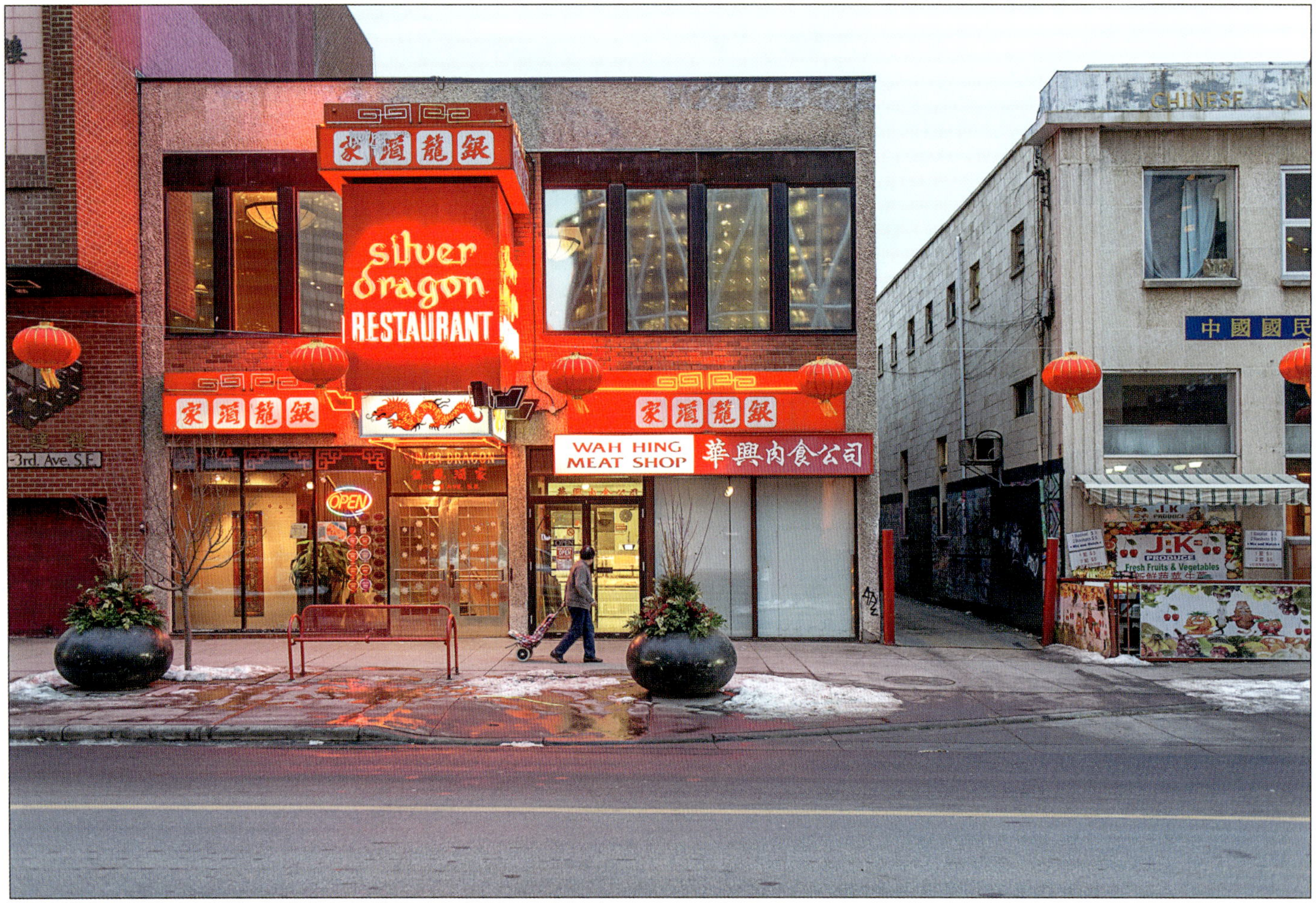

Chinatown, 2018

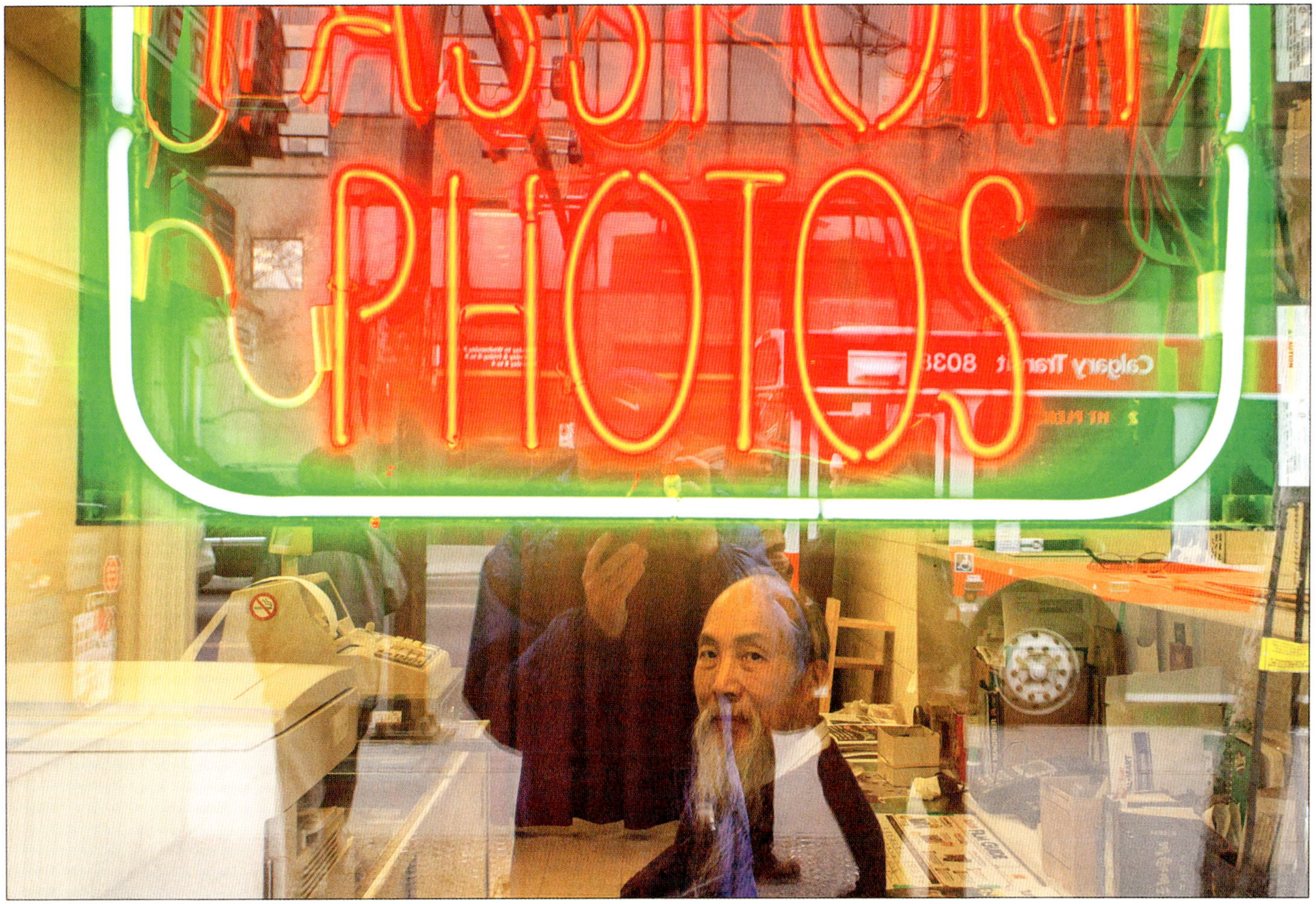

Chinatown, 2010

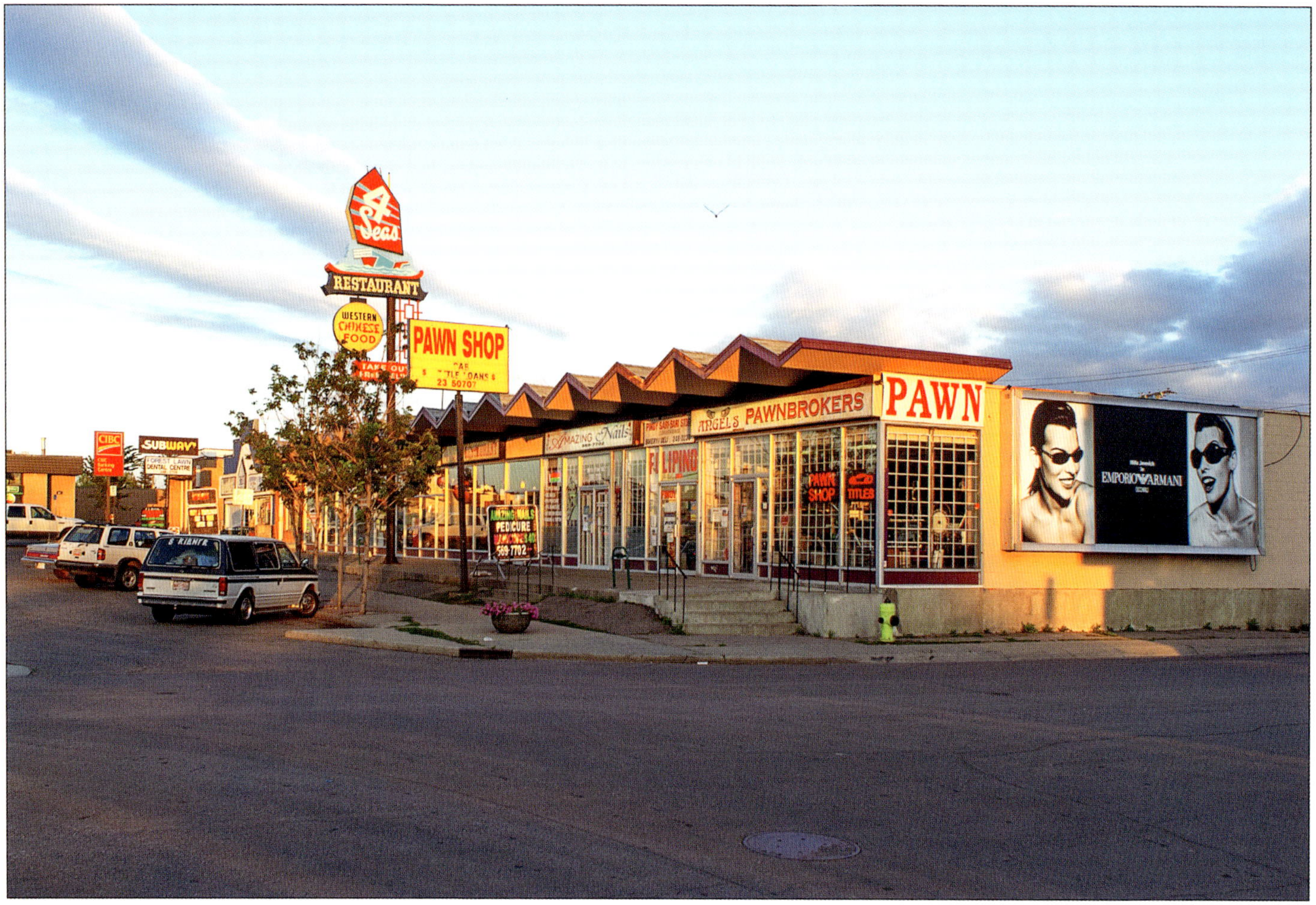

4 Seas Restaurant, 2005

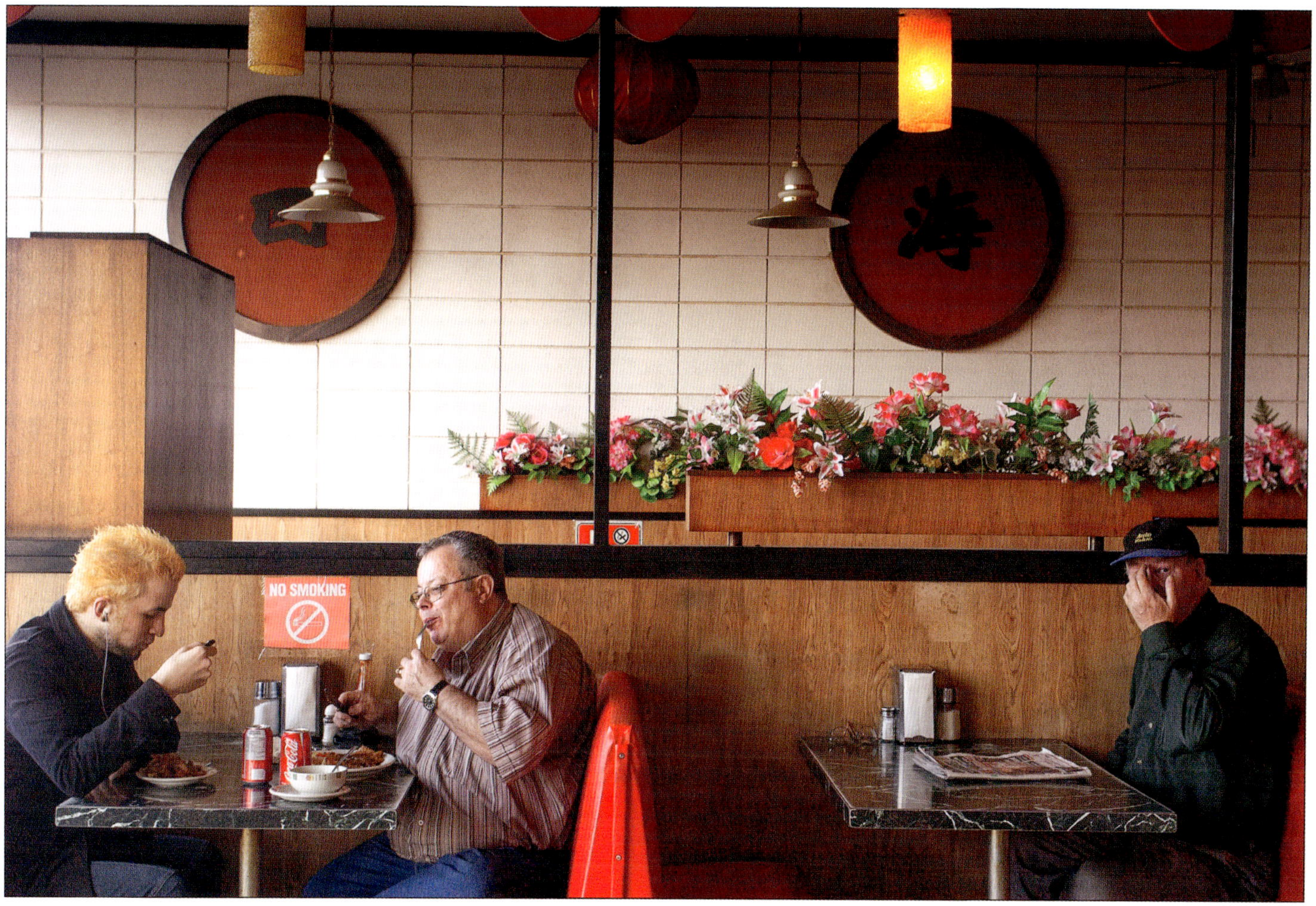

4 Seas Restaurant, 2009

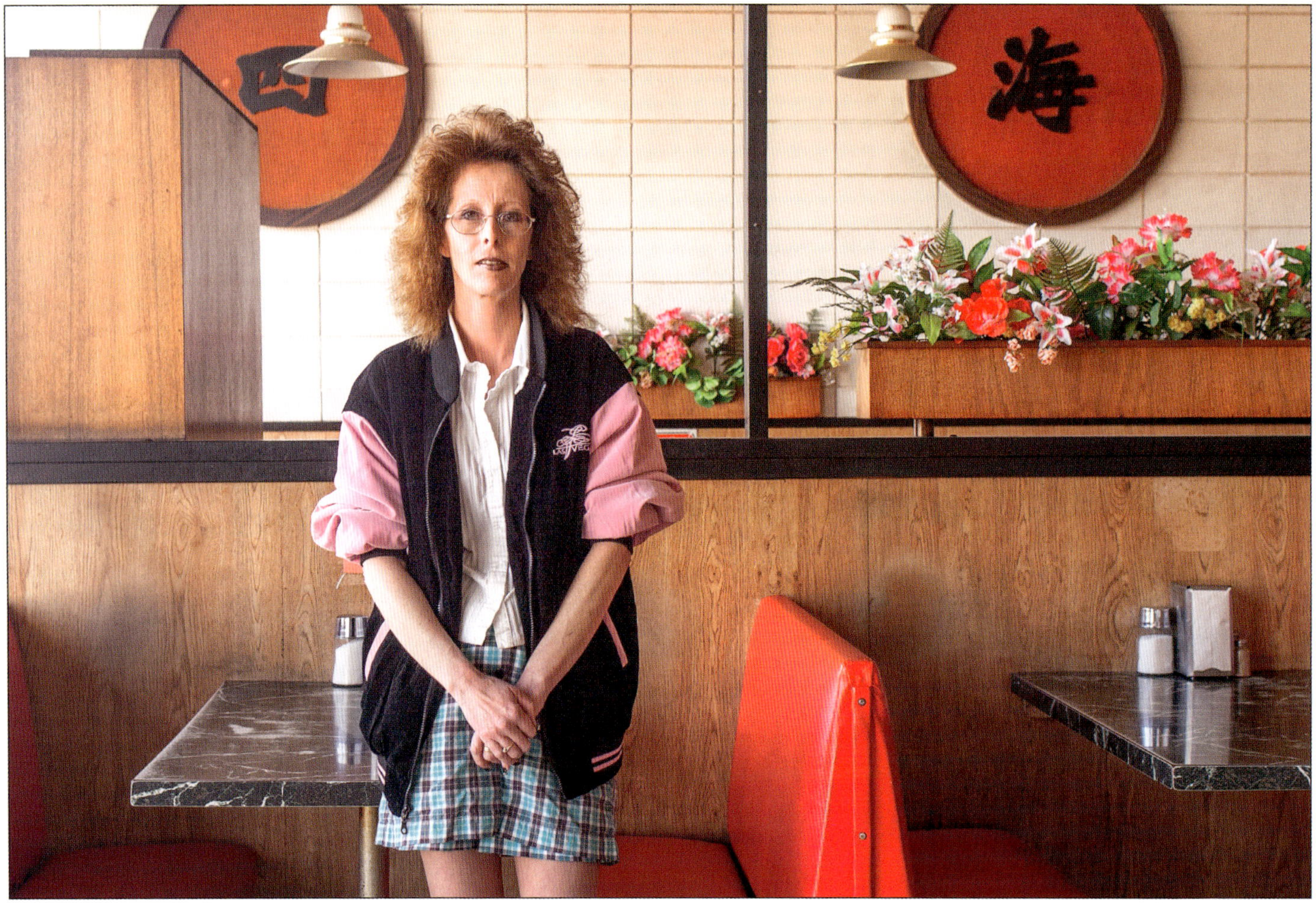

Marla Crowther, 4 Seas Restaurant, 2009

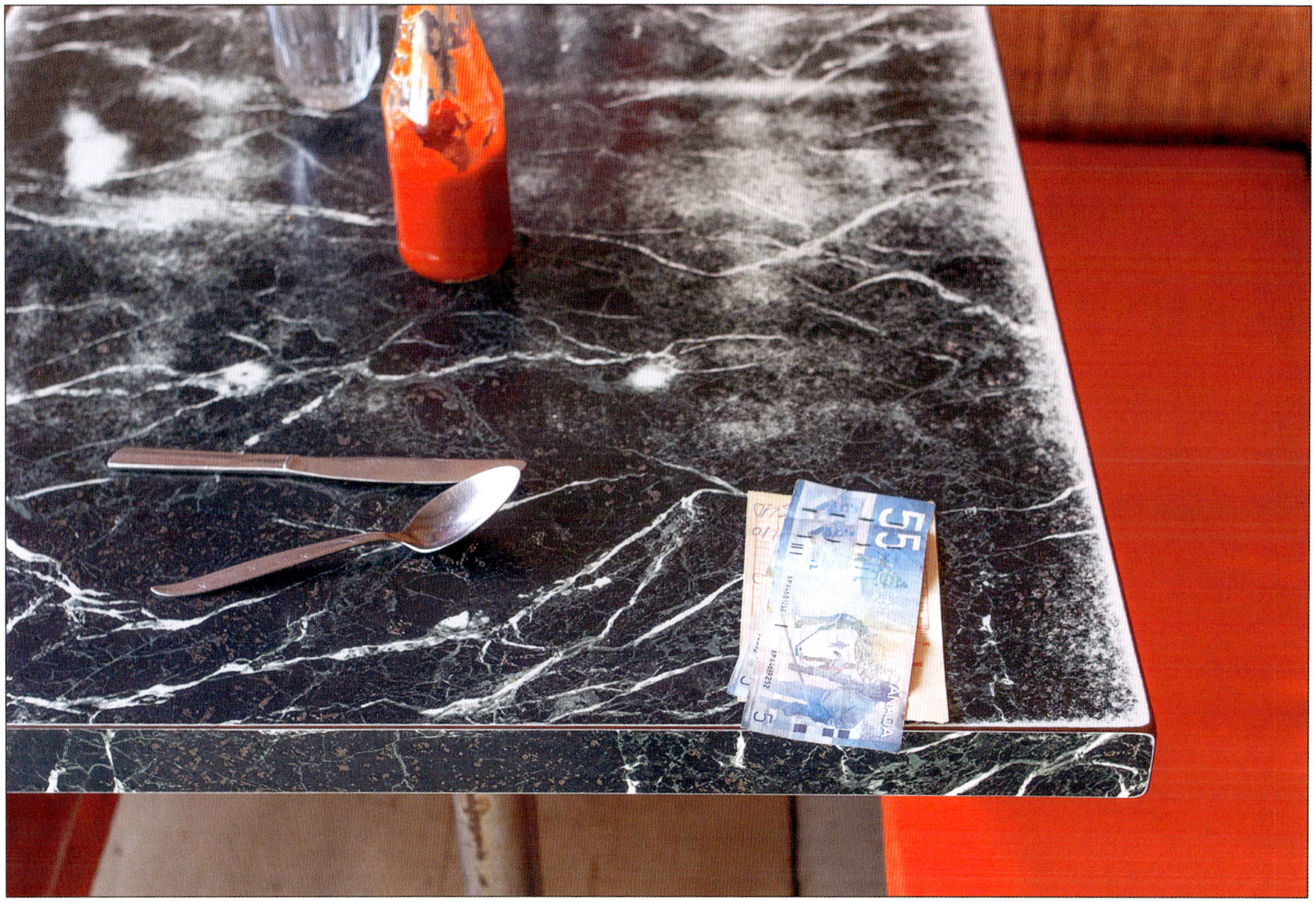

4 Seas Restaurant, 2009

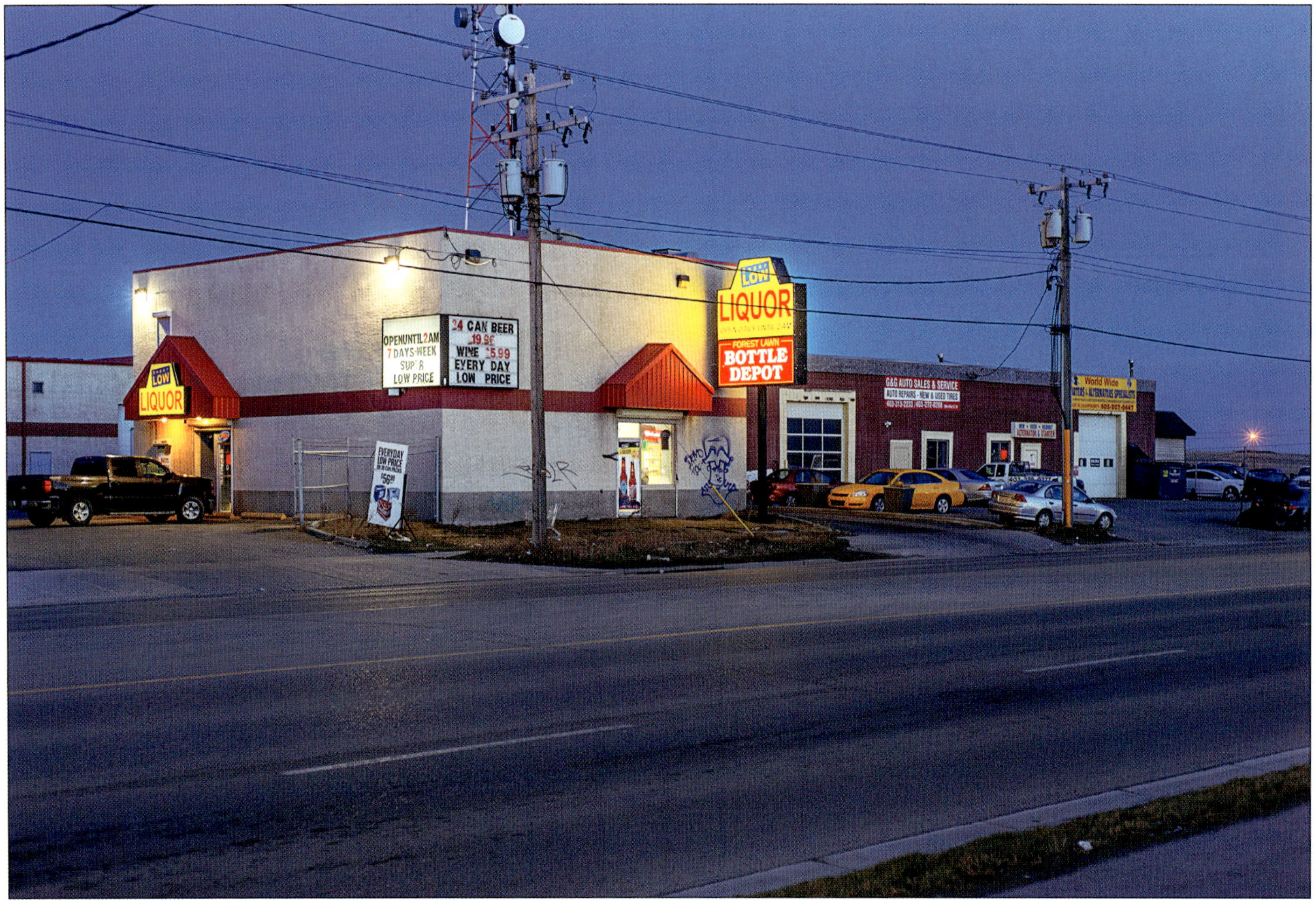

Near 21A Ave + 52 St SE, 2017

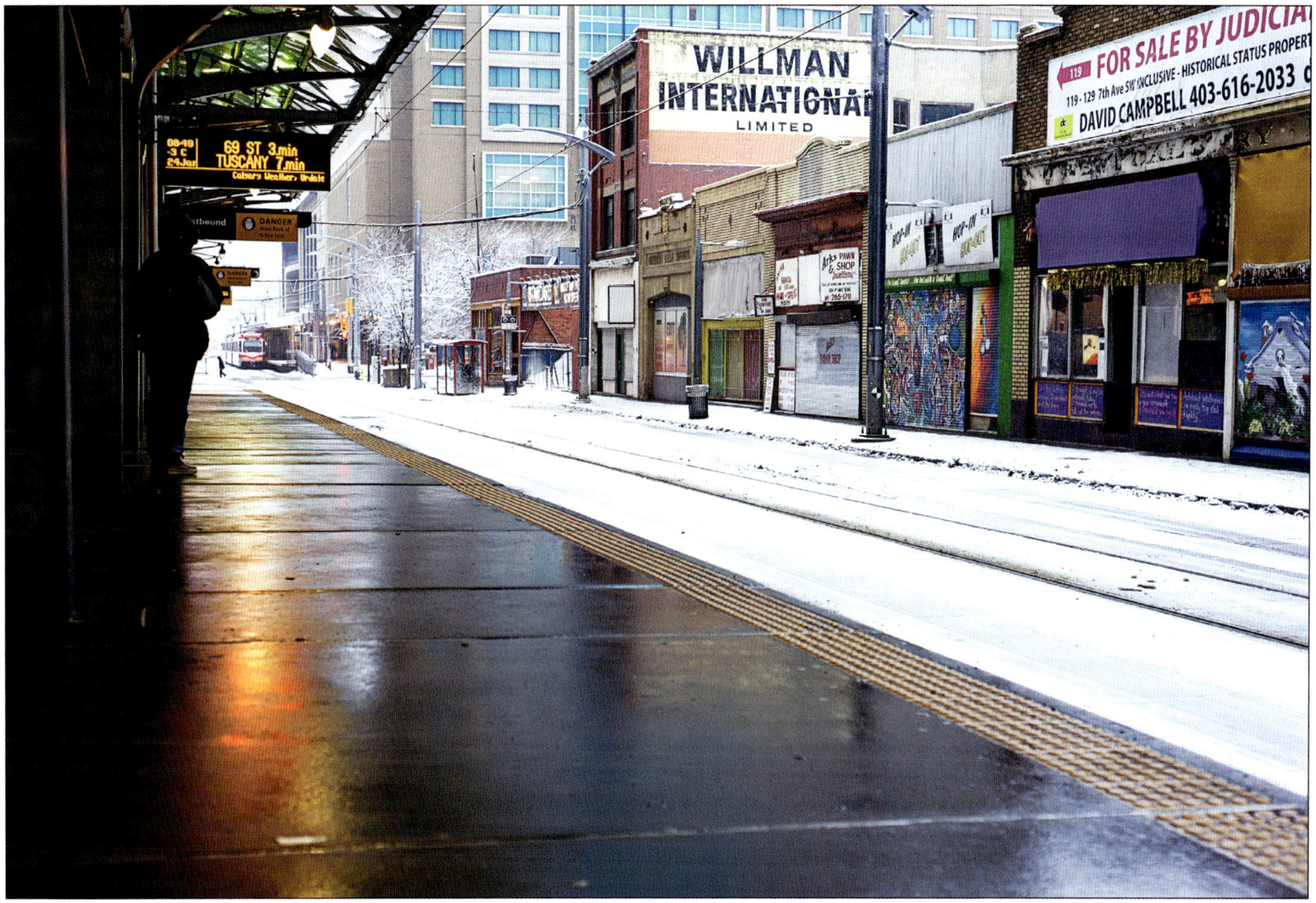

LRT, 7 Ave, 2016

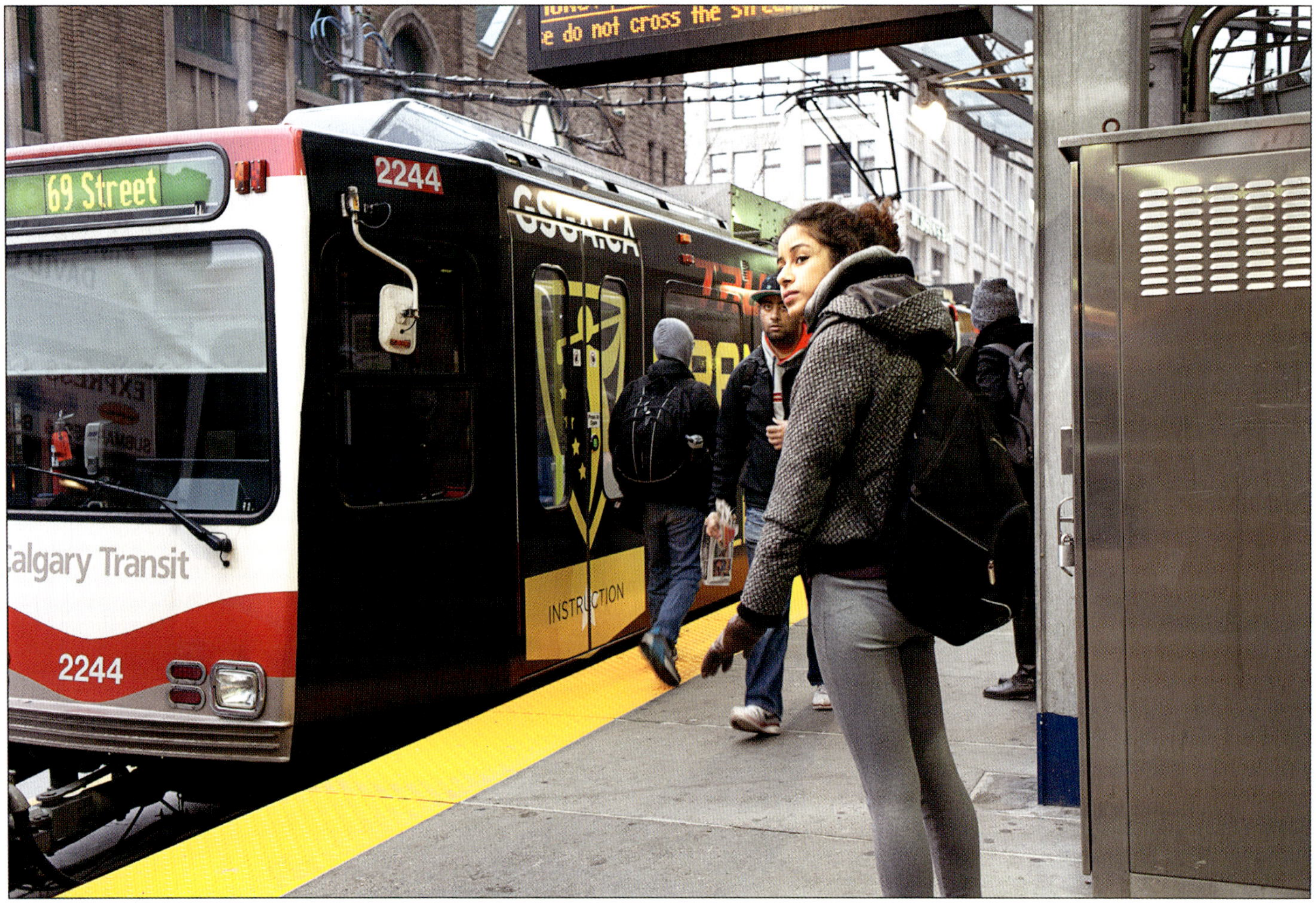

LRT, 7 Ave, 2016

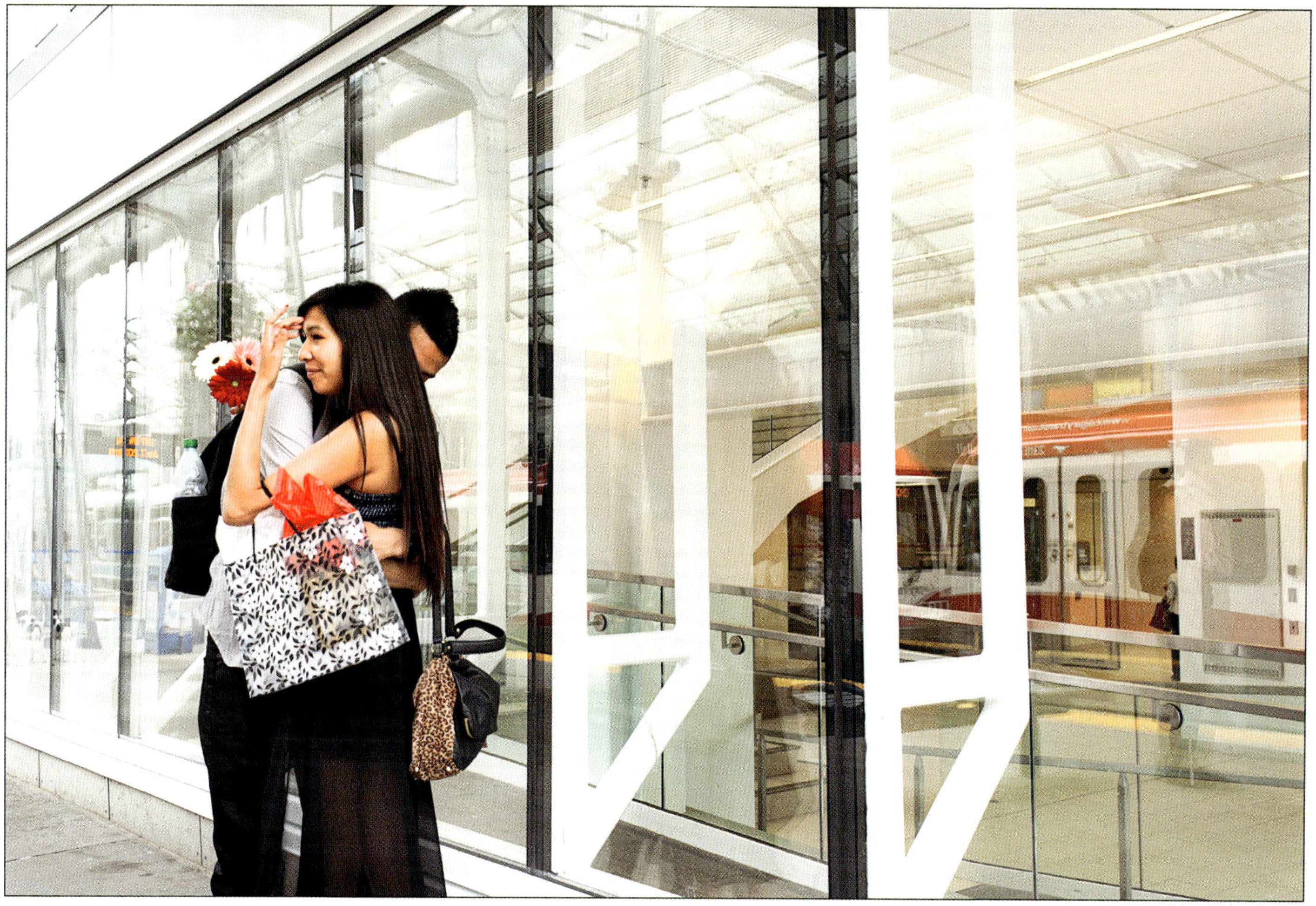

LRT, 7 Ave, 2013

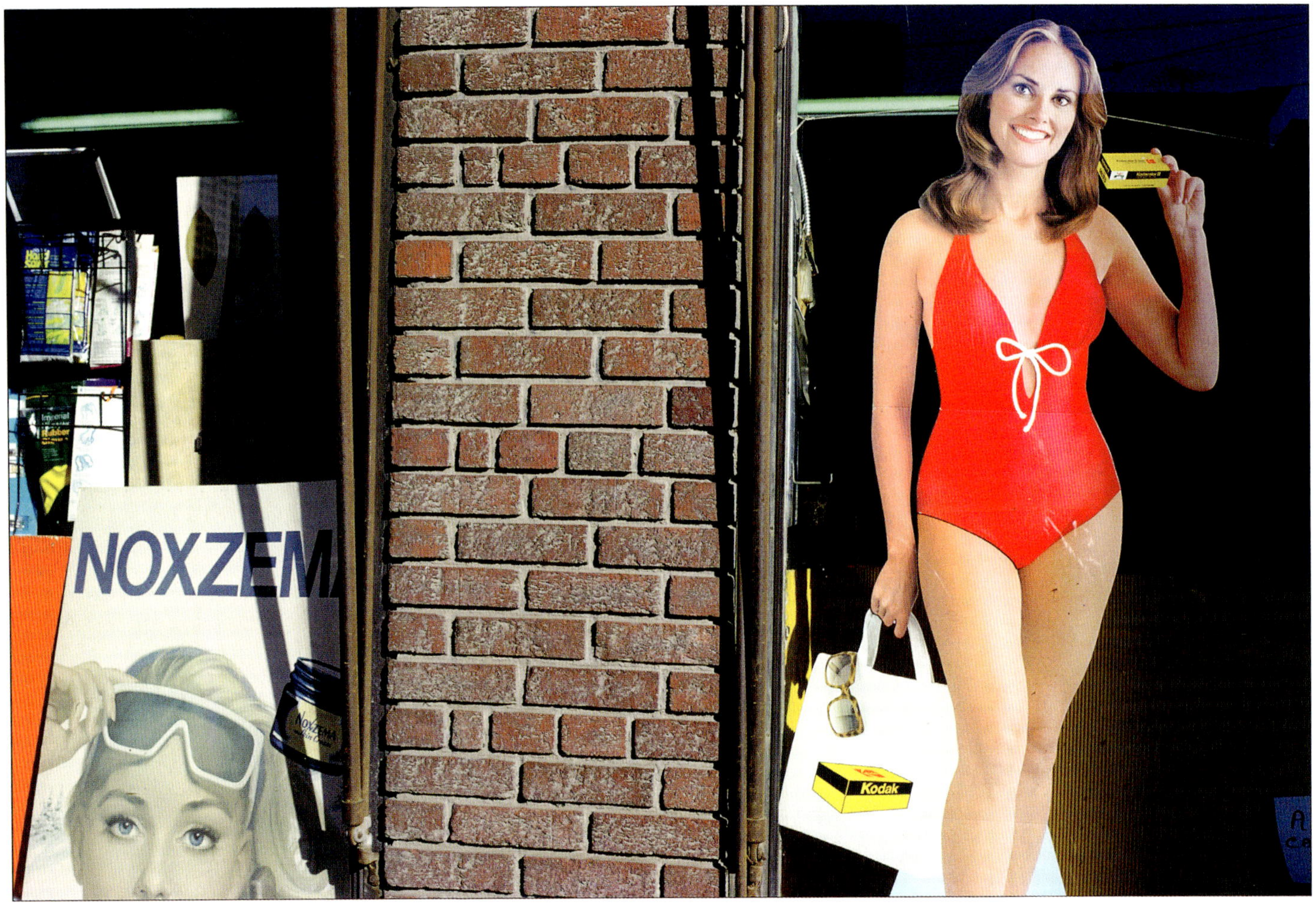

Downtown, 1978

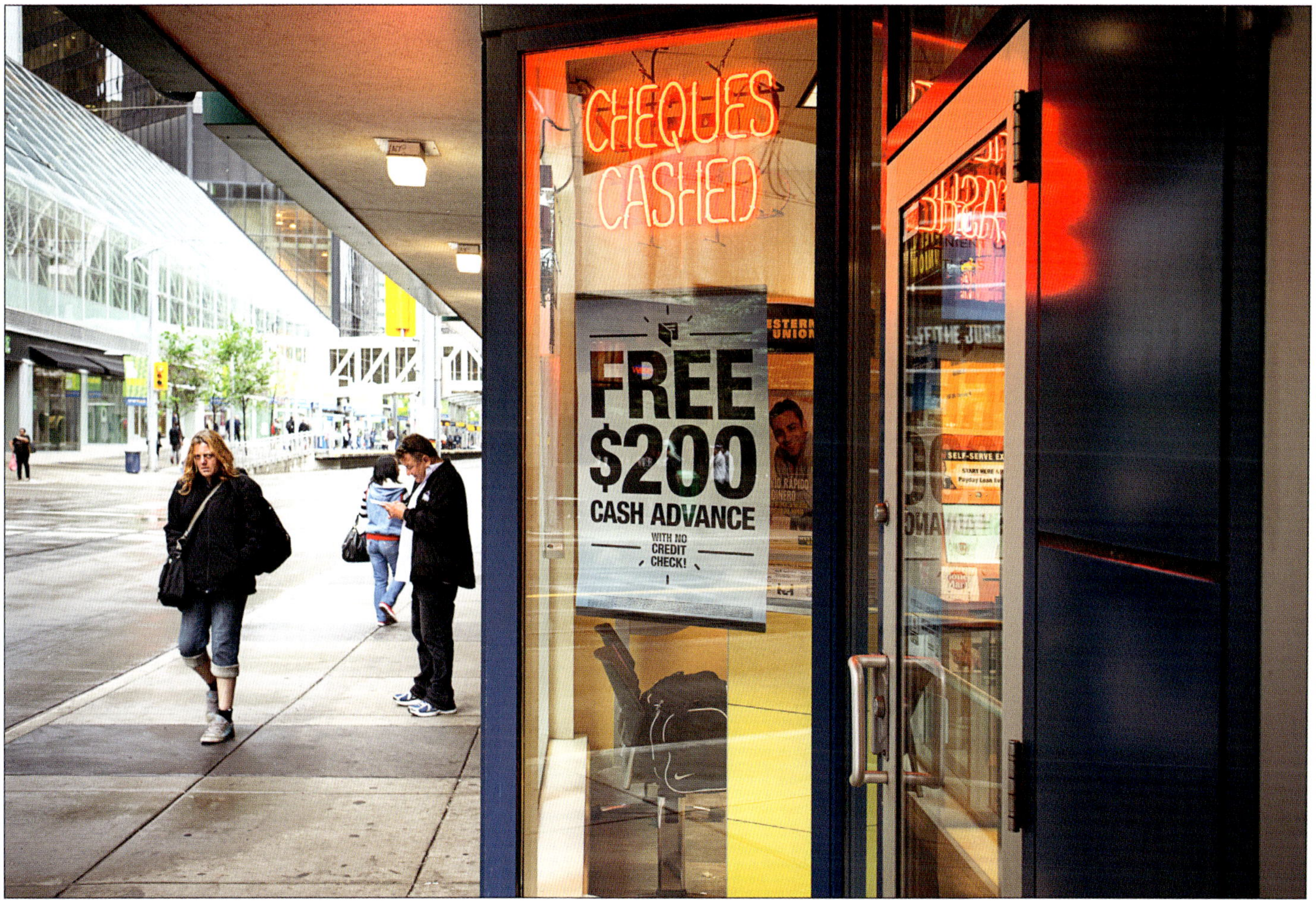

Downtown, 2013

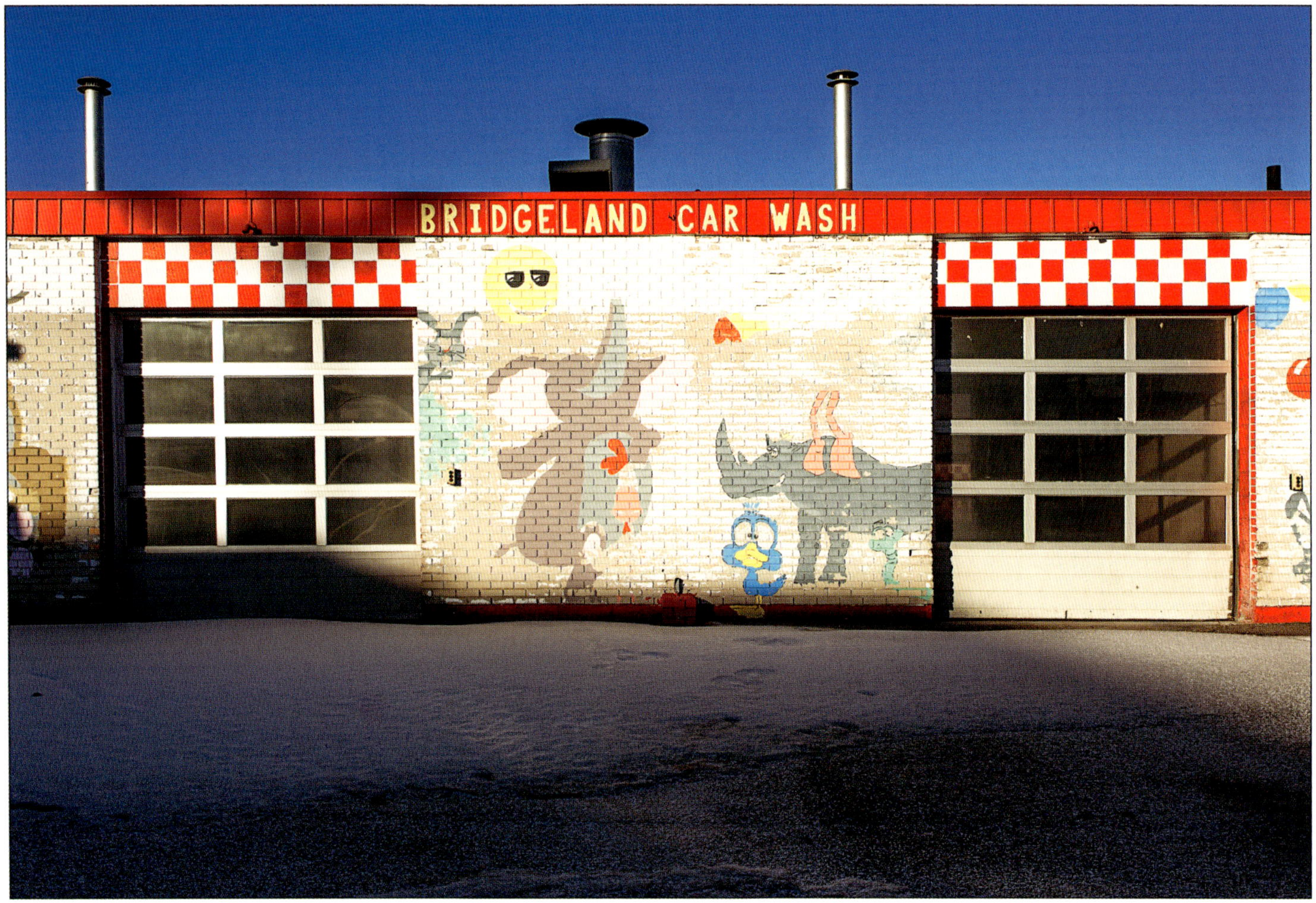

Bridgeland Car Wash, 2015

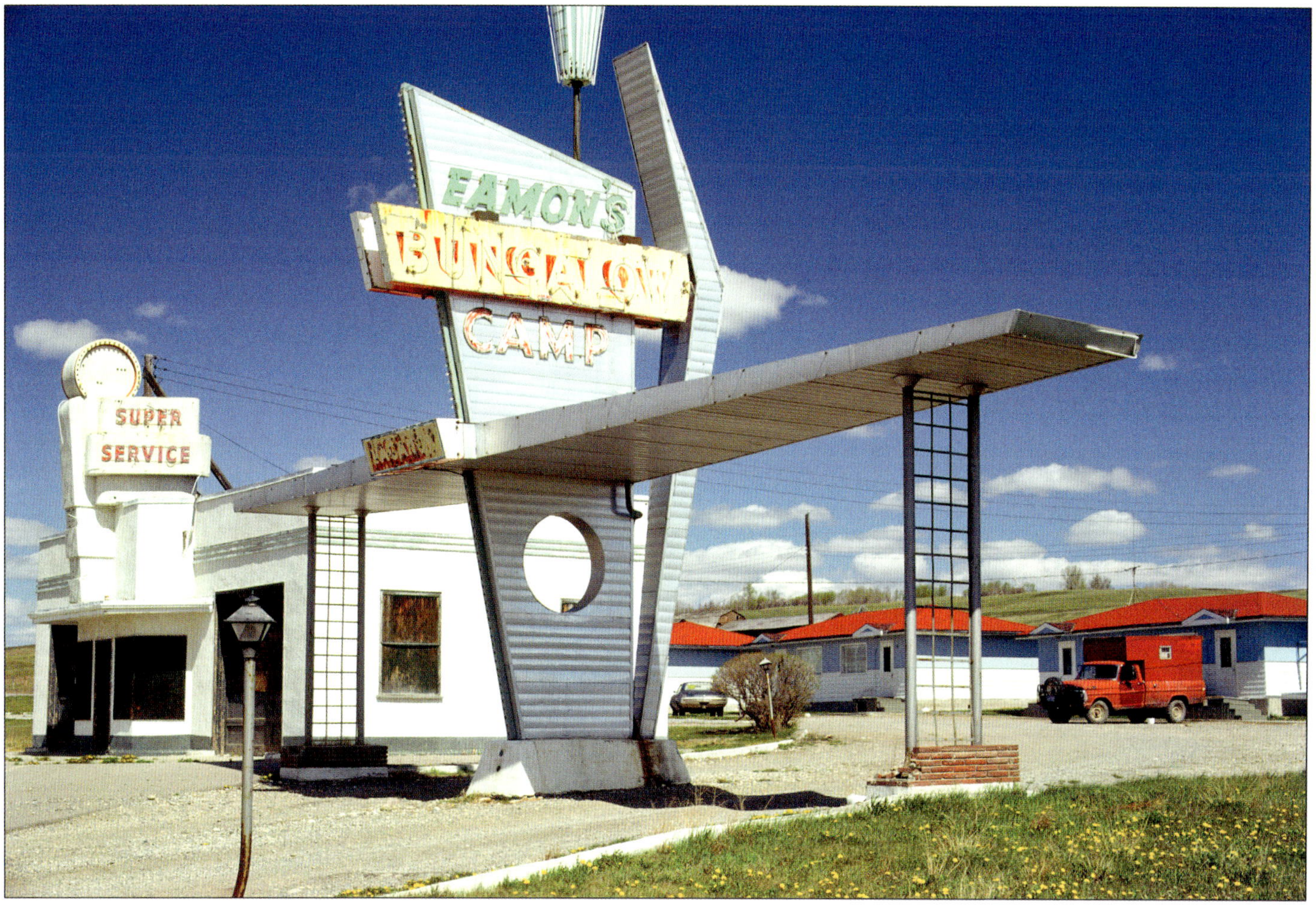

Eamon's, 1984

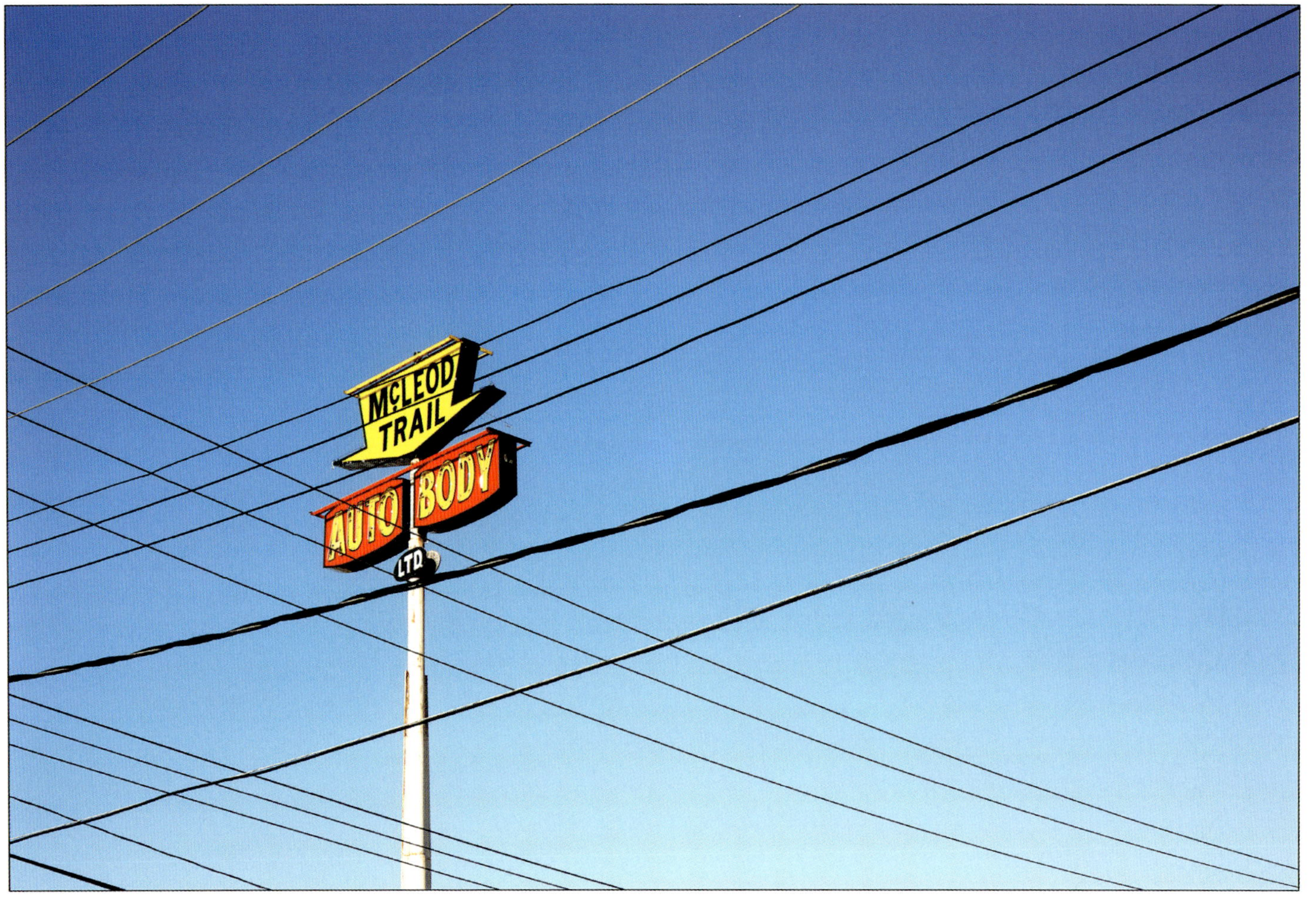

Macleod Trail Autobody, 2012

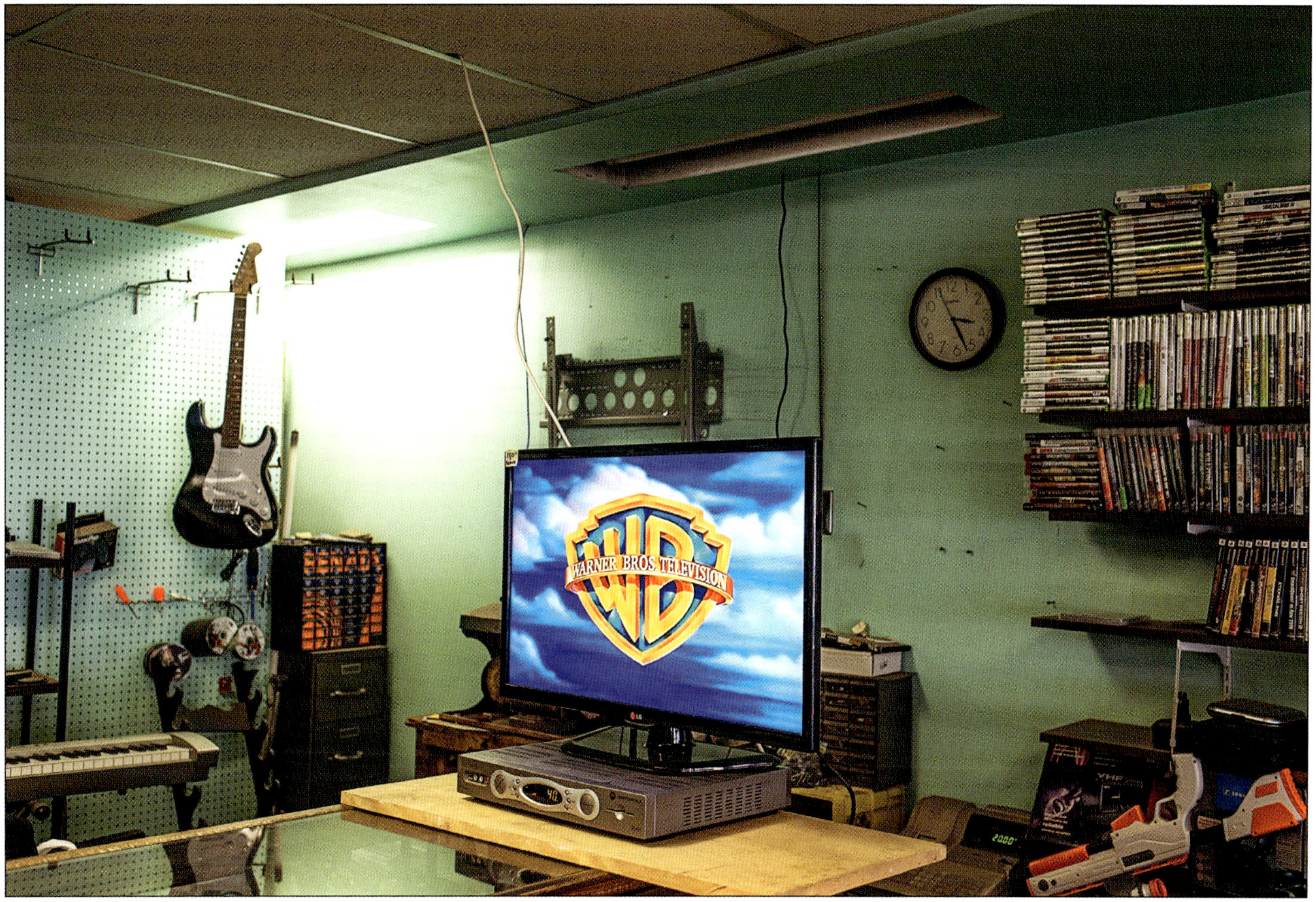

7 Ave SW, 2014

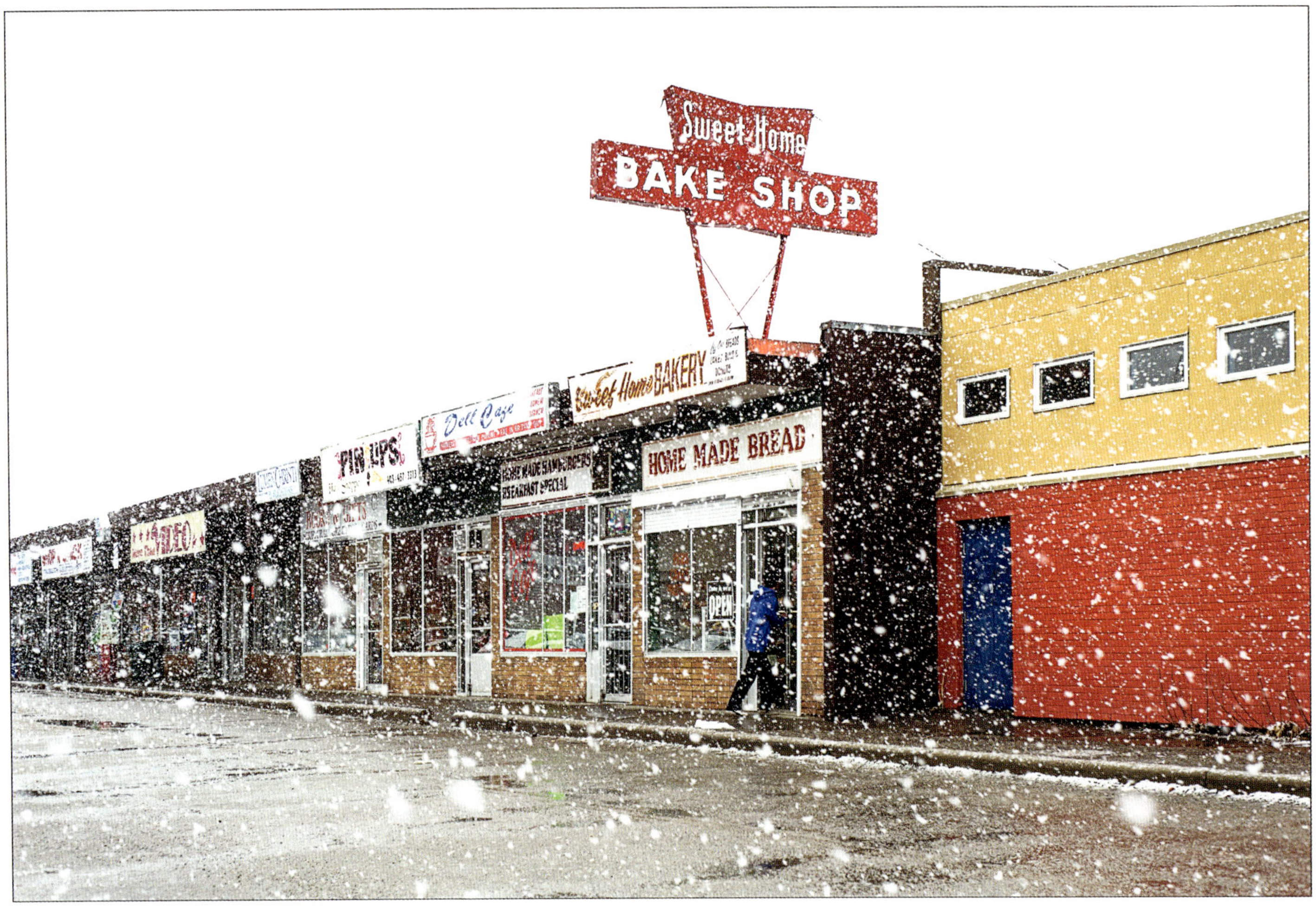

Sweet Home Bakeshop, 2014

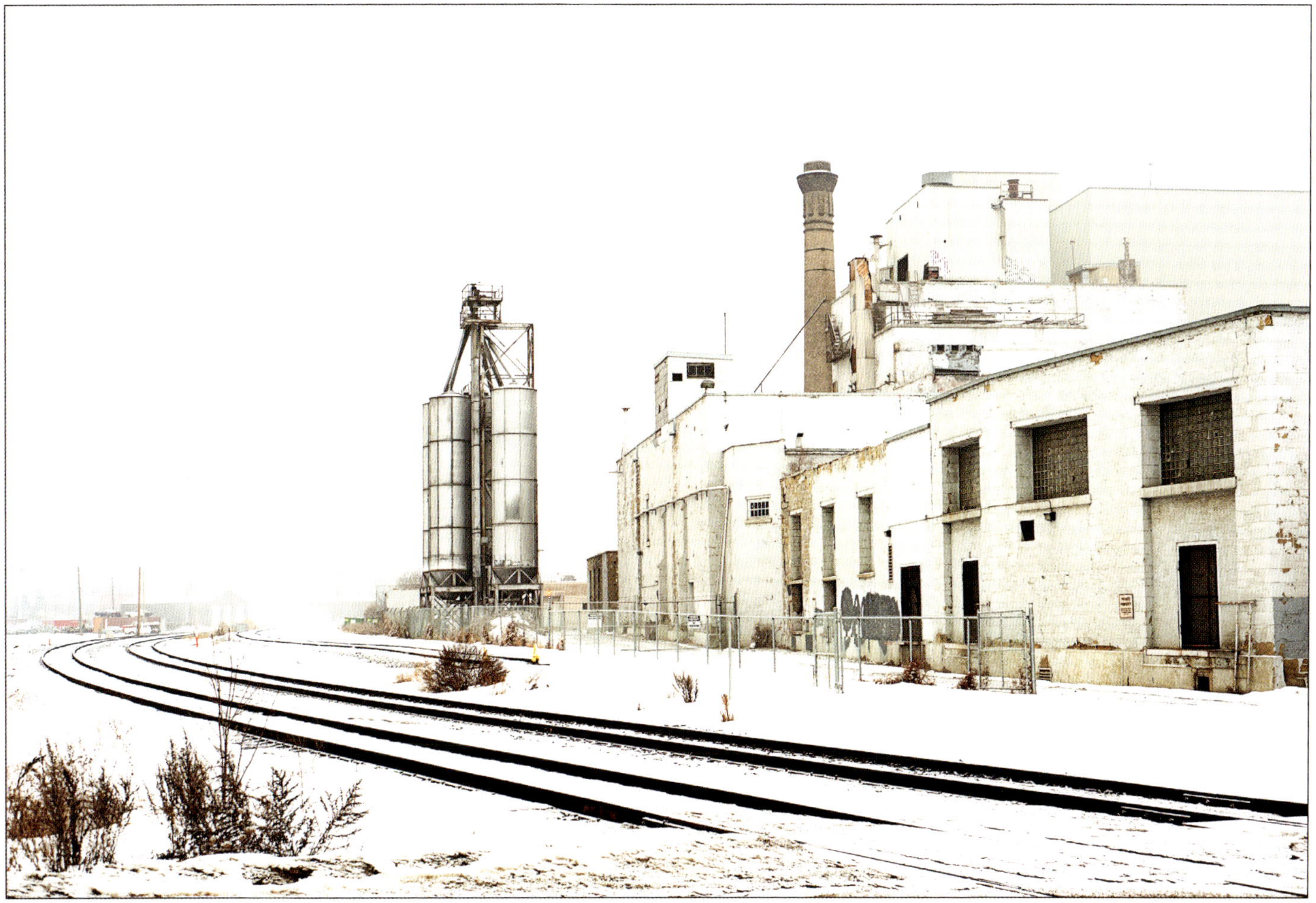

Abandoned brewery, 2017

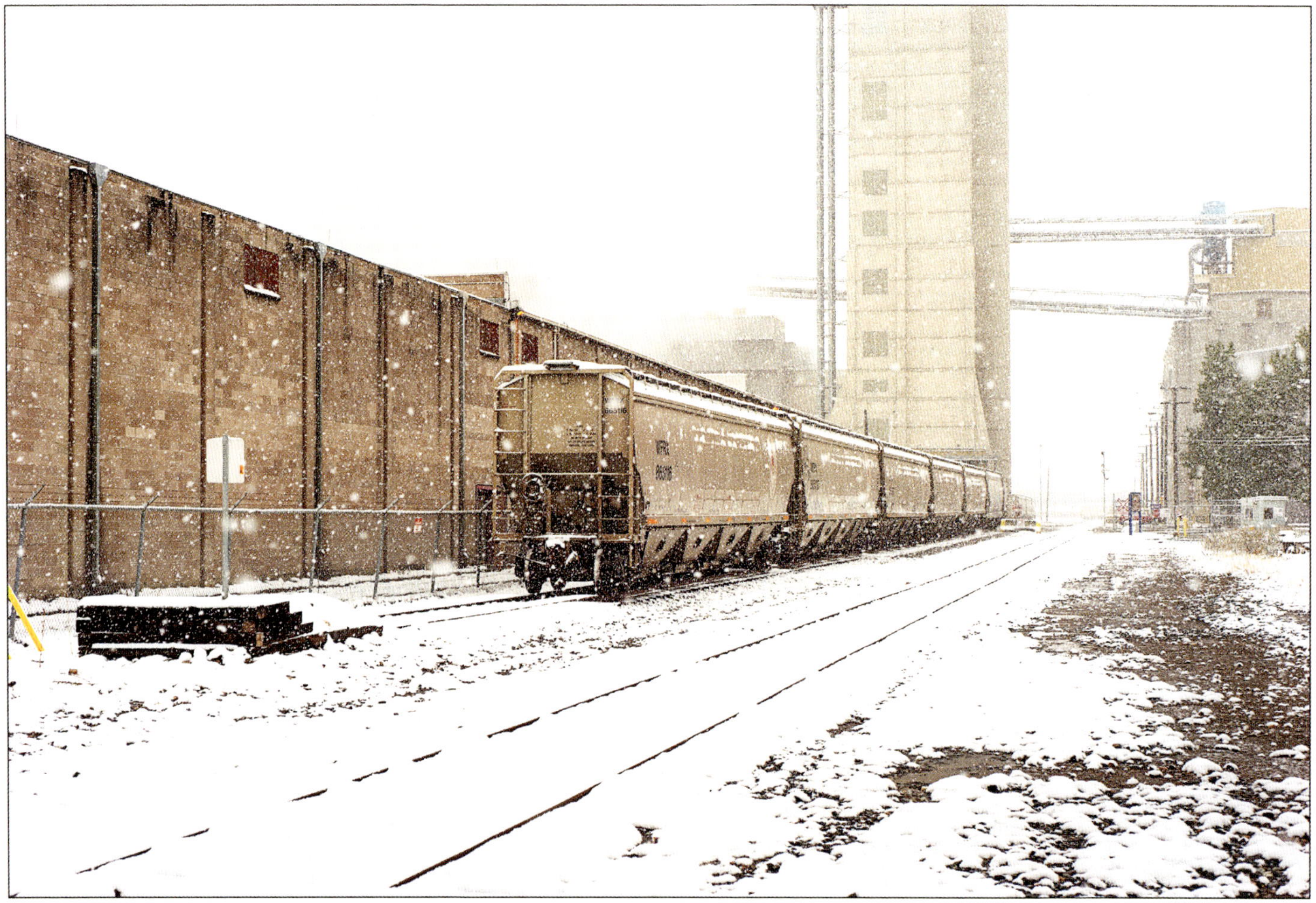

Near 15 St + 34 Ave SE, 2019

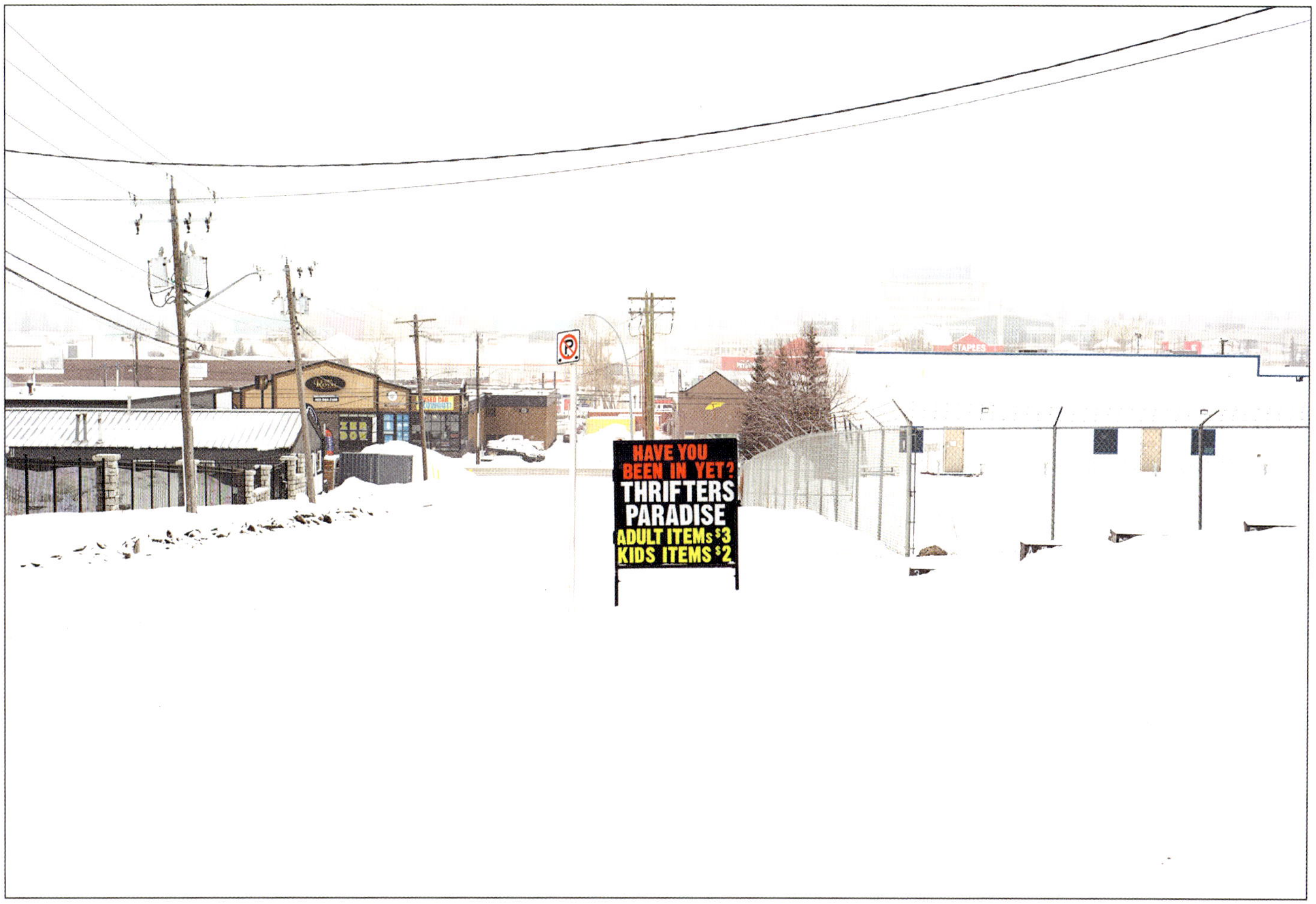

Thrifters Paradise, 2018

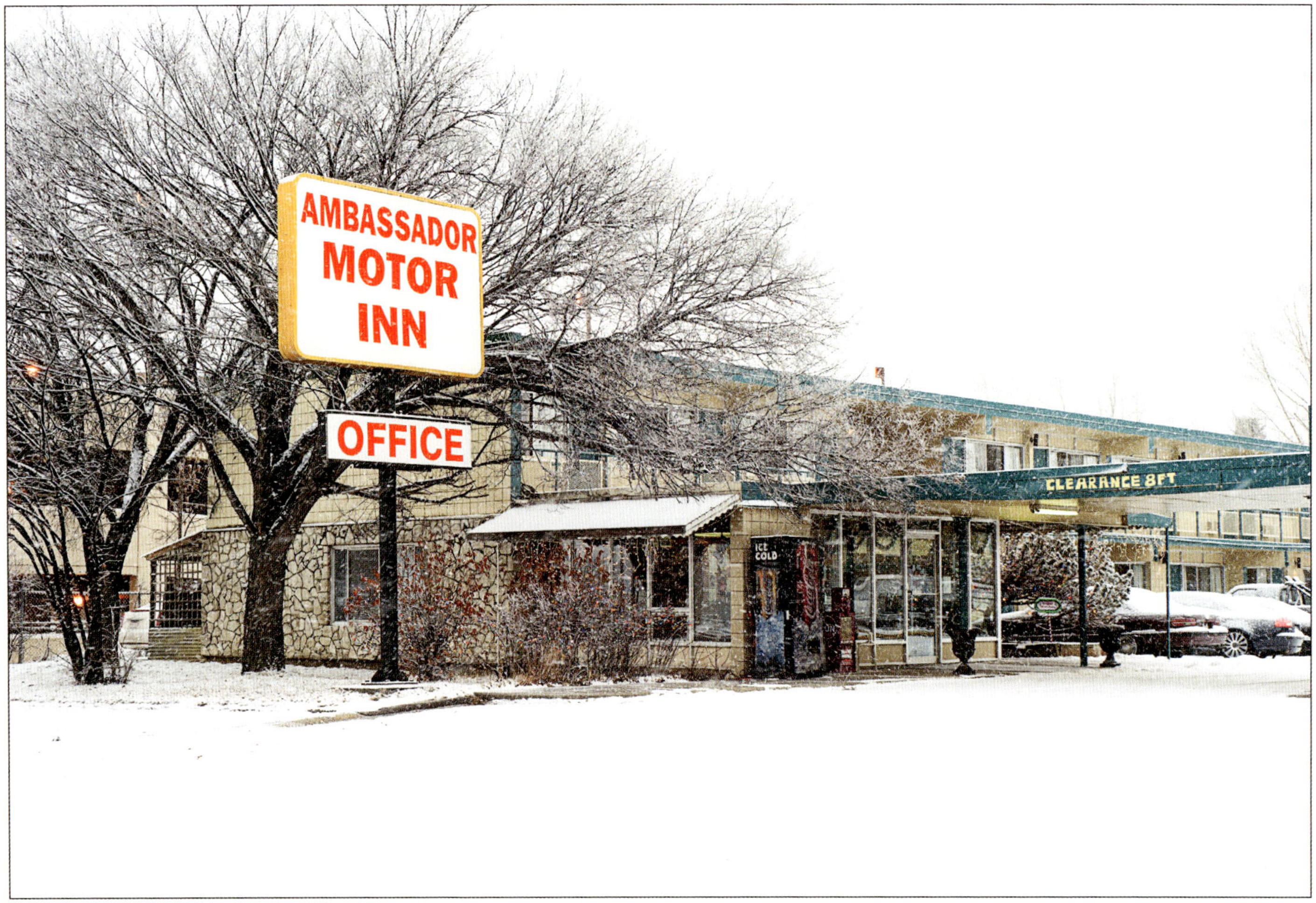

Ambassador Motor Inn, 2014

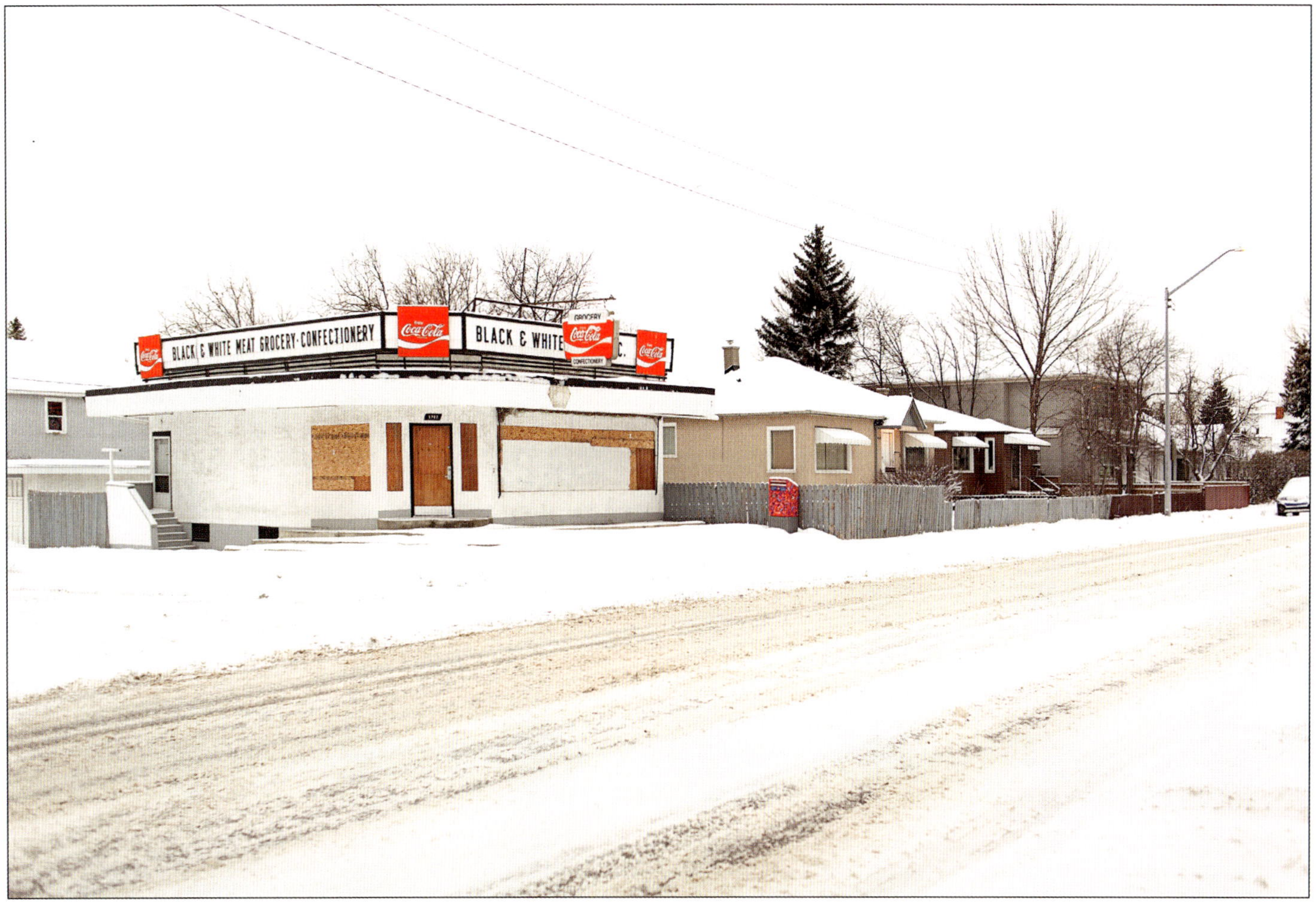

Black and White Confectionery, 2017

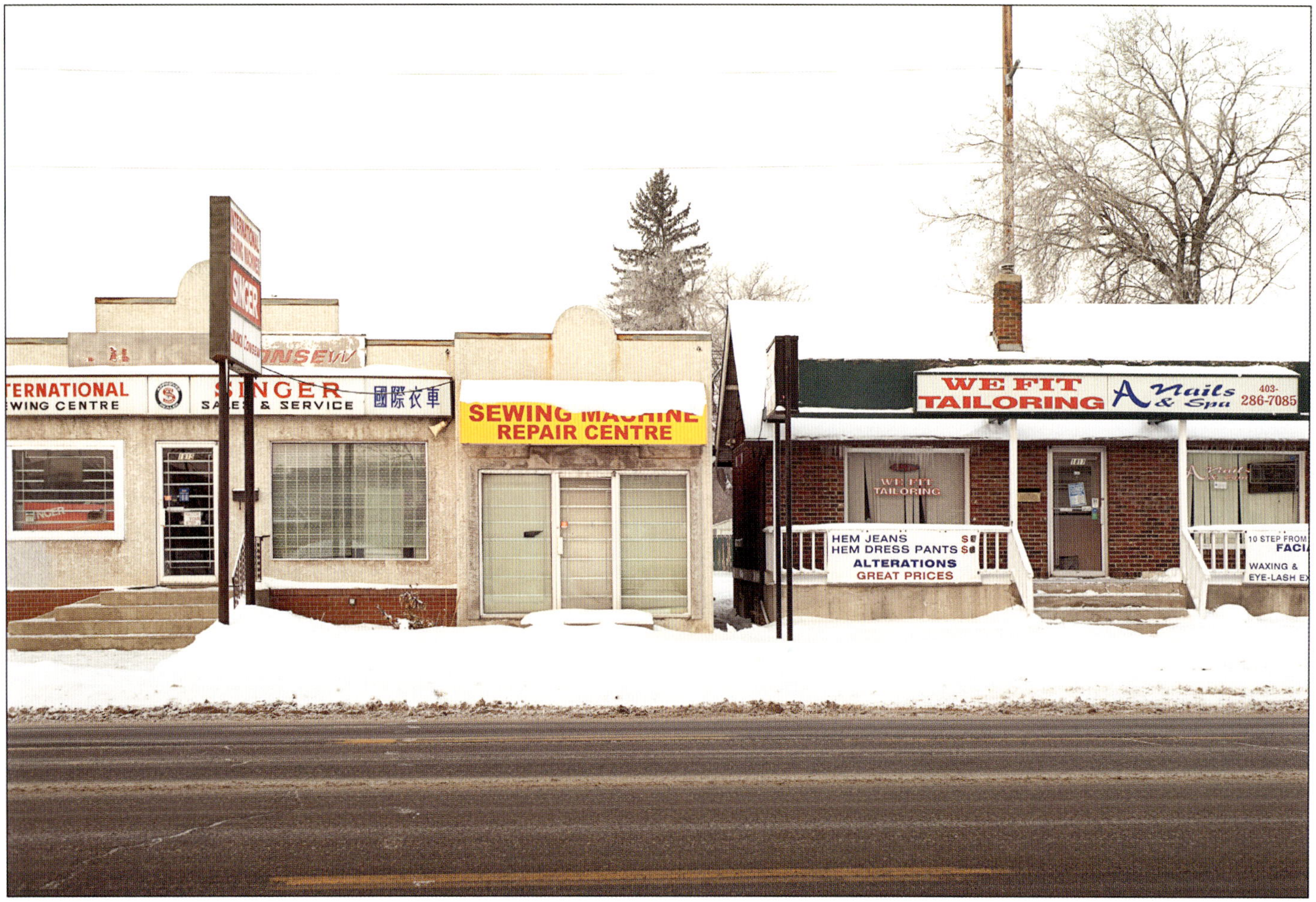

1815 Centre St, 2017

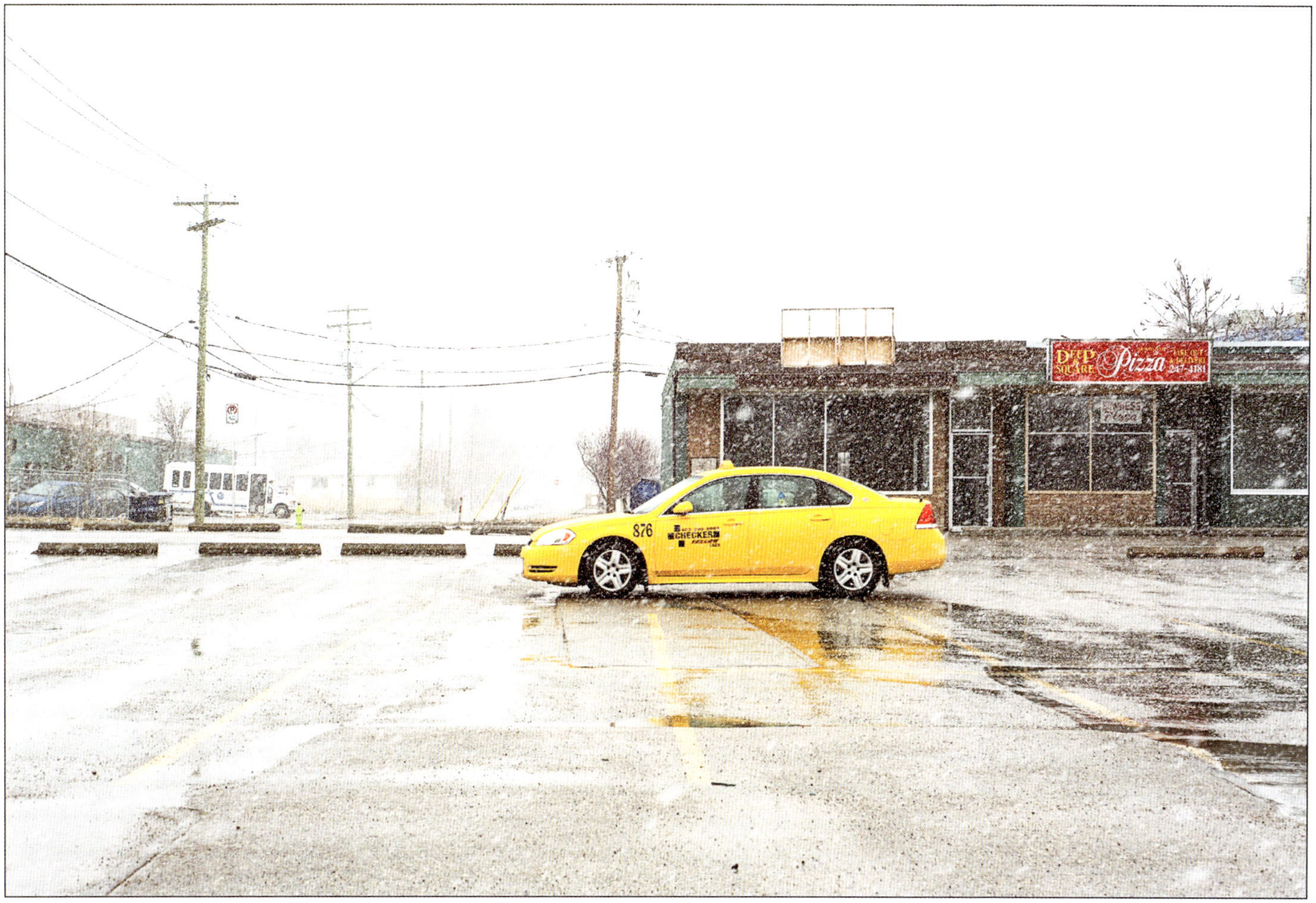

Near 41 Ave + 77 St NW, 2014

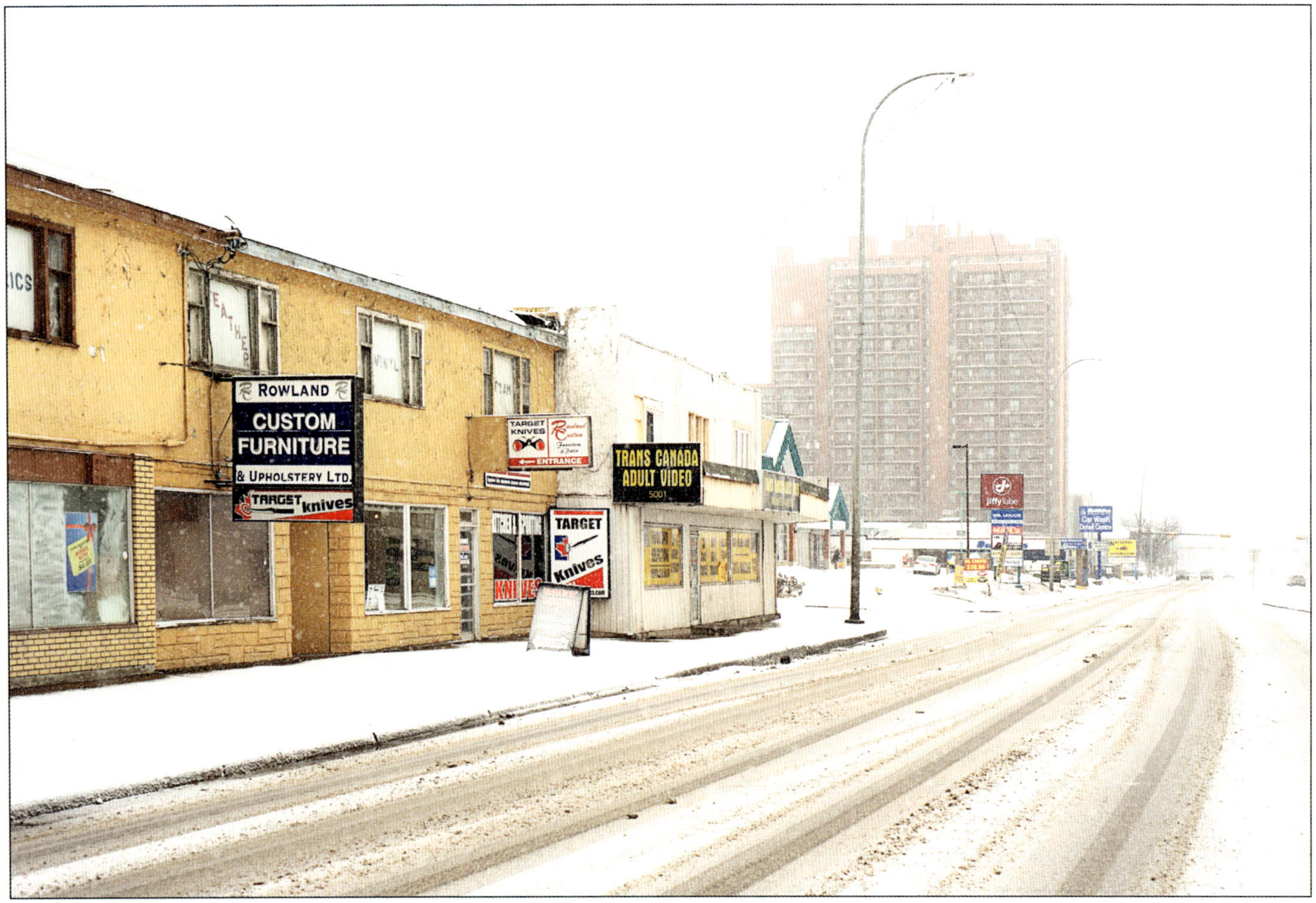

Macleod Trail, 2018

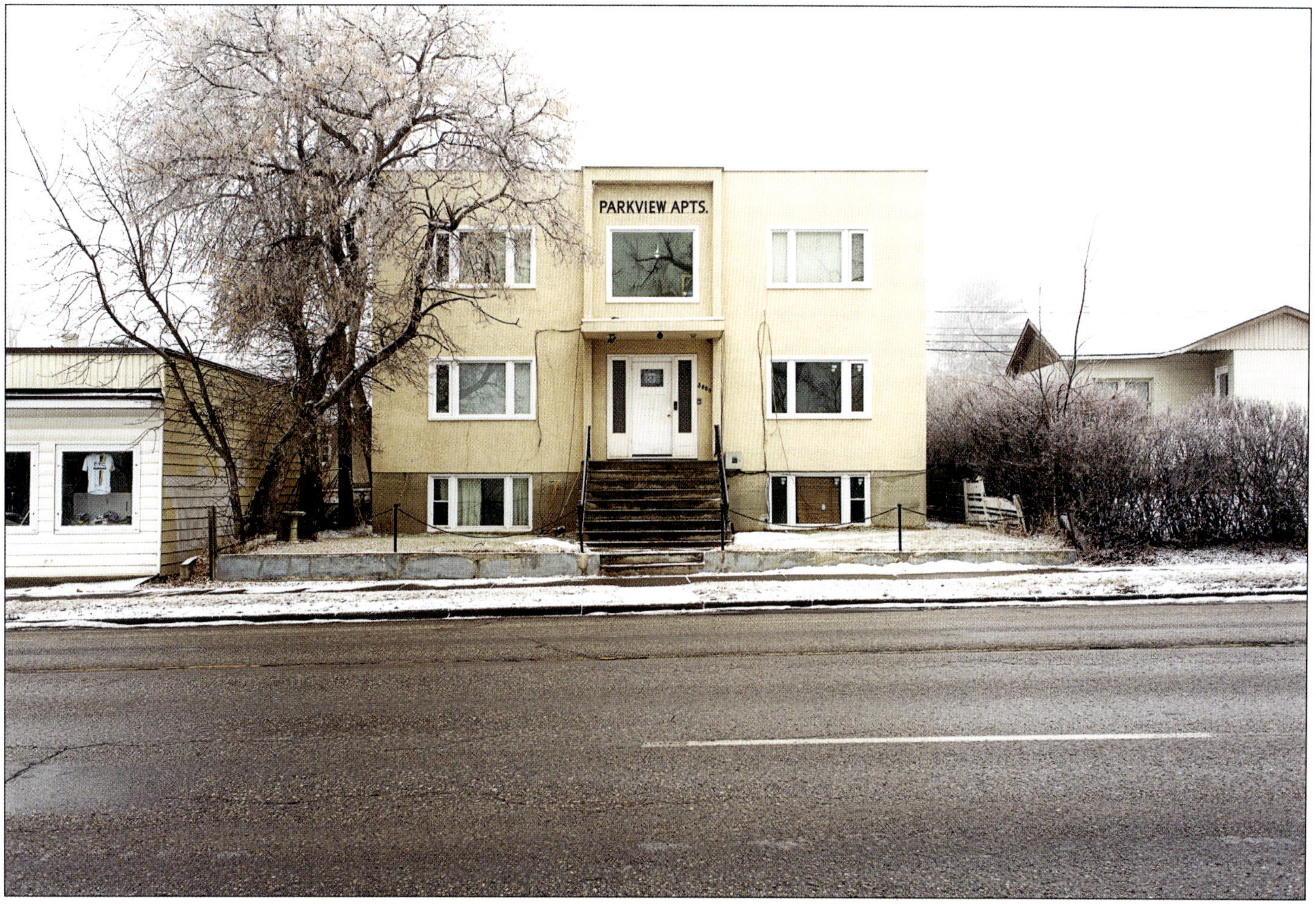

3009 Centre St NW, 2016

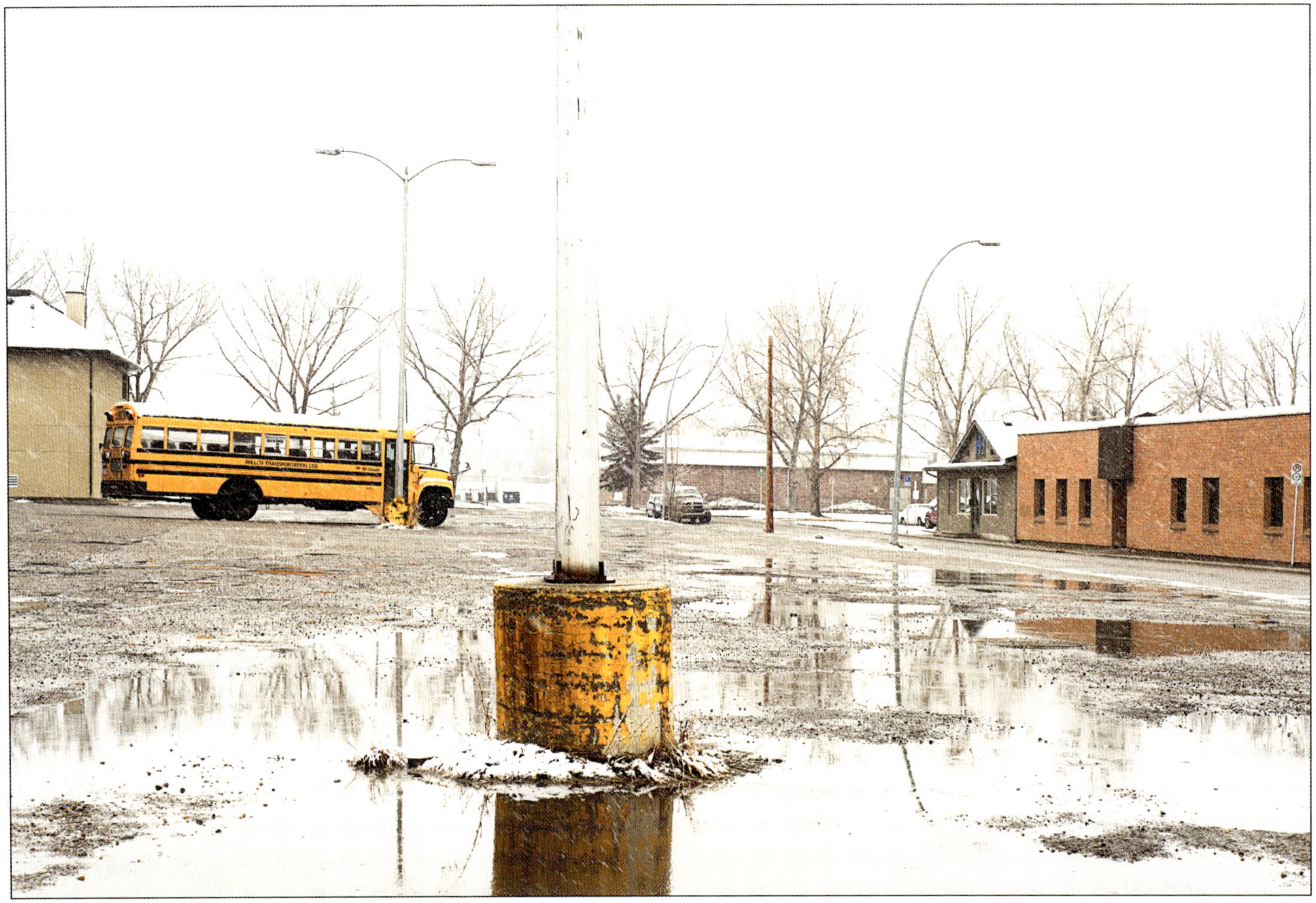

Bowness, 2014

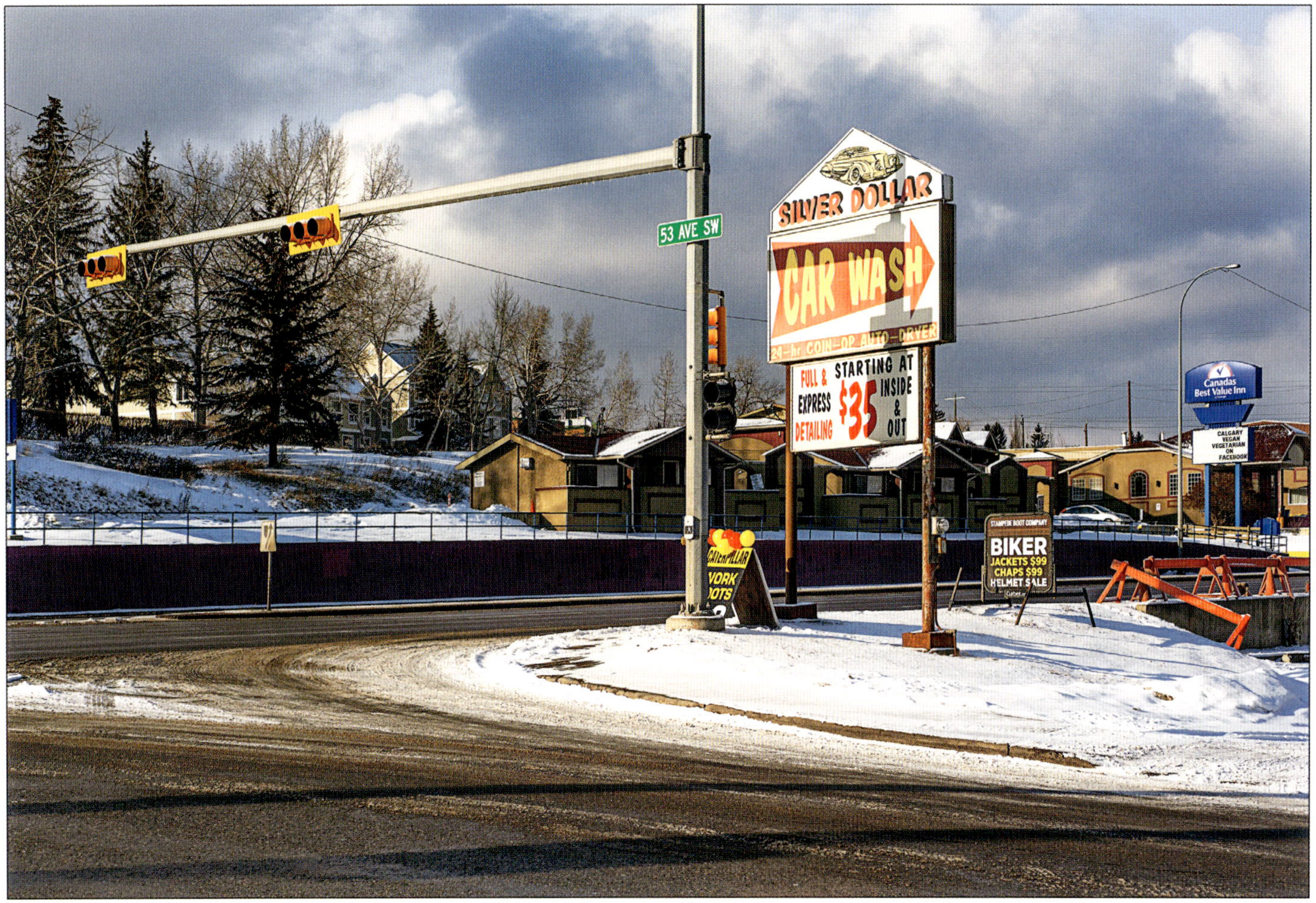

Macleod Trail, 2017

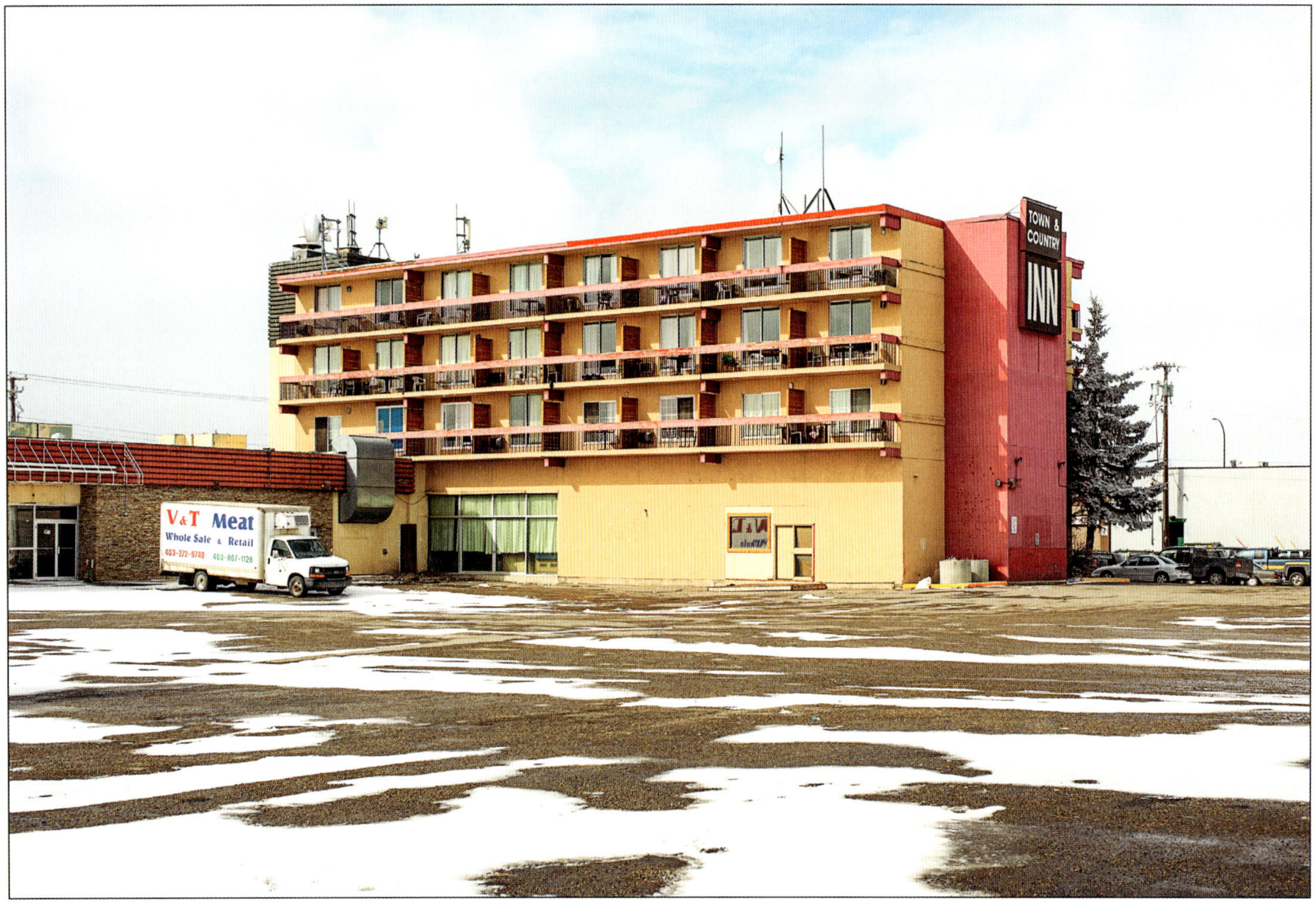

Town and Country Hotel, 2018

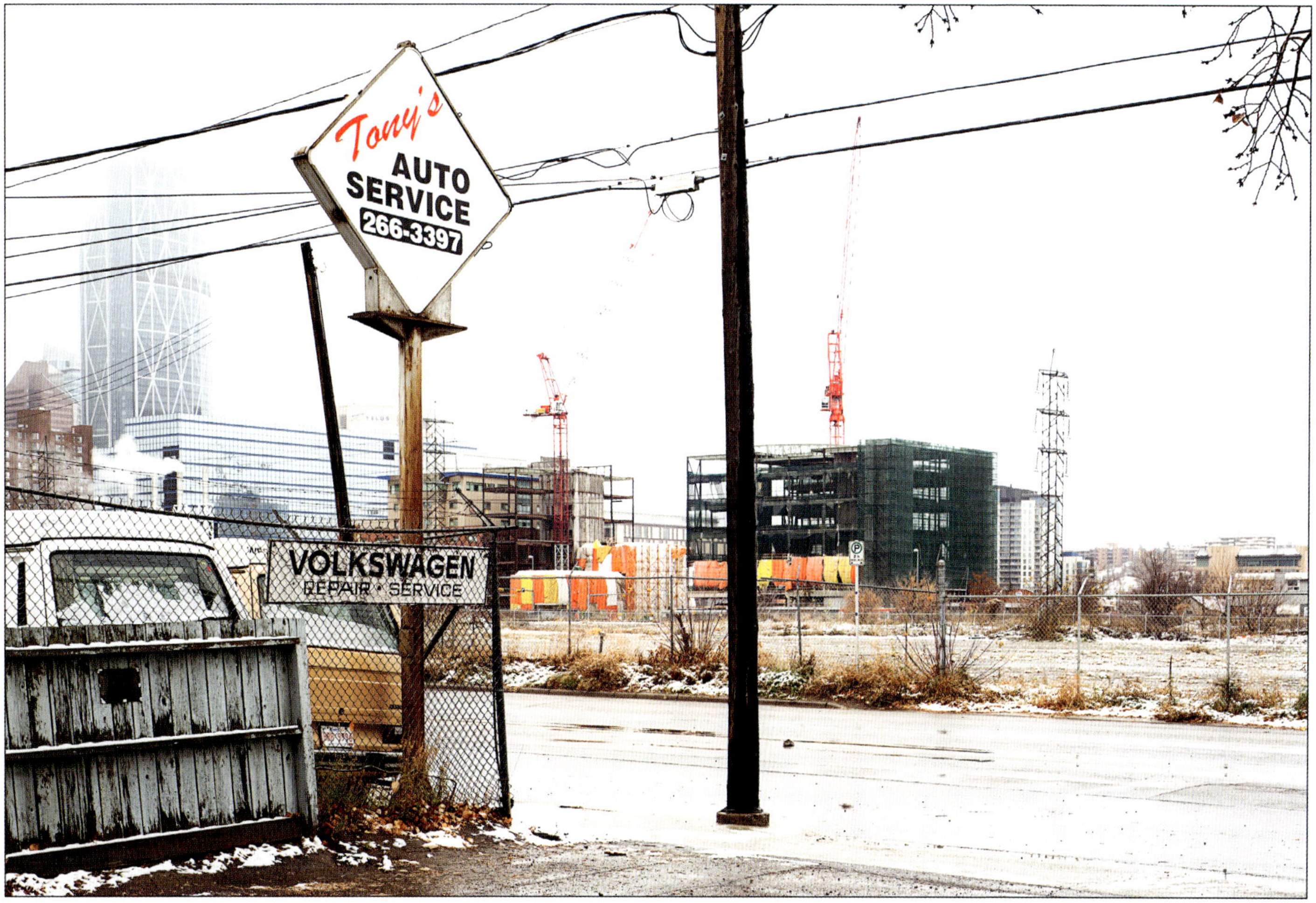

Tony's Auto Service, 2014

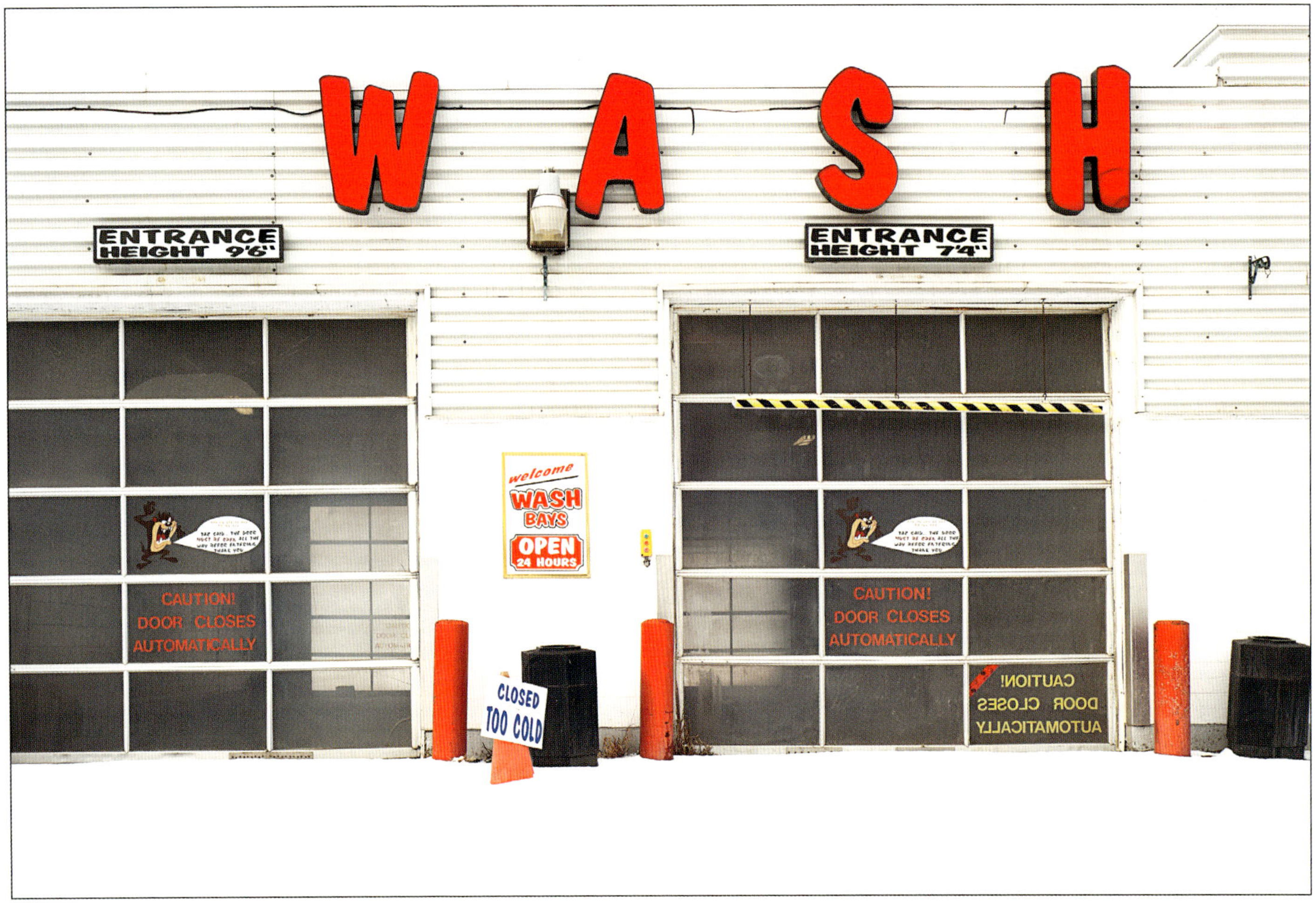

Near Macleod Trail + 53 Ave, 2017

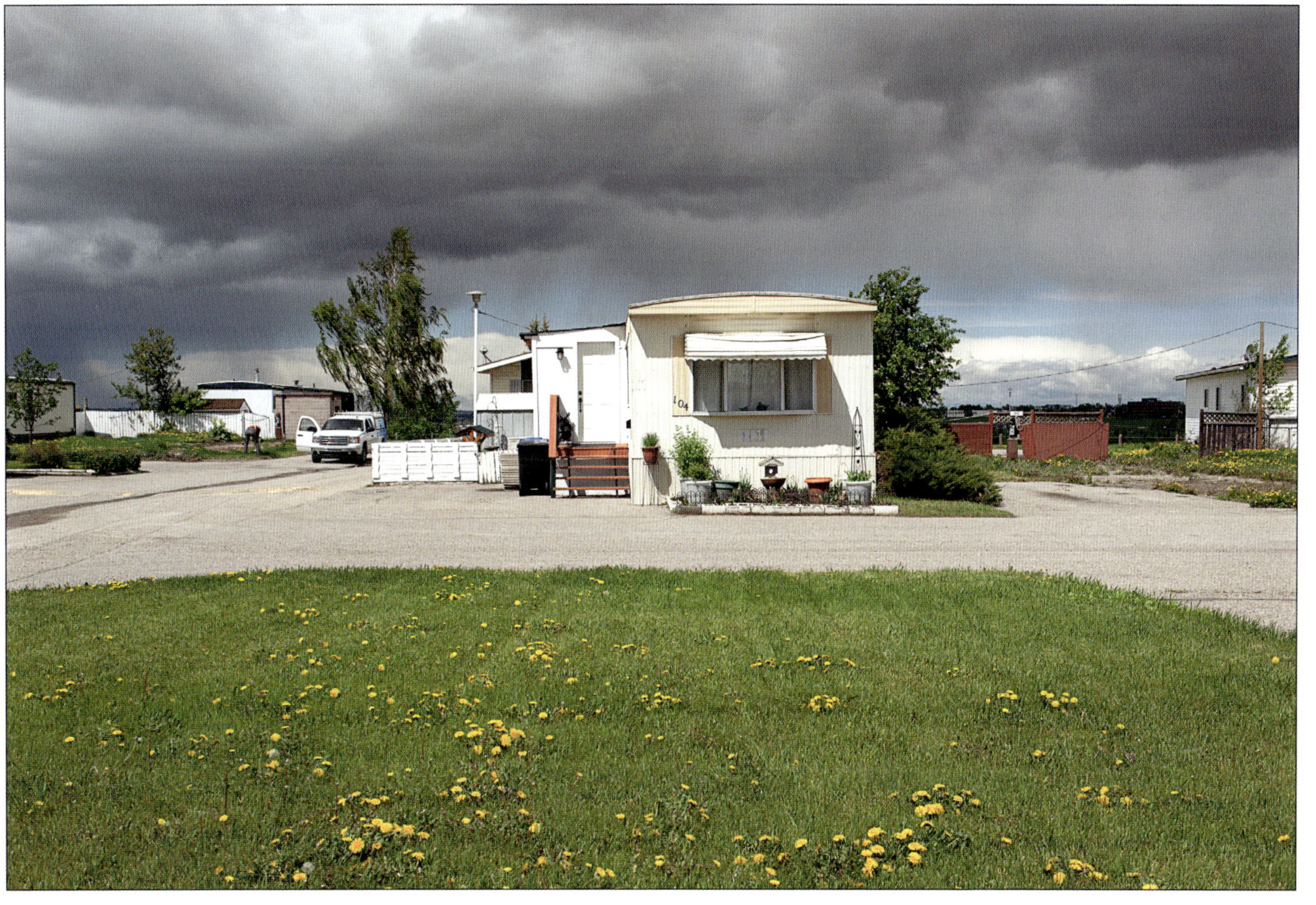

Midfield Mobile Home Park, 2017

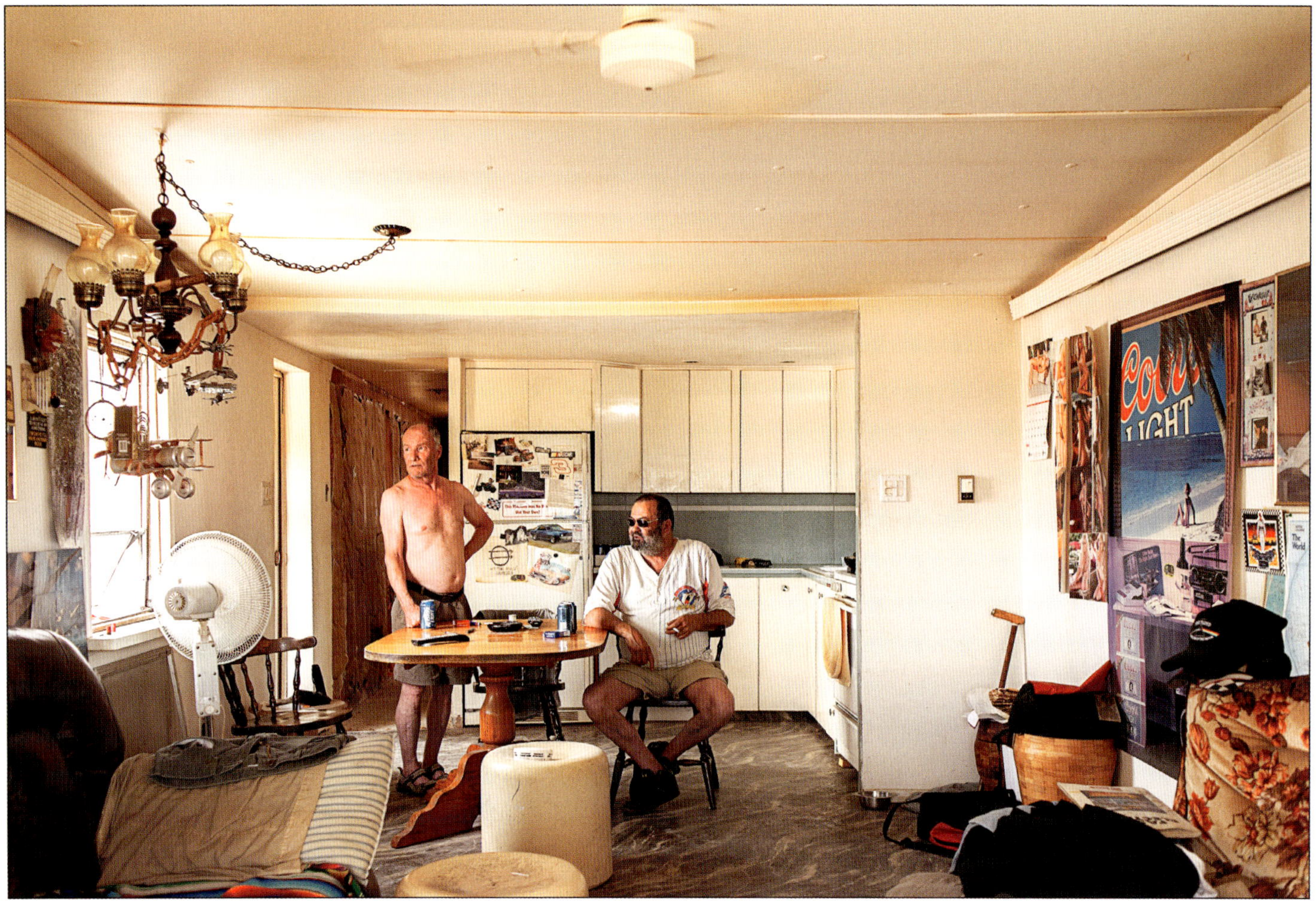

Ken Brohman and Gary Murphy, Midfield Mobile Home Park, 2017

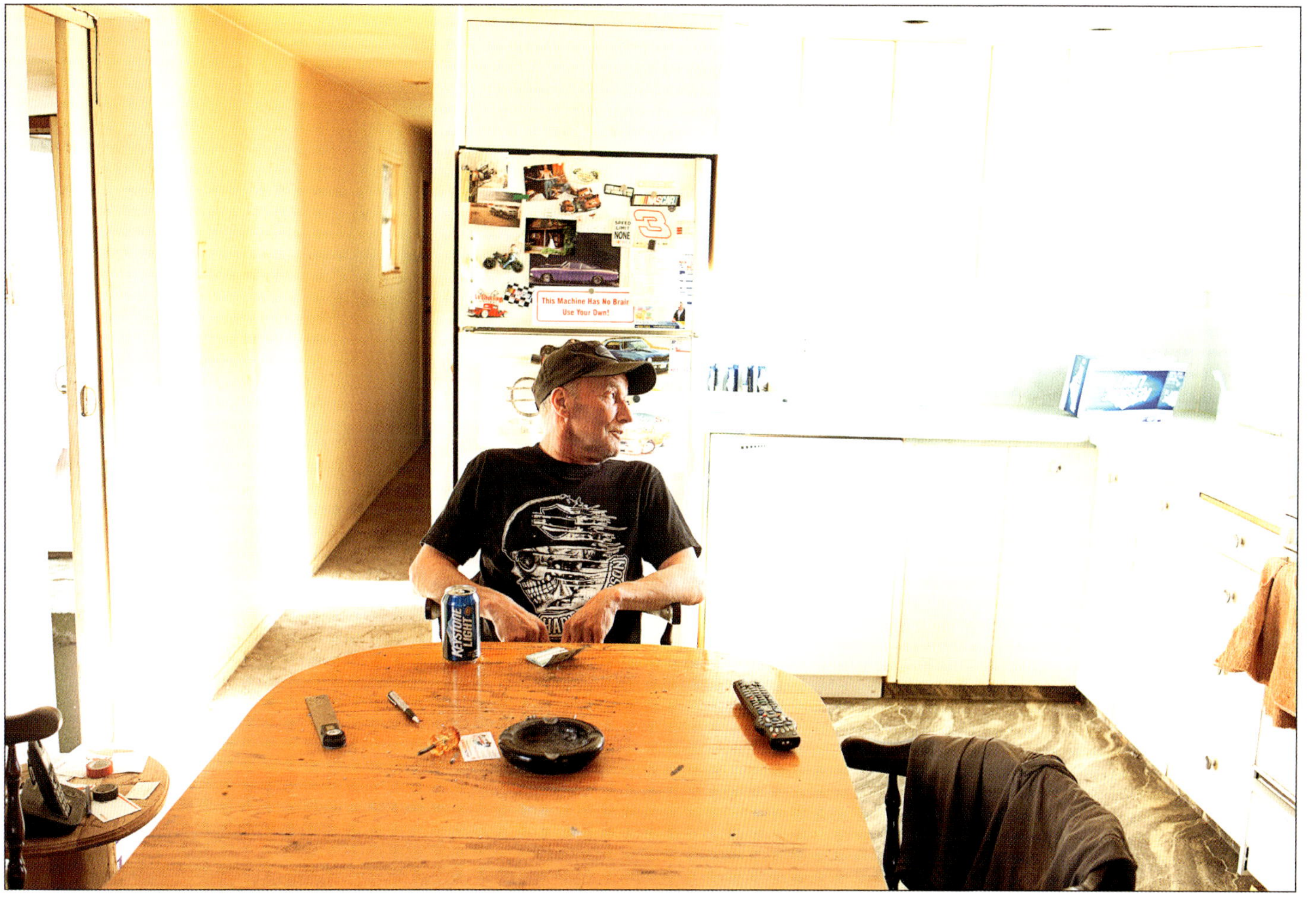

Ken Brohman, Midfield Mobile Home Park, 2017

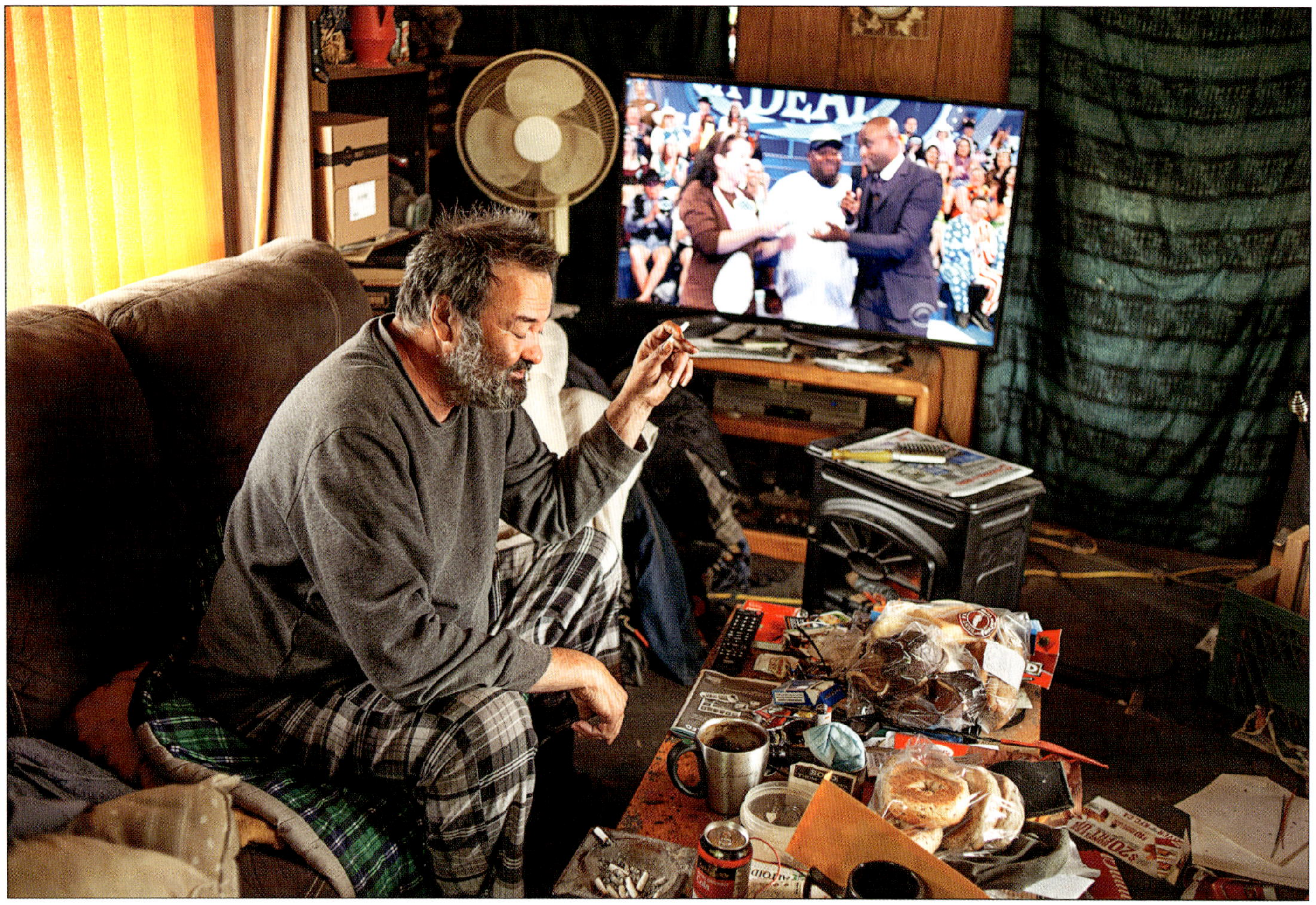

Gary Murphy, Midfield Mobile Home Park, 2017

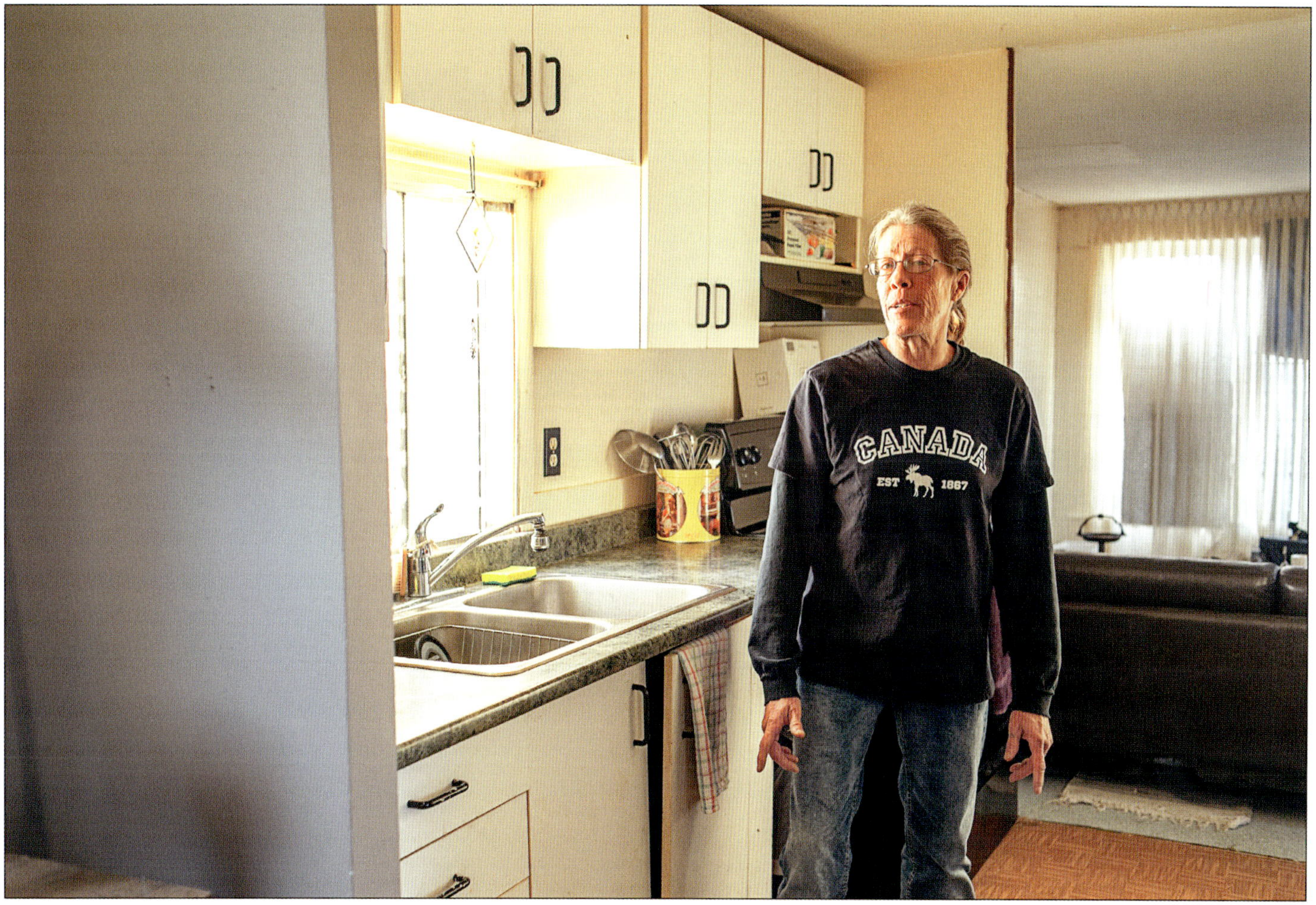

Lori Sperling, Midfield Mobile Home Park, 2017

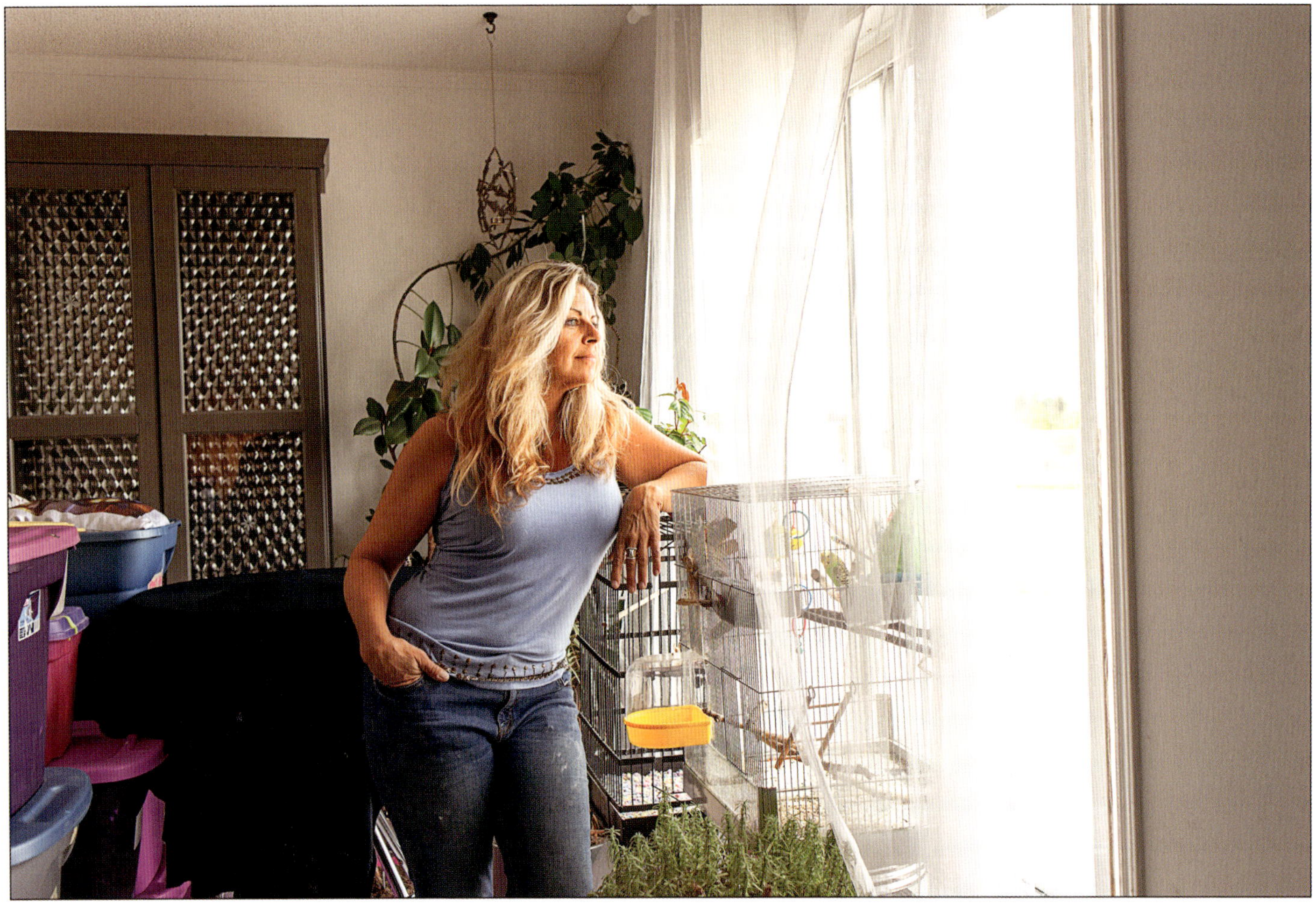

Kelly Schwab, Midfield Mobile Home Park, 2017

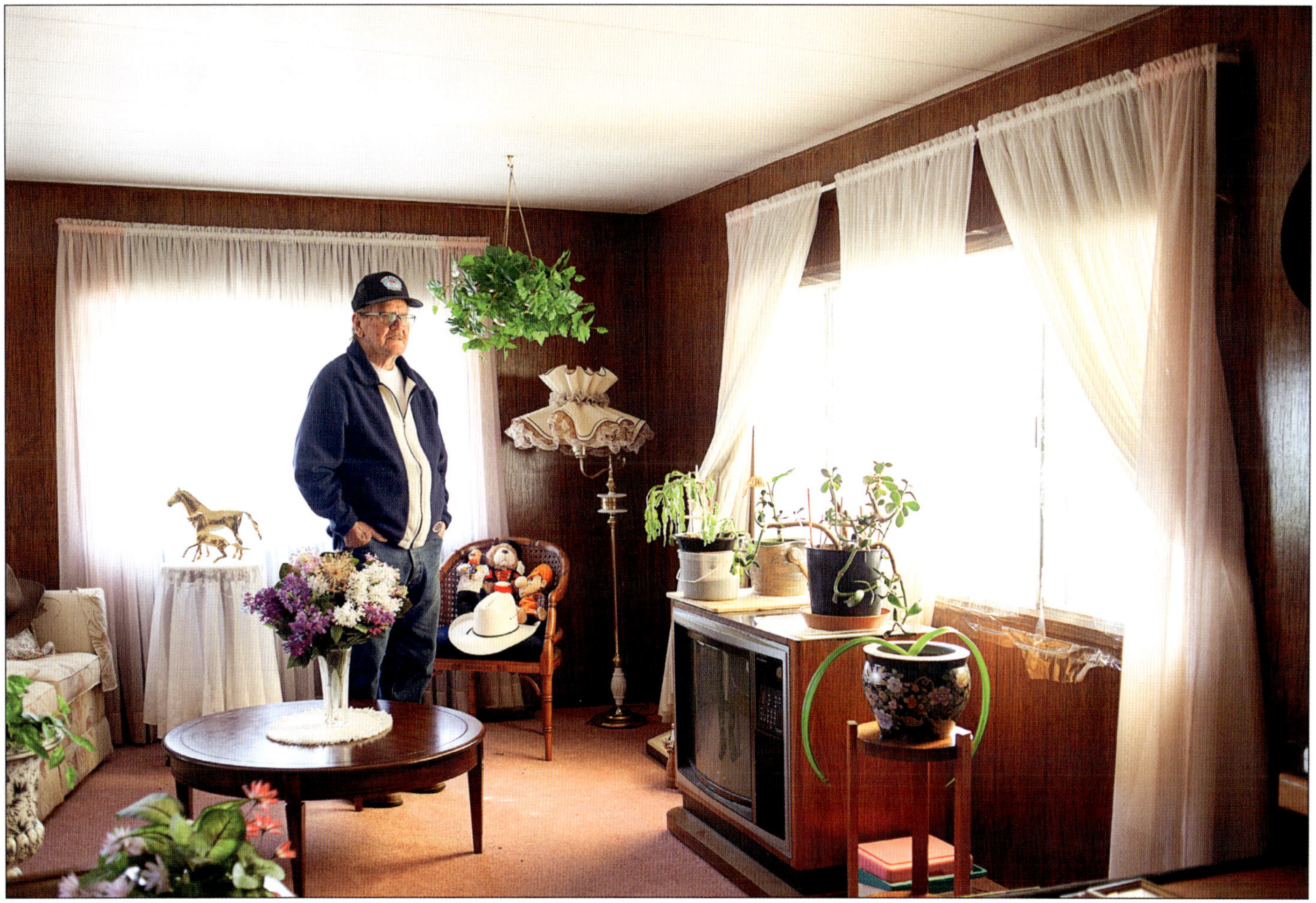

Rudy Prediger, Midfield Mobile Home Park, 2017

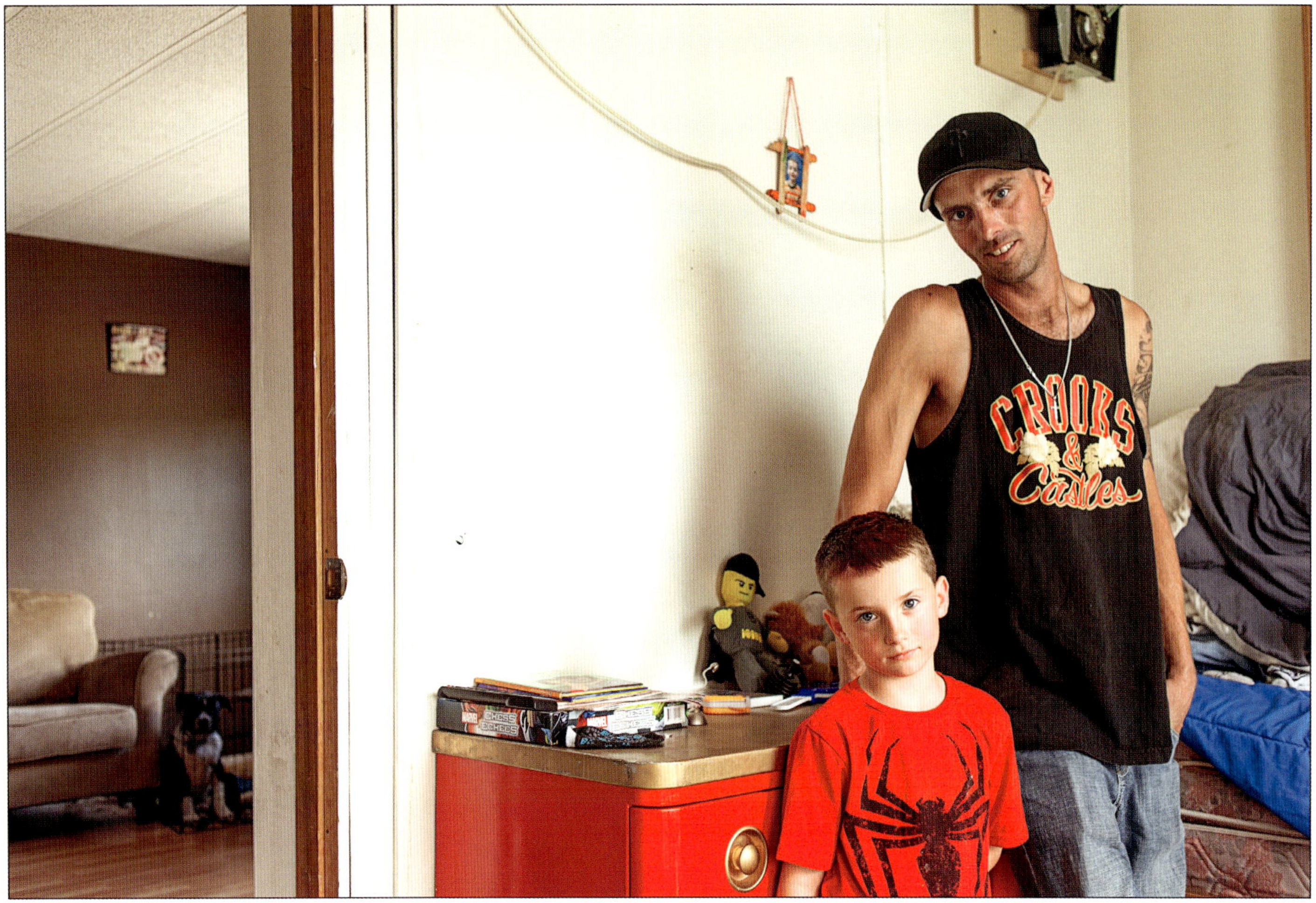

Desmond and son Brandon, Midfield Mobile Home Park, 2017

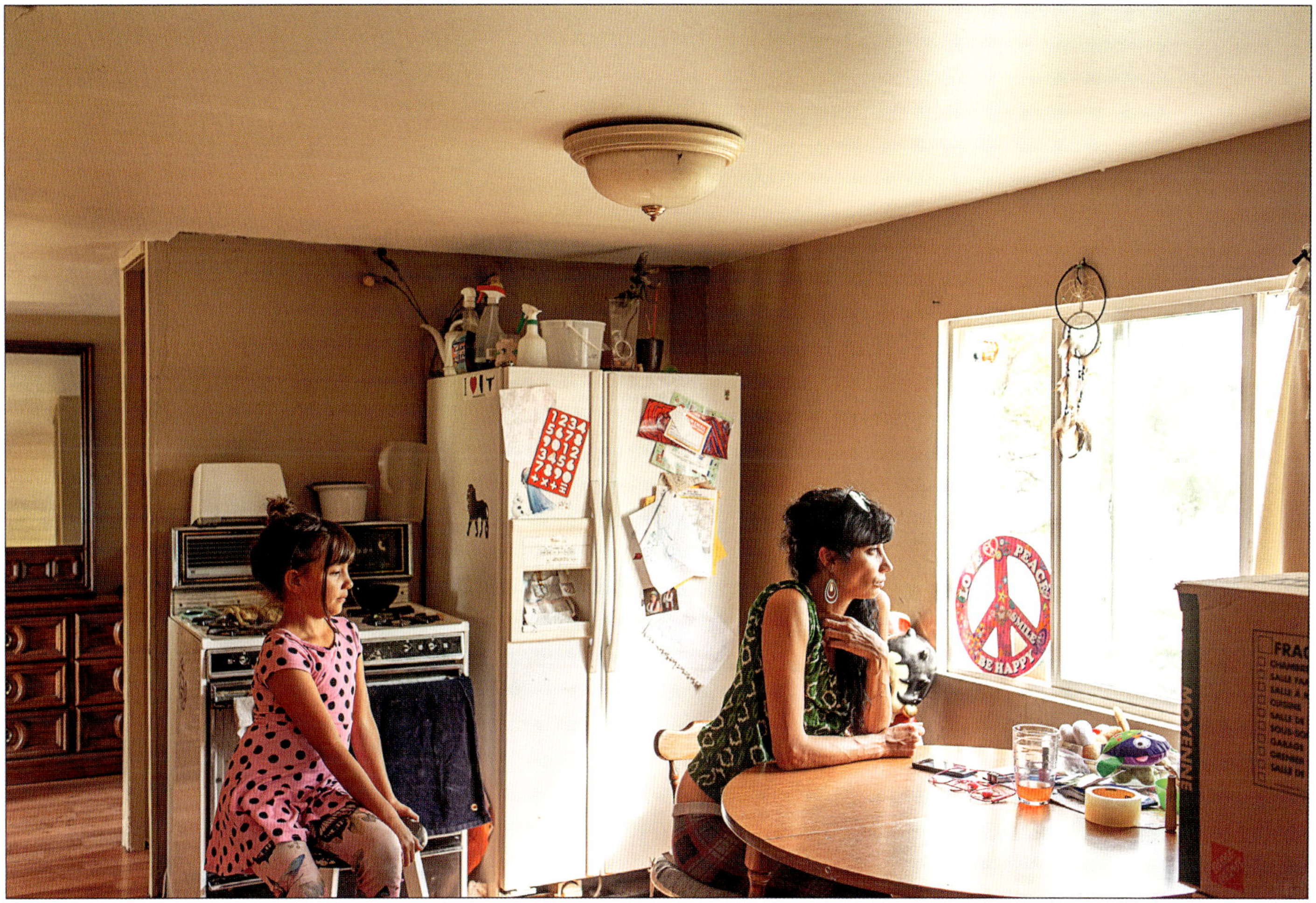

Naomi Anderson and daughter Chloe, Midfield Mobile Home Park, 2017

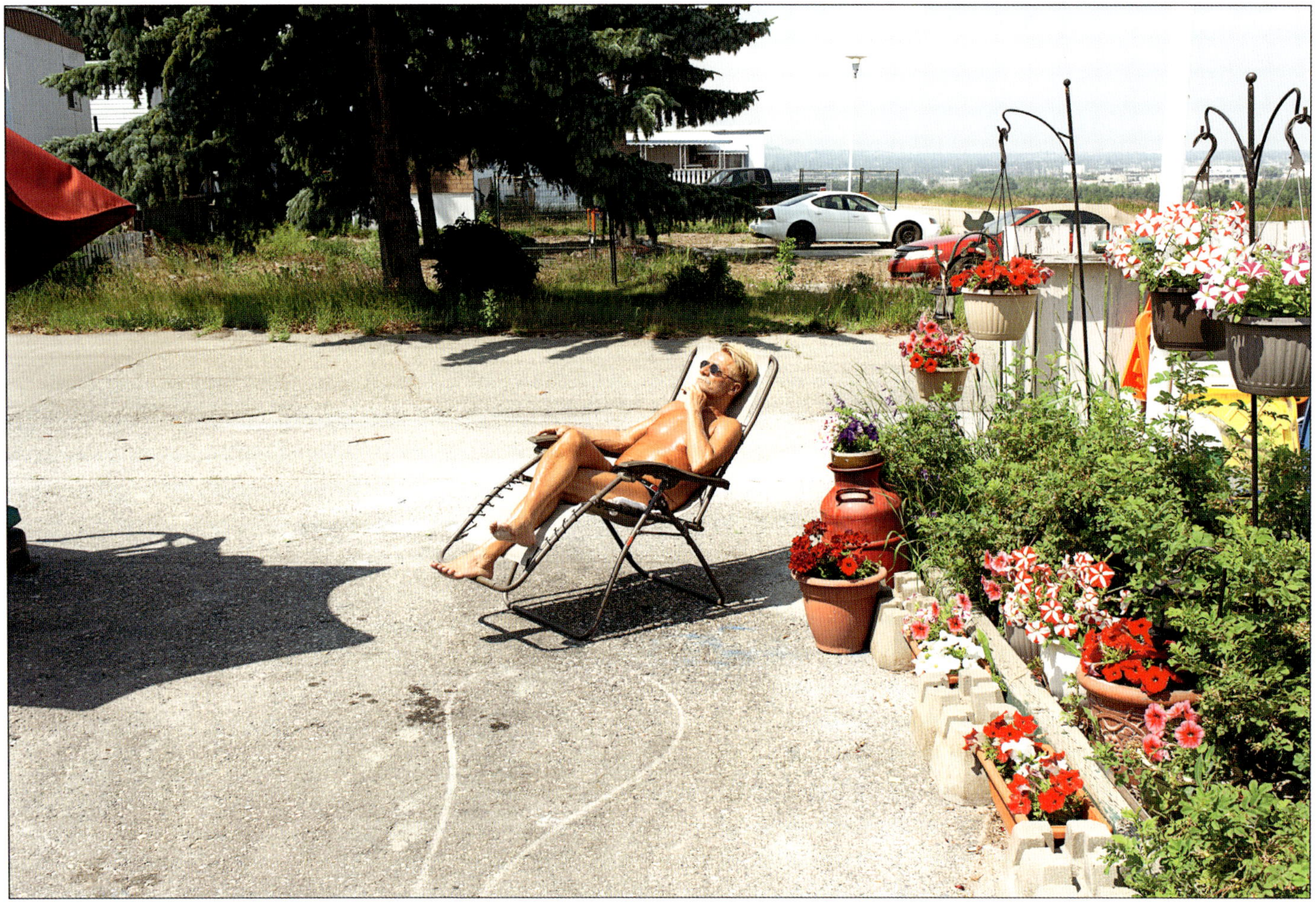

Yves Drouin, Midfield Mobile Home Park, 2017

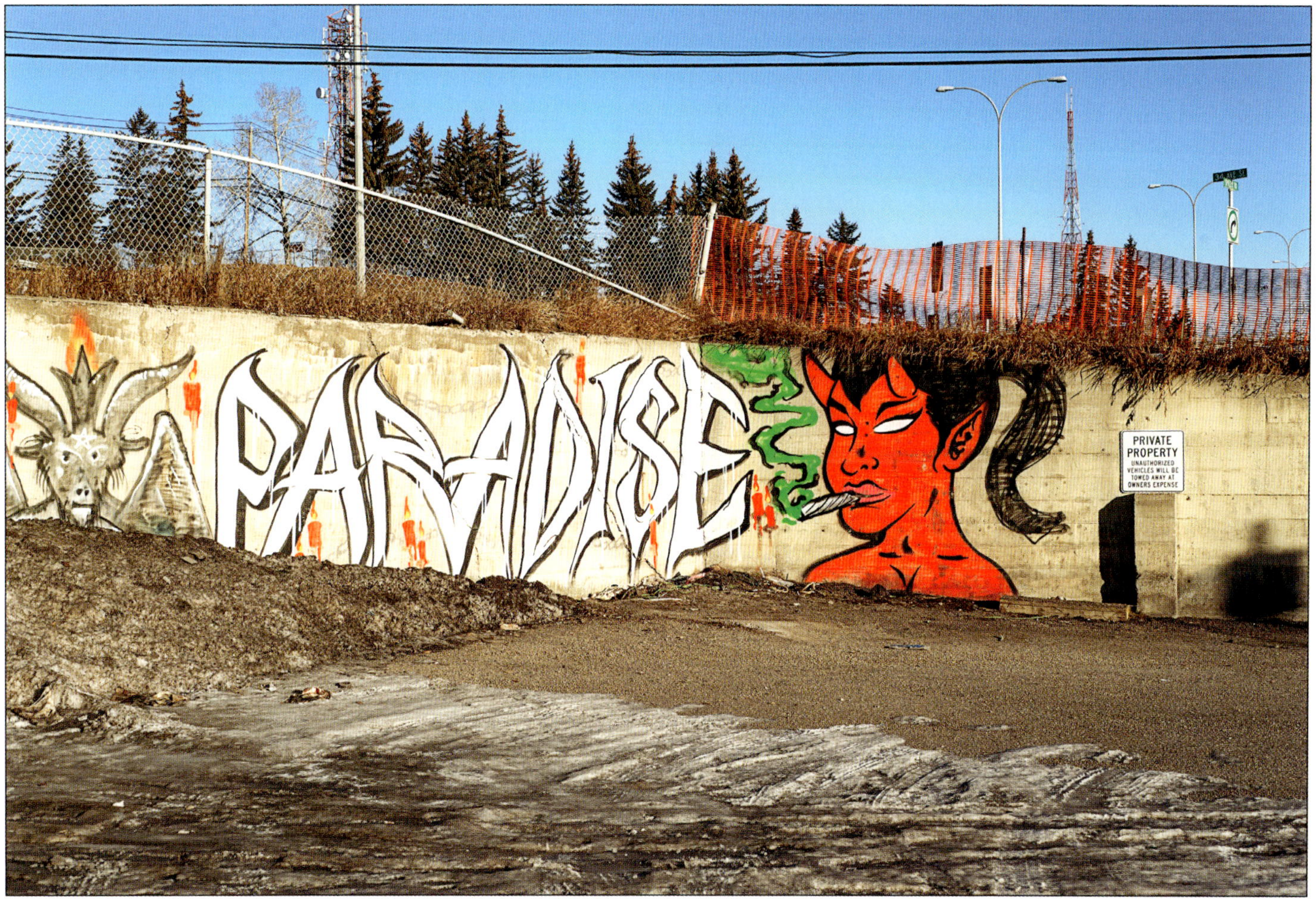

Near Macleod Trail + 34 Ave SE, 2016

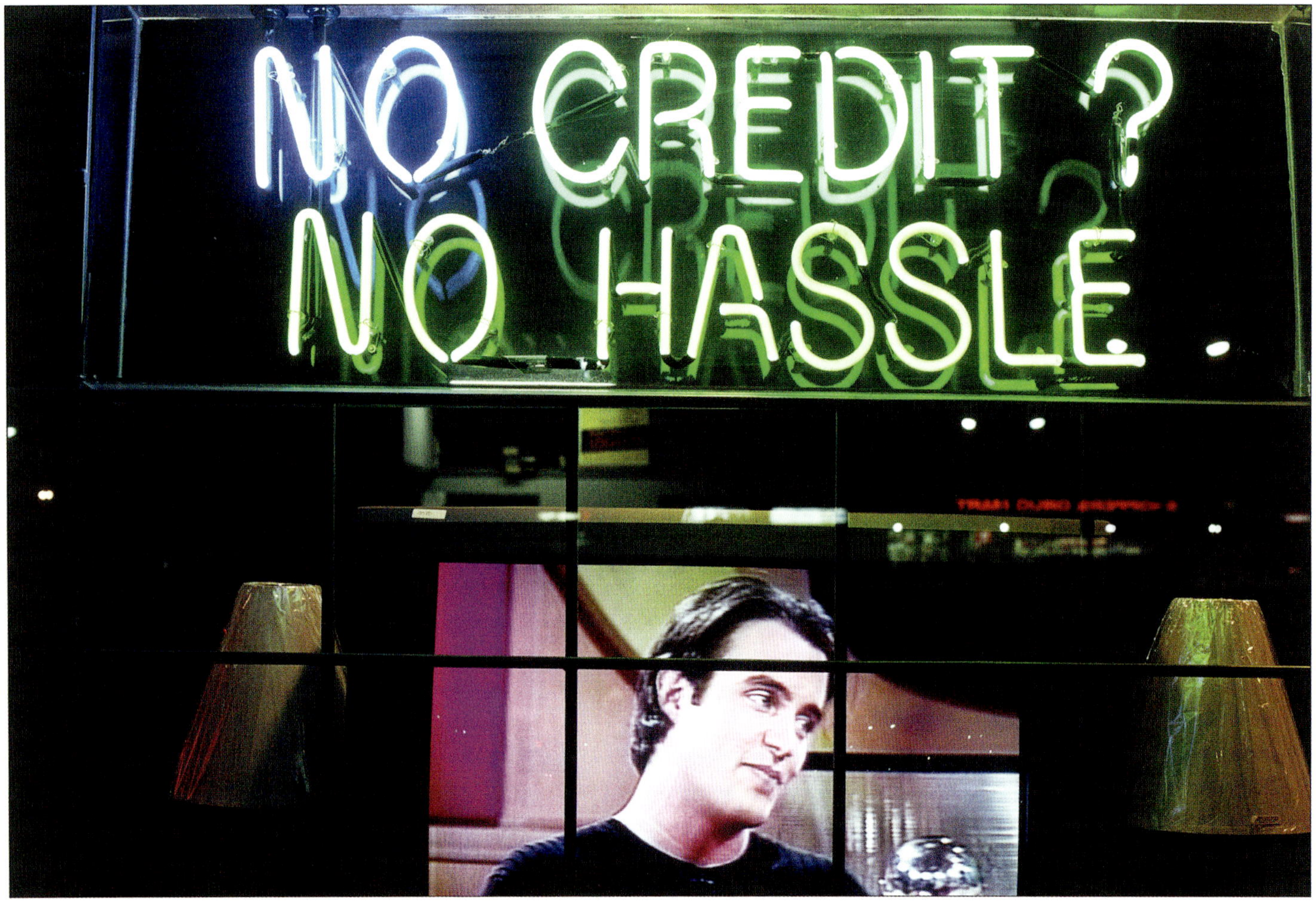

311 17 Ave SE, 2001

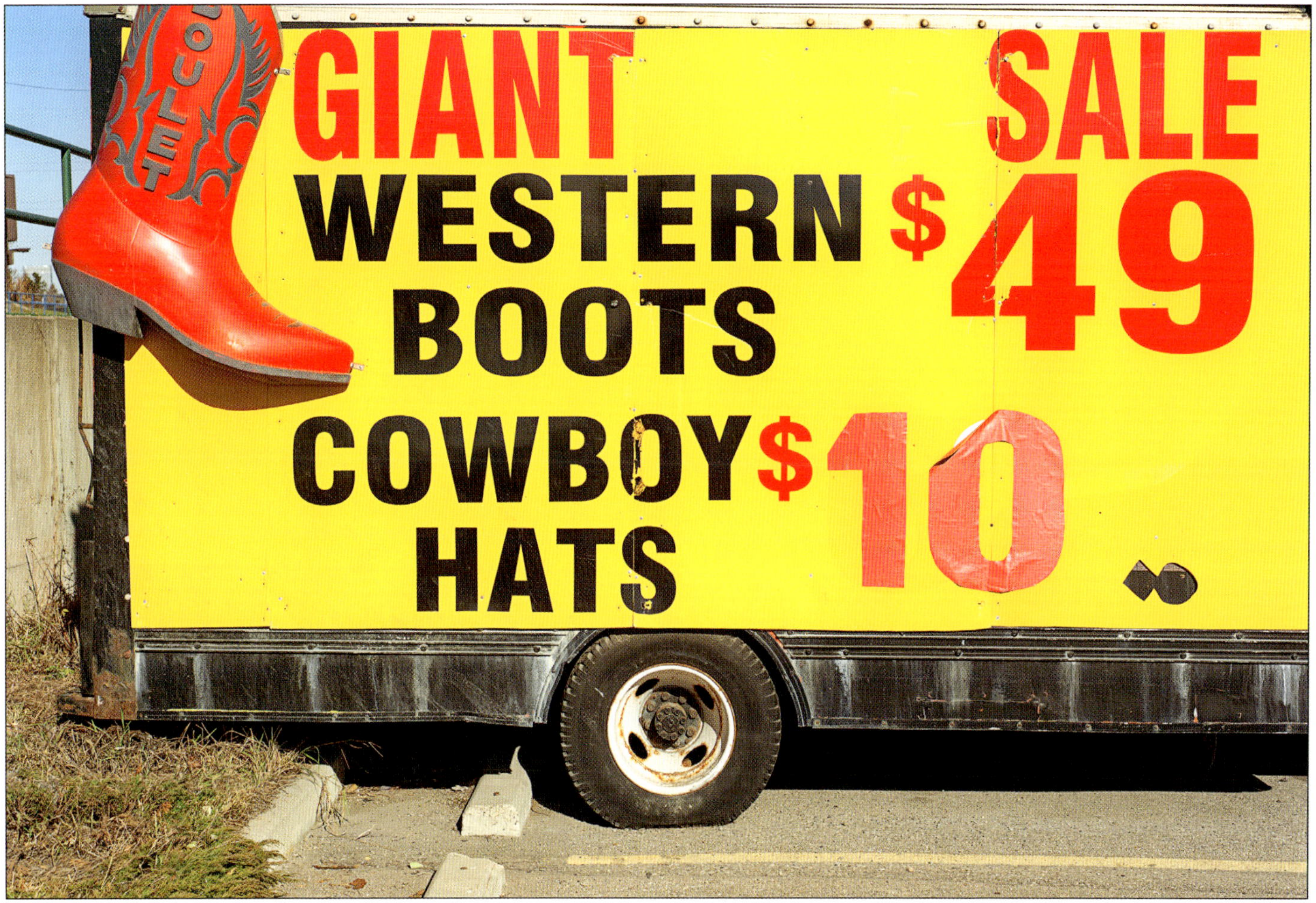

5327 Macleod Trail, 2018

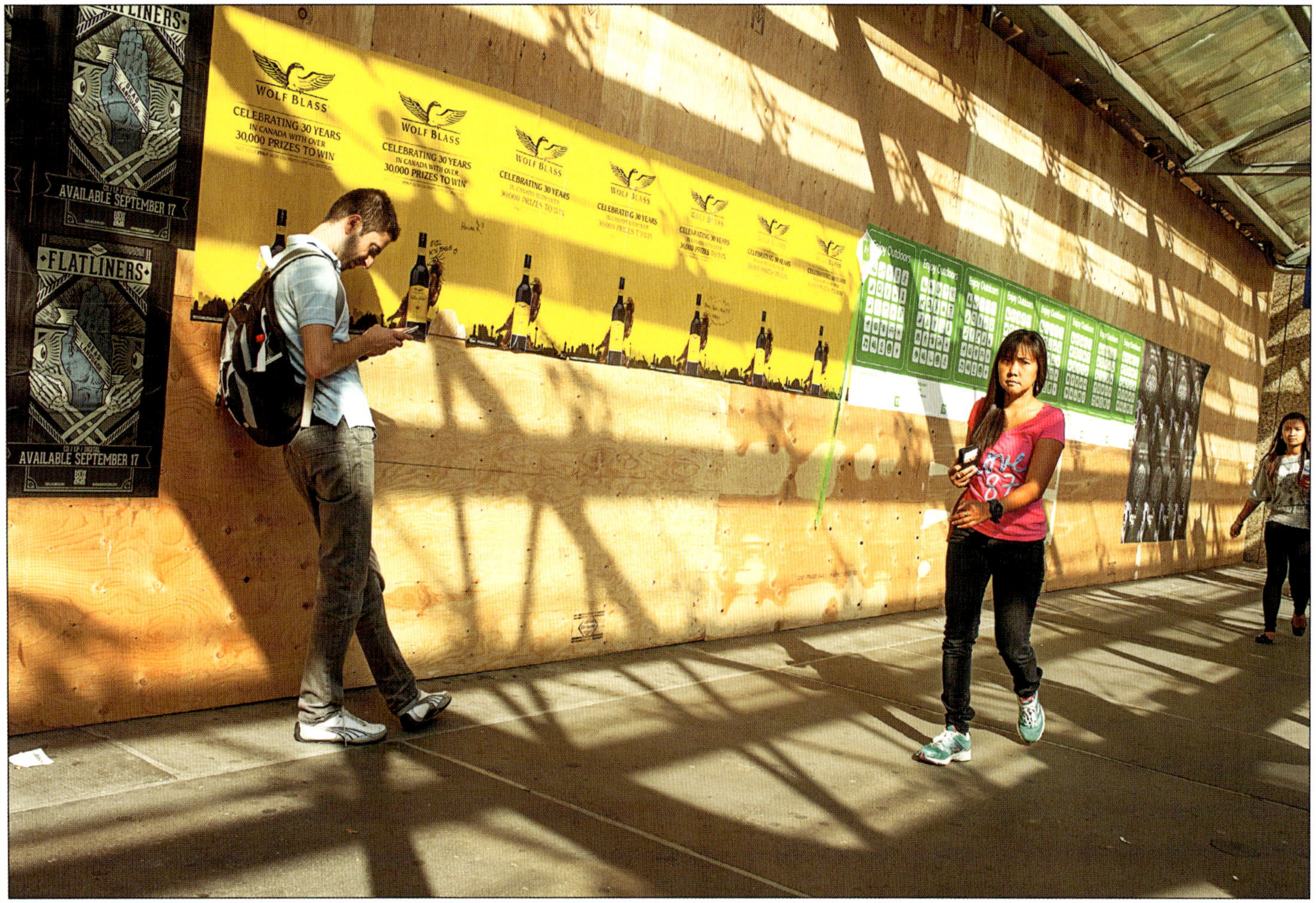
FLATLINERS
AVAILABLE SEPTEMBER 17
WOLF BLASS
CELEBRATING 30 YEARS
IN CANADA WITH OVER
30,000 PRIZES TO WIN
FLATLINERS
AVAILABLE SEPTEMBER 17

7 Ave SW, 2013

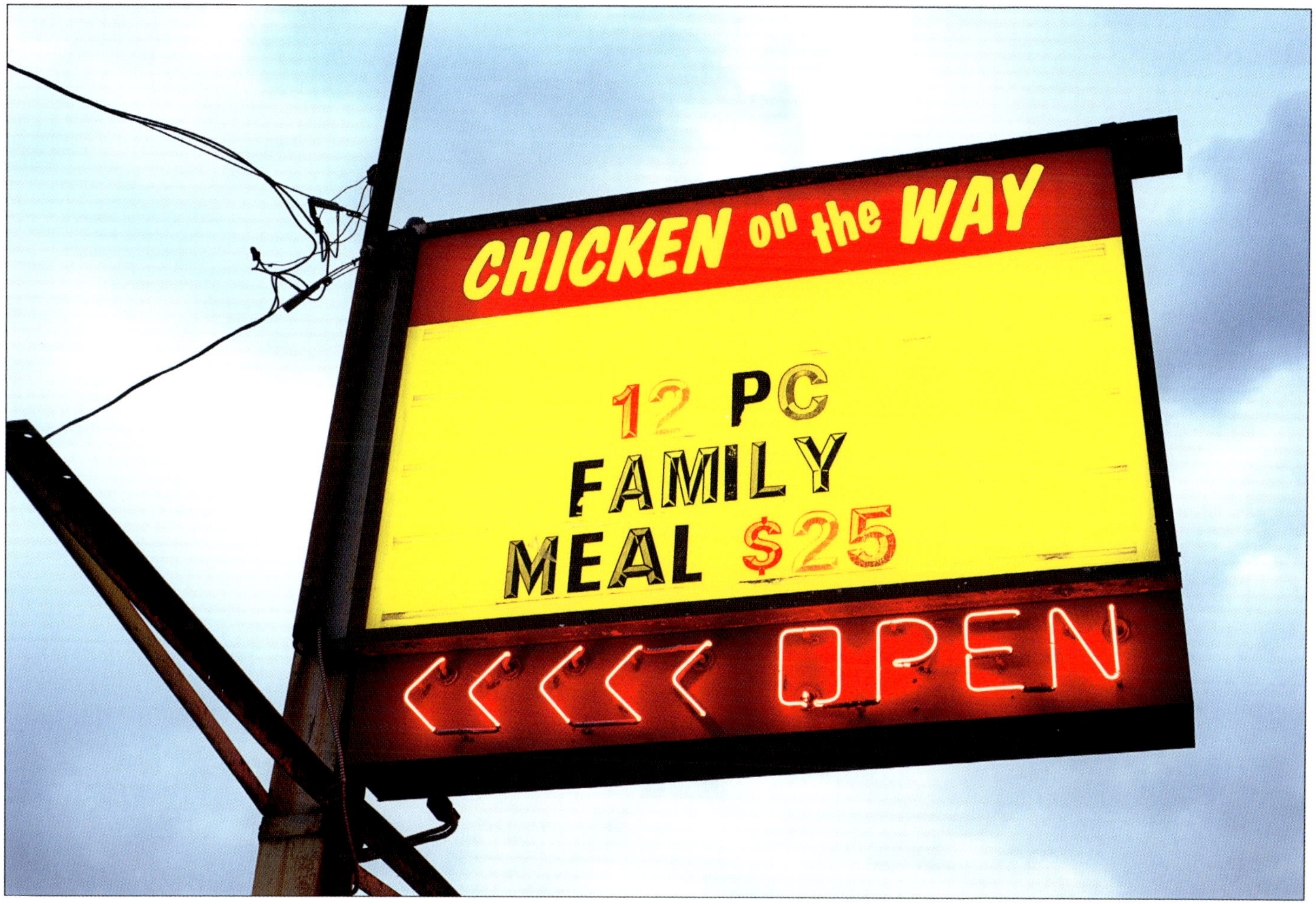

Chicken on the Way, 2016

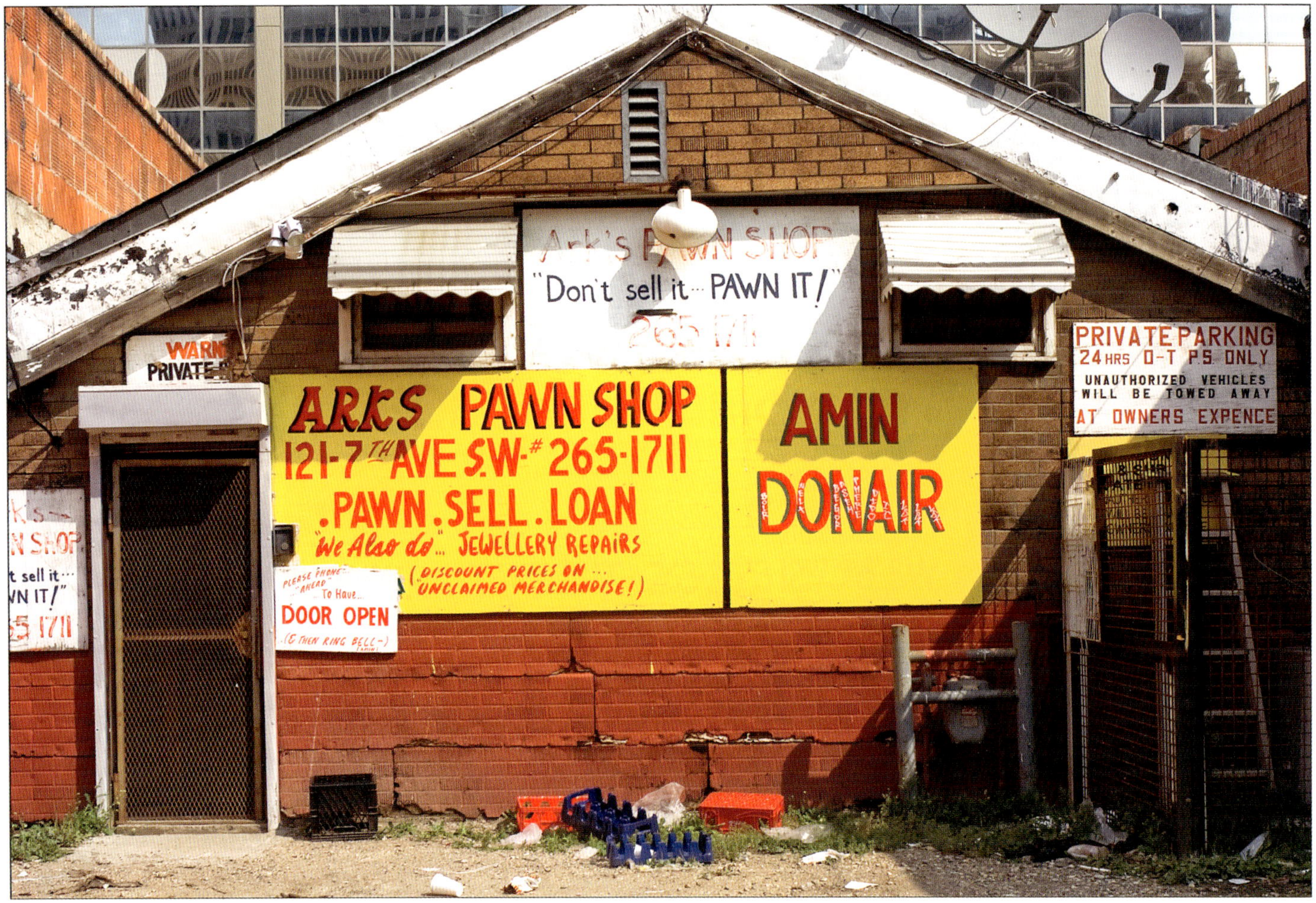

121 7 Ave SW, 2009

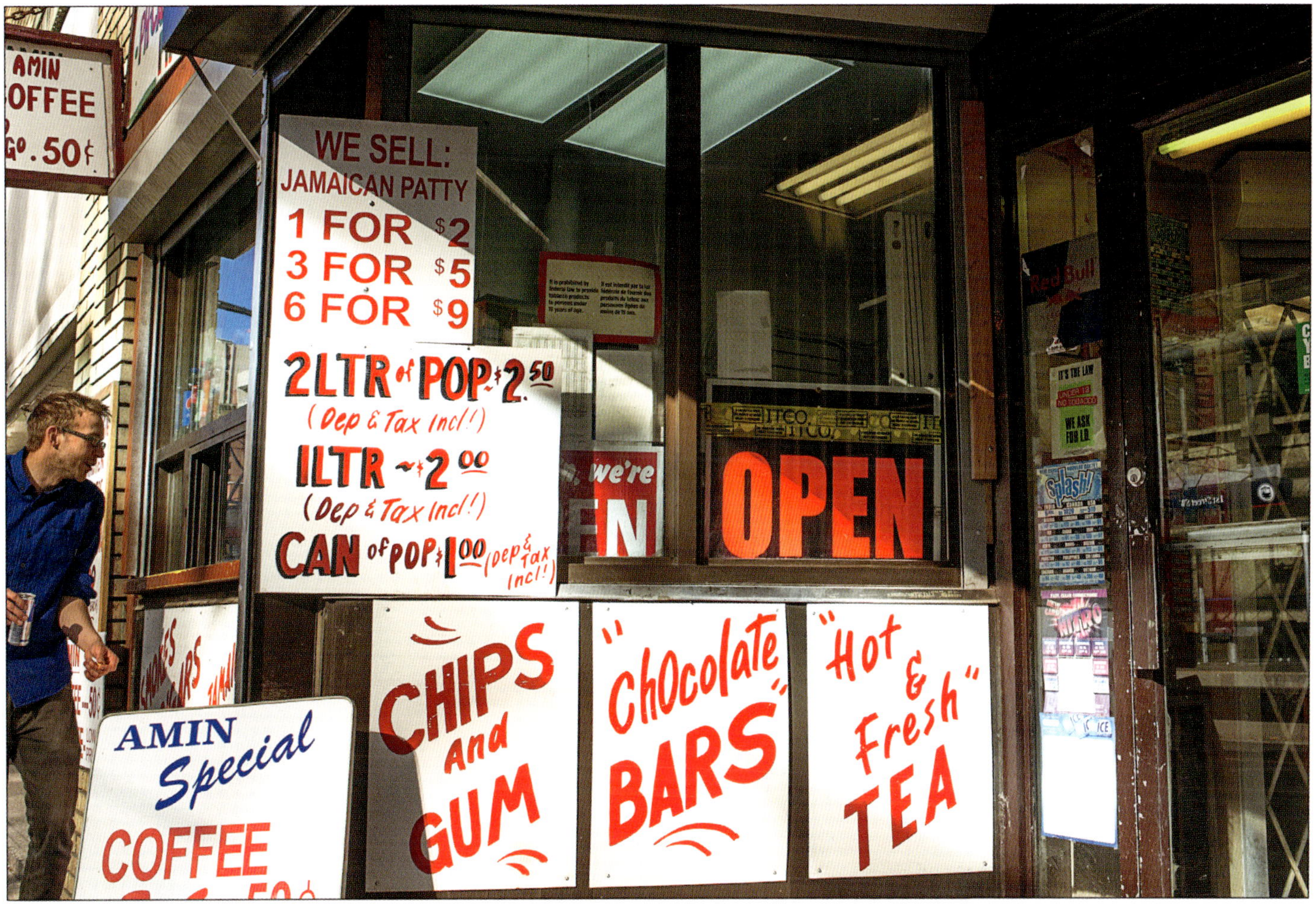
AMIN
COFFEE
WE SELL:
JAMAICAN PATTY
1 FOR $2
3 FOR $5
6 FOR $9
2LTR of POP $2.50
(Dep & Tax Incl!)
1LTR ~ $2.00
(Dep & Tax Incl!)
CAN of POP $1.00 (Dep & Tax Incl!)
OPEN
CHIPS And GUM
"Chocolate" BARS
"Hot & Fresh" TEA
AMIN Special
COFFEE

7 Ave SW, 2014

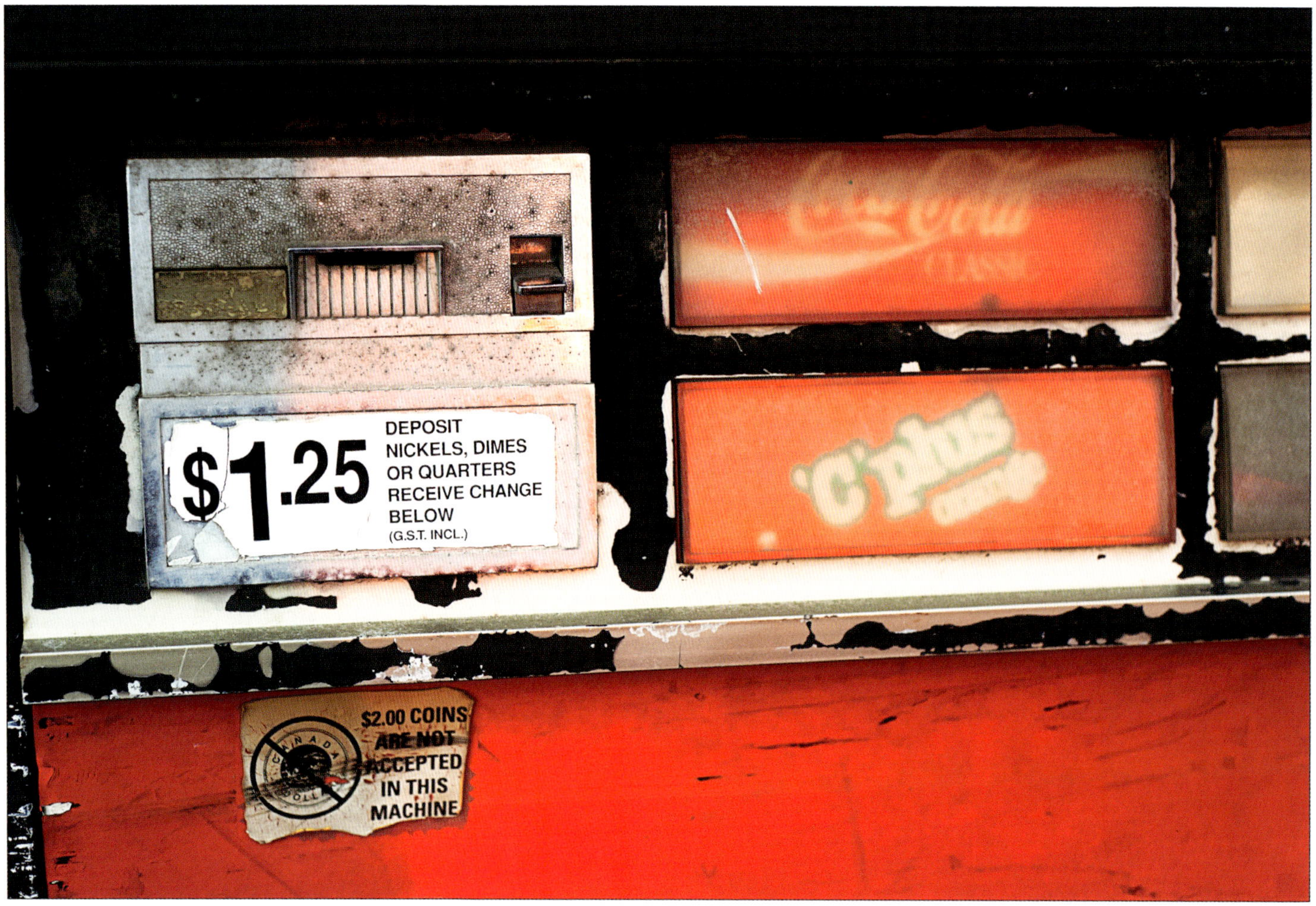

Town and Country Cold Beer Store, 2014

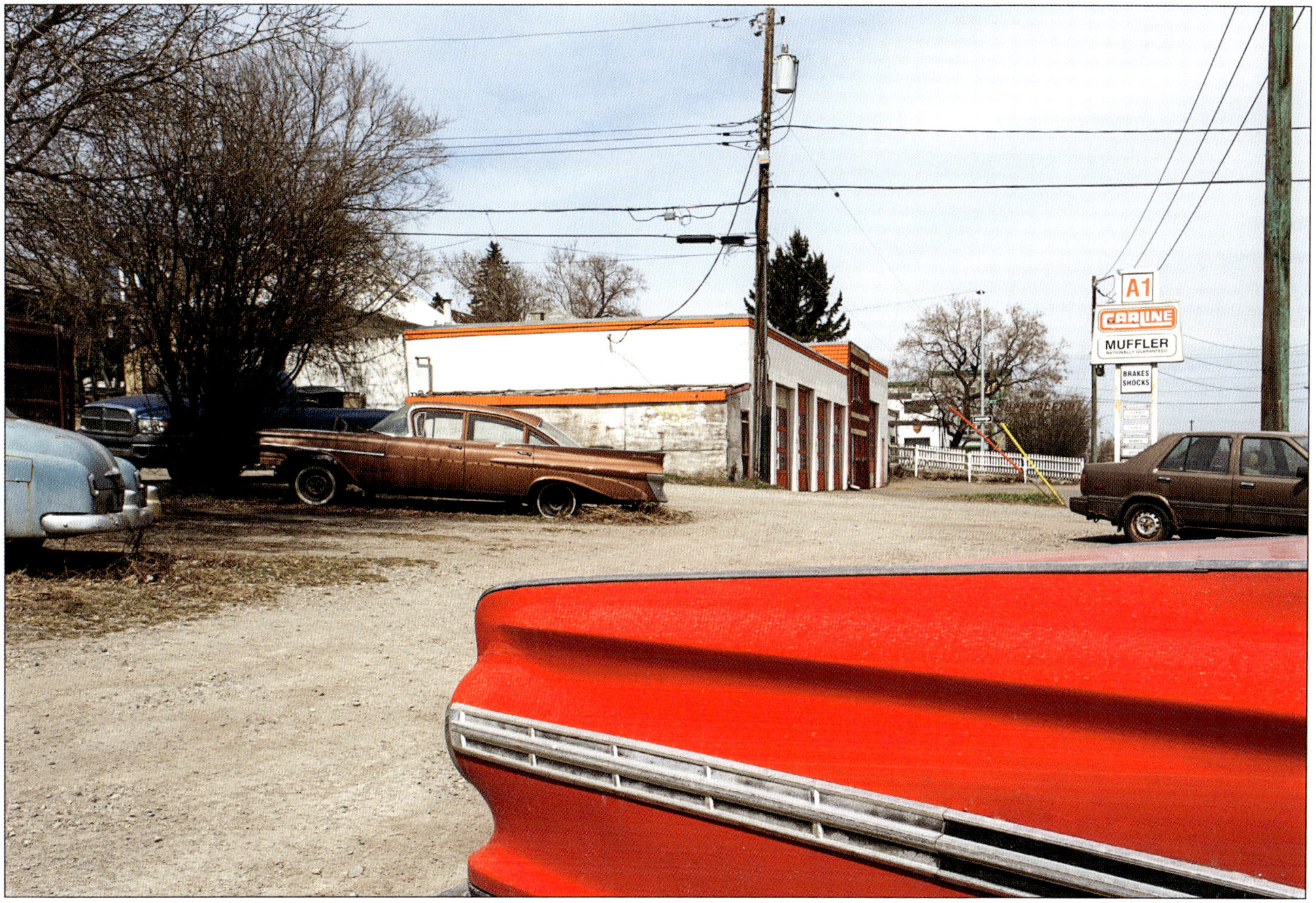

Near 19 Ave + 11 St SE, 2013

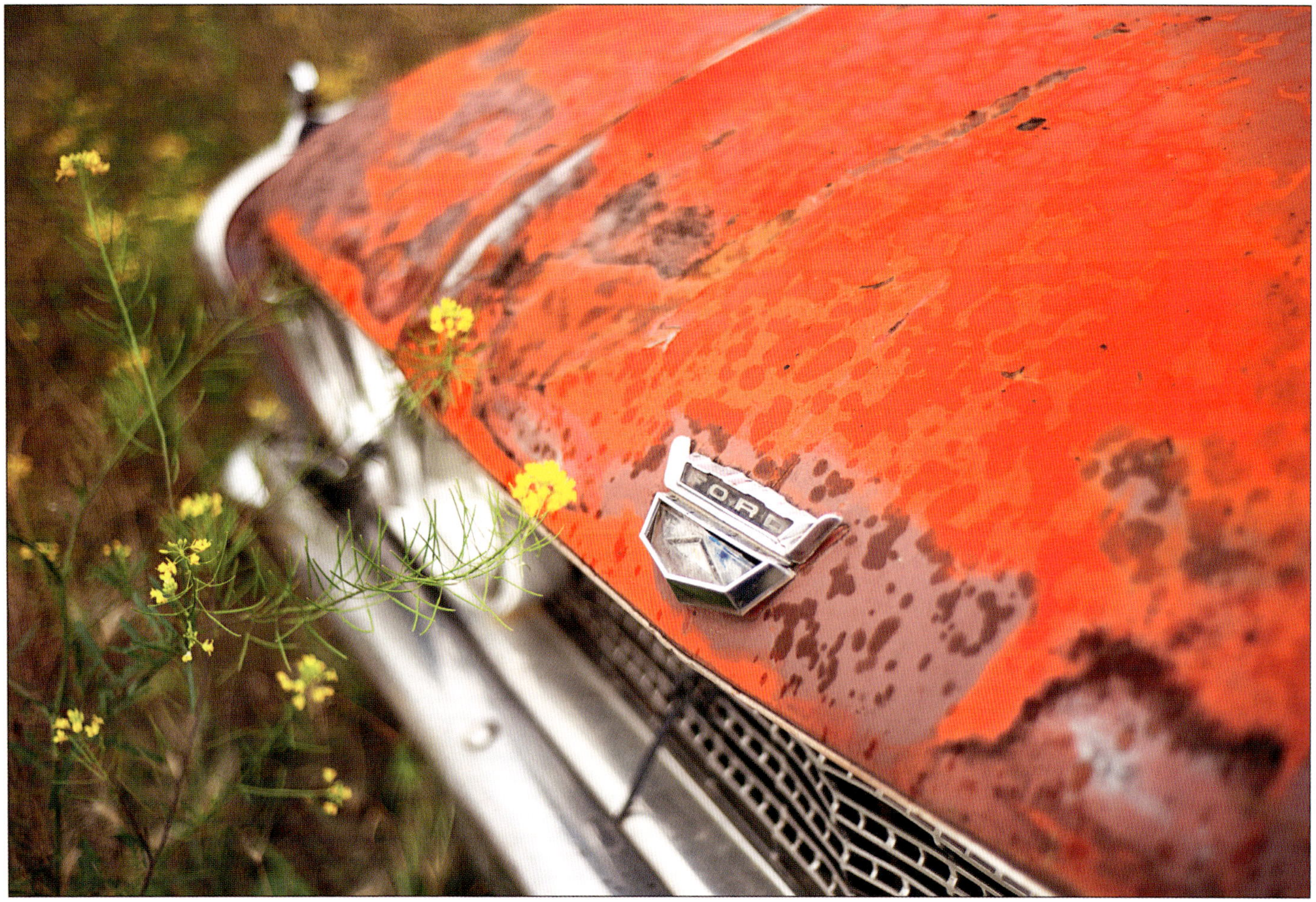

2828 Bonnybrook Rd SE, 2018

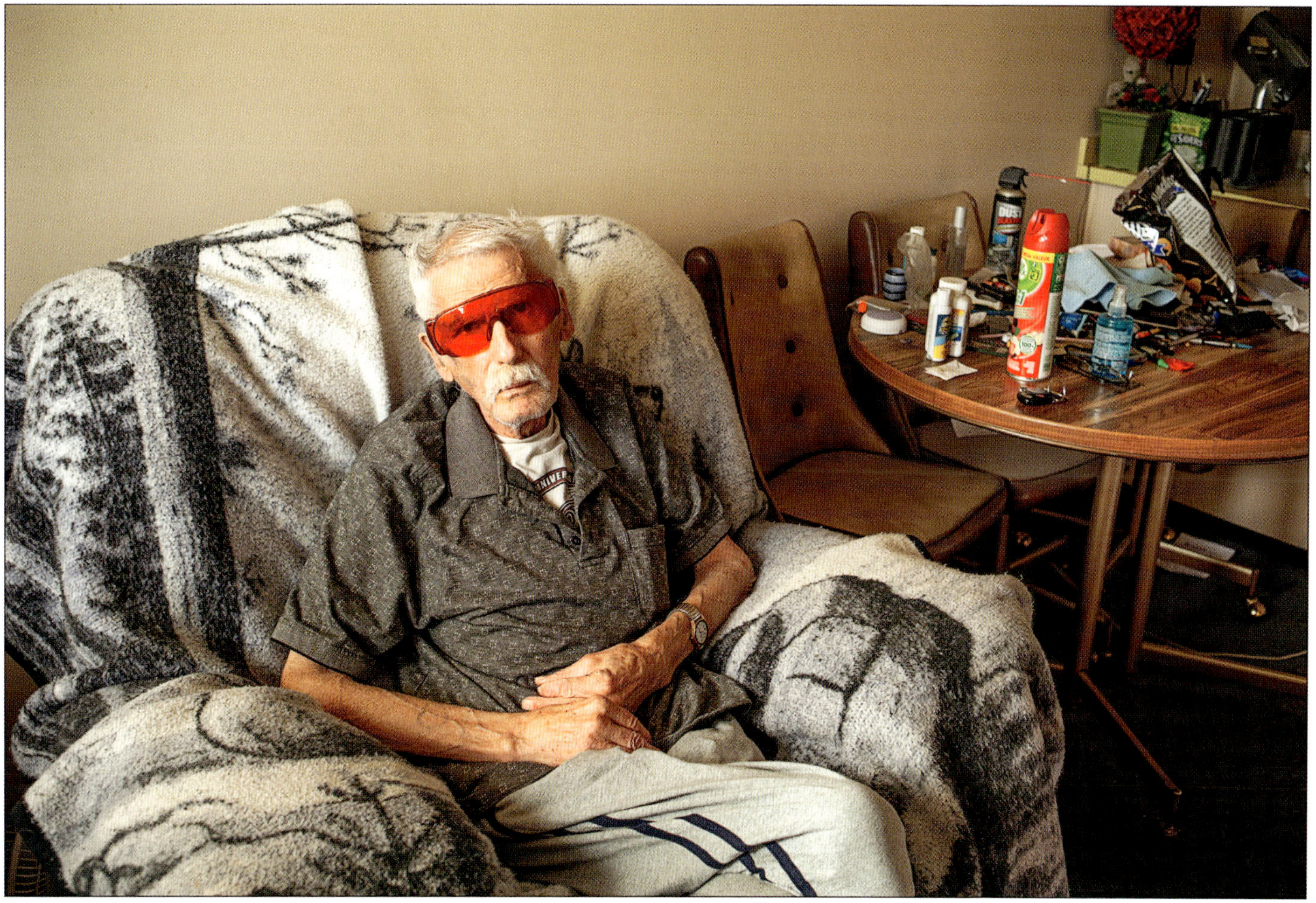

Gary Hoskins, Murdoch Manor, 2016

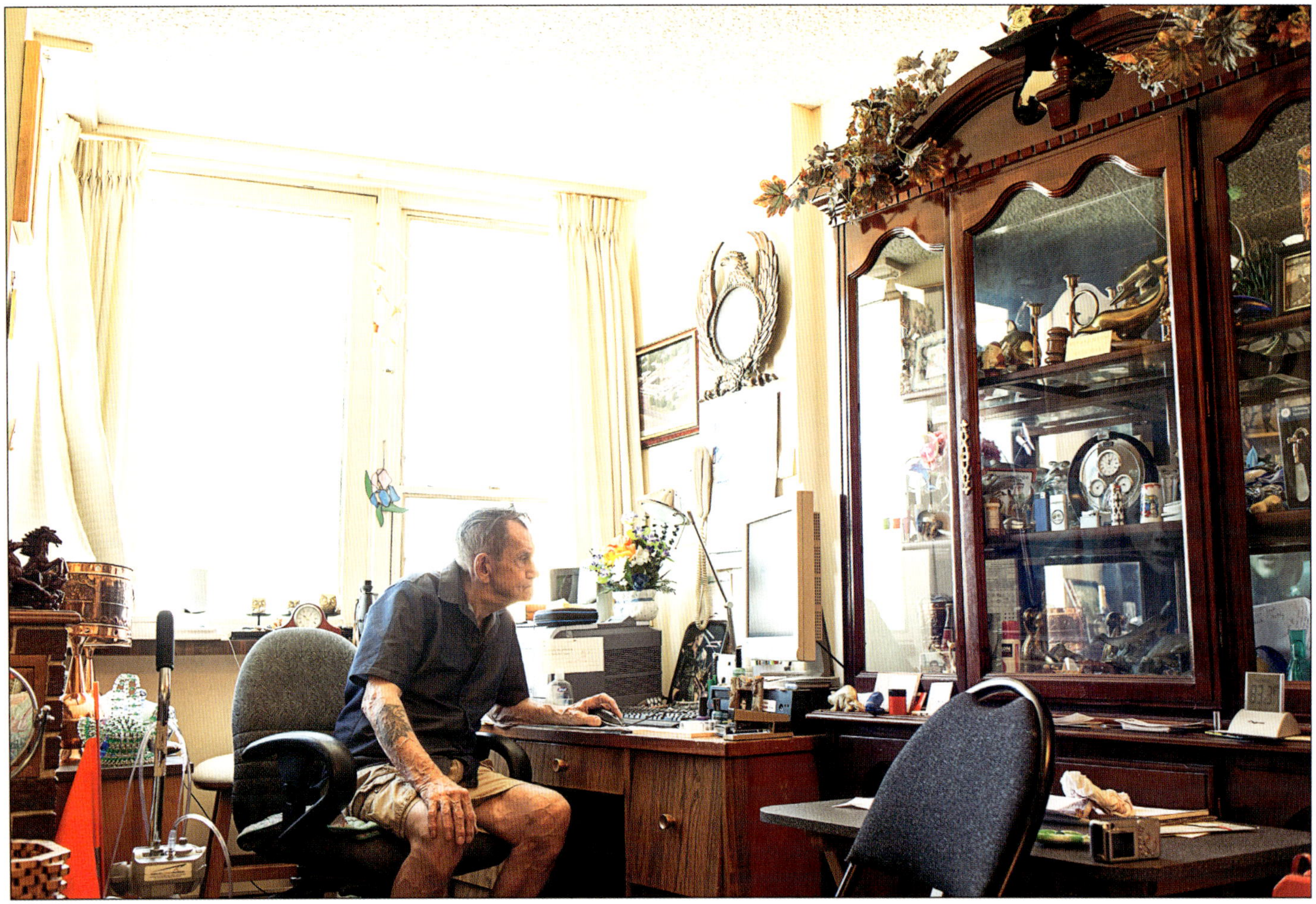

Fred Gowan, Murdoch Manor, 2015

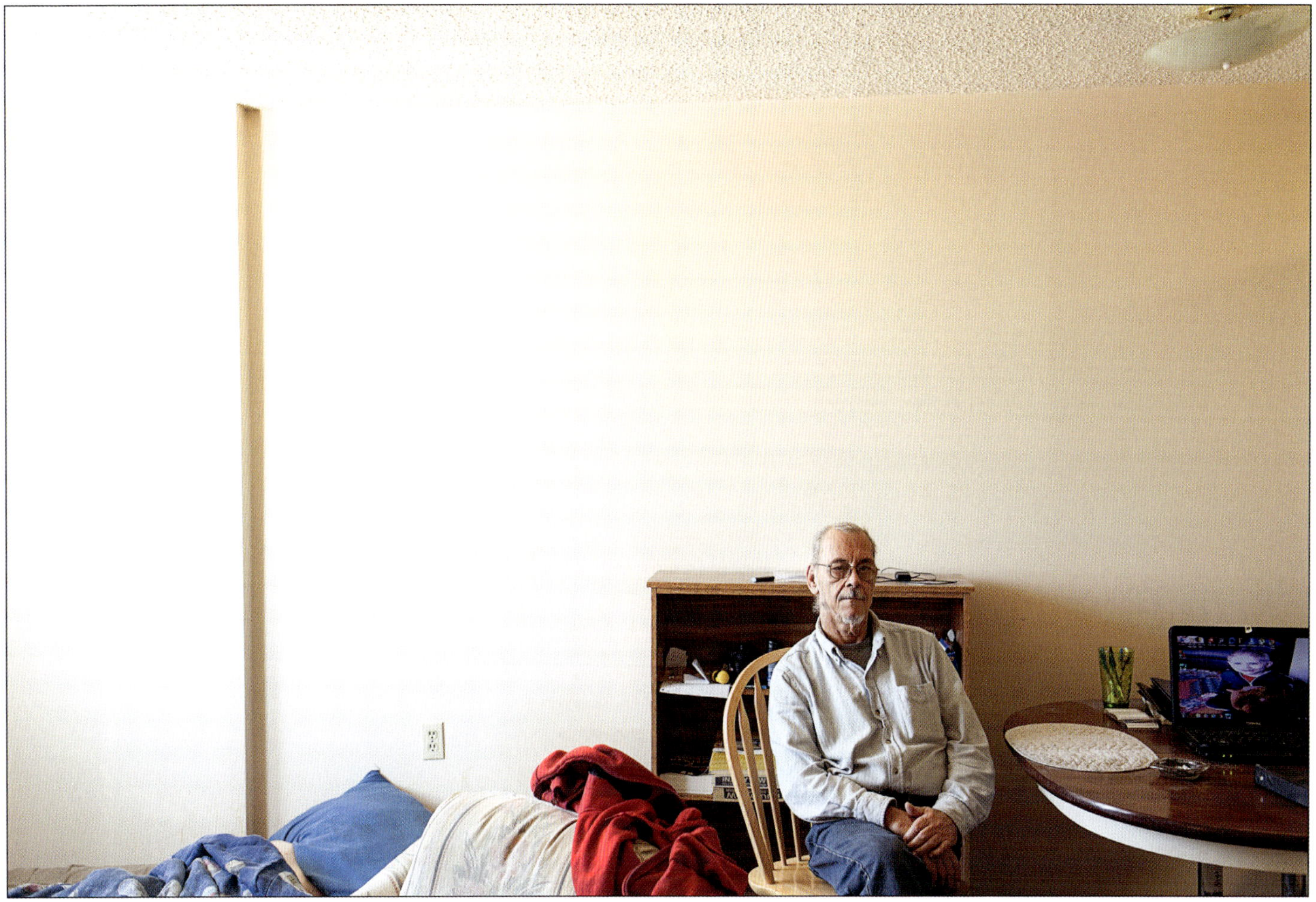

Jack Lamarre, Murdoch Manor, 2015

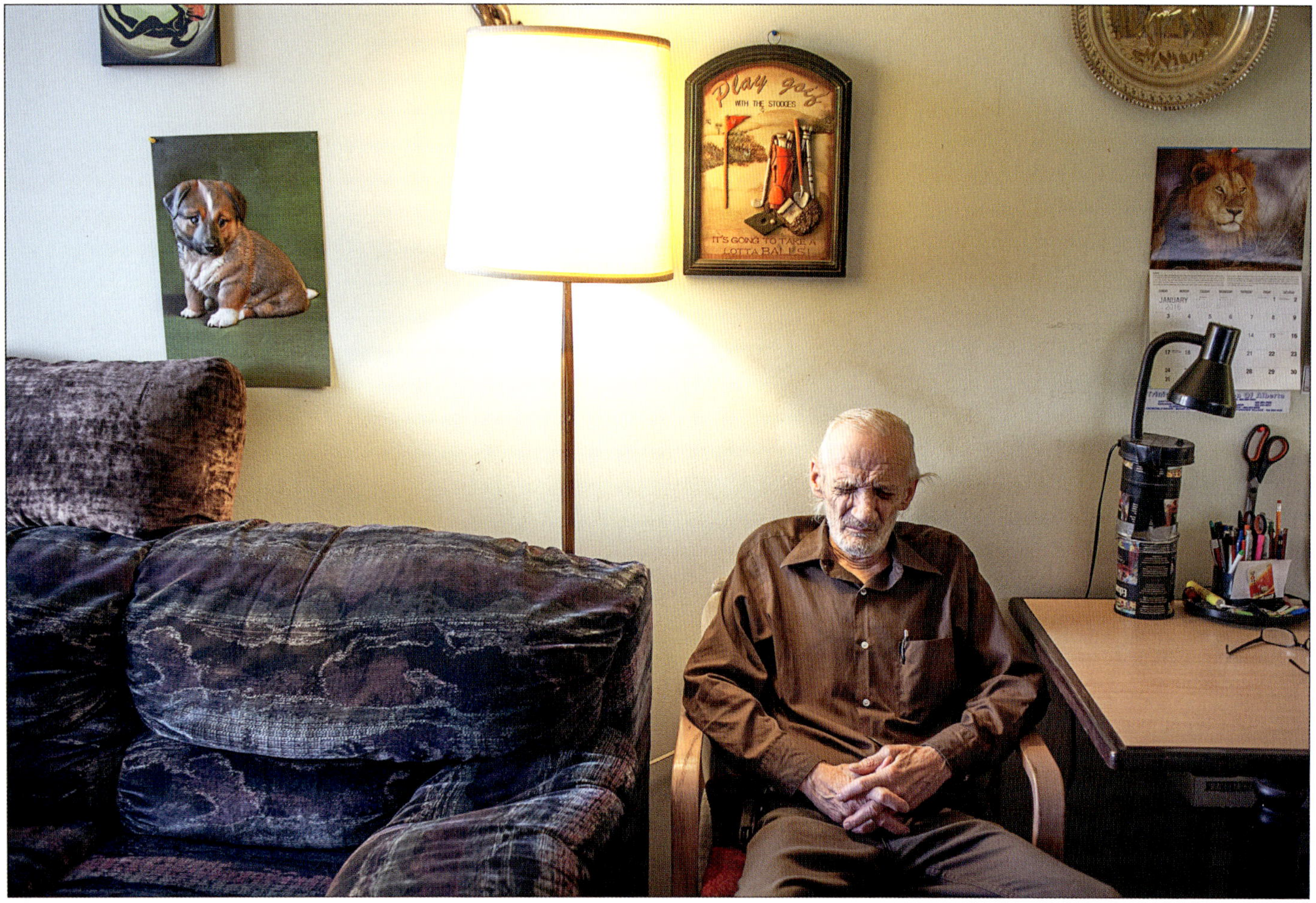

Doug Edwards, Murdoch Manor, 2016

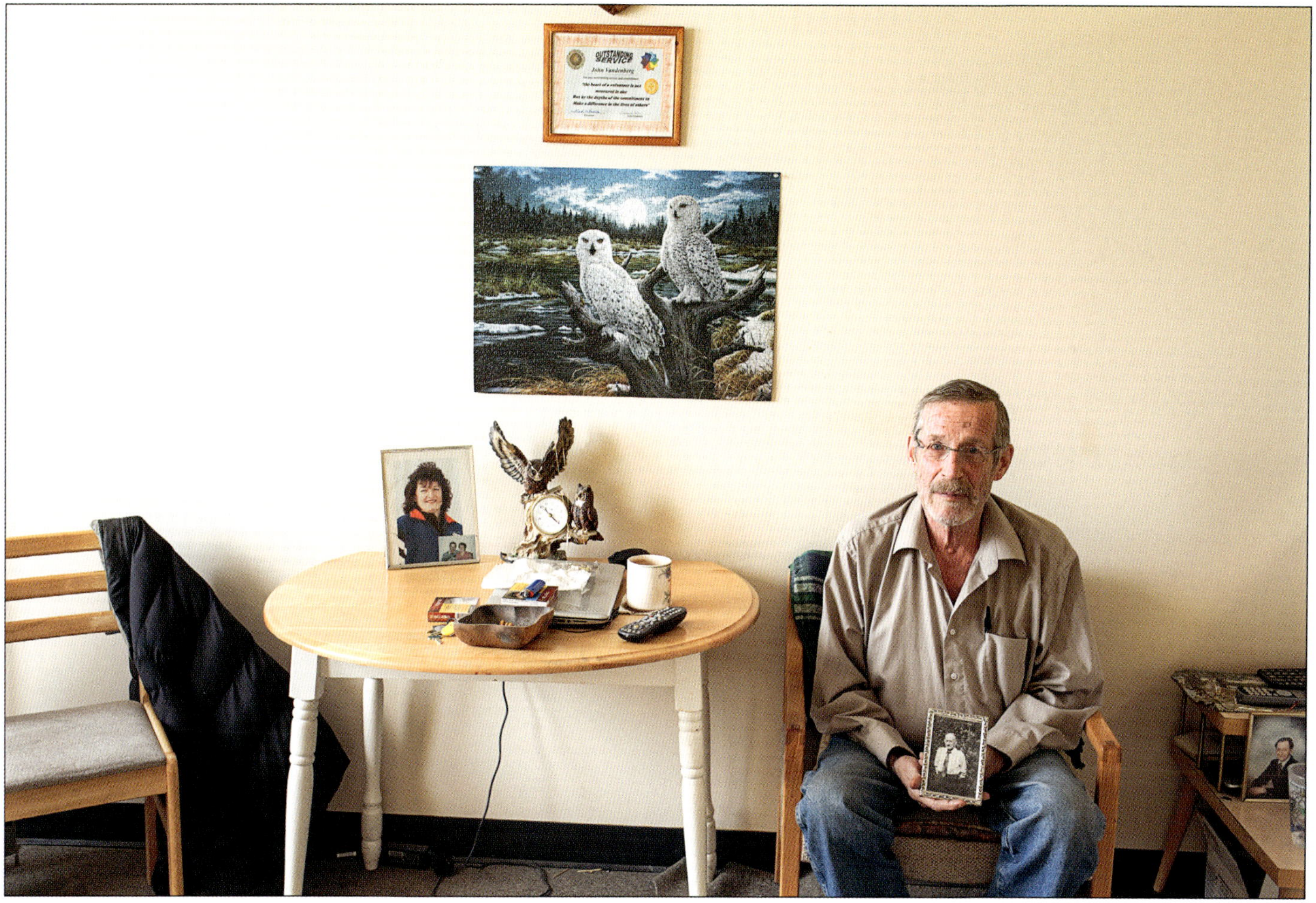

John Vandenberg, Murdoch Manor, 2015

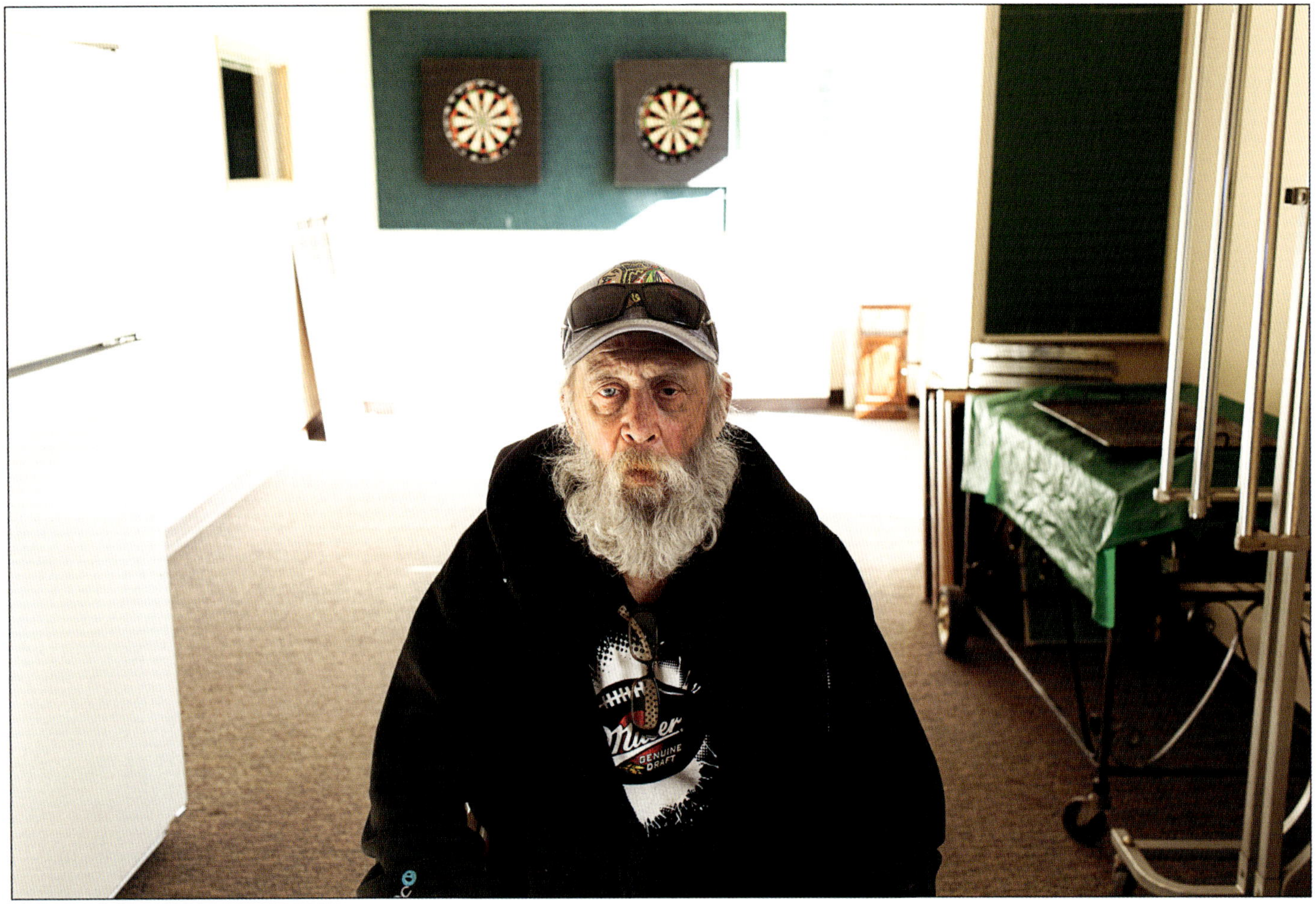

Jim Yurkiewicz, Murdoch Manor, 2015

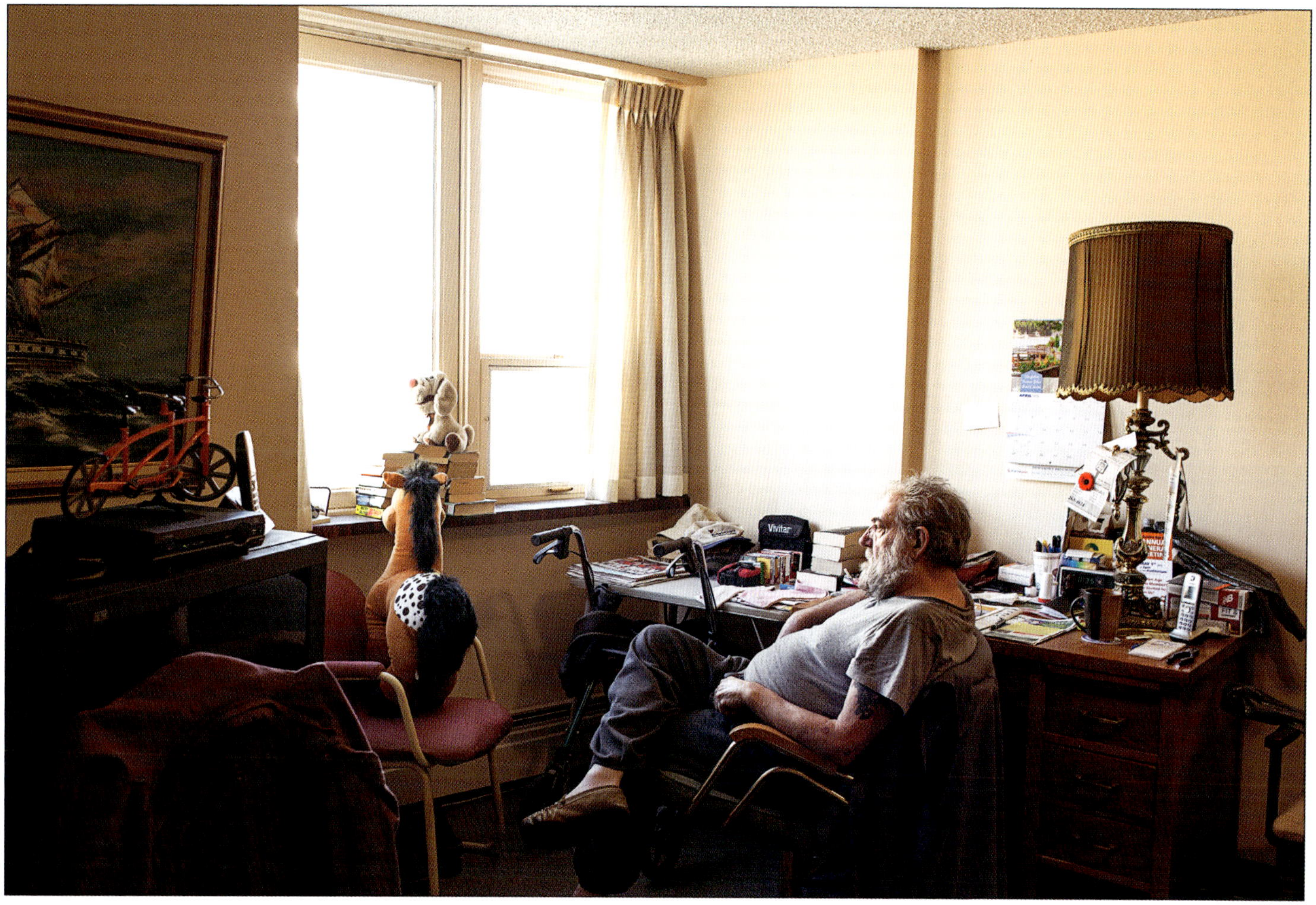

Michael Simpson, Murdoch Manor, 2015

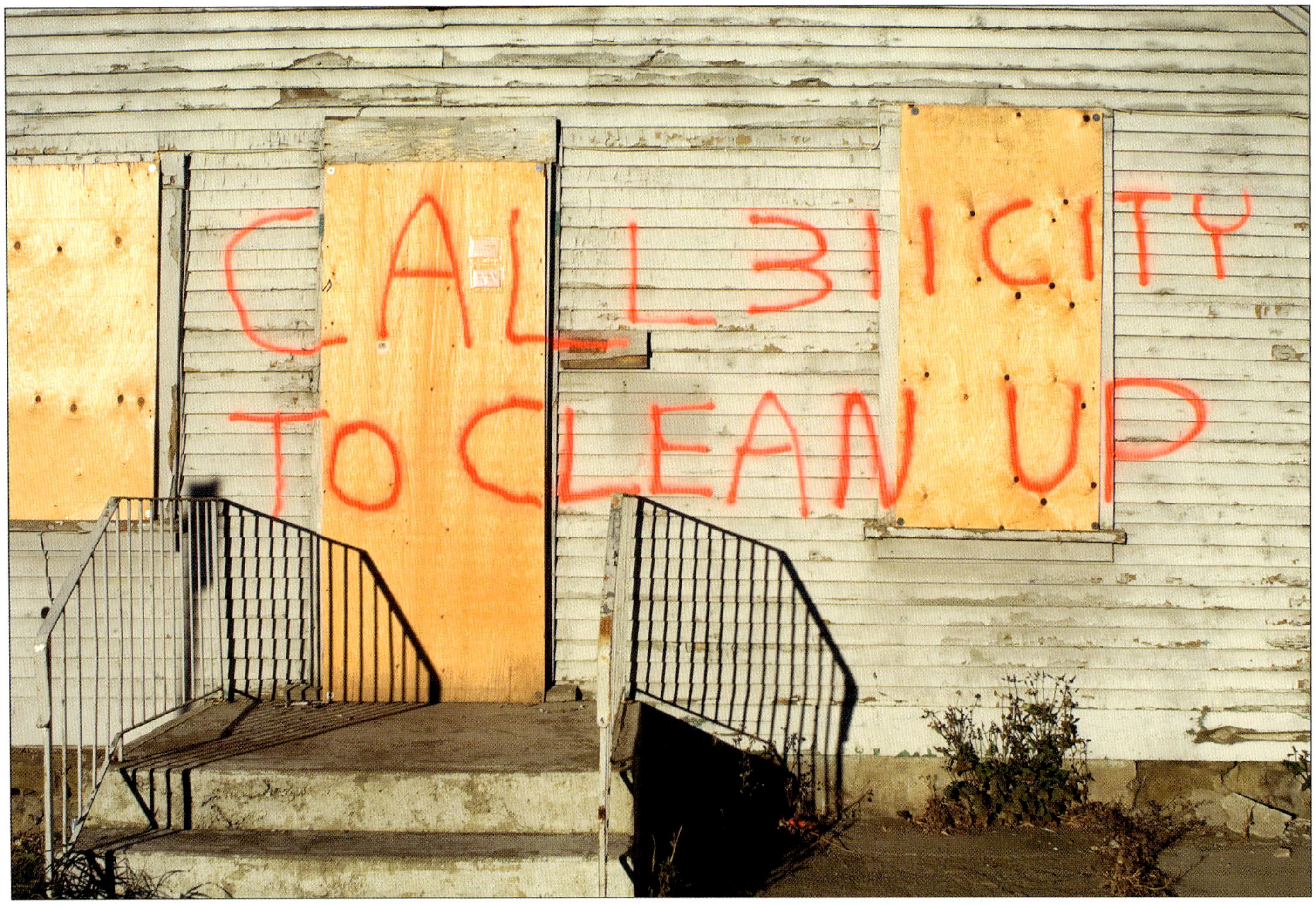

Near 5 St + 11 Ave SE, 2007

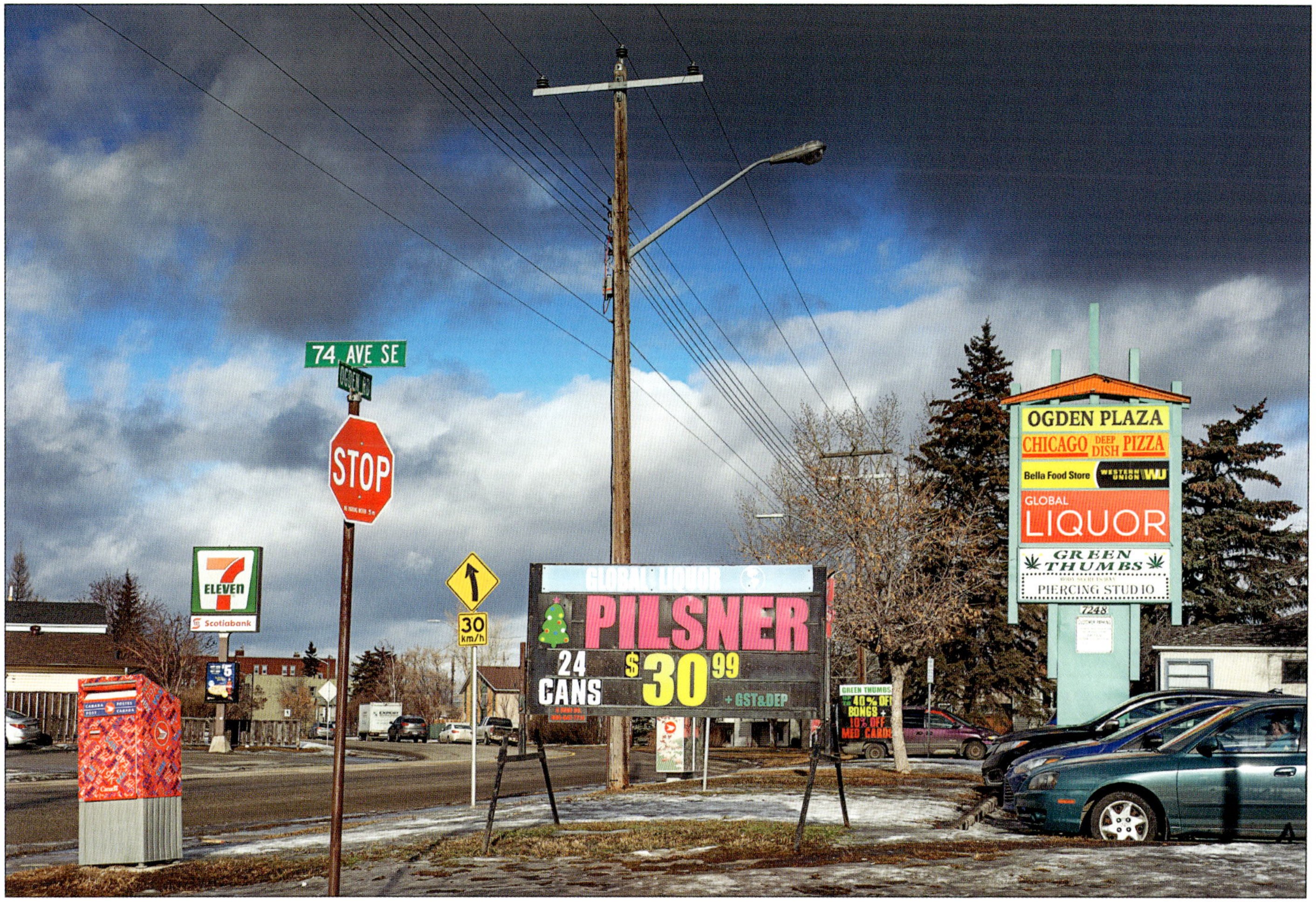

74 Ave + Ogden Rd. SE, 2019

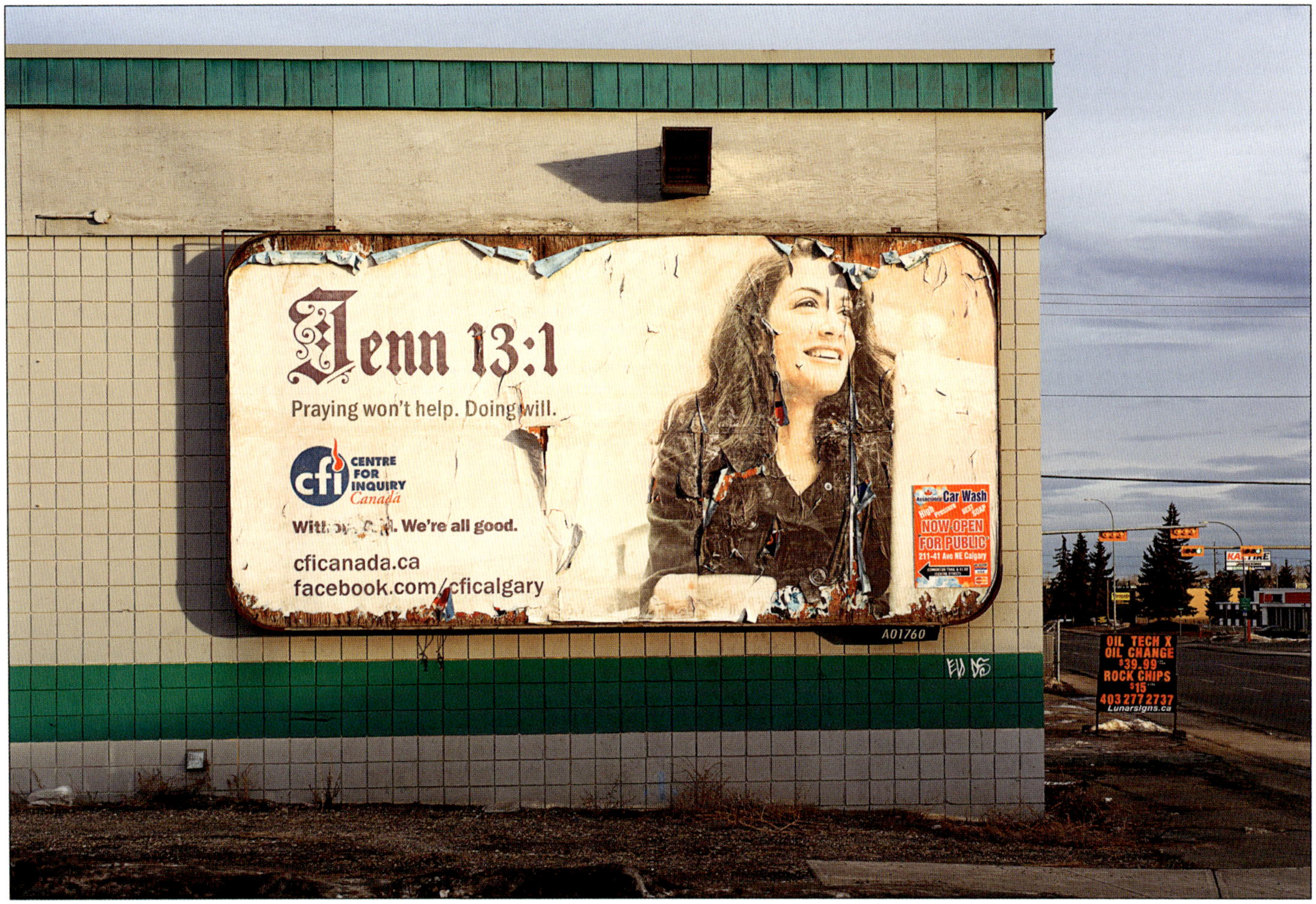

3603 Edmonton Trail, 2017

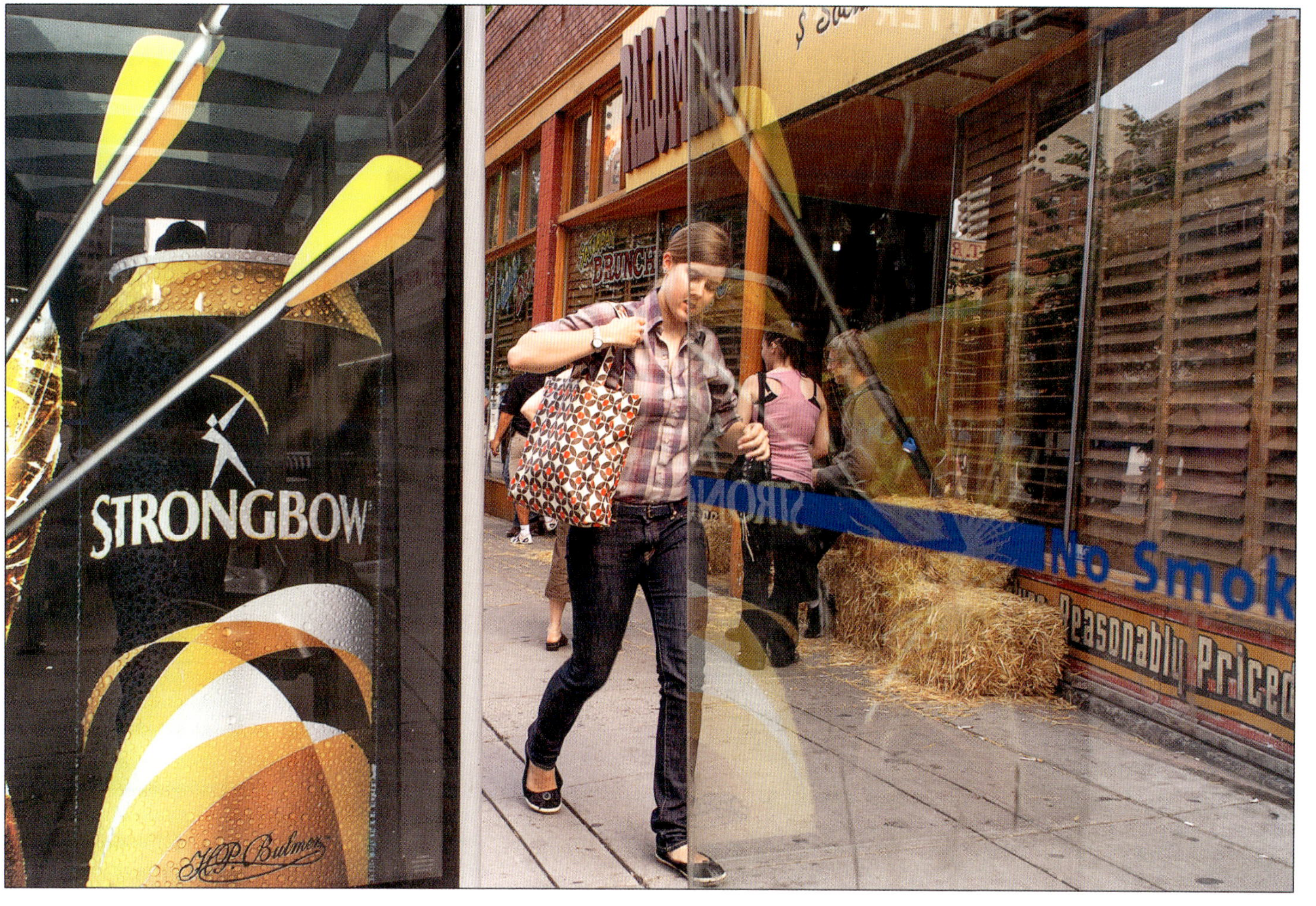

7 Ave SW, 2008

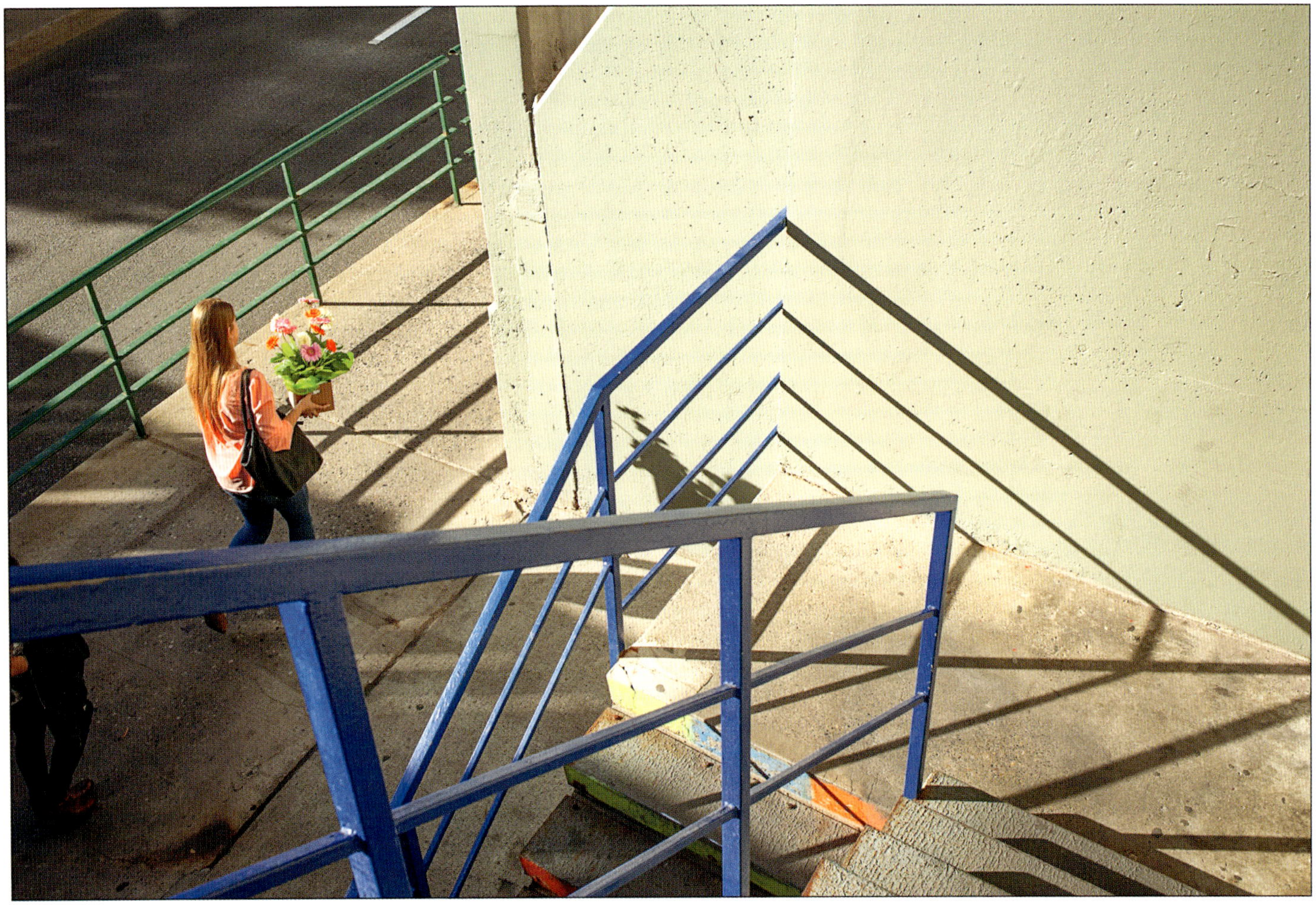

Downtown, 2016

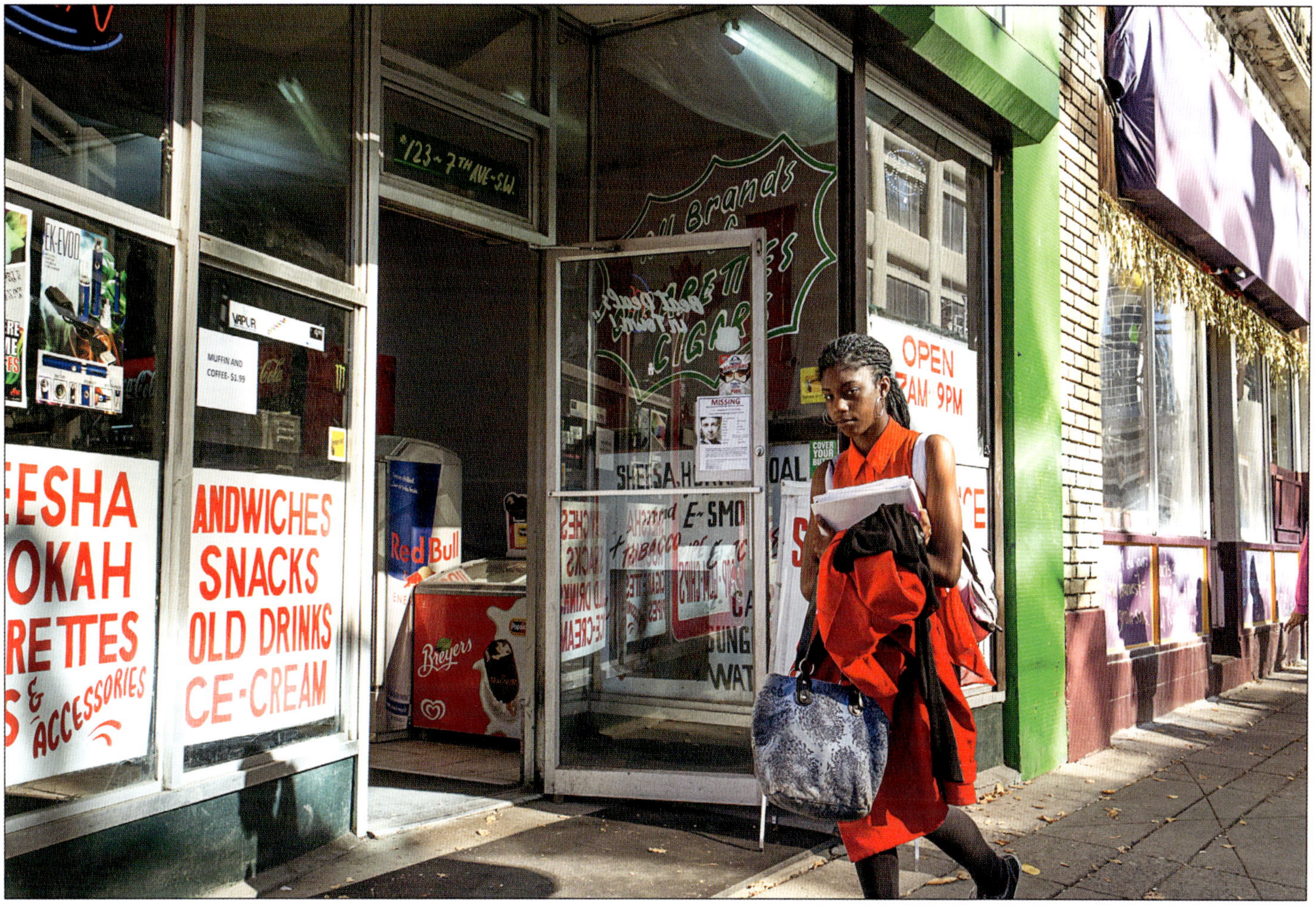
#123 - 7TH AVE-S.W.
EESHA
OKAH
RETTES
& ACCESSORIES
ANDWICHES
SNACKS
OLD DRINKS
CE-CREAM
MUFFIN AND COFFEE- $1.99
OPEN
7AM 9PM
Red Bull
Breyers
MISSING
E-SMO

7 Ave SW, 2014

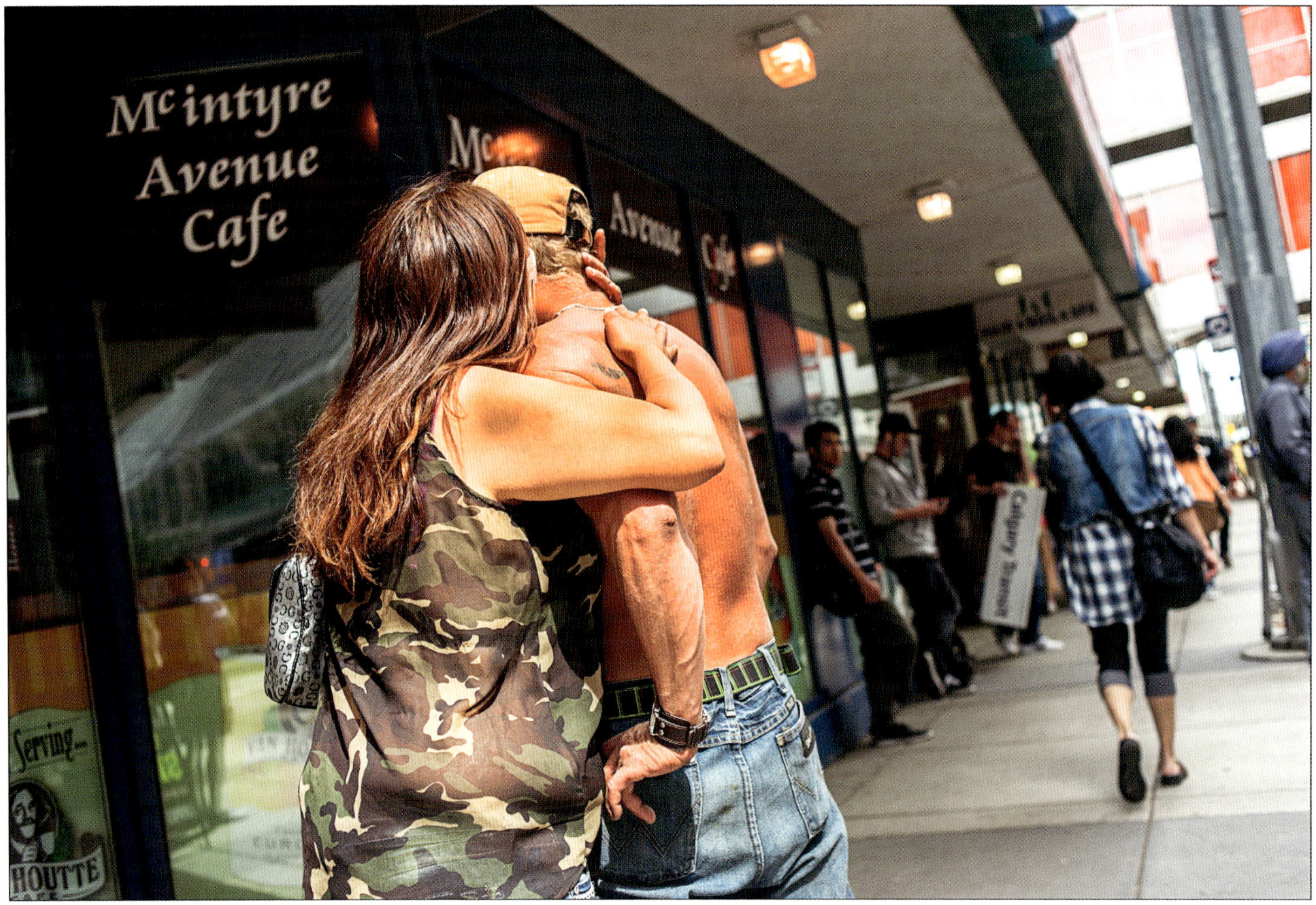

7 Ave SW, 2013

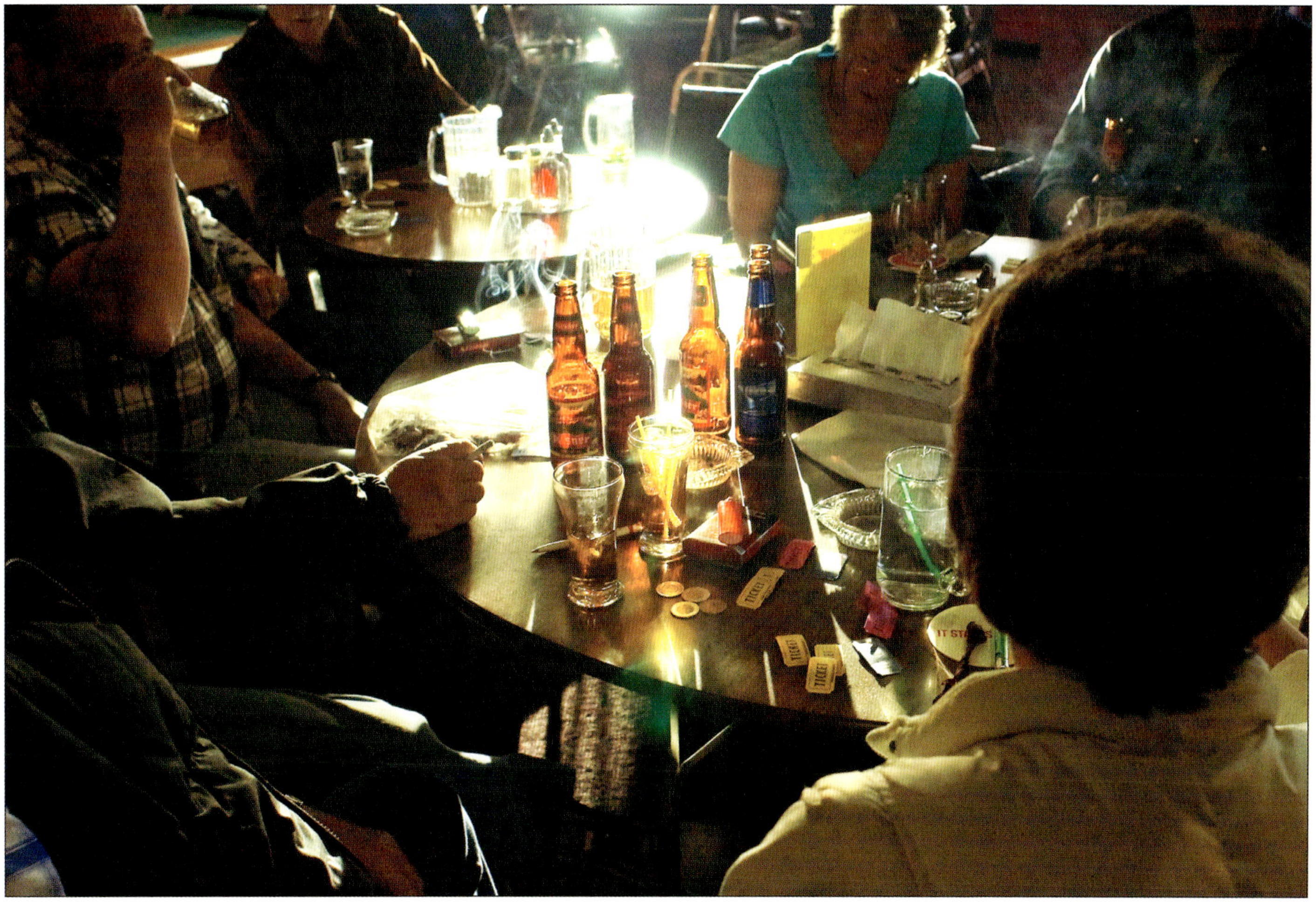

Ogden Legion, 2007

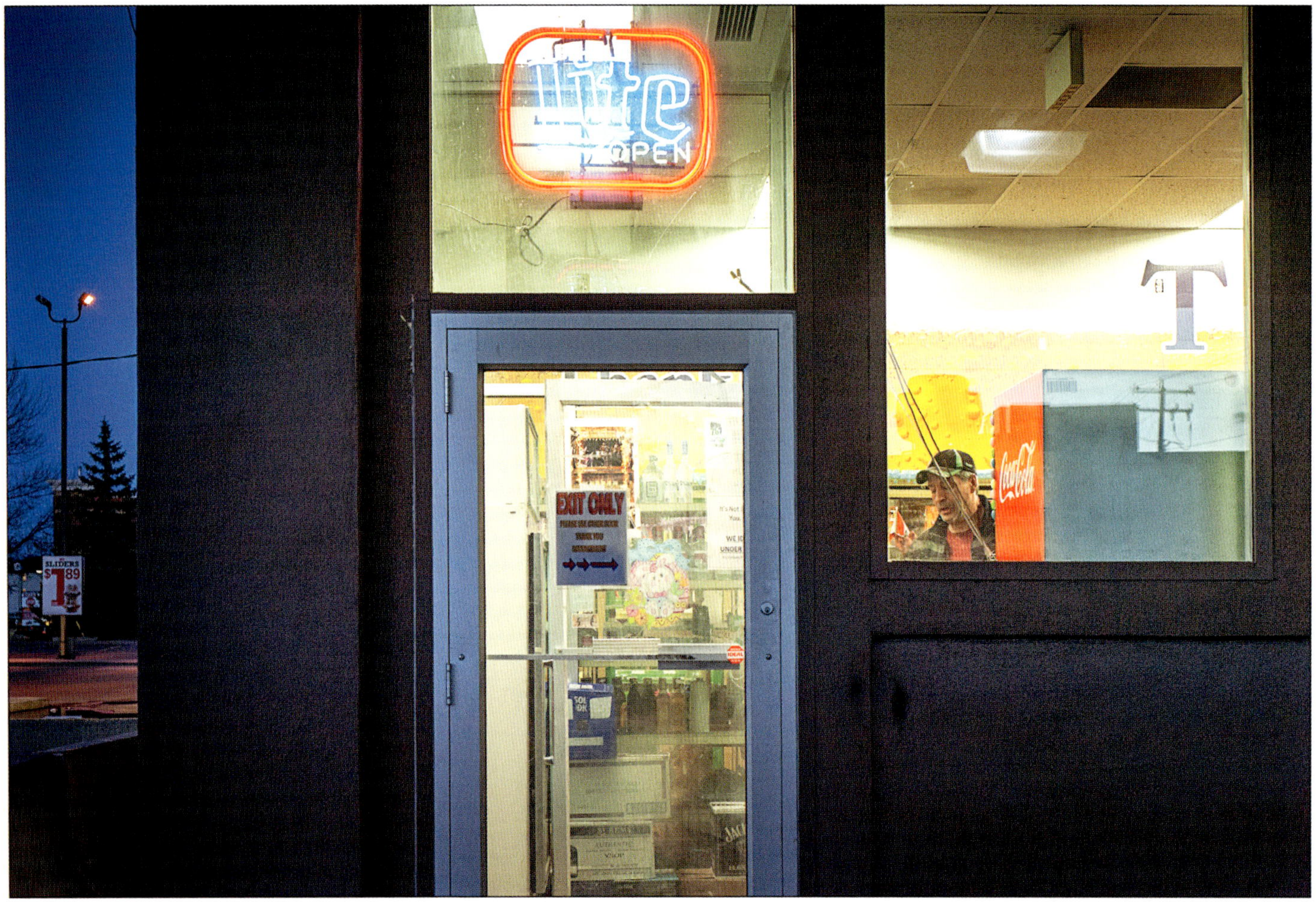

Town and Country Cold Beer Store, 2017

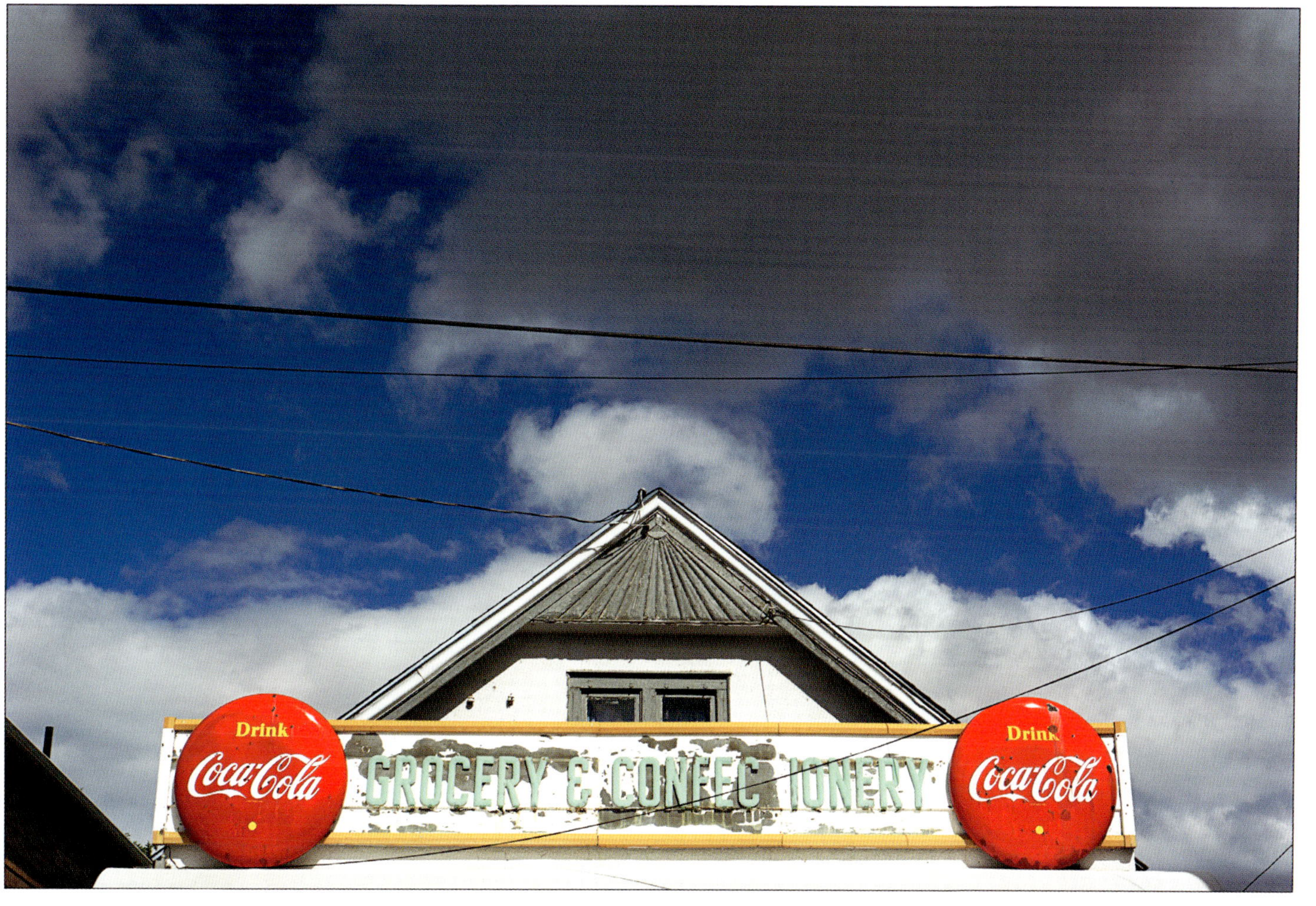

2718 17 St SW, 2015

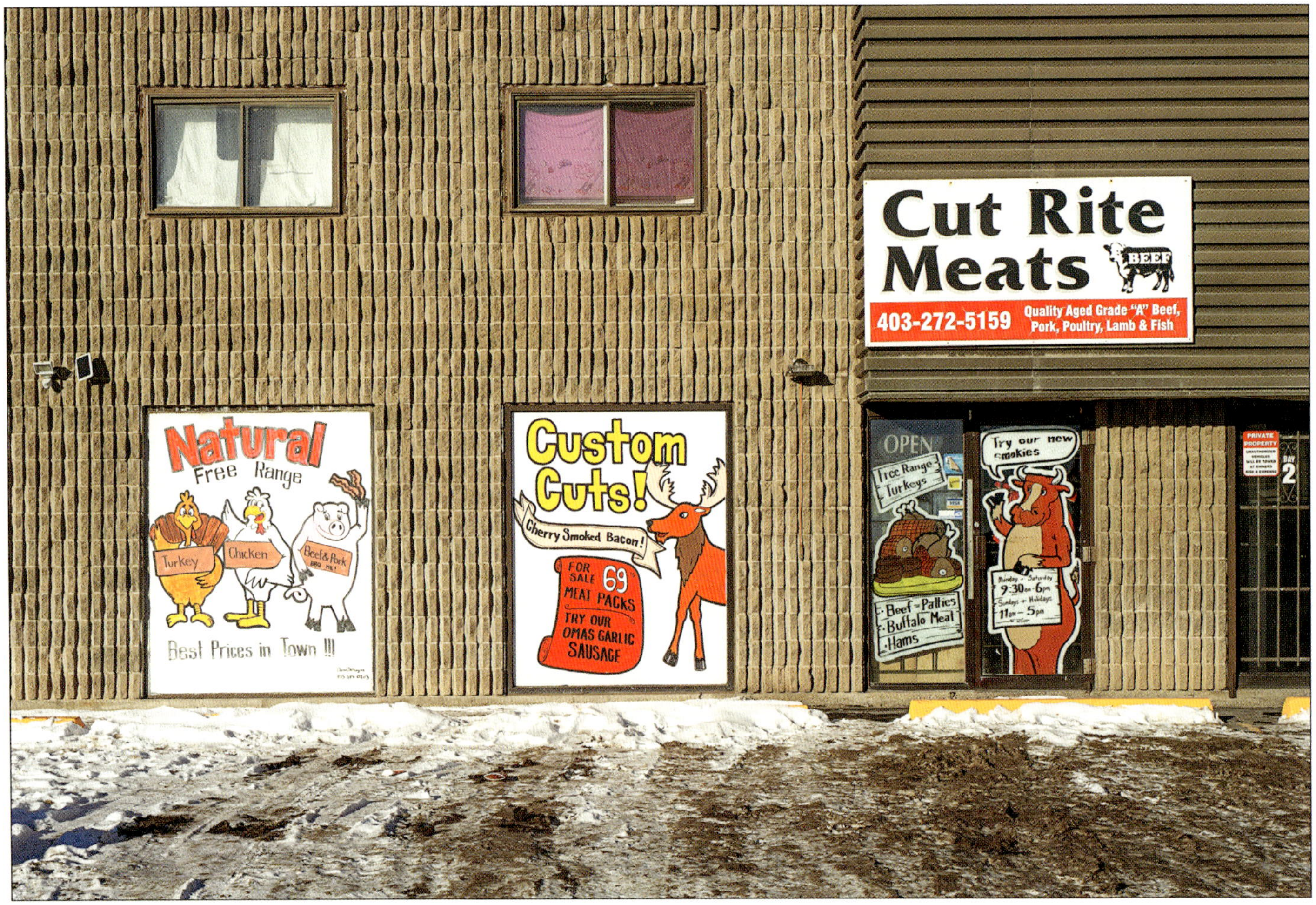

Cut Rite Meats, 2016

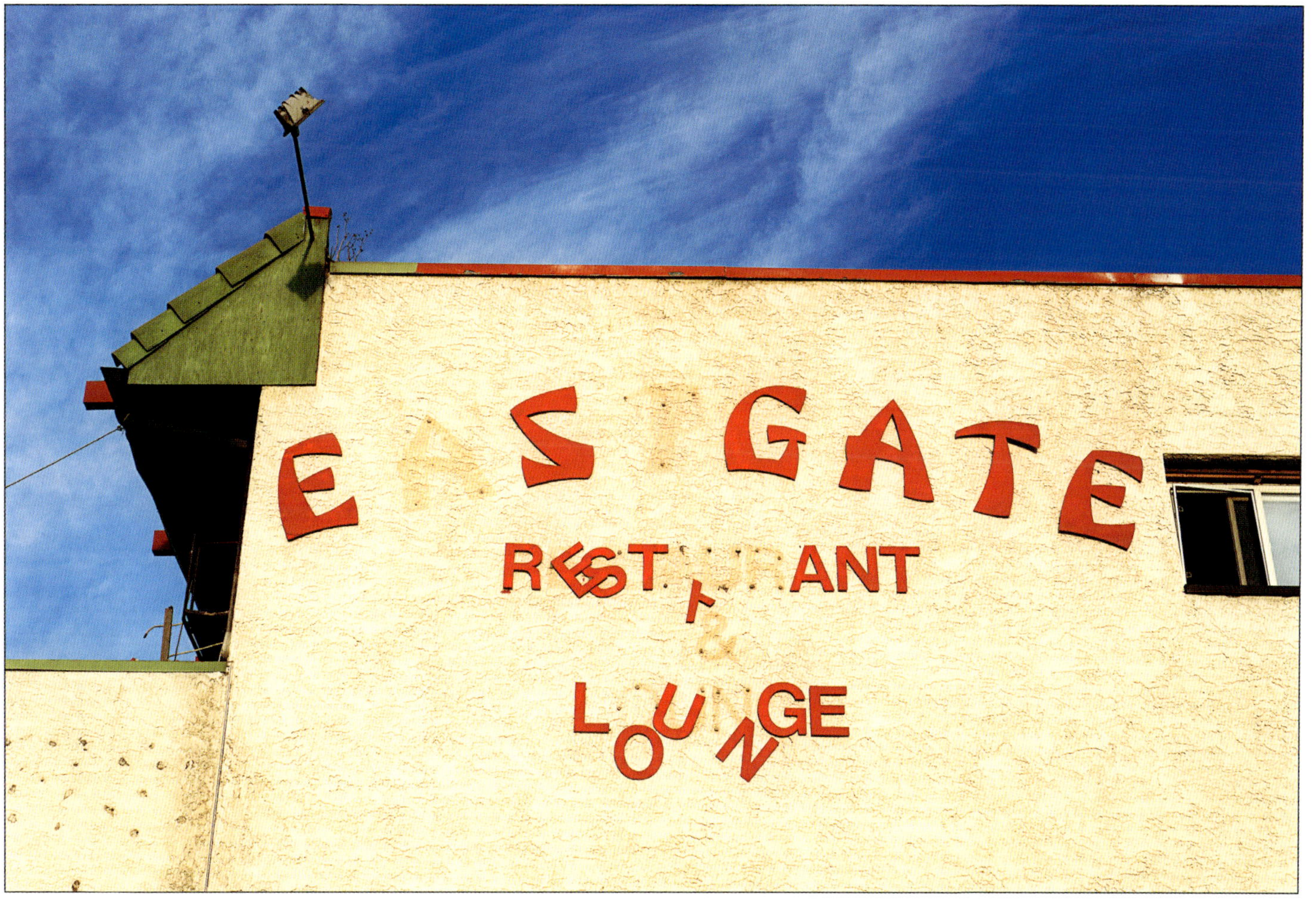

East Gate Restaurant, 2013

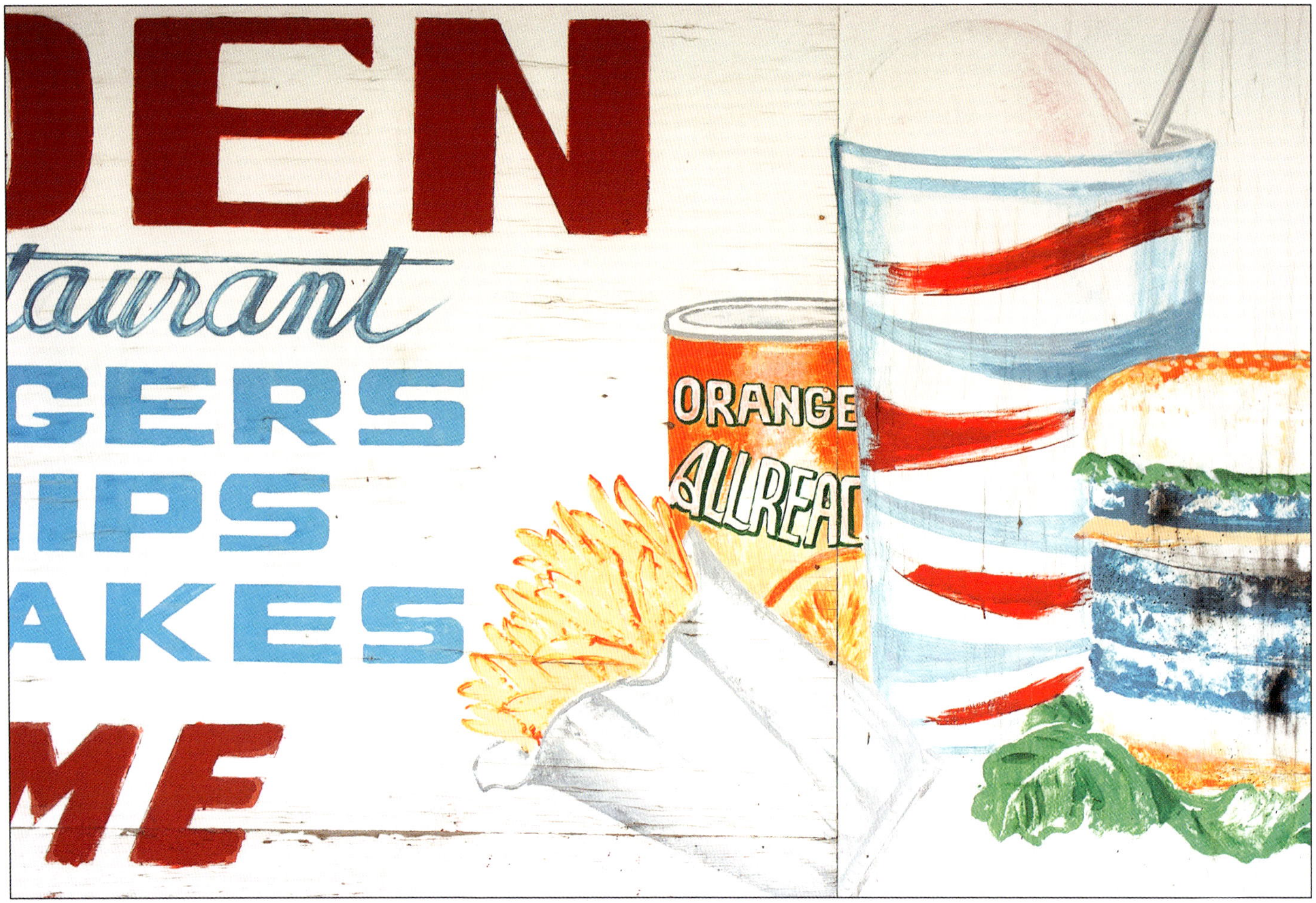

24 St + Ogden Rd SE, 2007

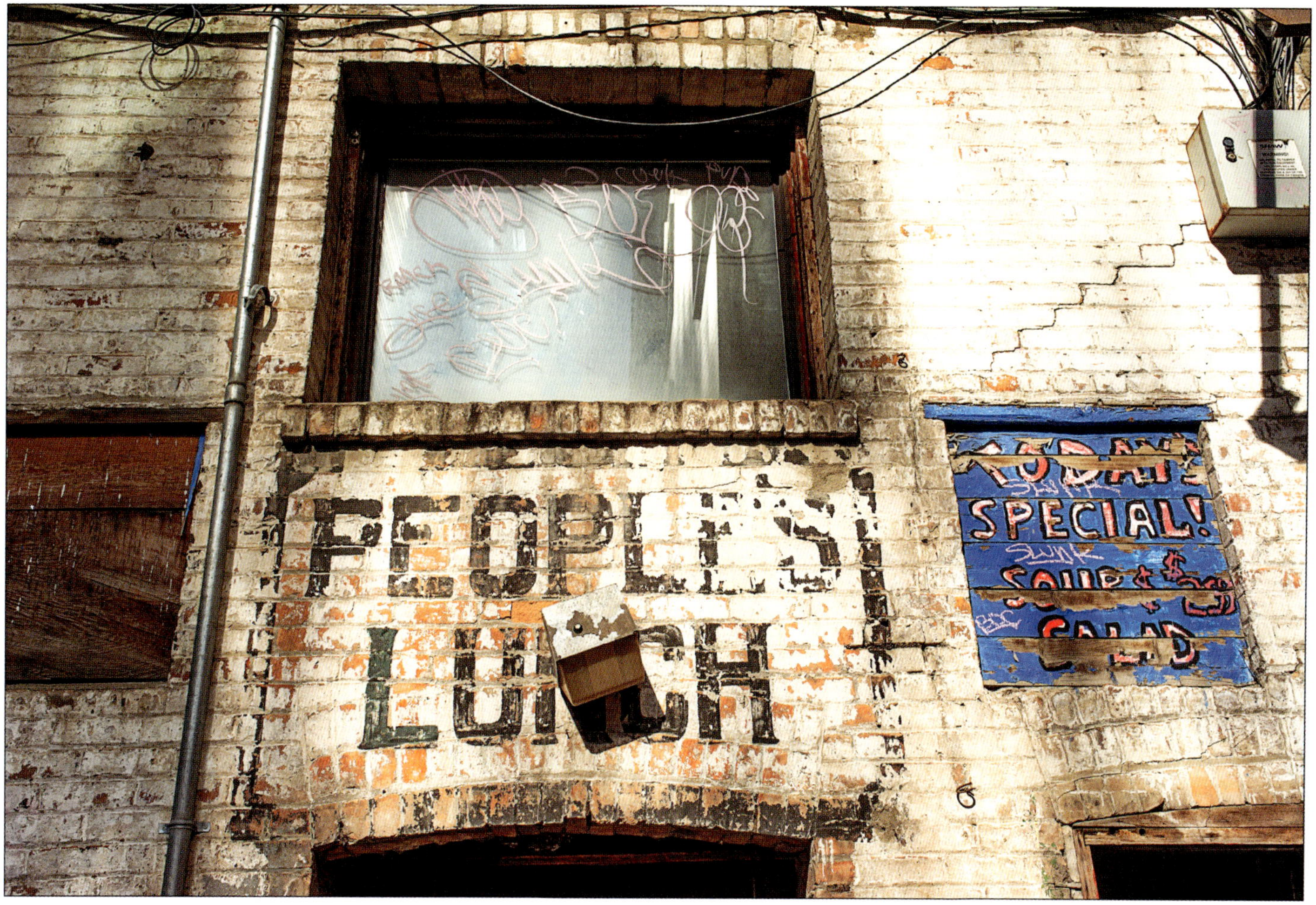

People's Lunch, 2017

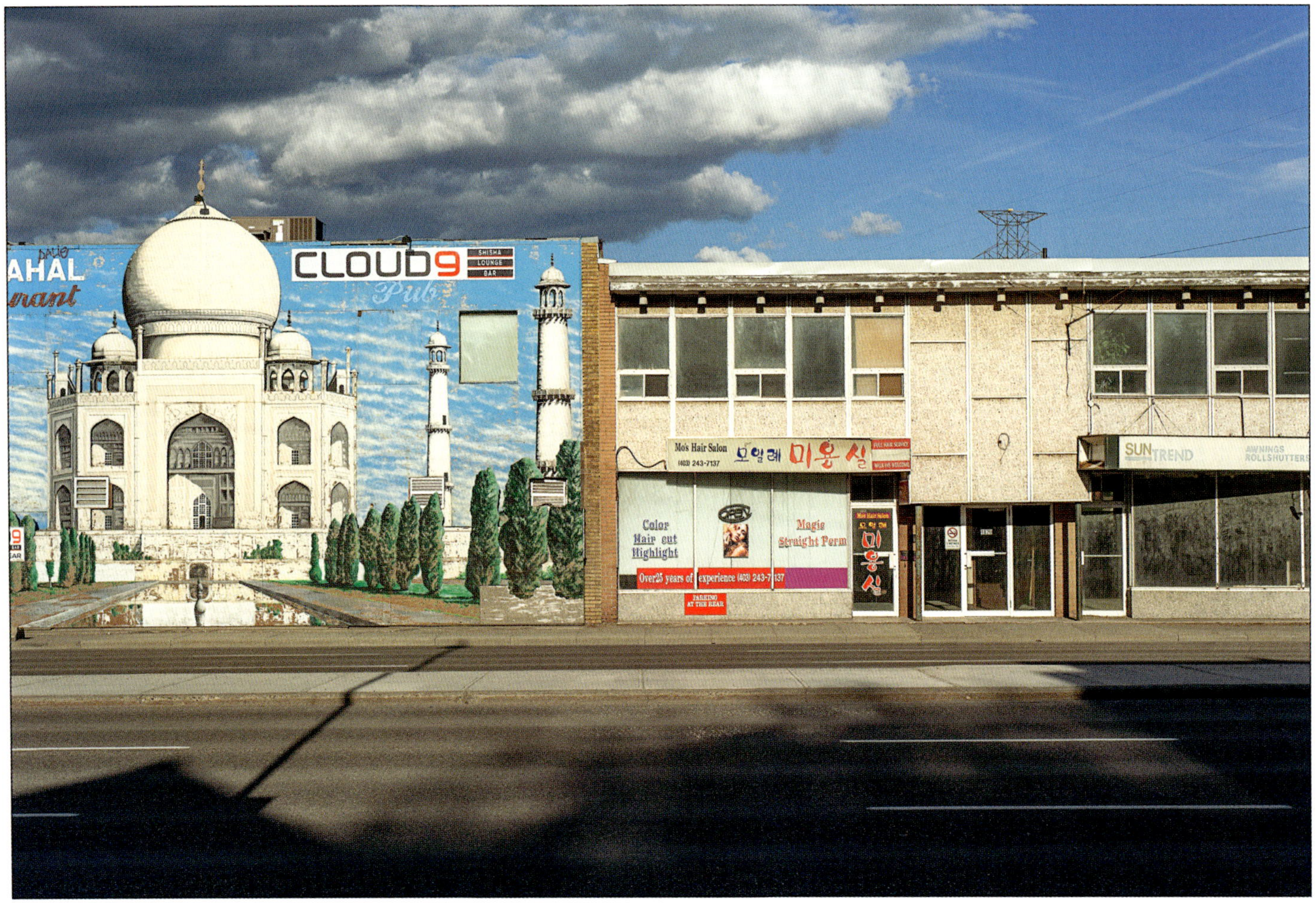

Taj Mahal Restaurant, 2019

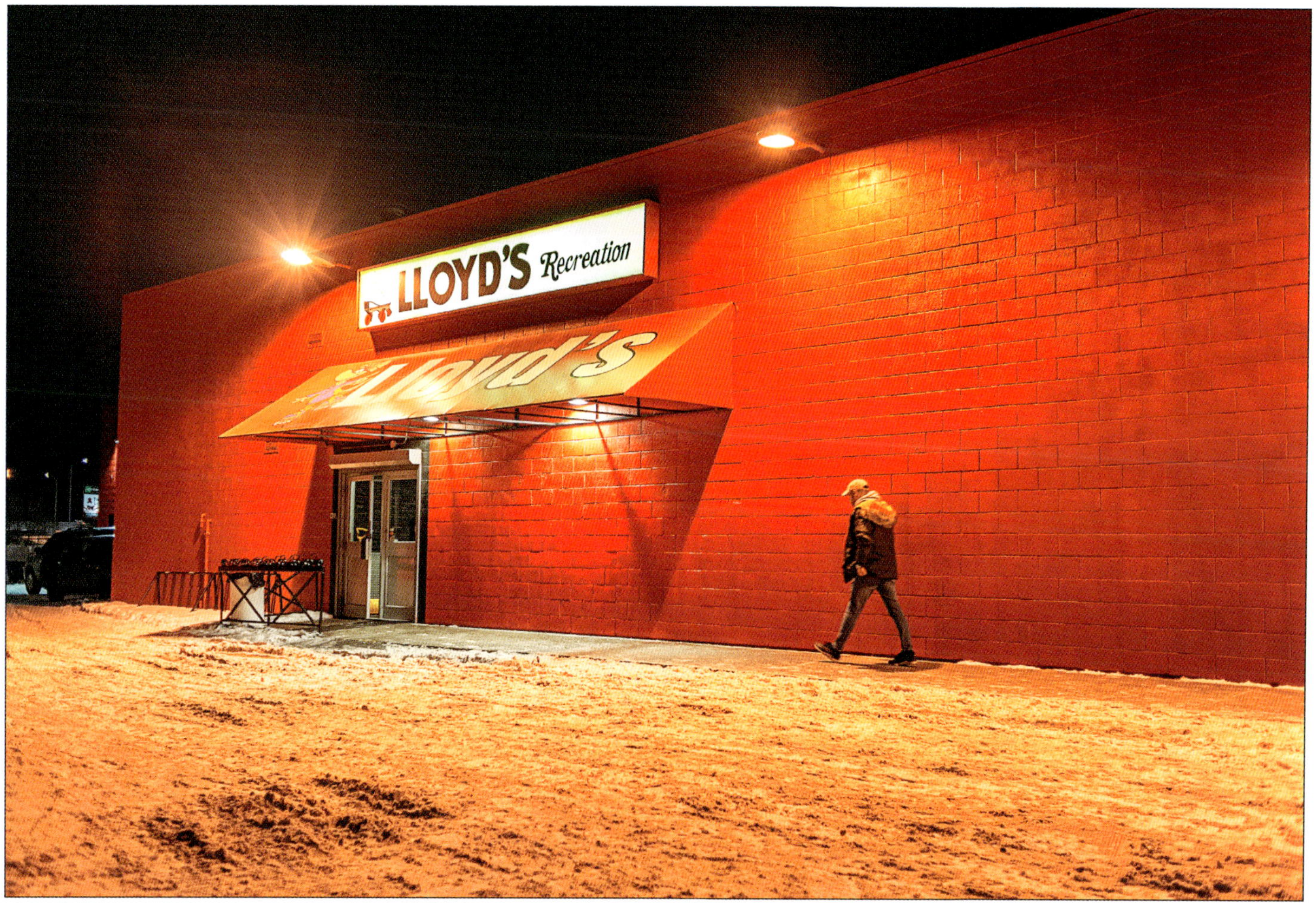

Lloyd's, 2018

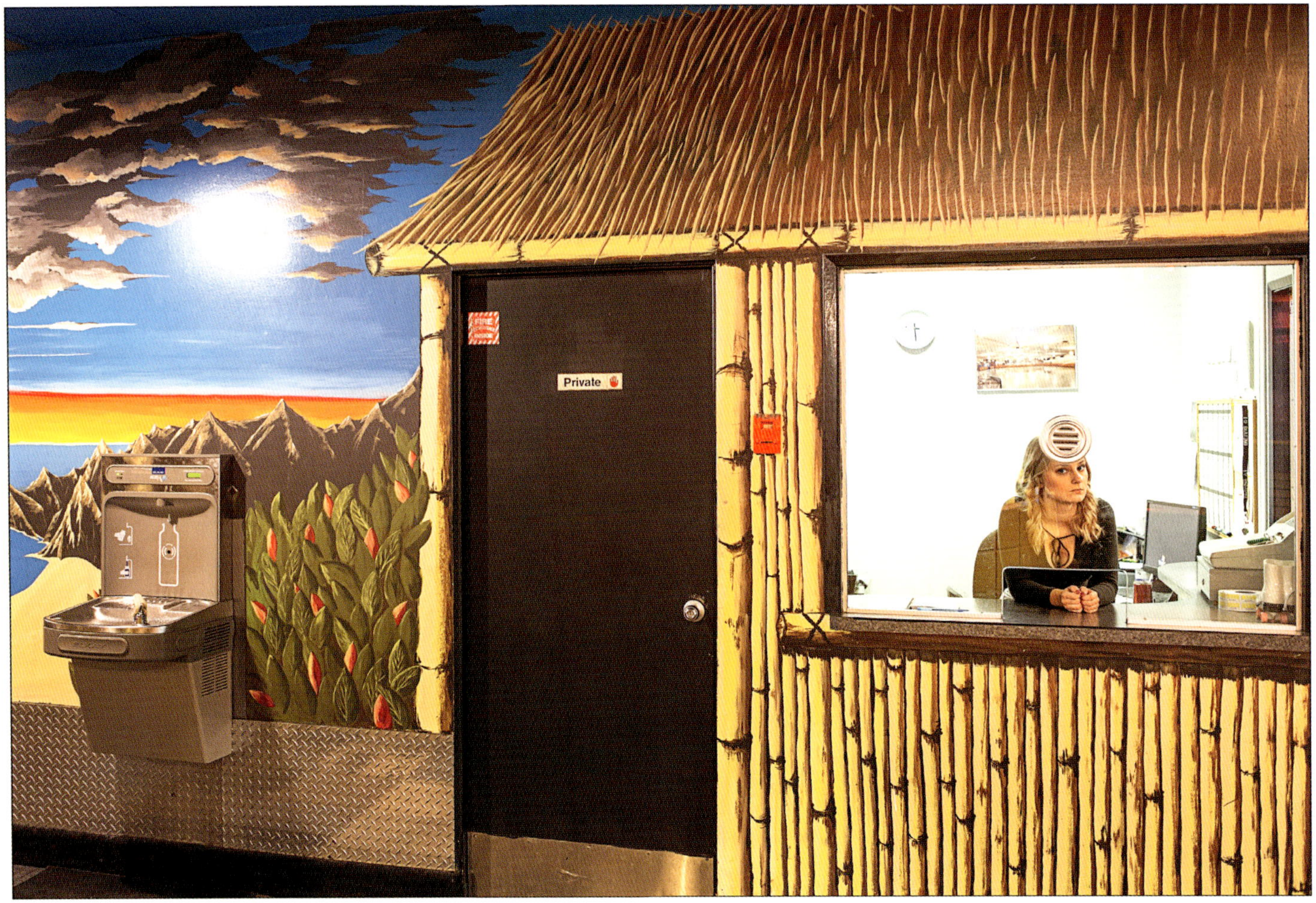

Lloyd's, 2017

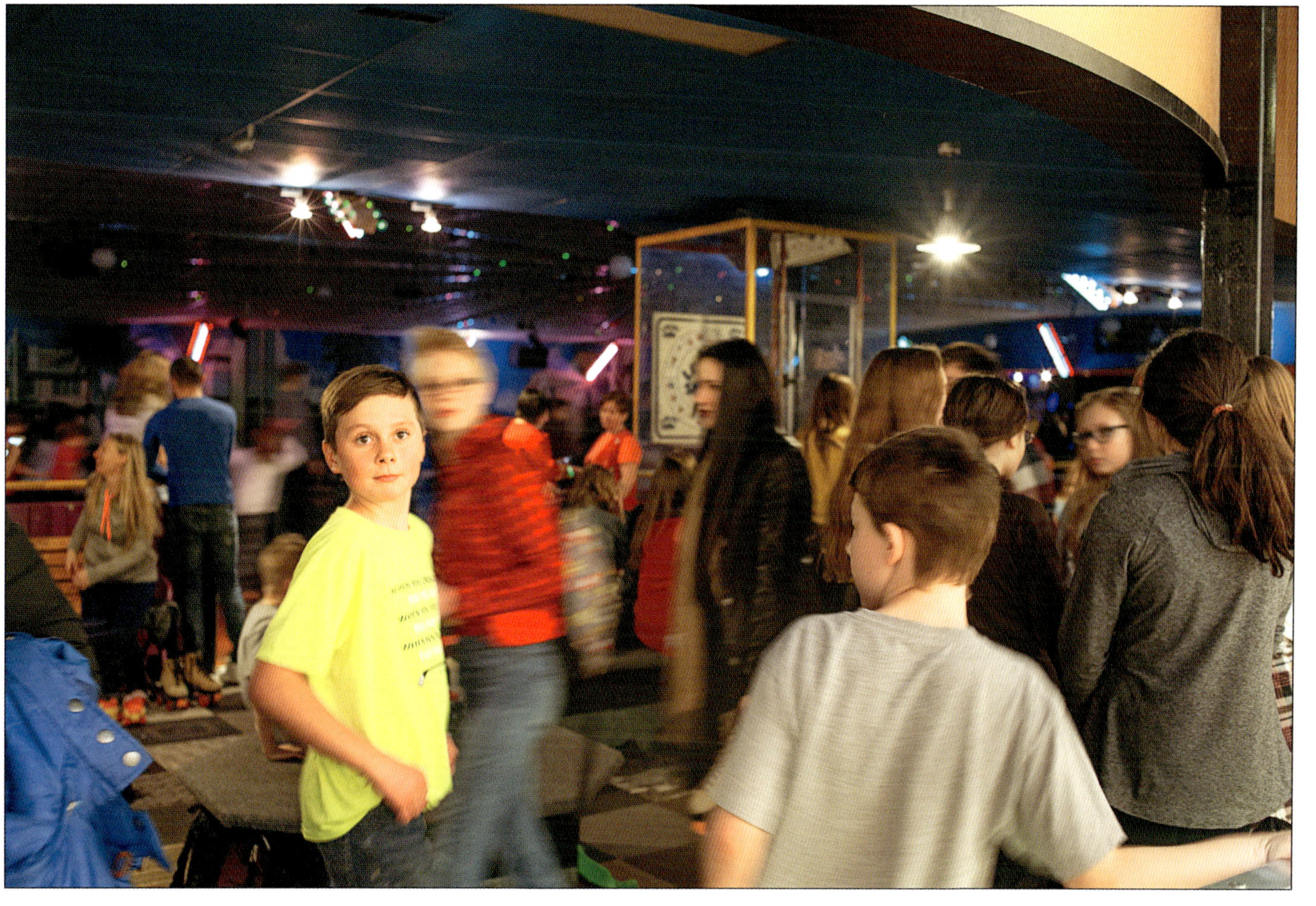

Lloyd's, 2017

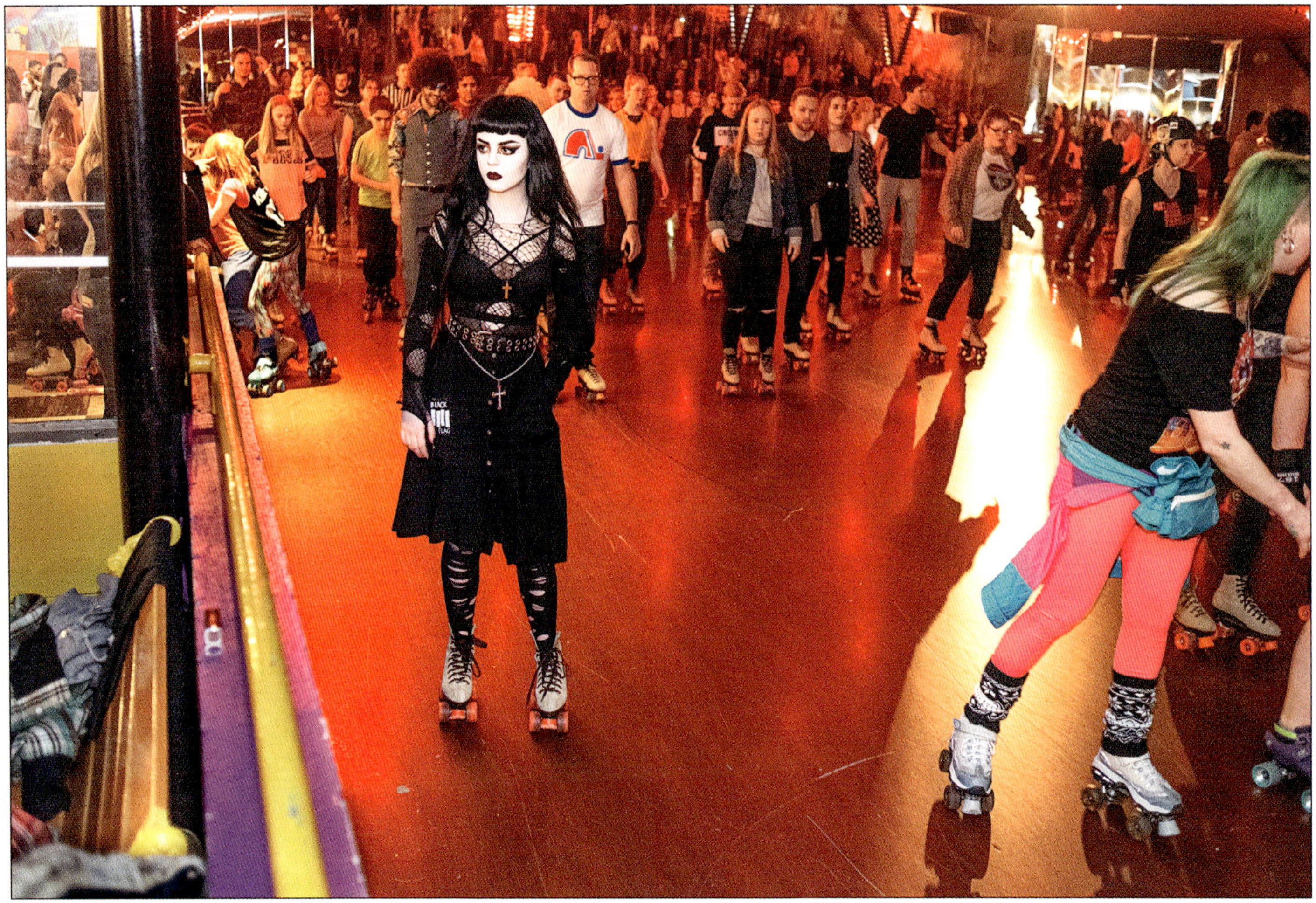

Lloyd's, 2018

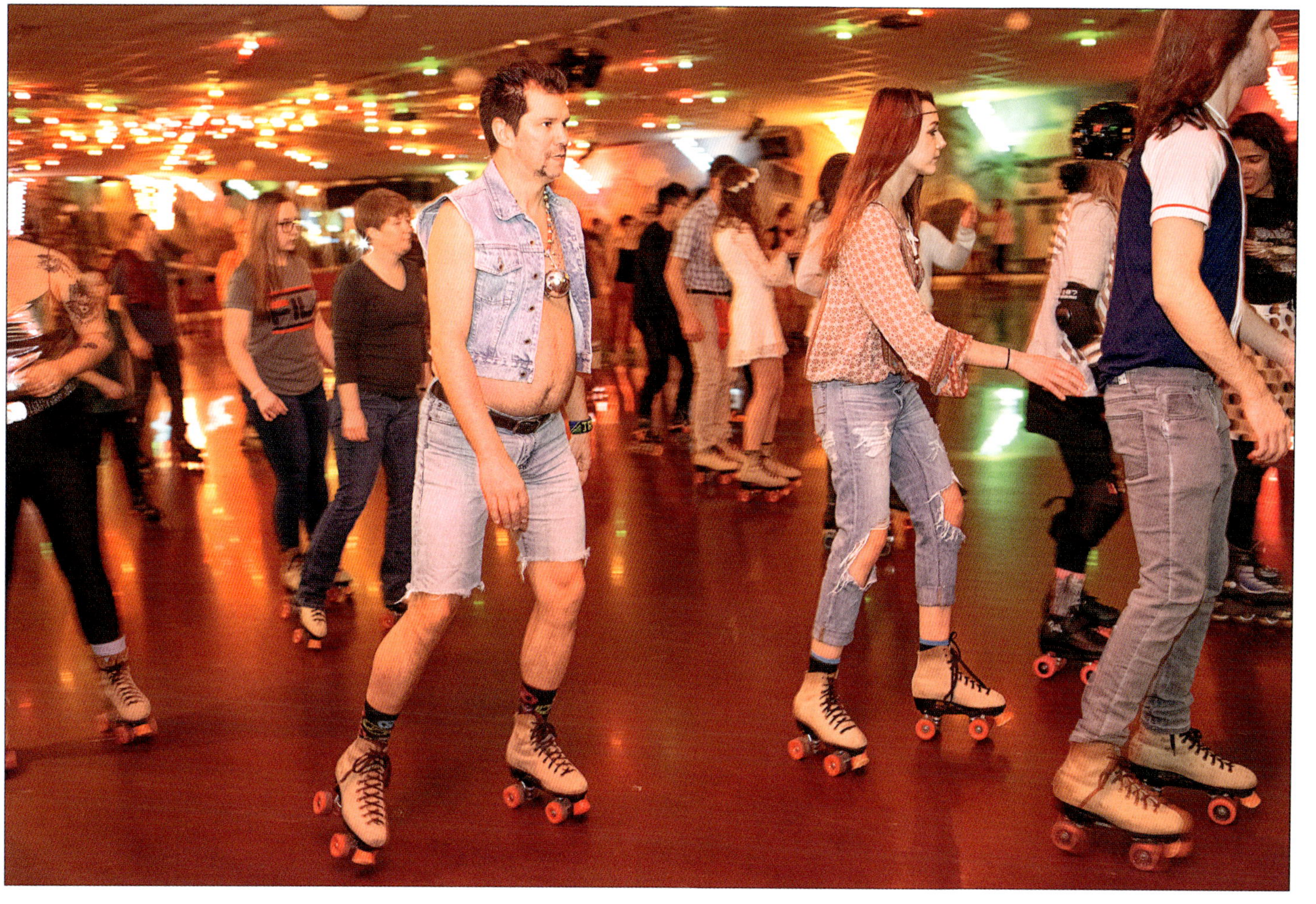

Lloyd's, 2018

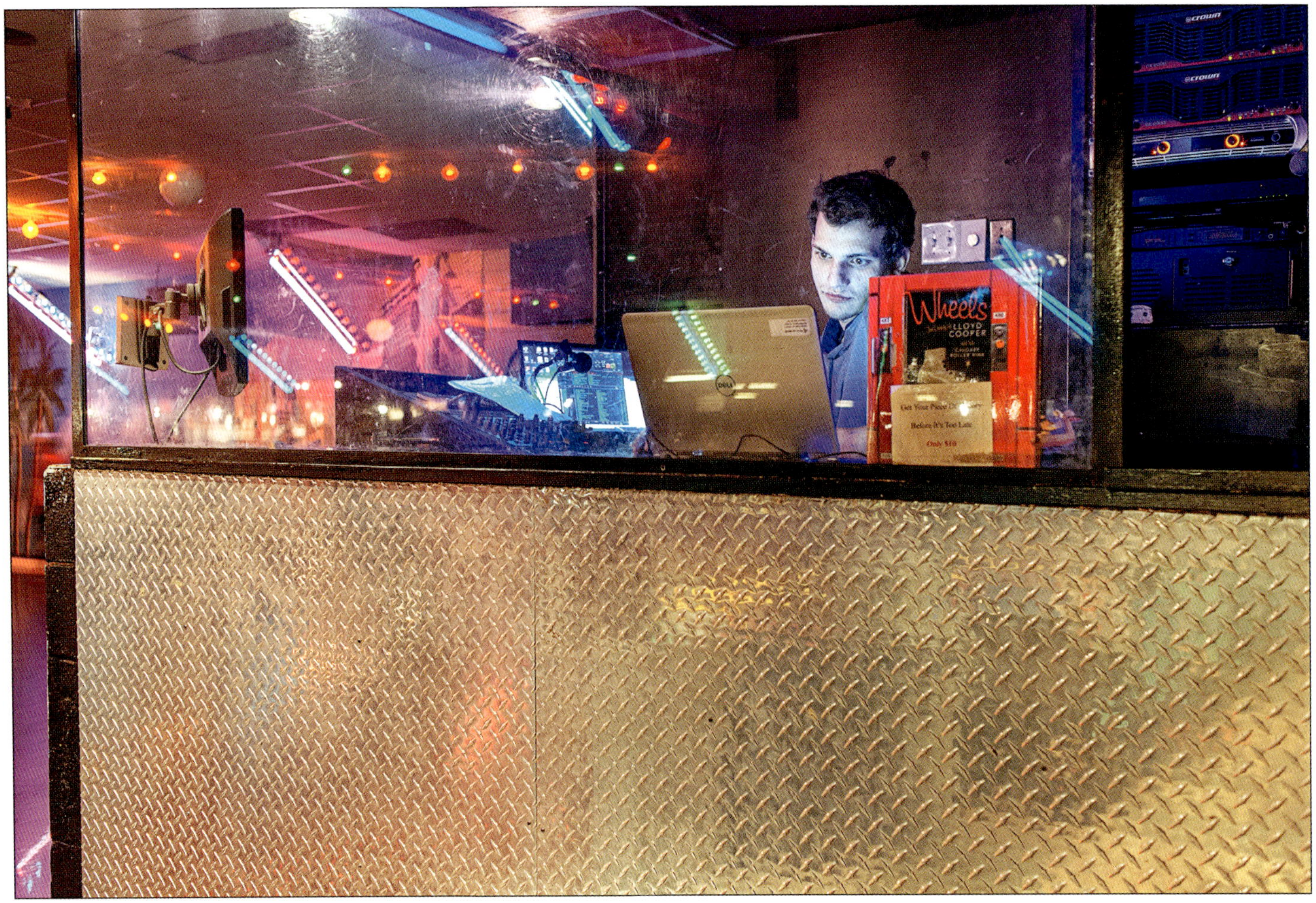

Lloyd's, 2018

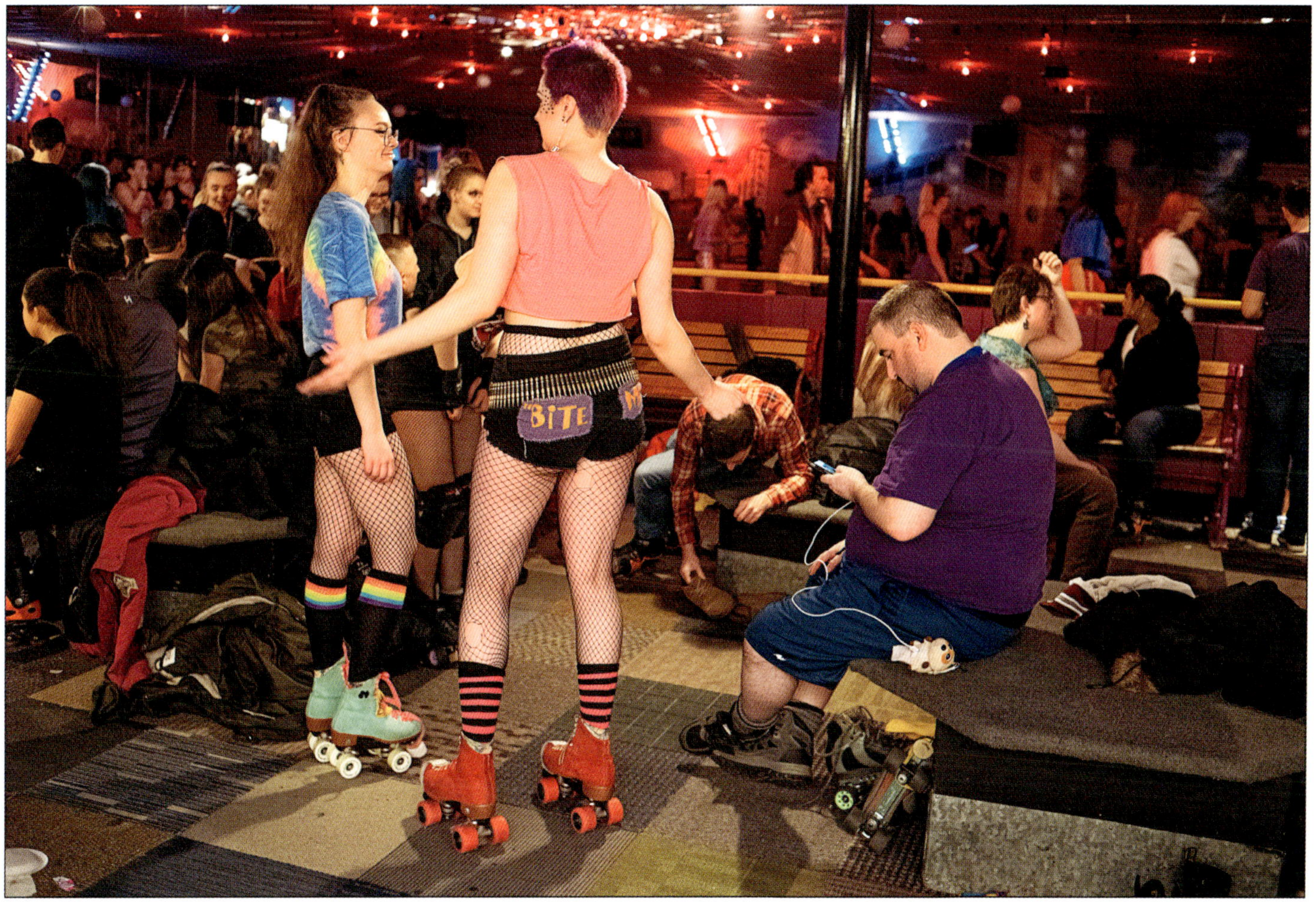

Lloyd's, 2018

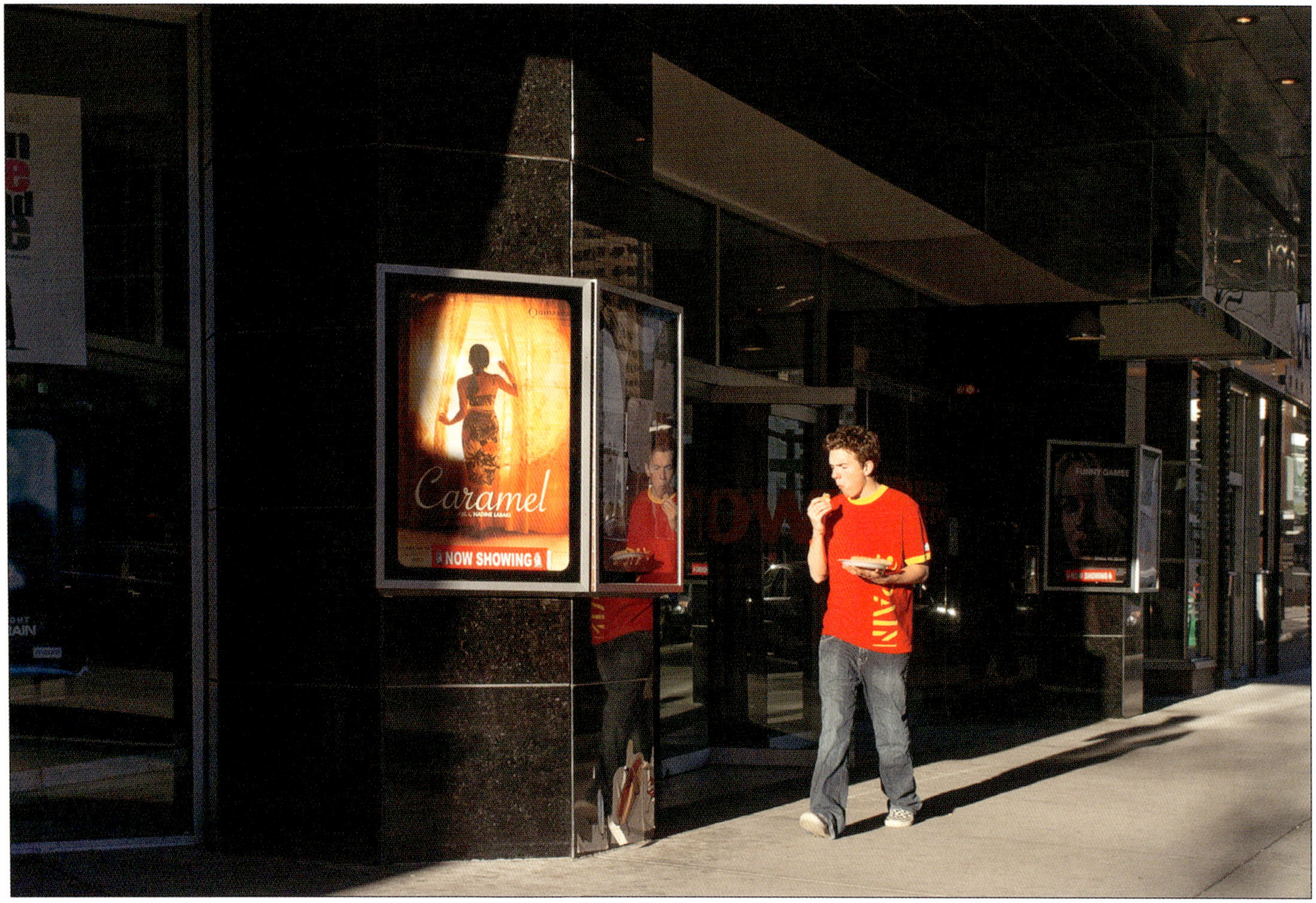

The Uptown Theatre, 2008

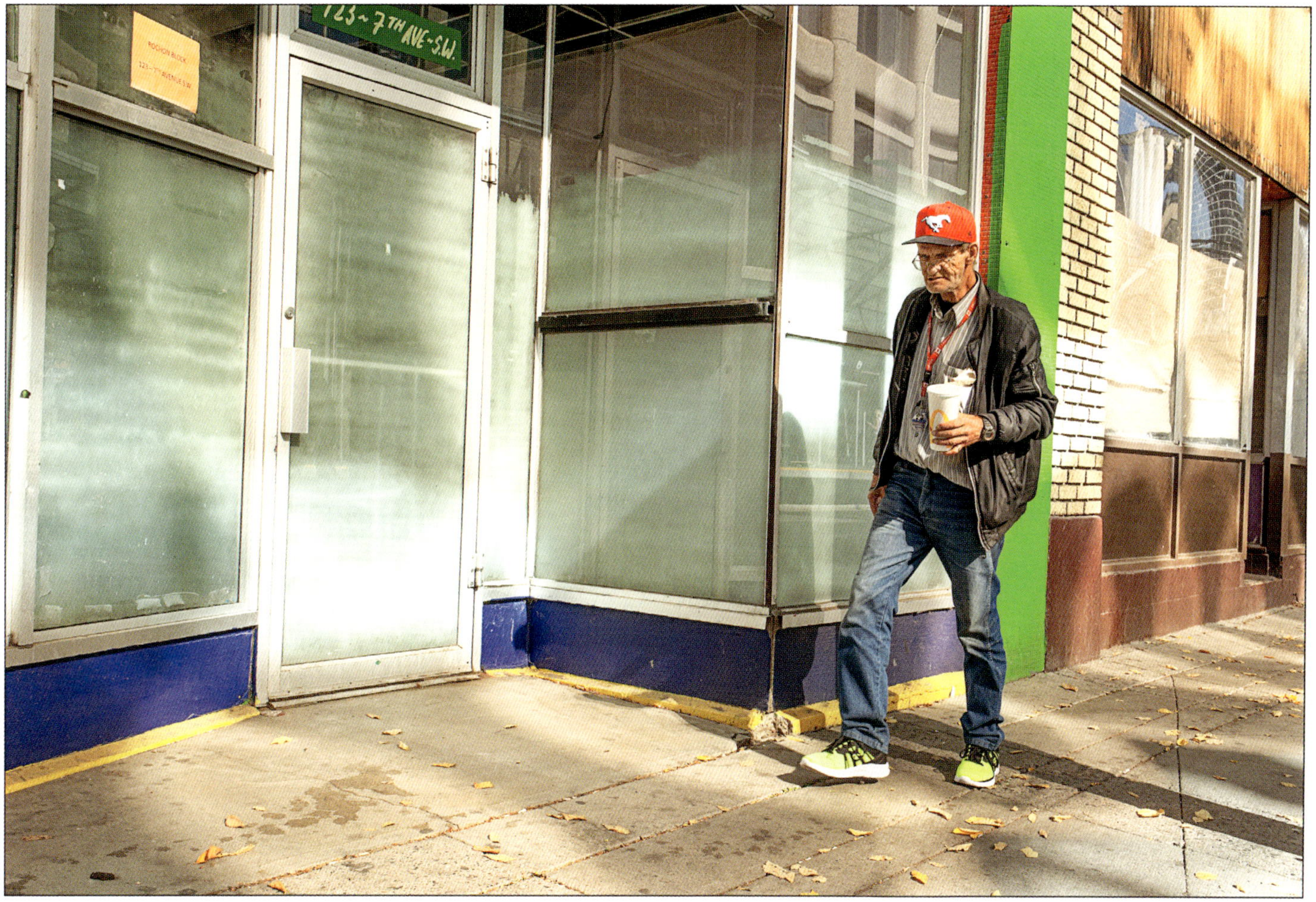

7 Ave SW, 2017

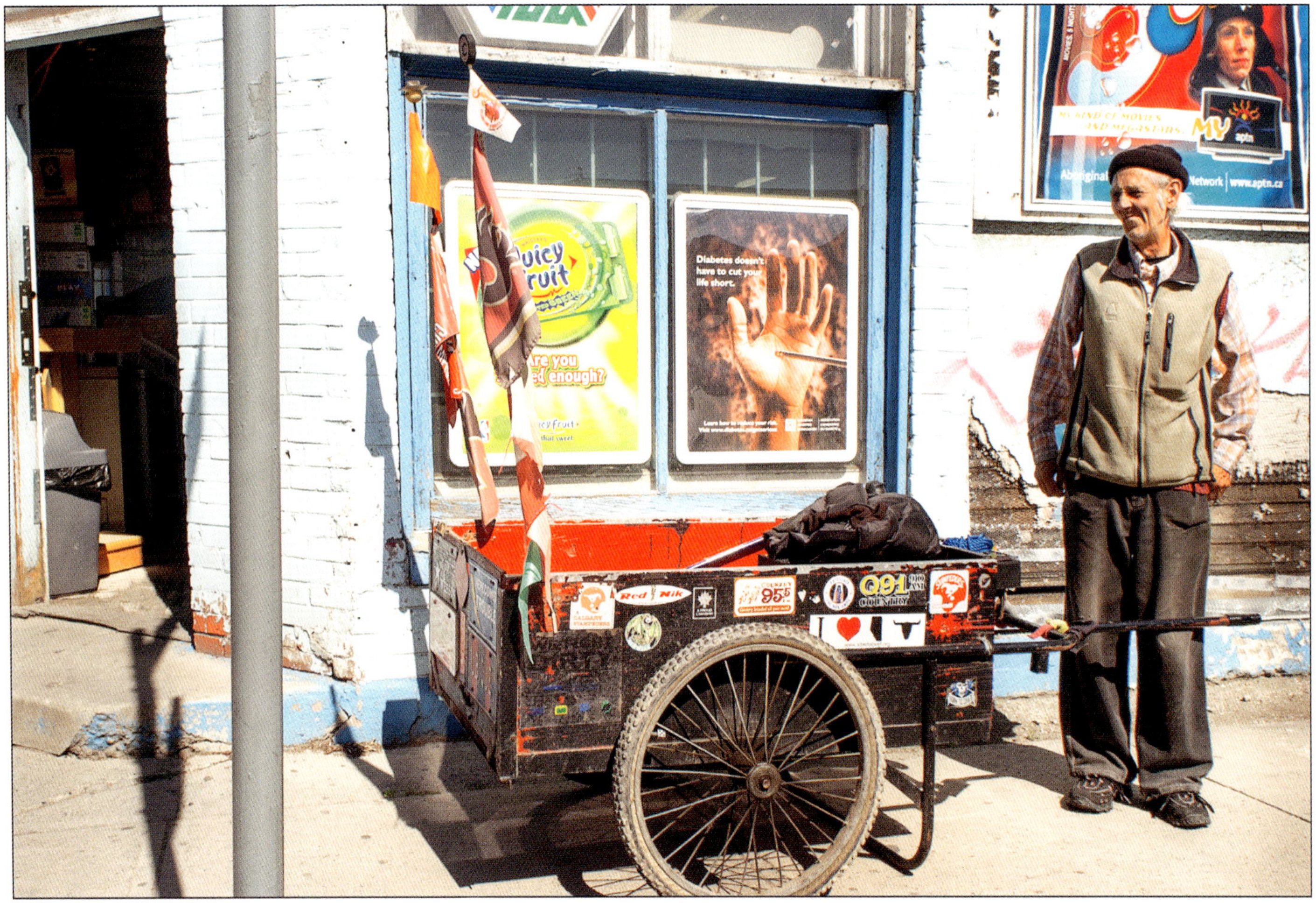

Frank Schroeder, 2006

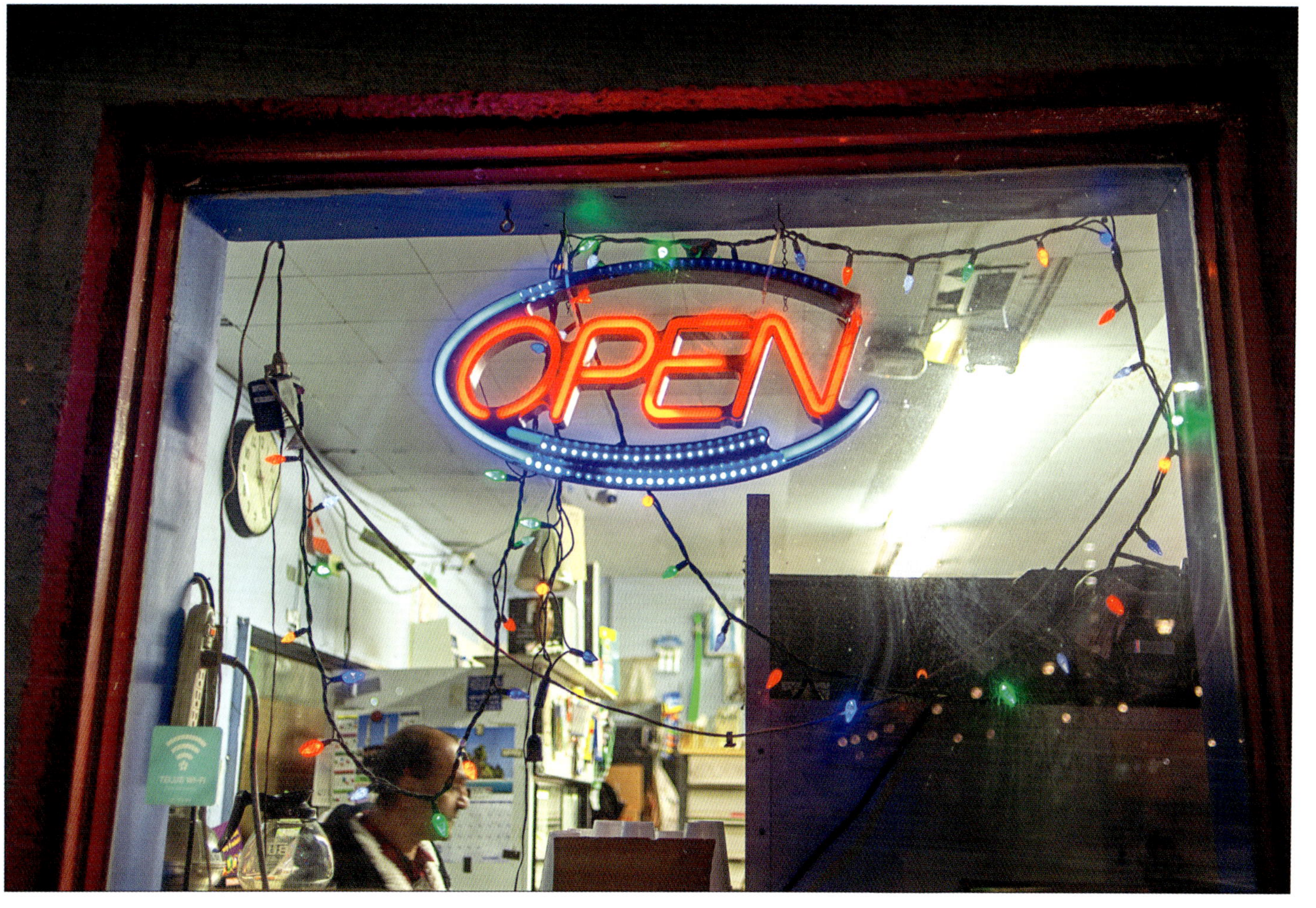

Canpro, 2016

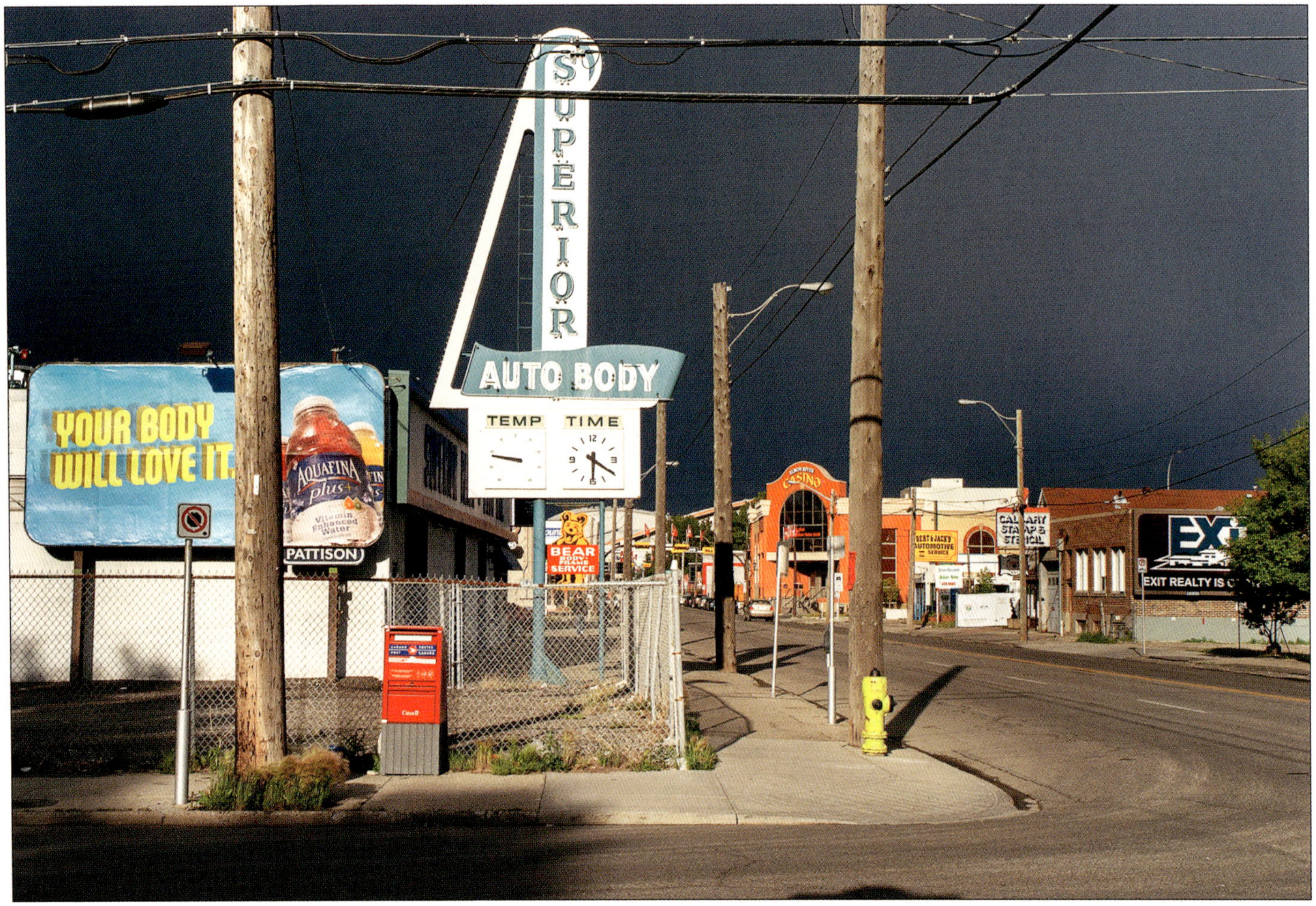

Superior Autobody, 2007

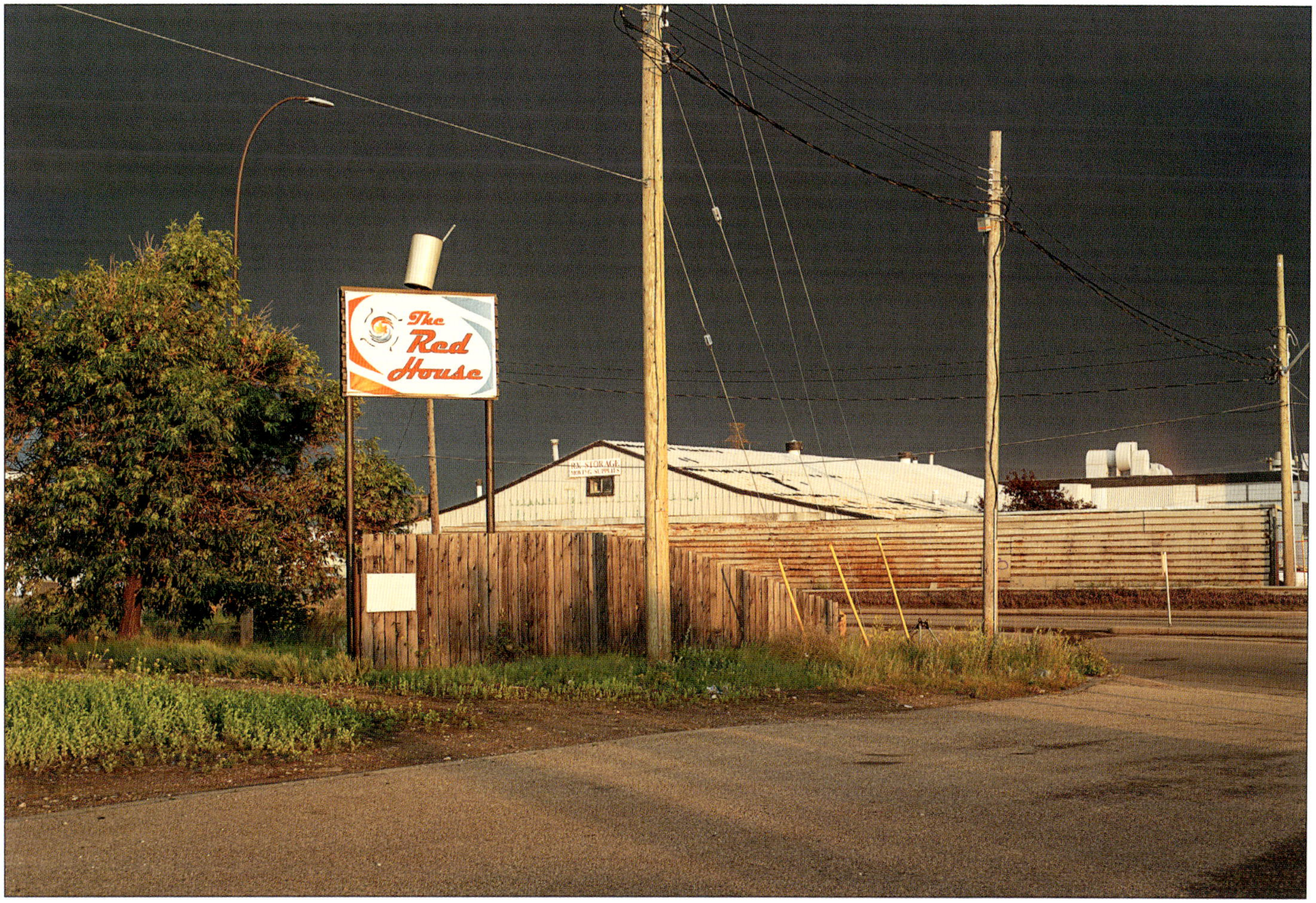

The Red House, 2019

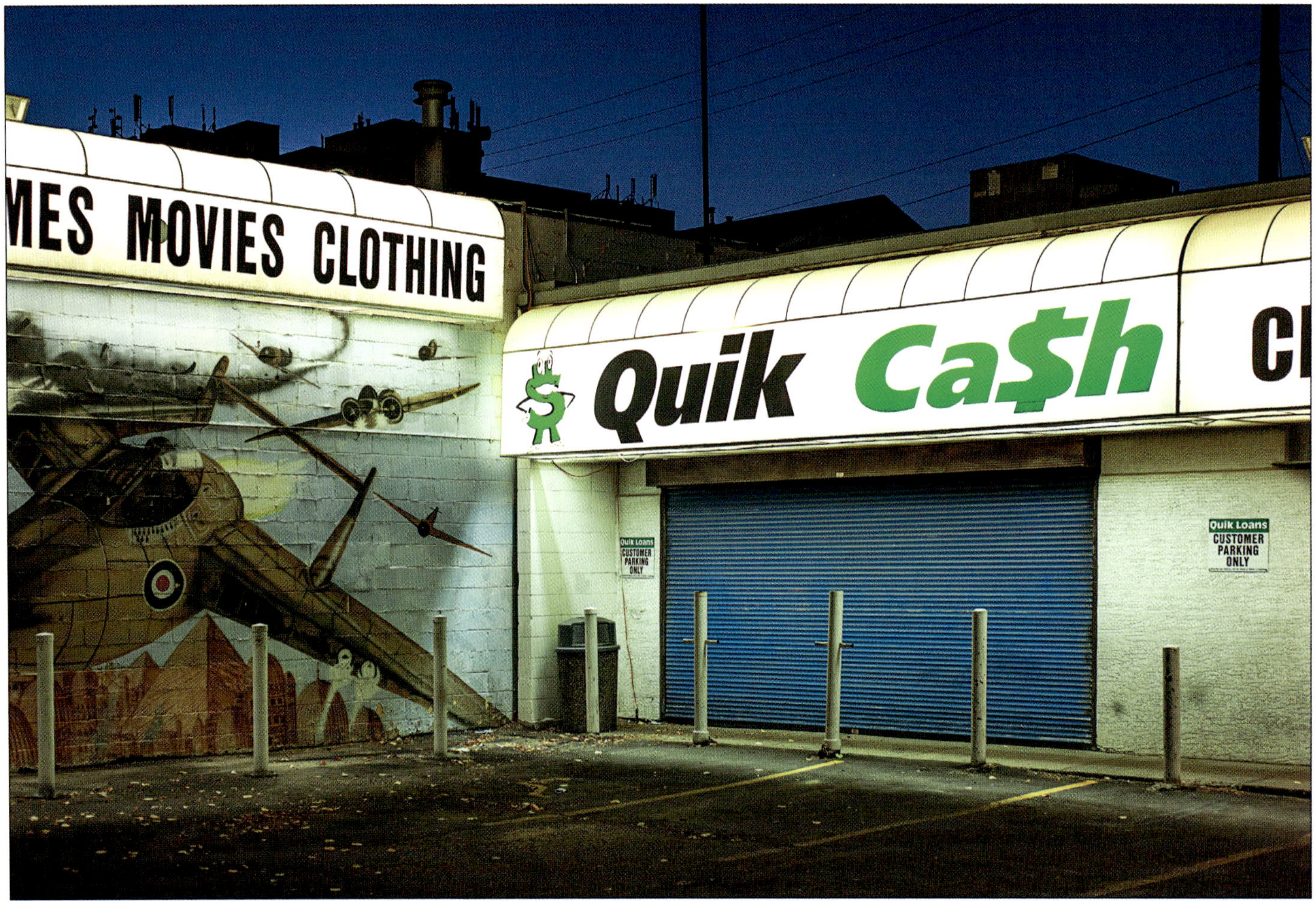

Quik Cash, 2016

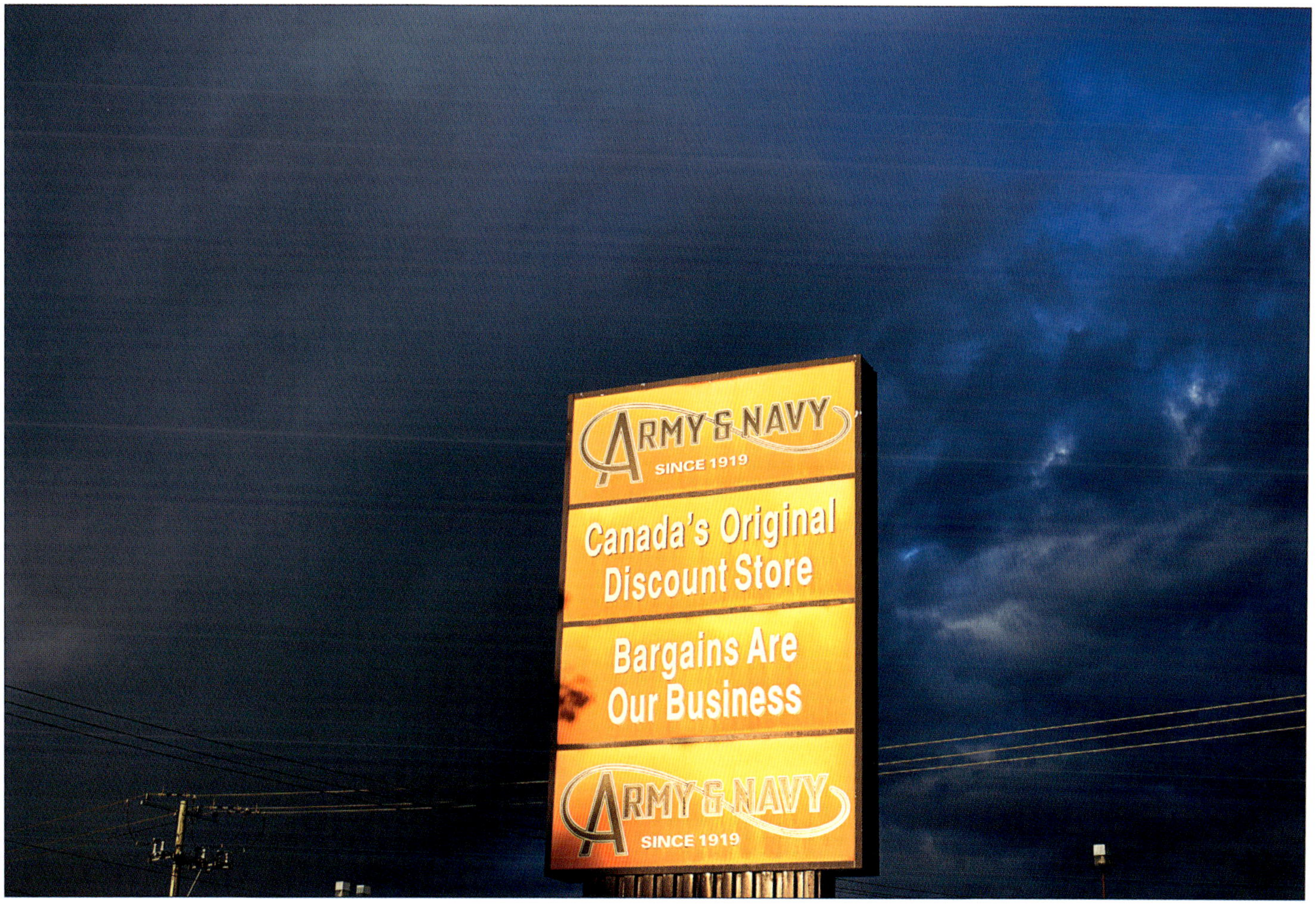

Army and Navy, 2015

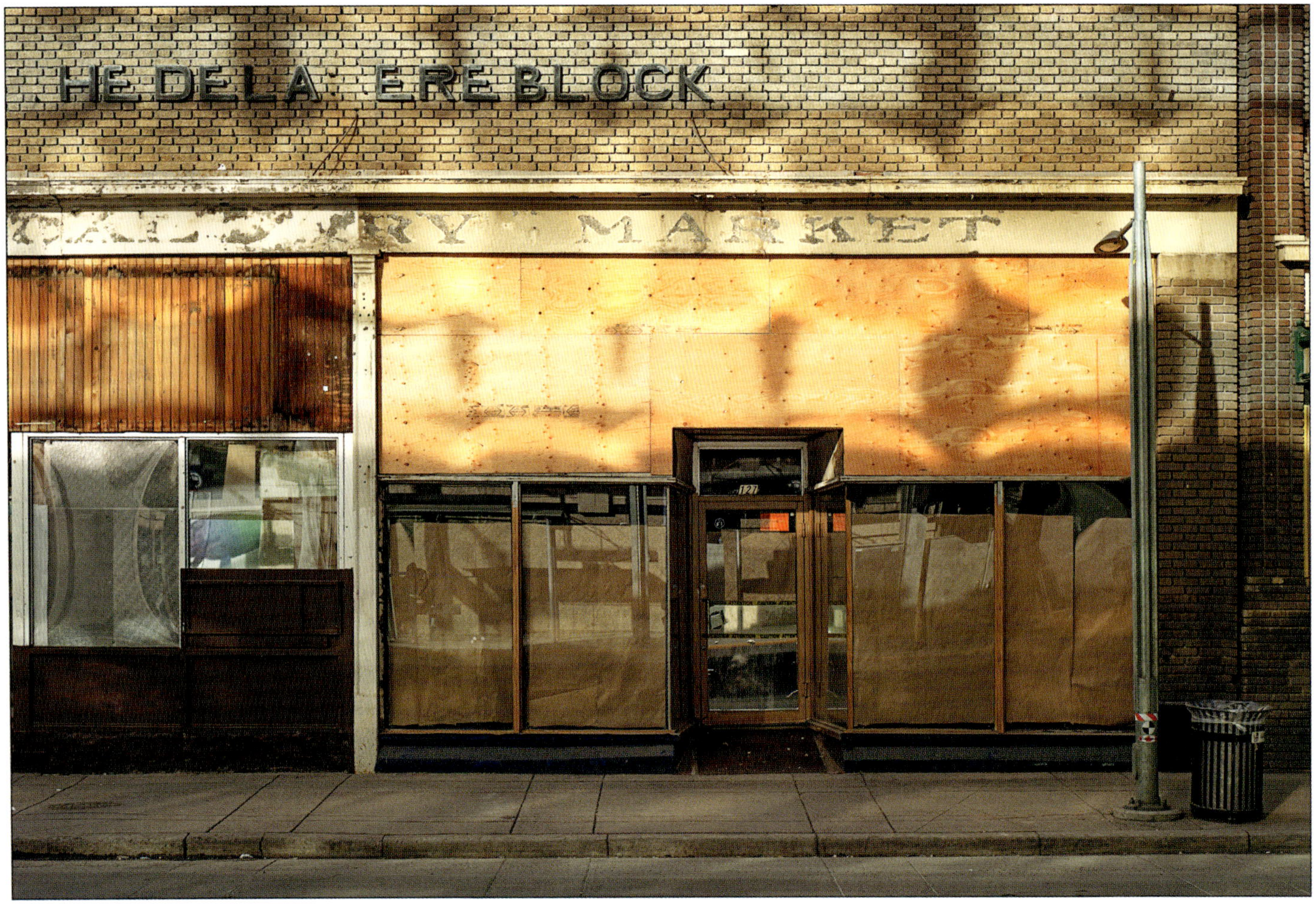

127 7 Ave SW, 2017

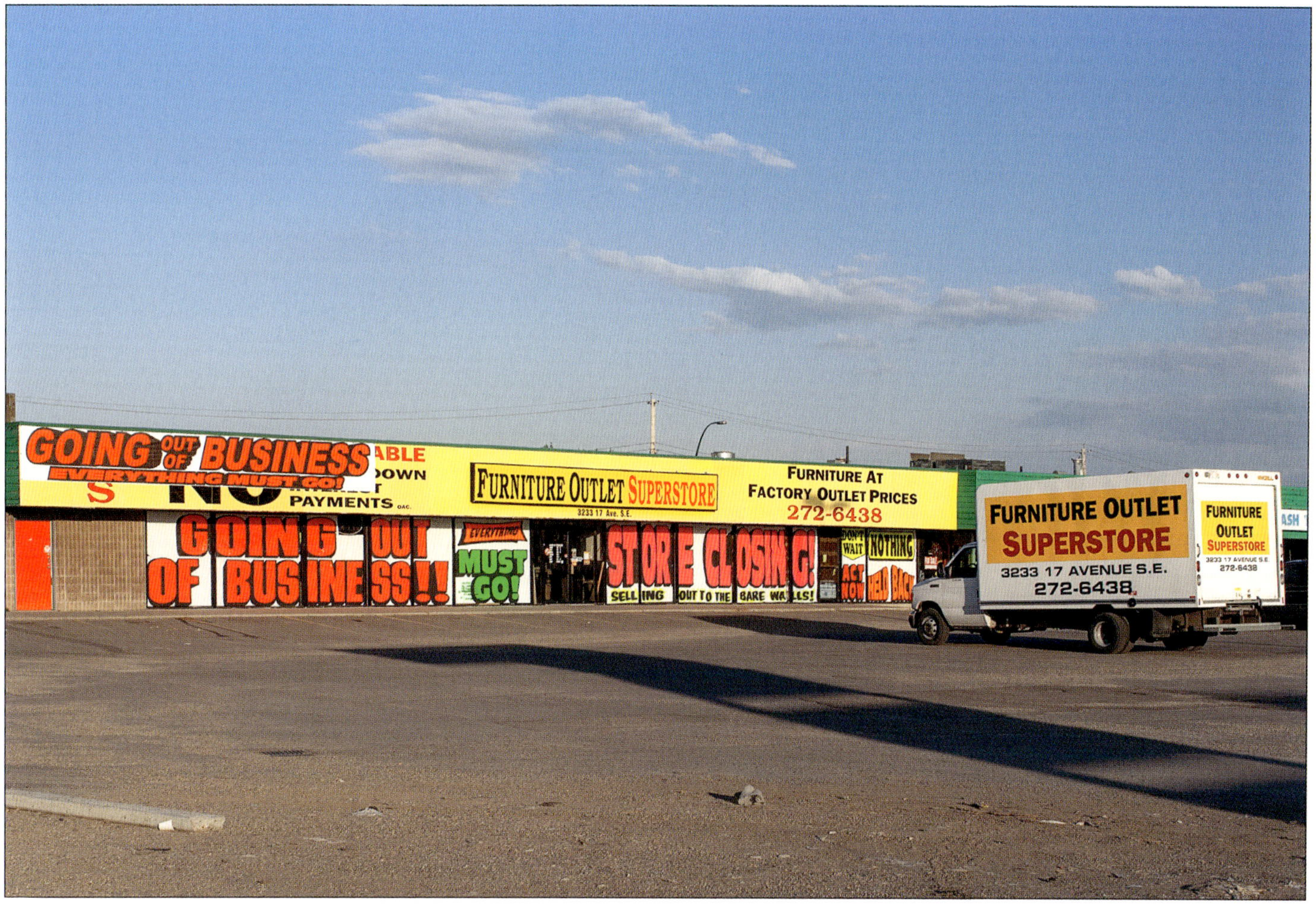

Furniture Outlet Superstore, 2009

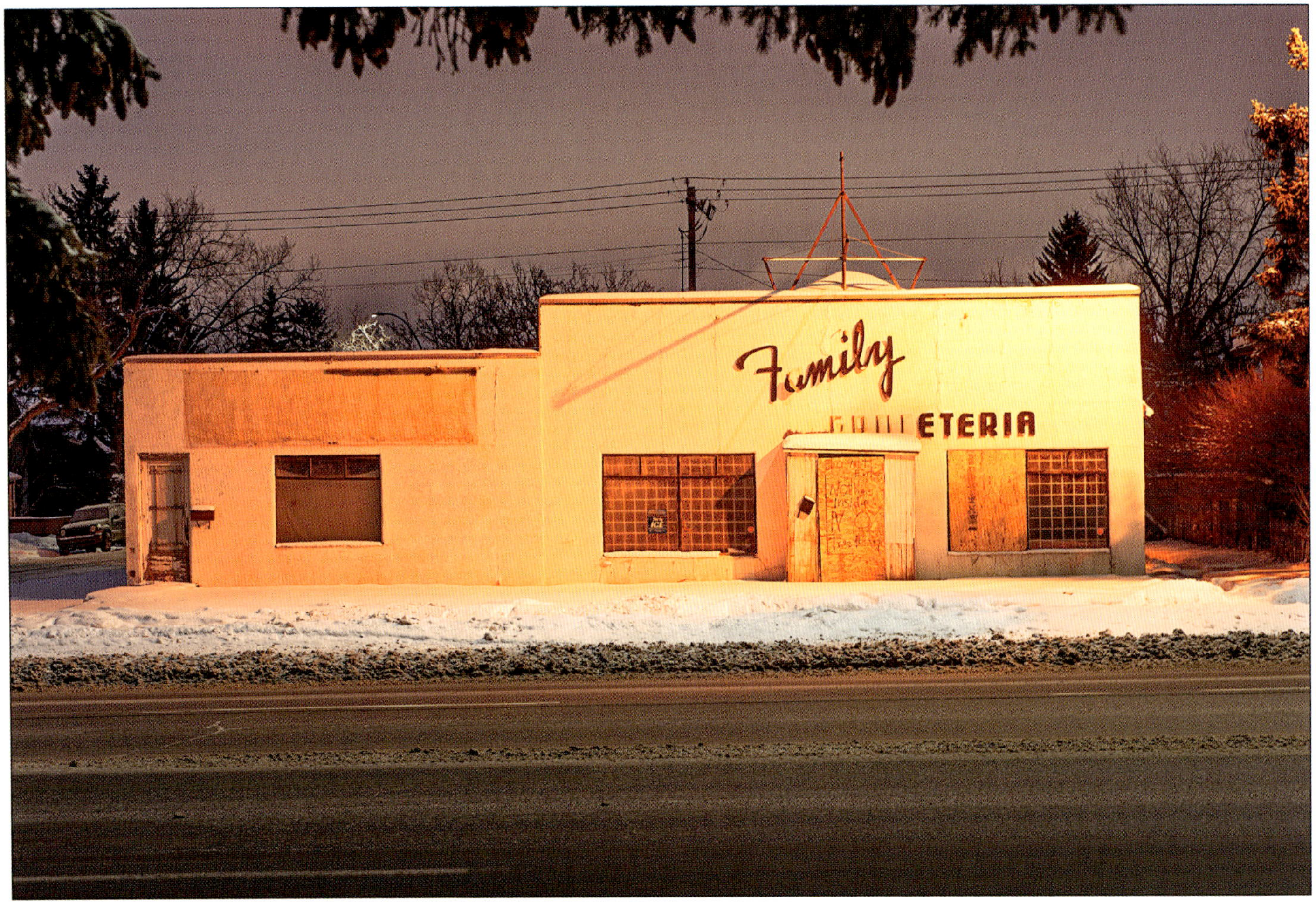

Family Groceteria, 2017

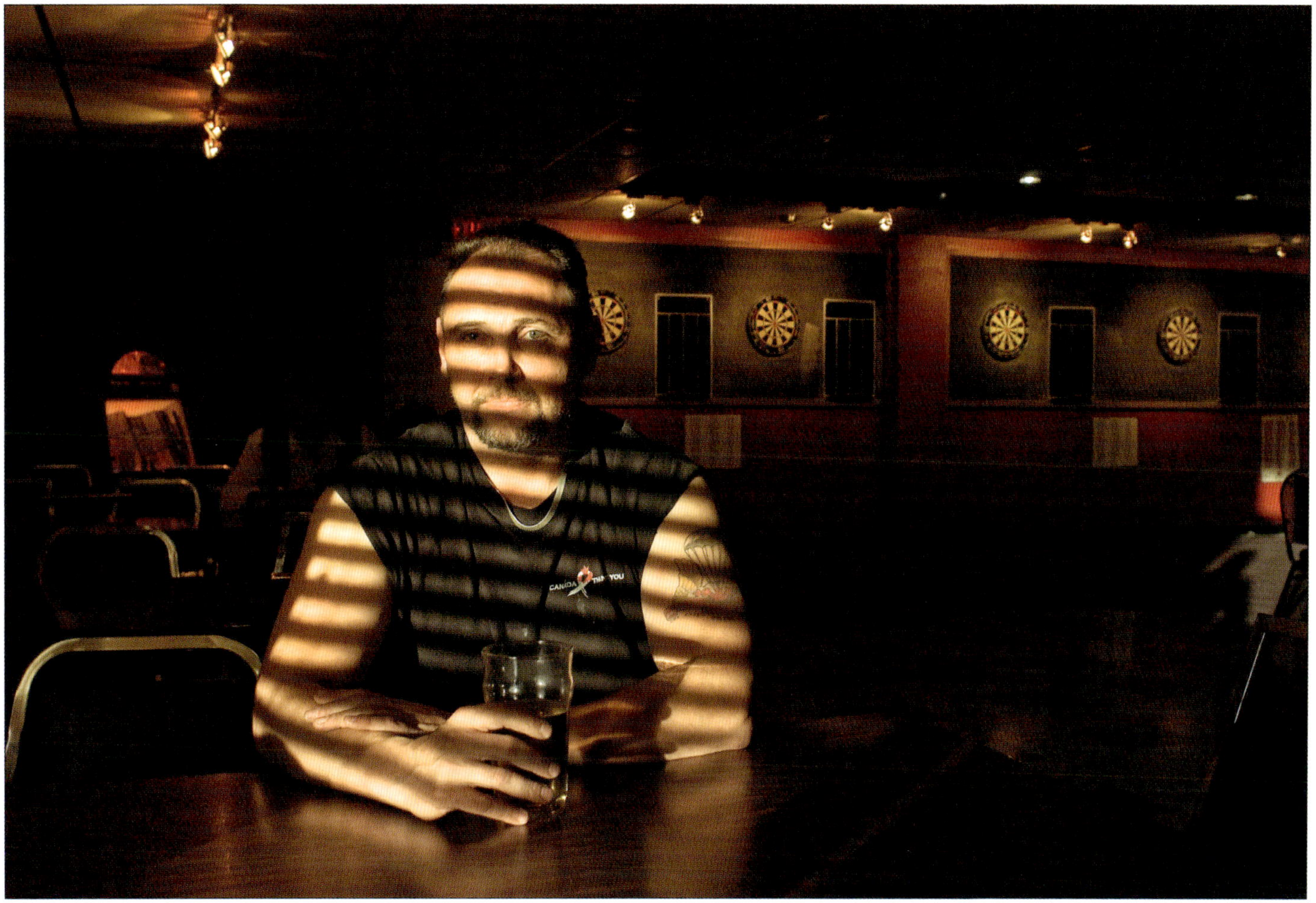

Todd Davies, Ogden Legion, 2007

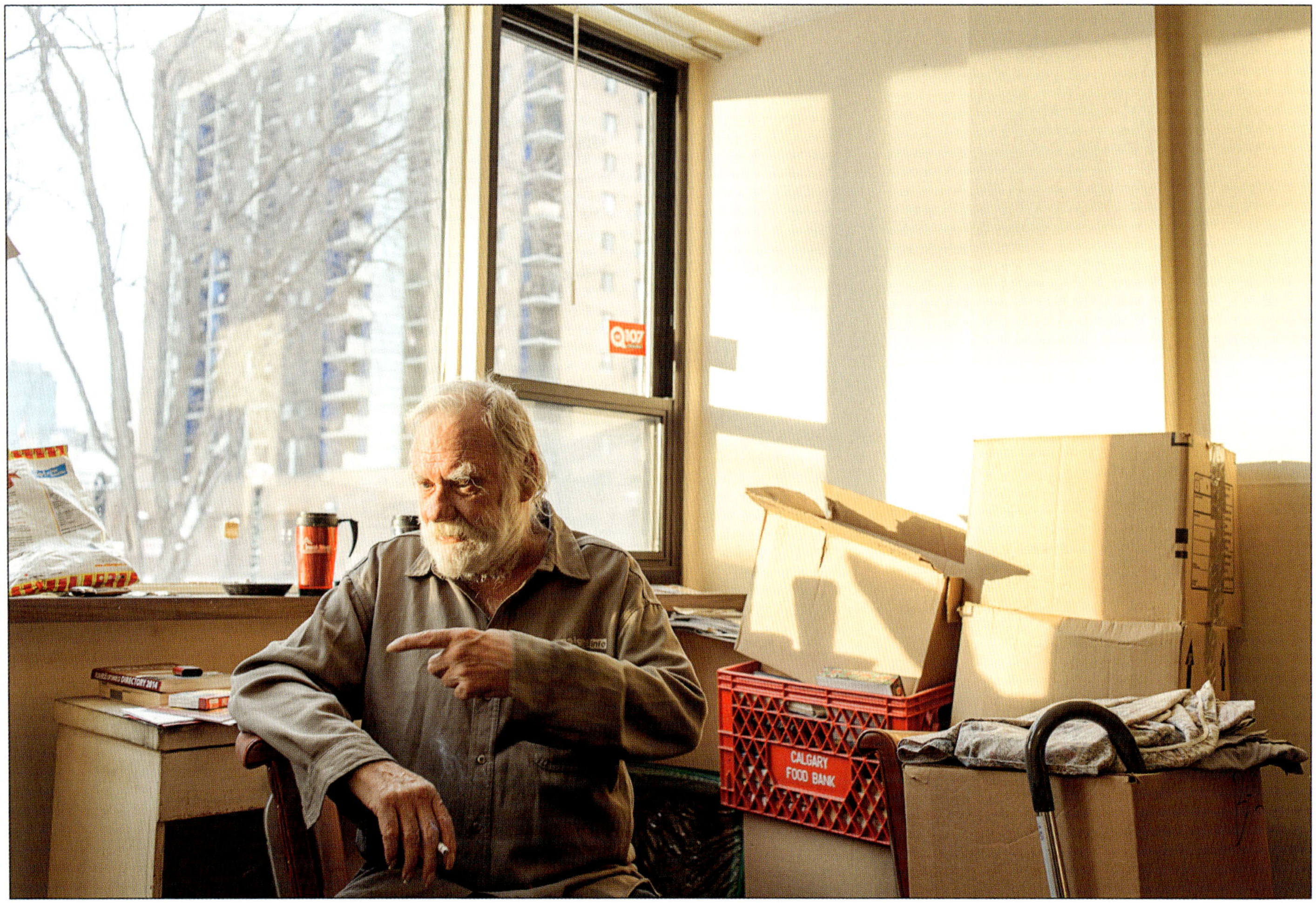

Robin Randell, George King Tower, 2015

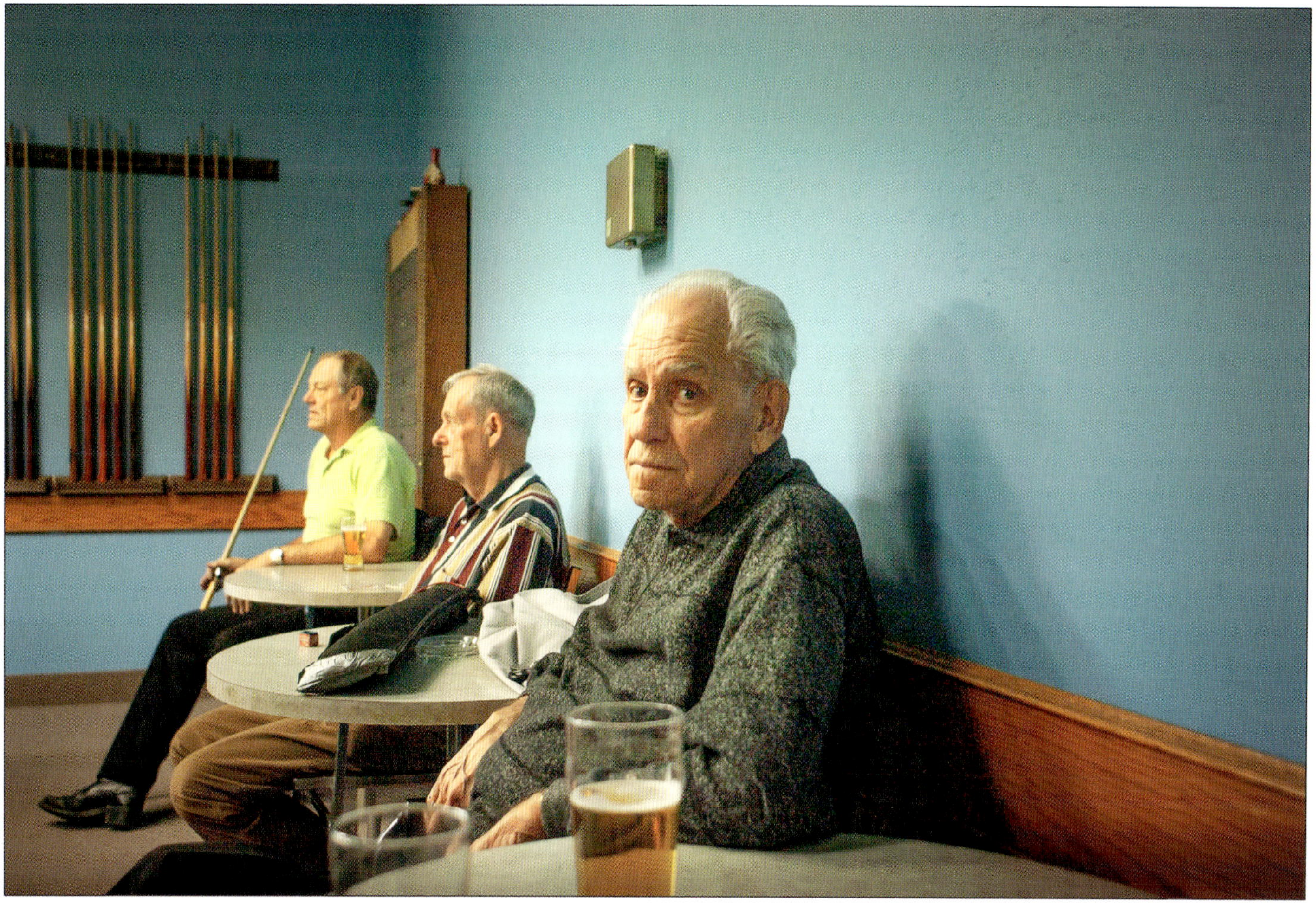

Centennial Legion, 2007

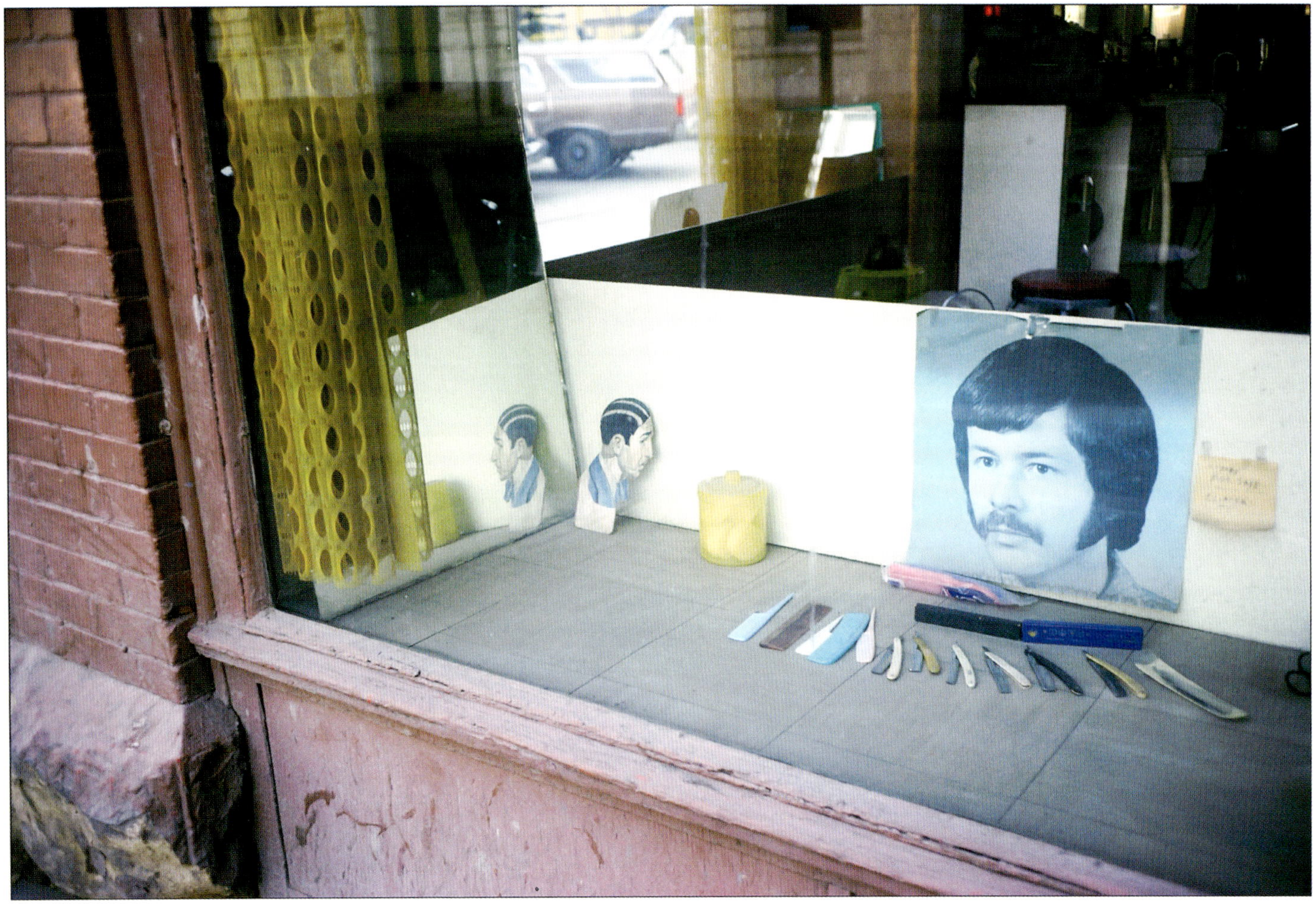

Downtown, 1984

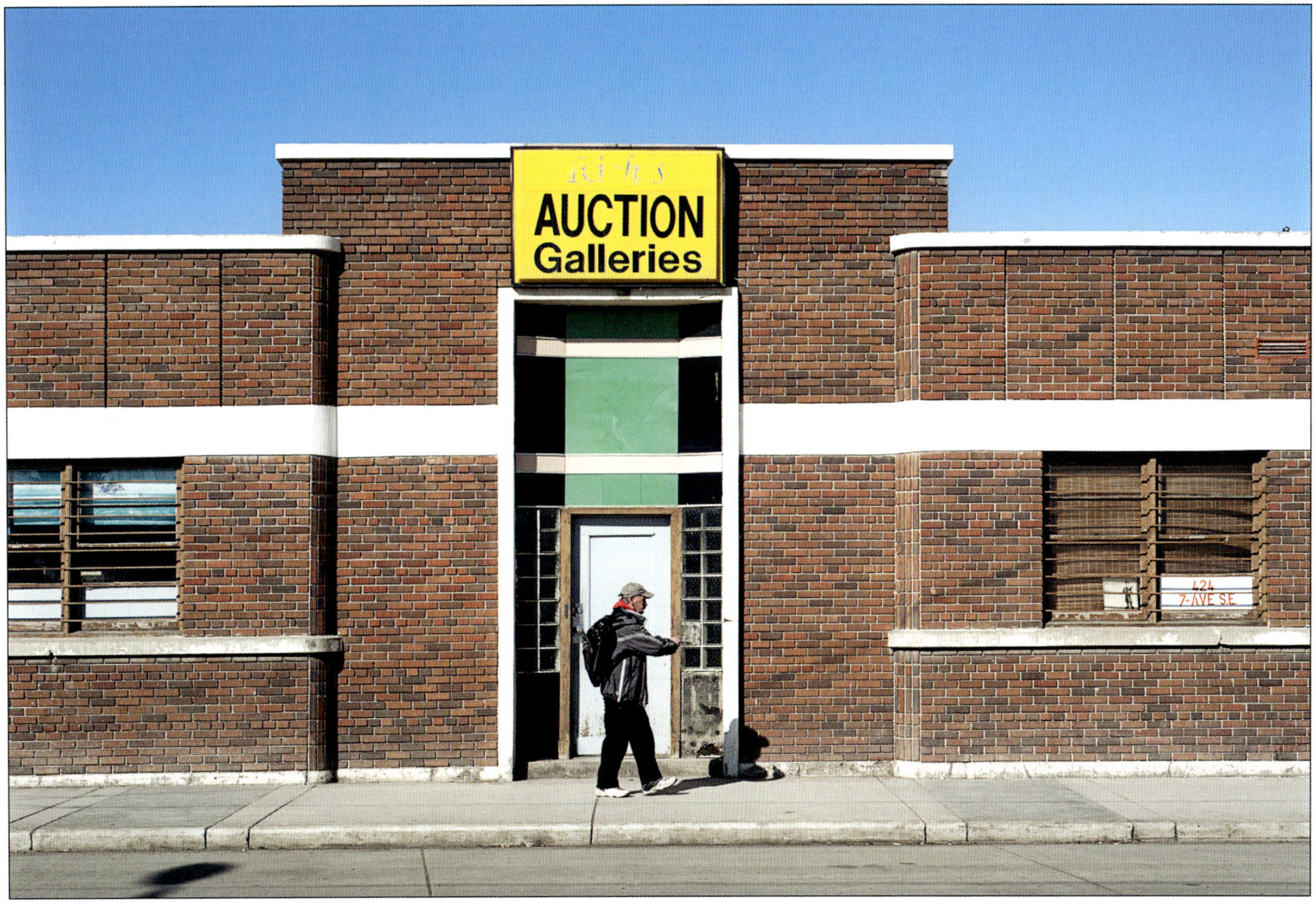

424 7 AVE SE, 2013

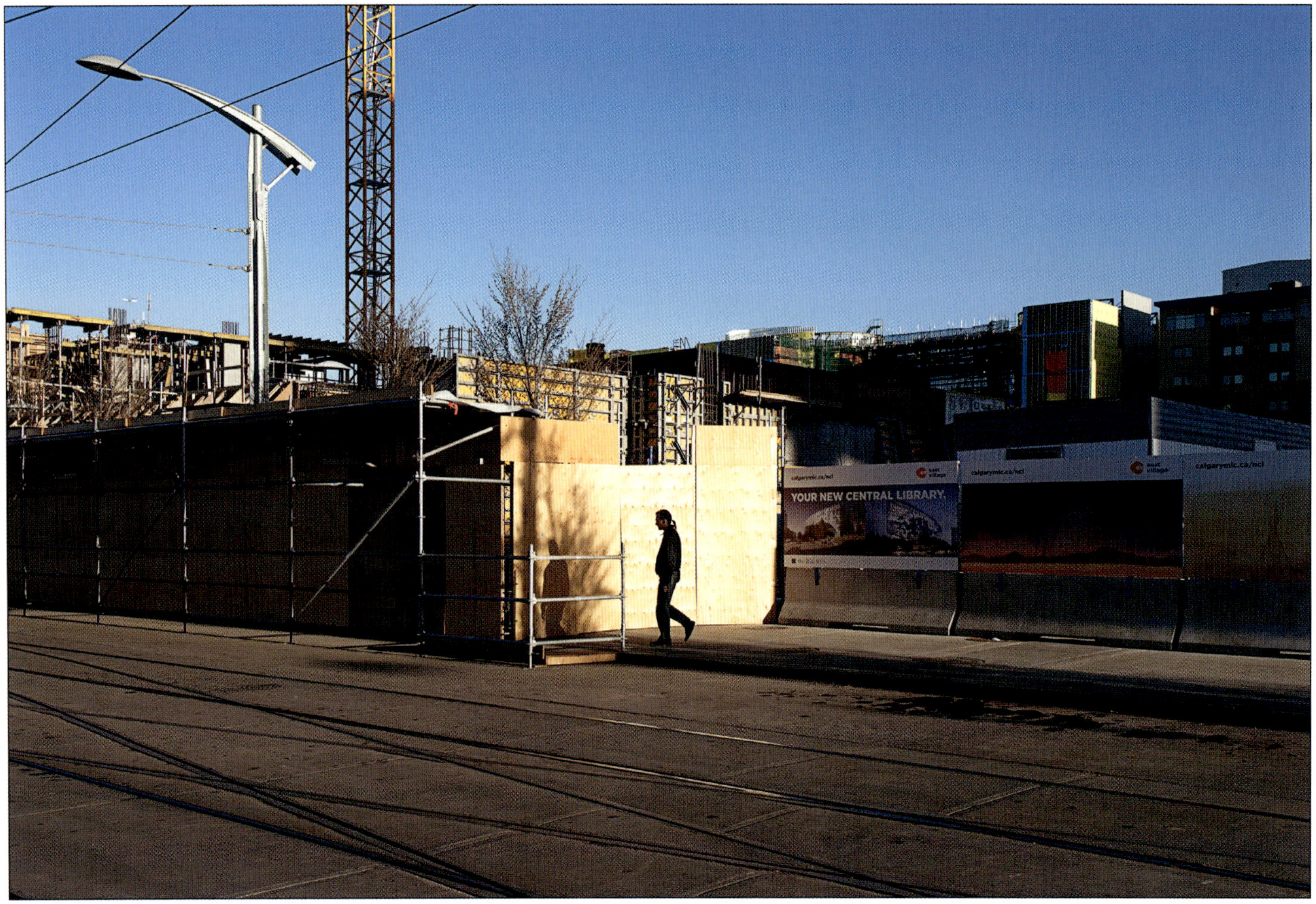

East Village, 2015

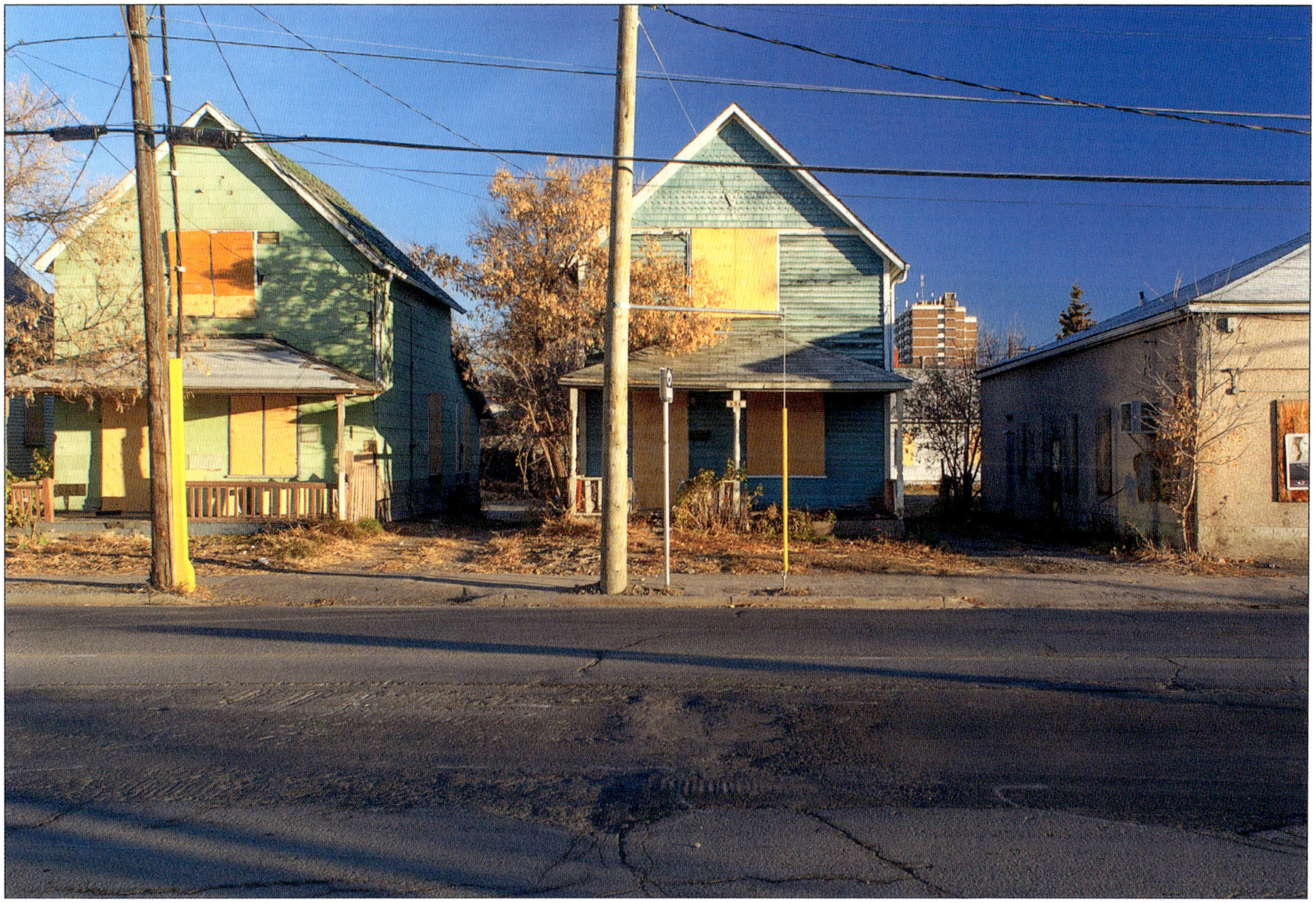

534 12 Ave SE, 2007

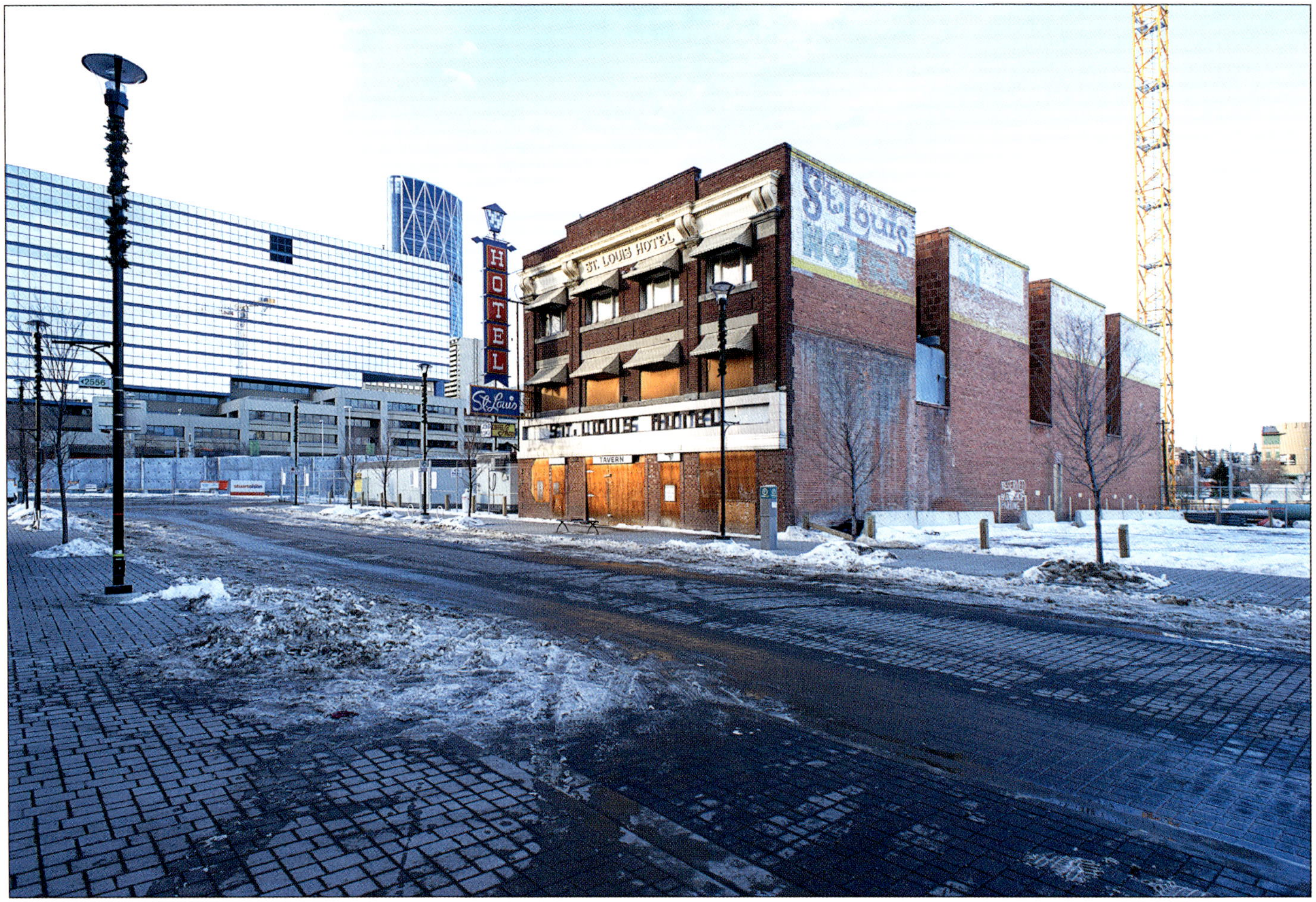

St Louis Hotel, 2015

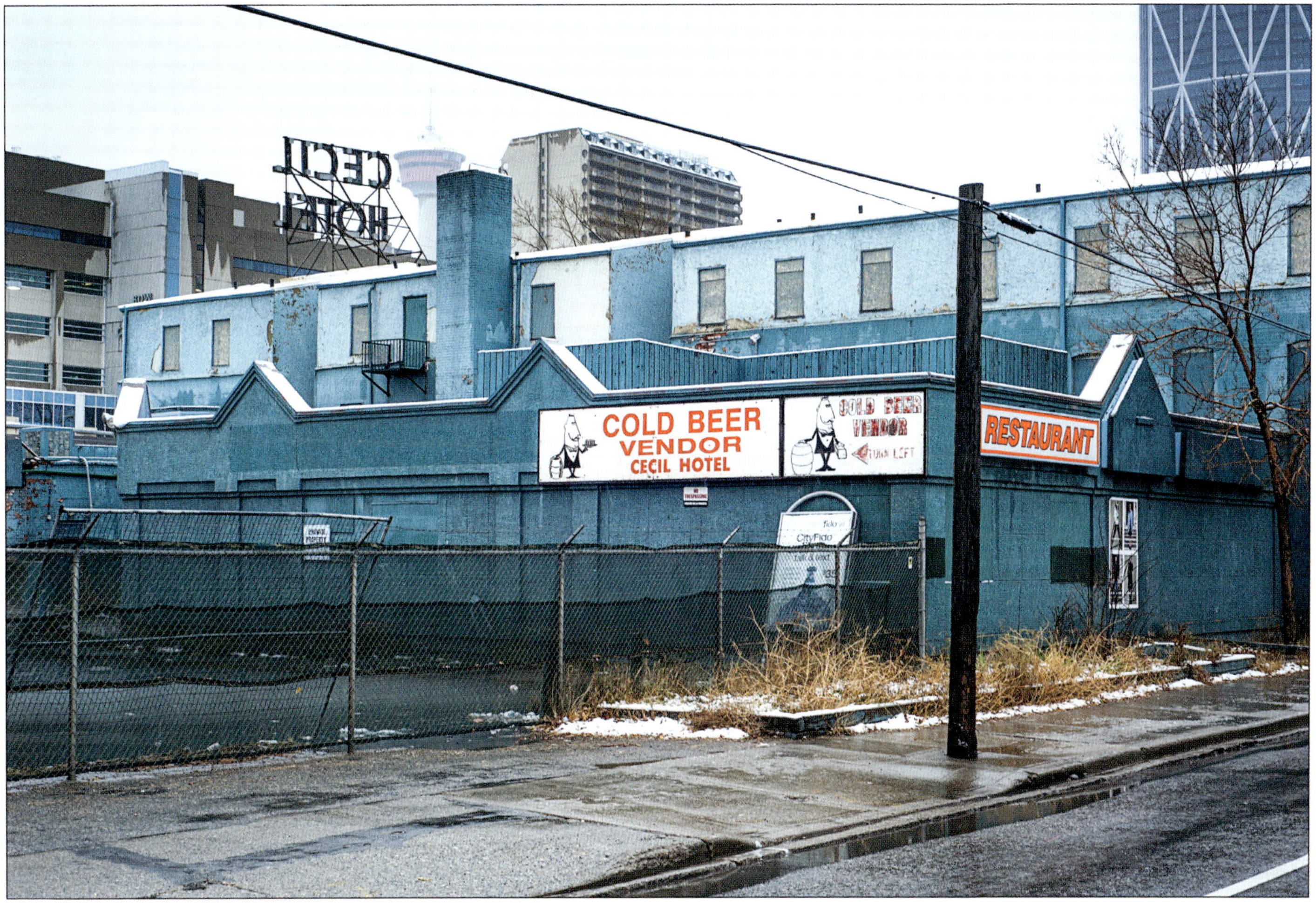

Cecil Hotel, 2014

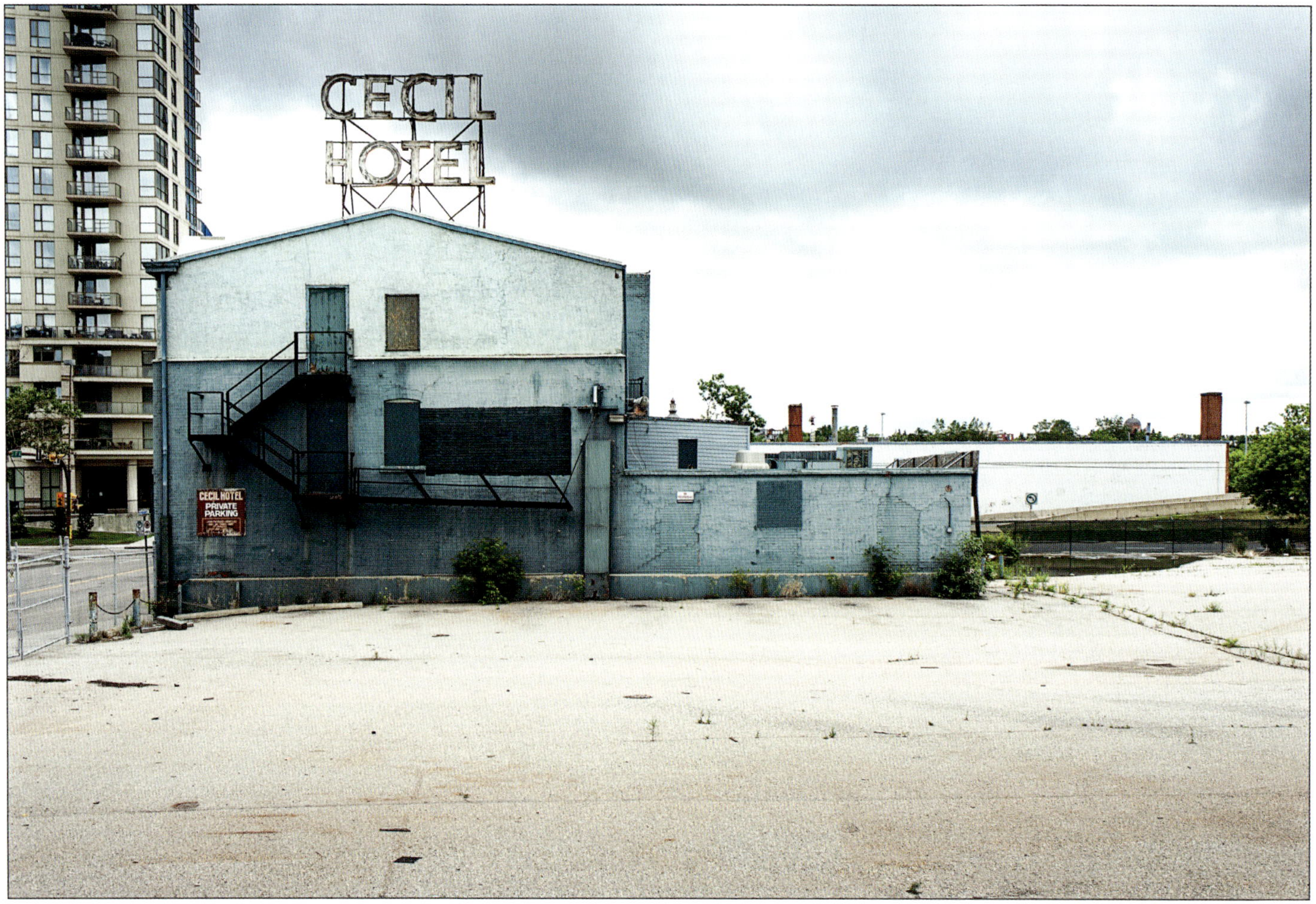

Cecil Hotel, 2015

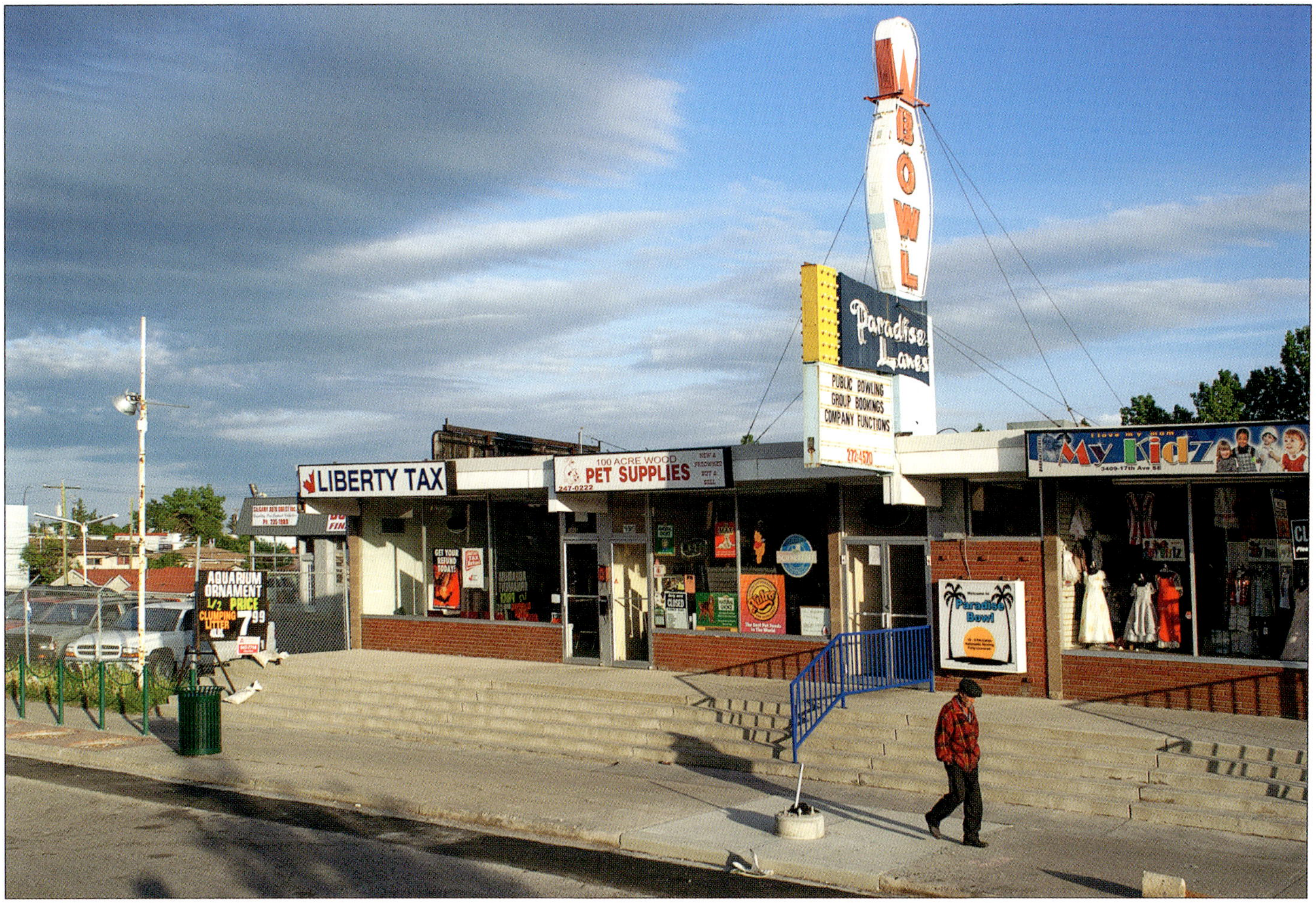

Paradise Lanes, 2006

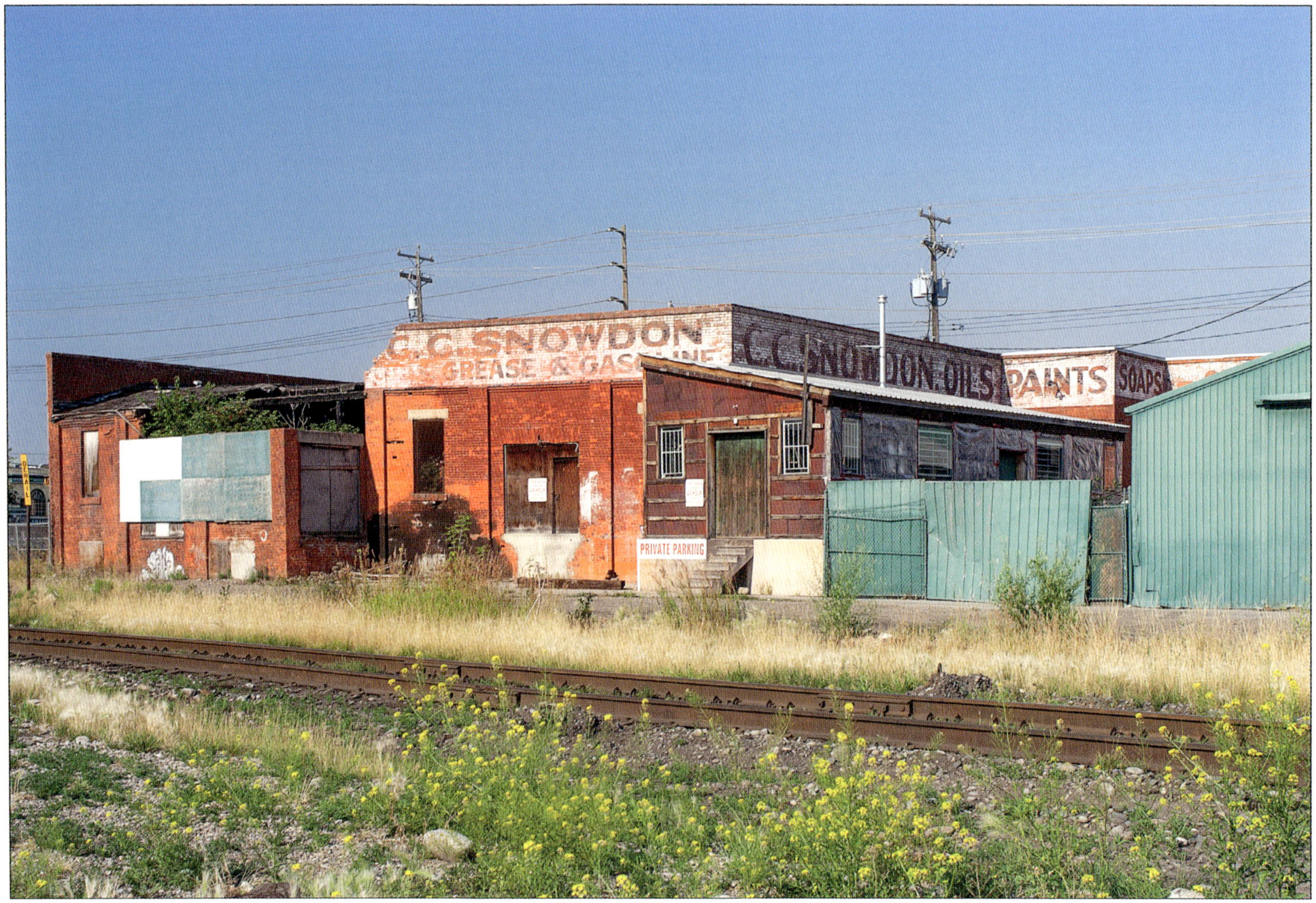

2010 11 Ave SE, 2007

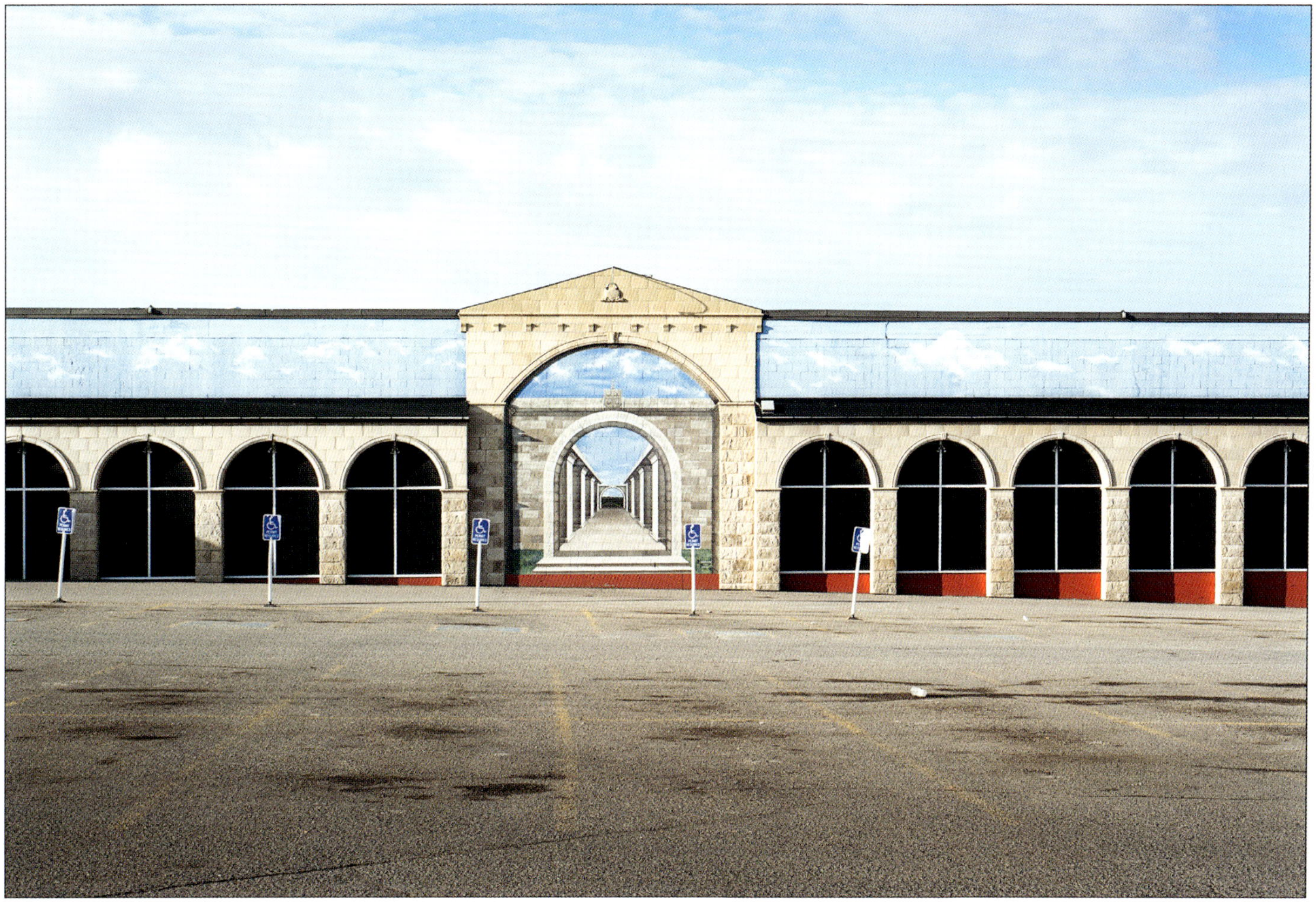

Cash Casino, 2014

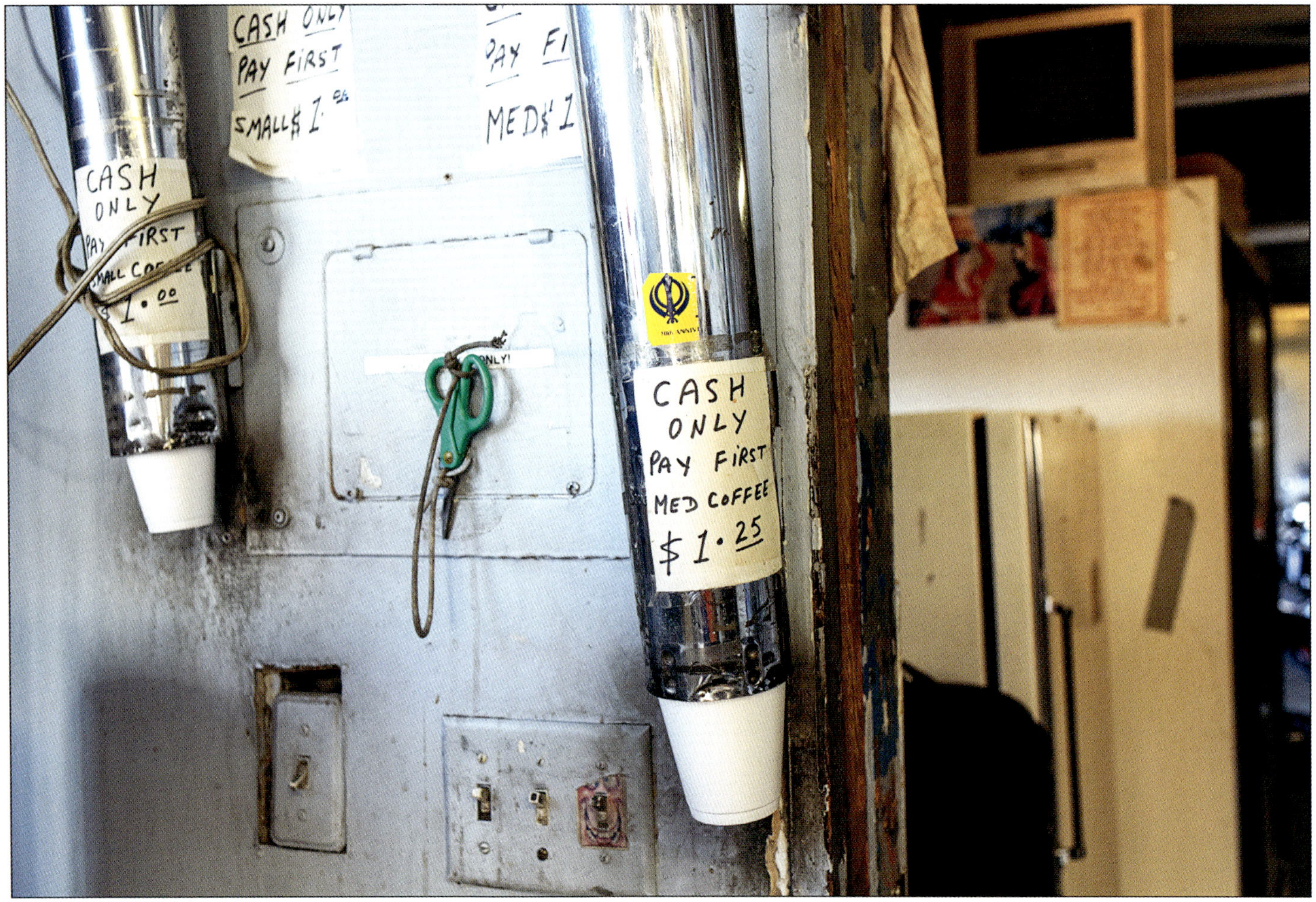

Canpro, 2016

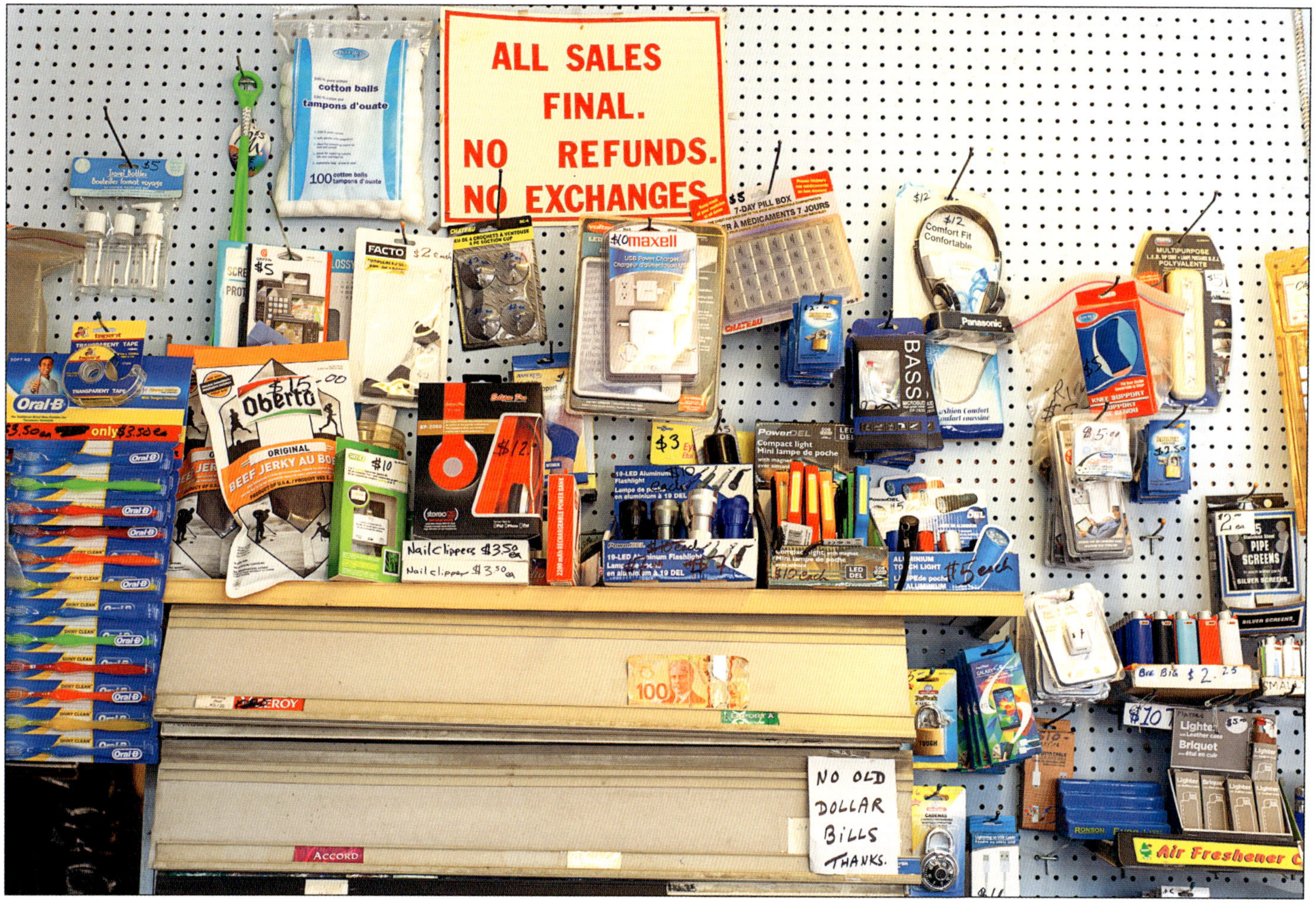
ALL SALES FINAL. NO REFUNDS. NO EXCHANGES
NO OLD DOLLAR BILLS THANKS.

Canpro, 2016

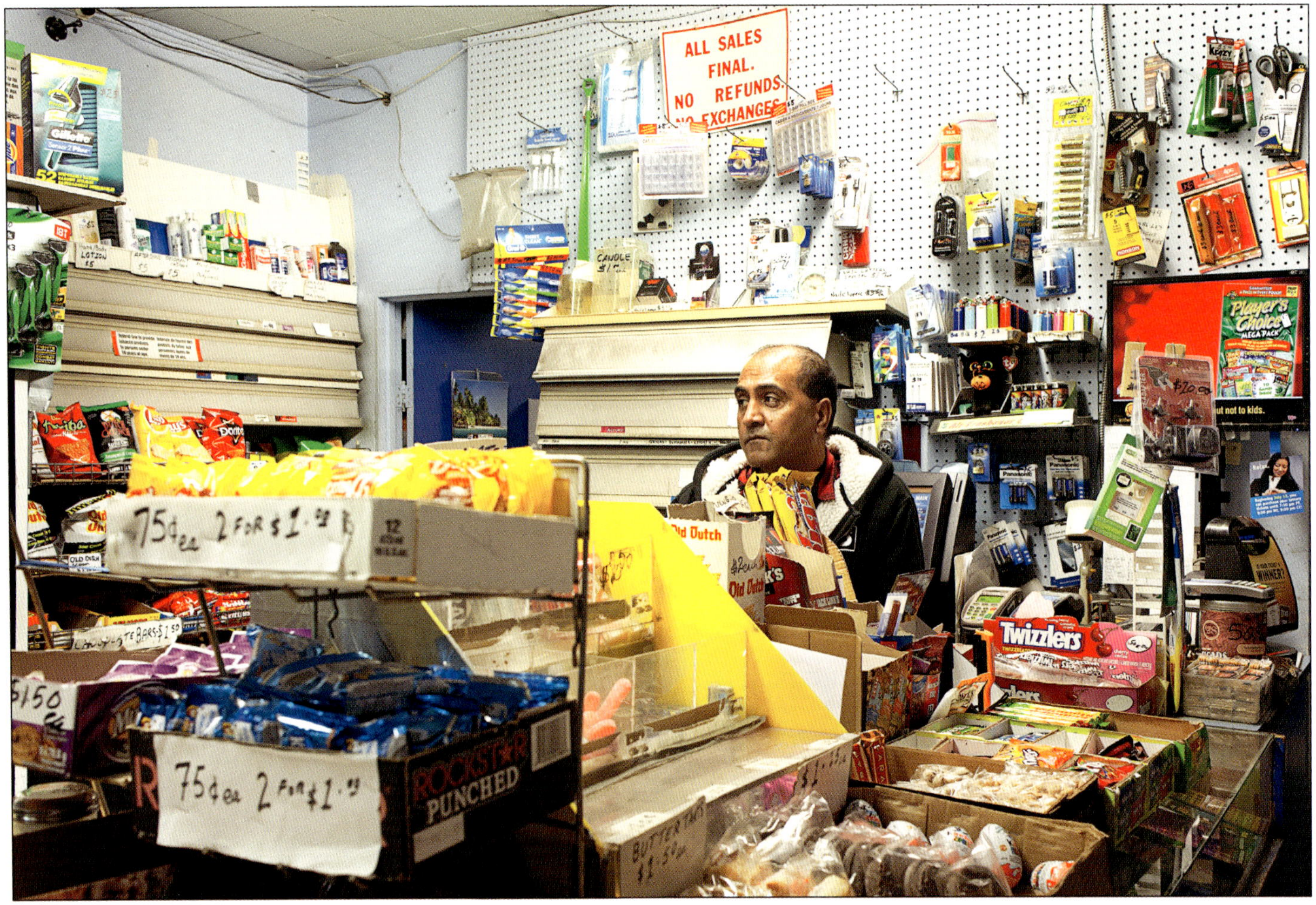
ALL SALES FINAL. NO REFUNDS. NO EXCHANGES
Old Dutch
Twizzlers
ROCKSTAR PUNCHED

Canpro, 2016

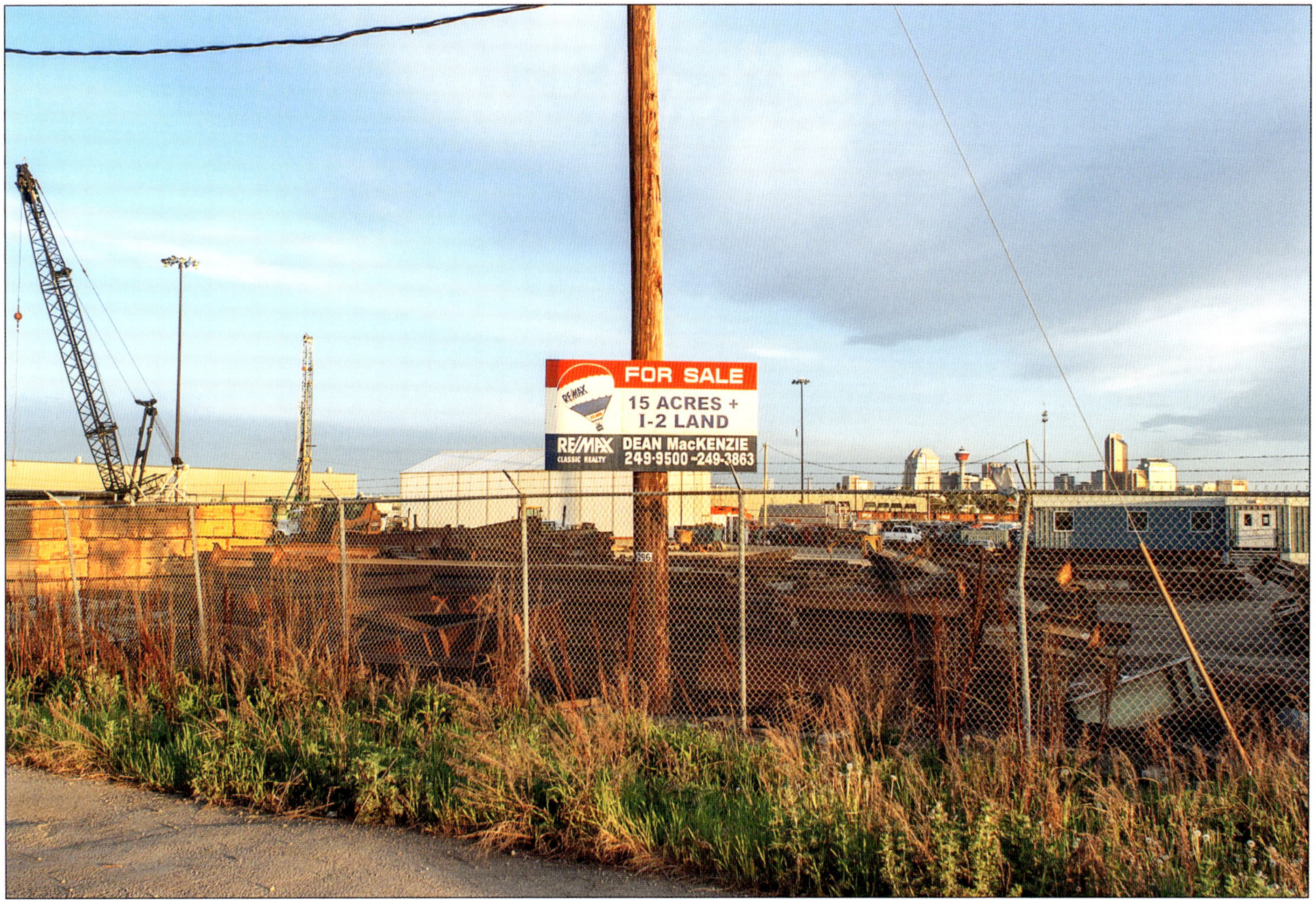

Alyth Yards, 2006

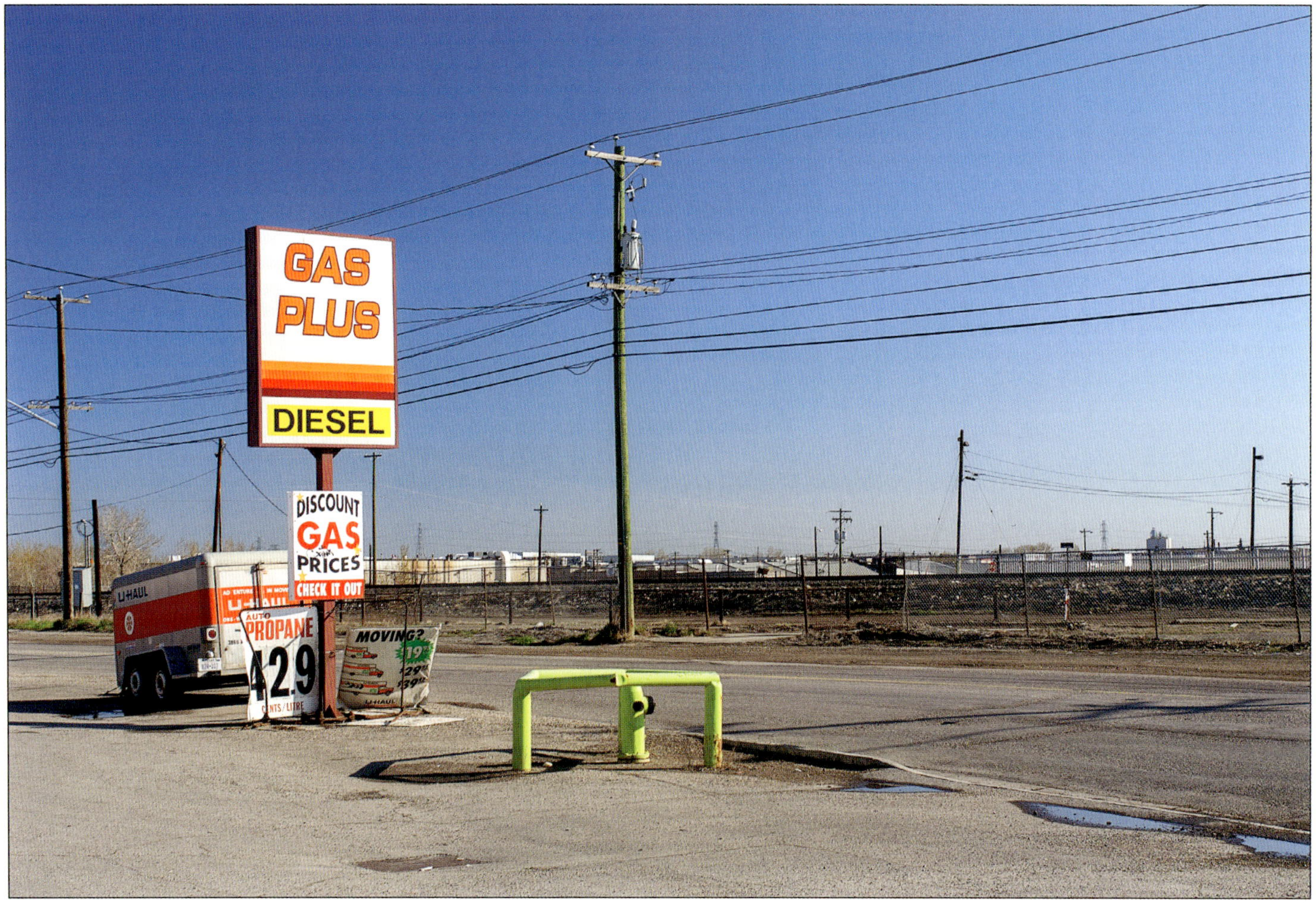

Gas Plus, 2009

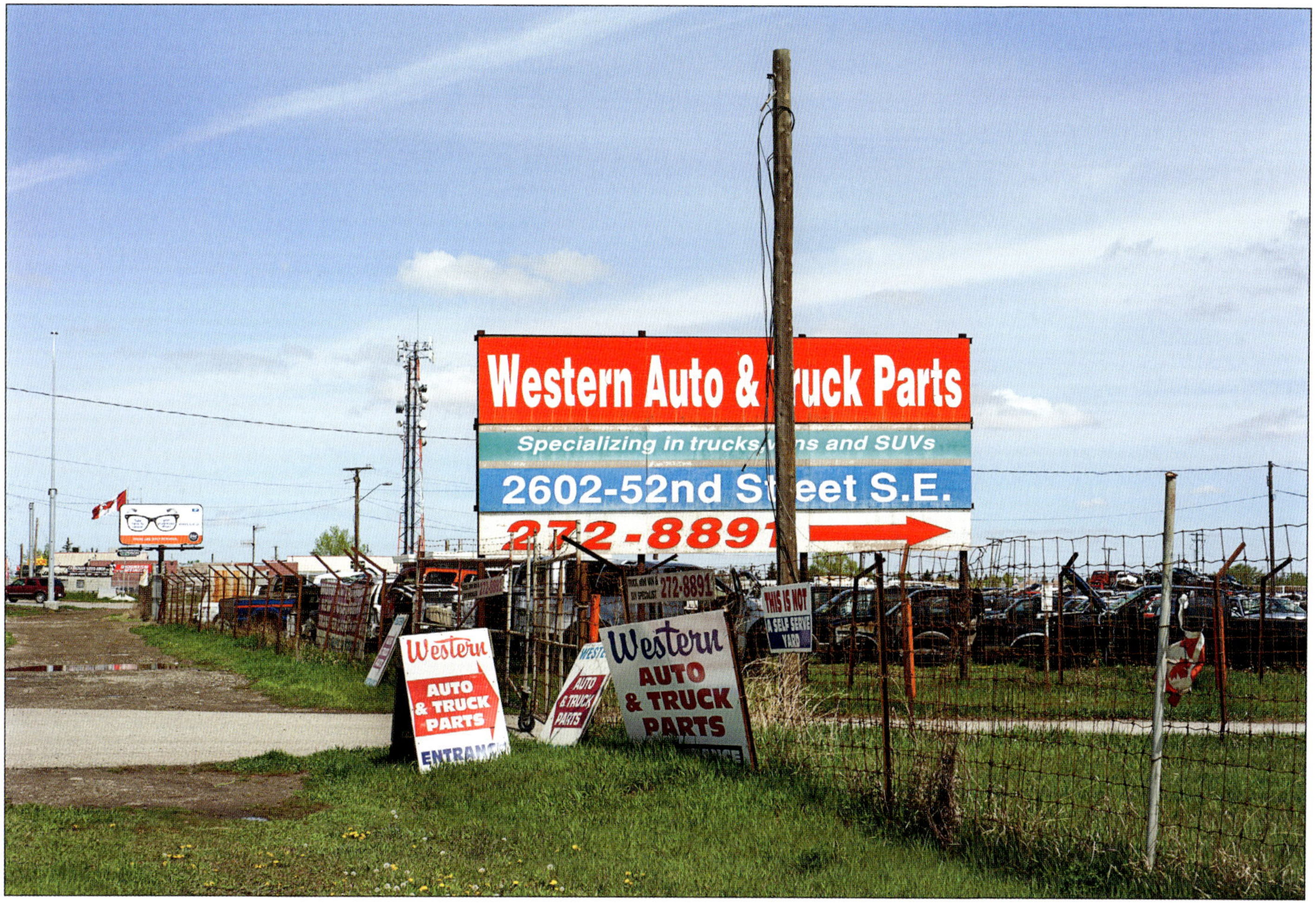

Western Auto and Truck Parts, 2015

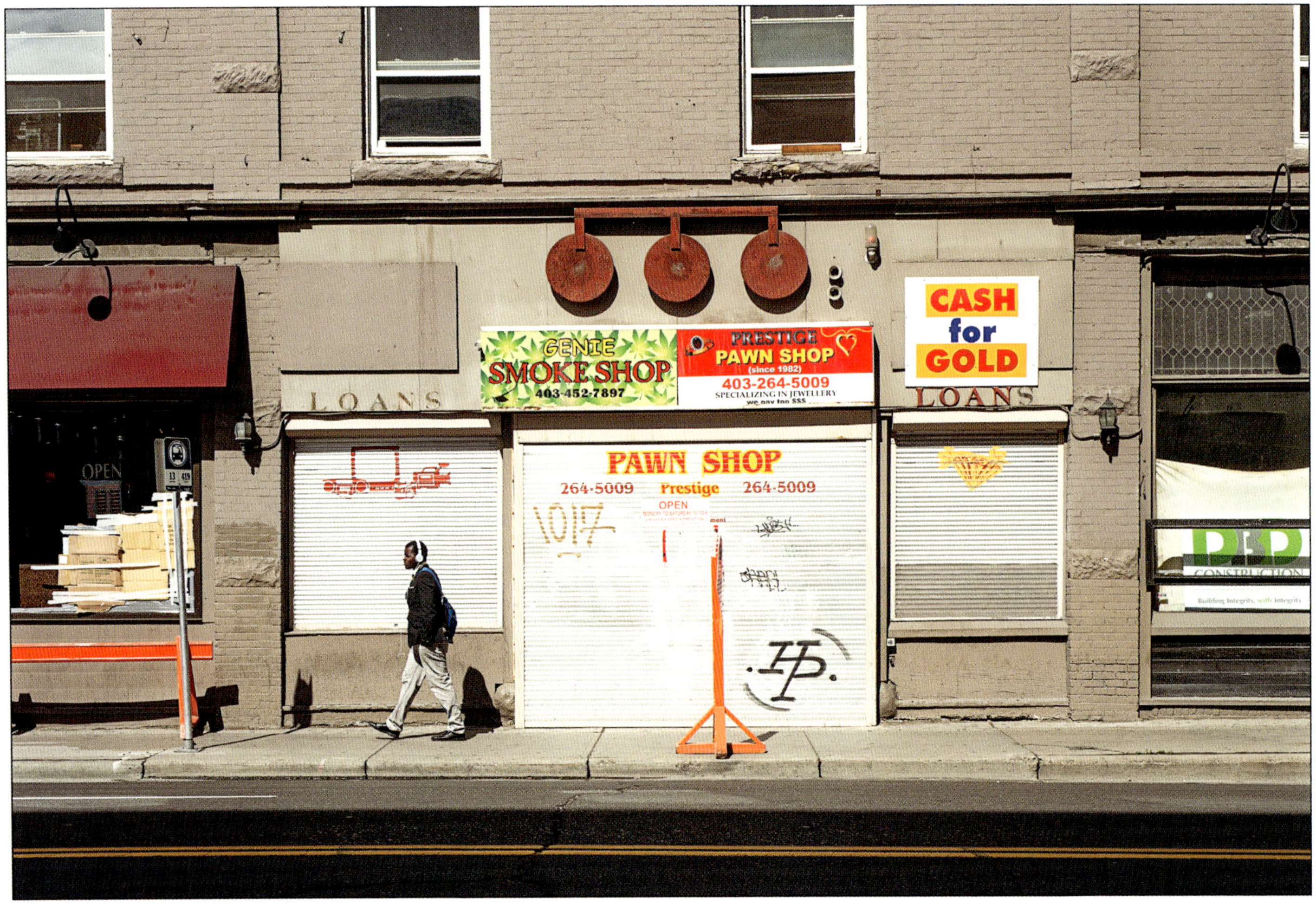

Prestige Pawn Shop, 2016

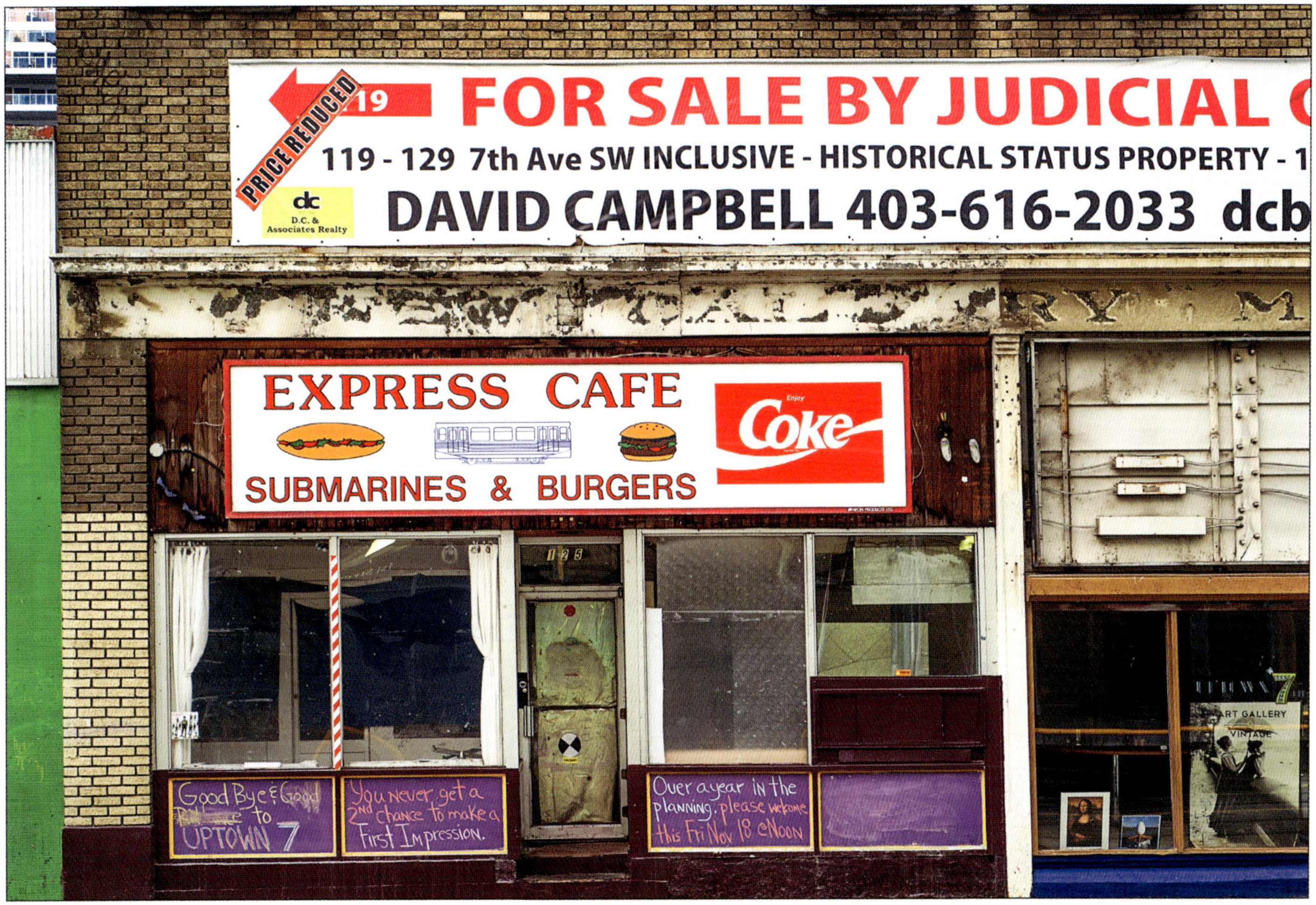

Express Café, 2016

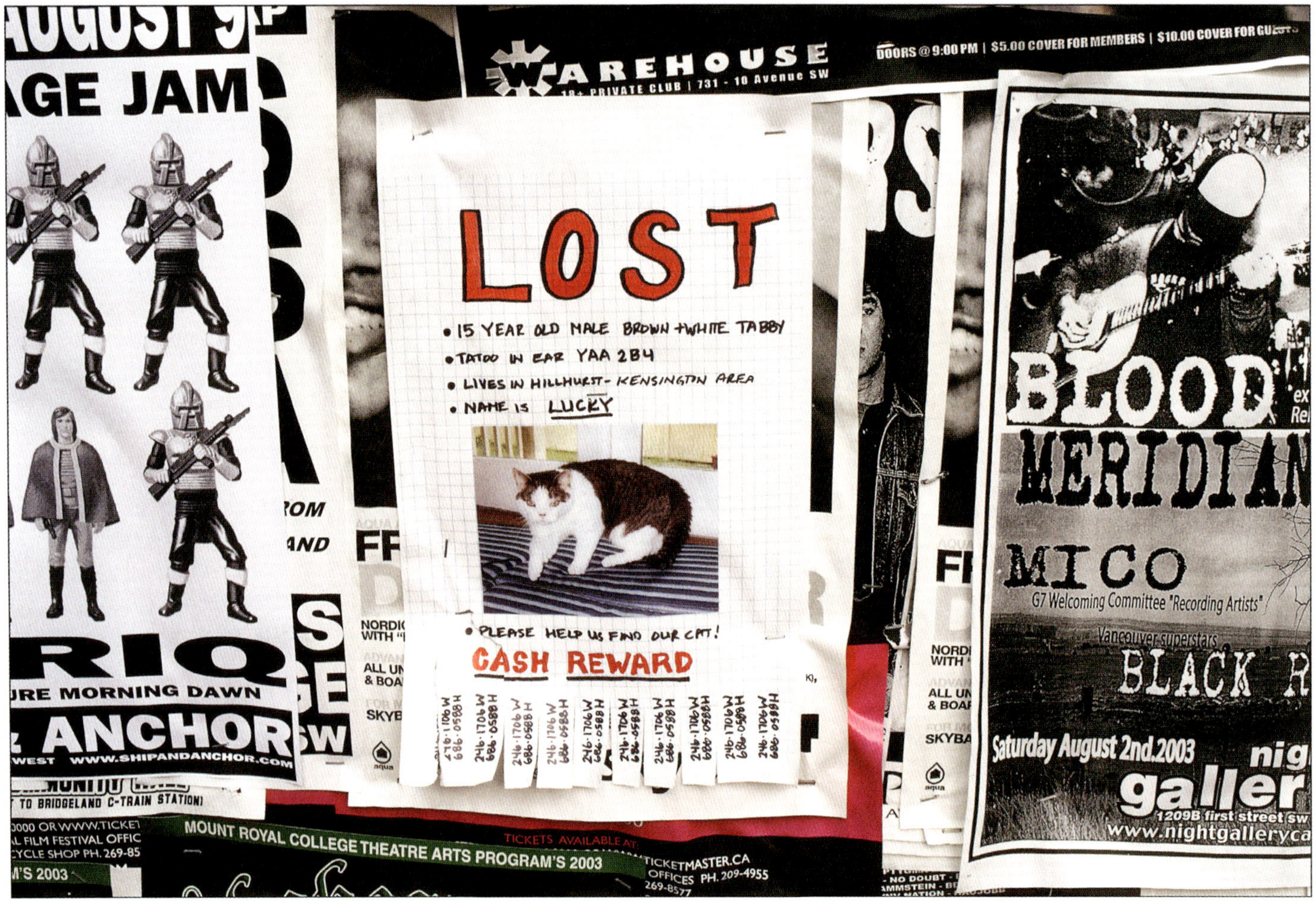
AUGUST 9
AGE JAM
RIQ
URE MORNING DAWN
ANCHOR
WWW.SHIPANDANCHOR.COM
TO BRIDGELAND C-TRAIN STATION
WAREHOUSE
18+ PRIVATE CLUB | 731 - 10 Avenue SW
DOORS @ 9:00 PM | $5.00 COVER FOR MEMBERS | $10.00 COVER FOR GU
LOST
• 15 YEAR OLD MALE BROWN + WHITE TABBY
• TATOO IN EAR YAA 2B4
• LIVES IN HILLHURST - KENSINGTON AREA
• NAME IS LUCKY
• PLEASE HELP US FIND OUR CAT!
CASH REWARD
246-1706 W
686-0588 H
BLOOD
MERIDIAN
MICO
G7 Welcoming Committee "Recording Artists"
Vancouver superstars
BLACK R
Saturday August 2nd.2003
galler
1209B first street sw
www.nightgalleryca
MOUNT ROYAL COLLEGE THEATRE ARTS PROGRAM'S 2003
TICKETS AVAILABLE AT
TICKETMASTER.CA

9 St SW, 2003

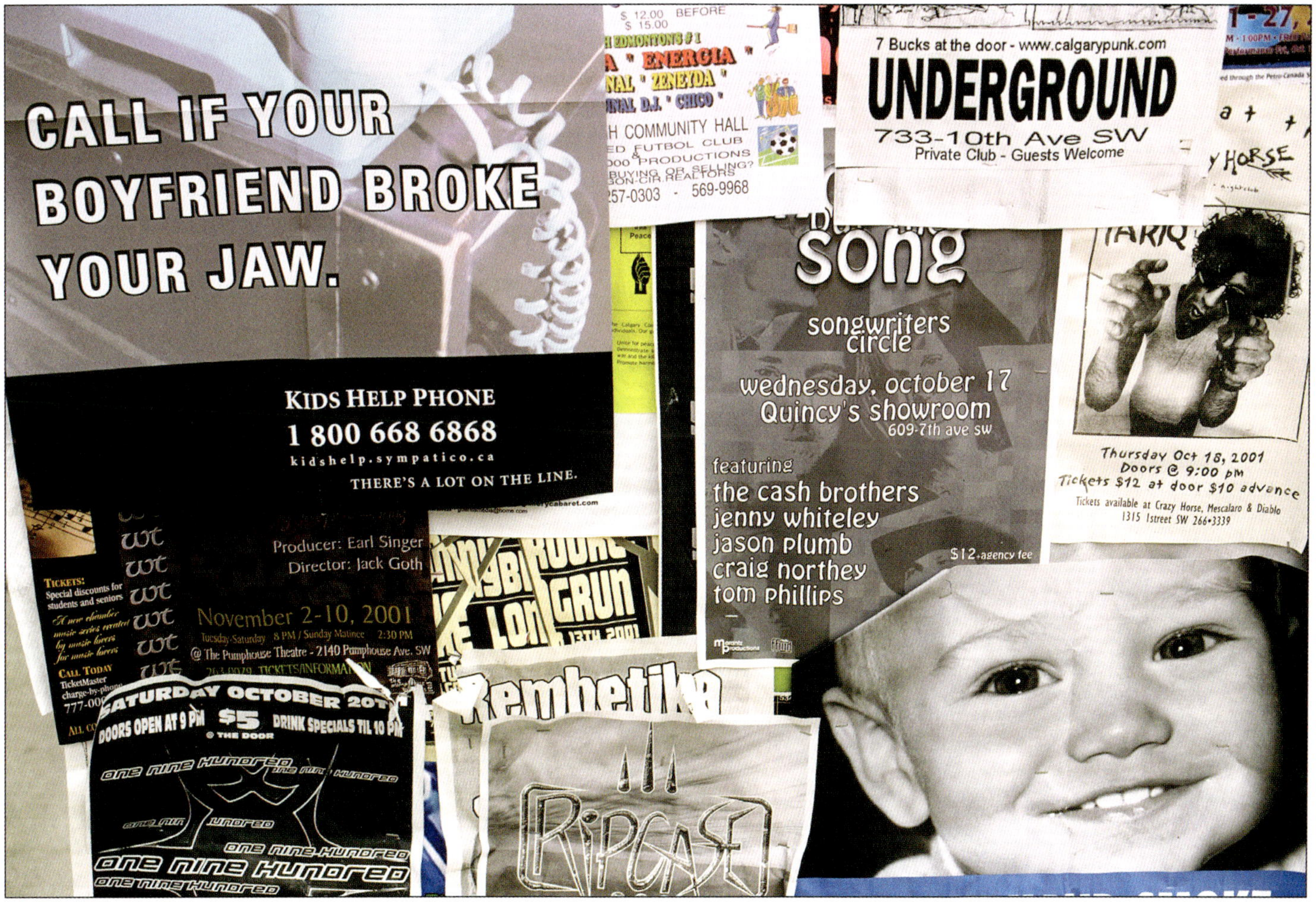

Centre St, 2001

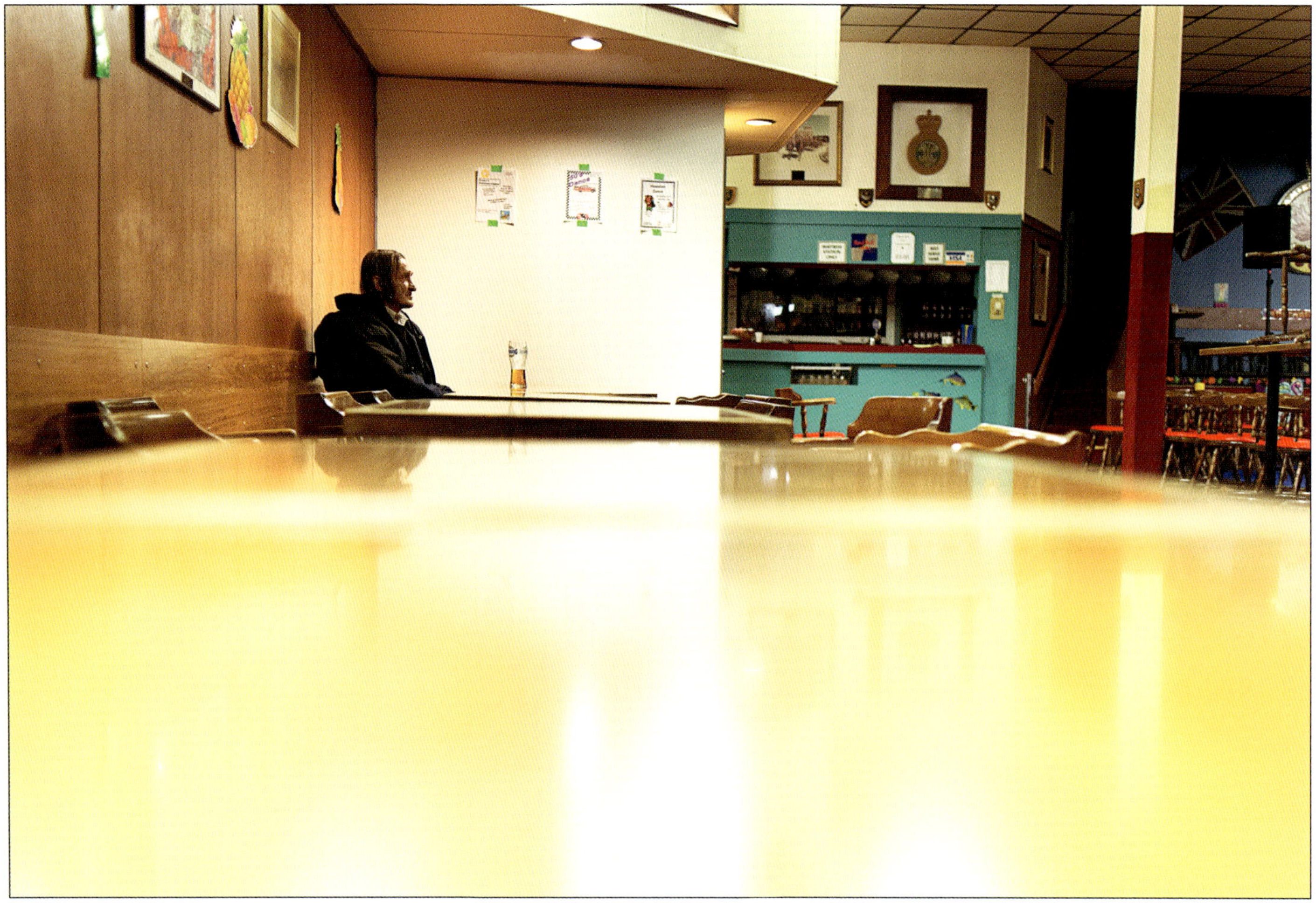

Raymond, Legion #1, 2013

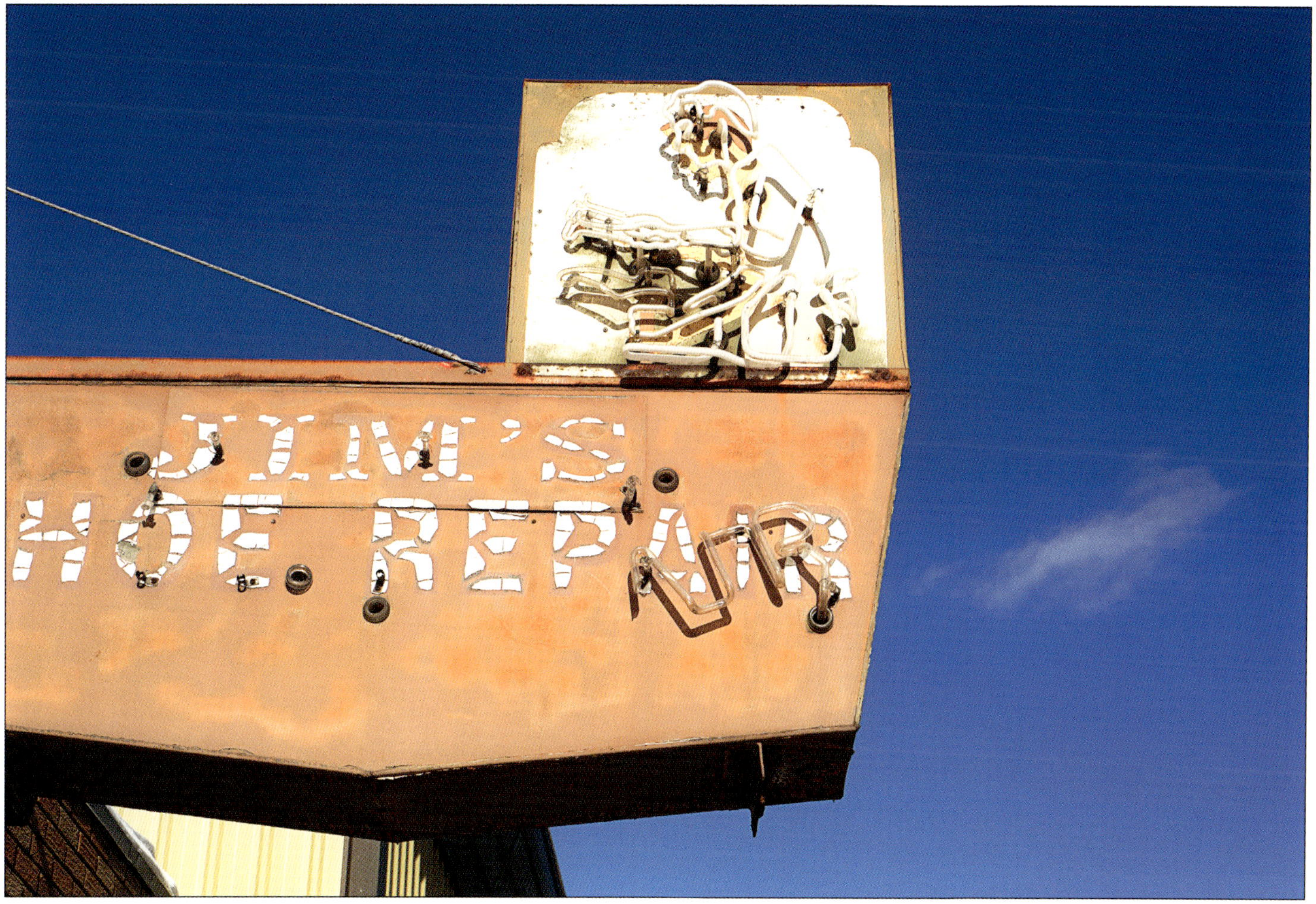

Jim's Shoe Repair, 2014

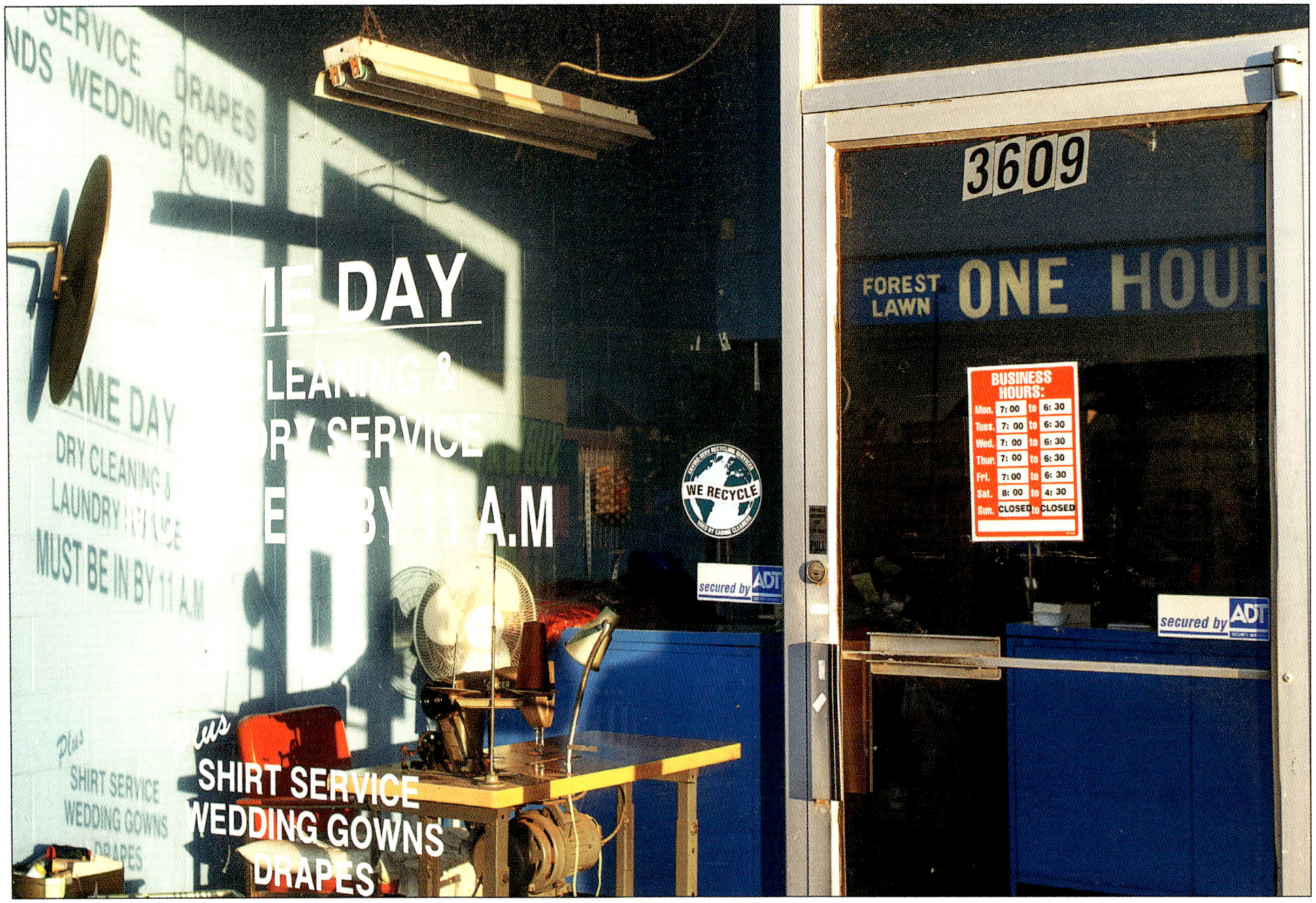

3609 17 Ave SE, 2008

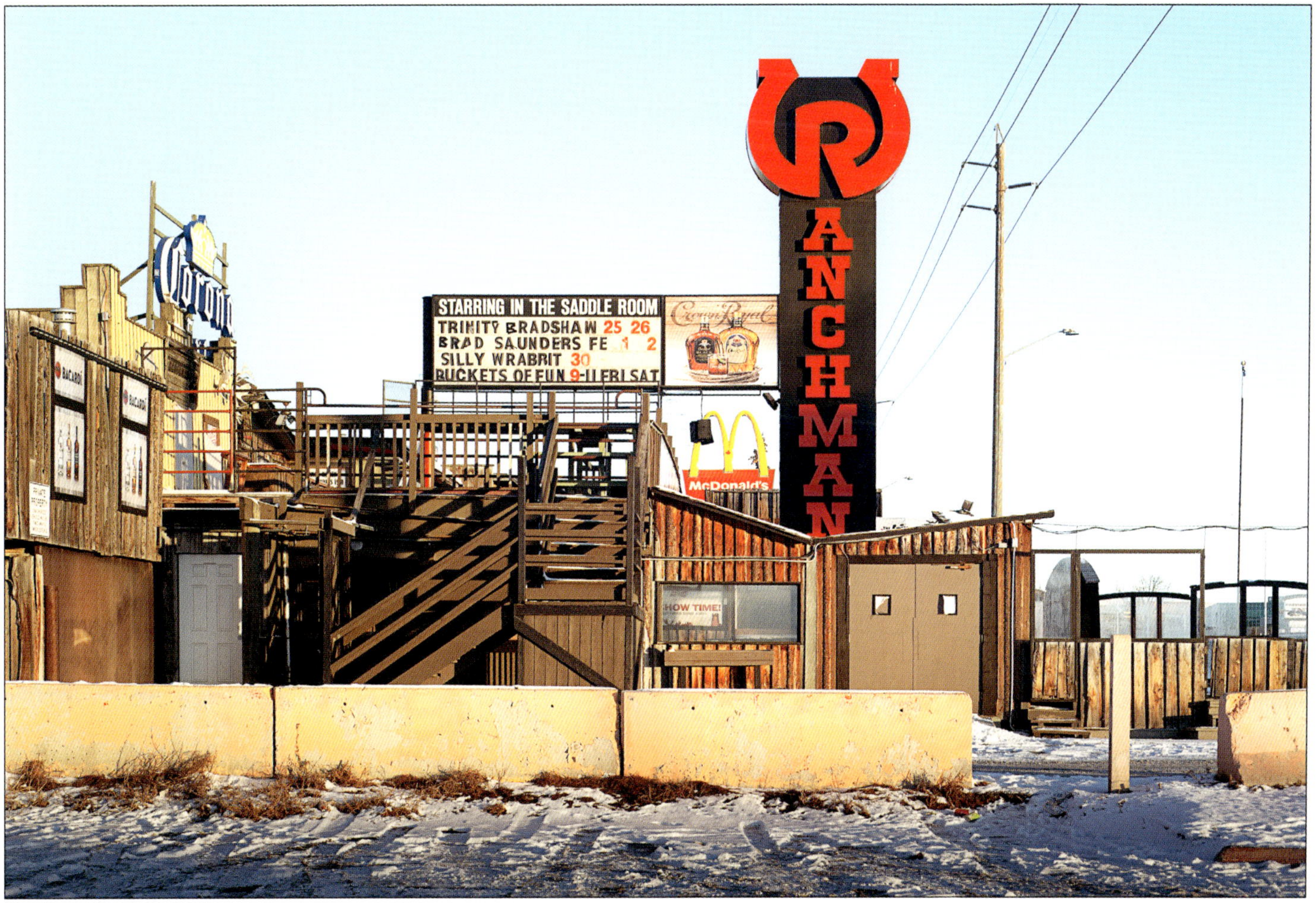

Ranchman's, 2019

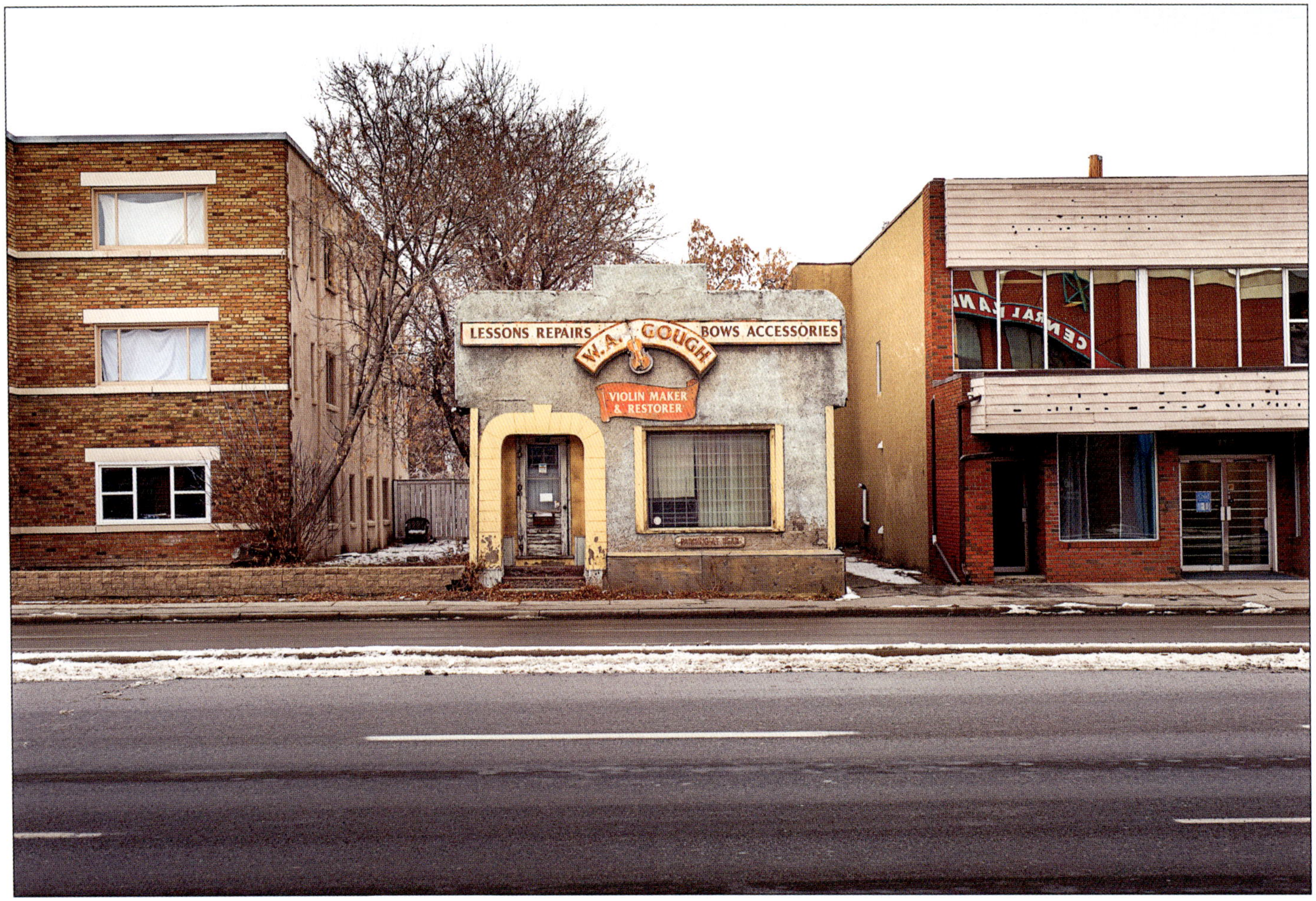

W.A. Gough Violin Maker and Restorer, 2013

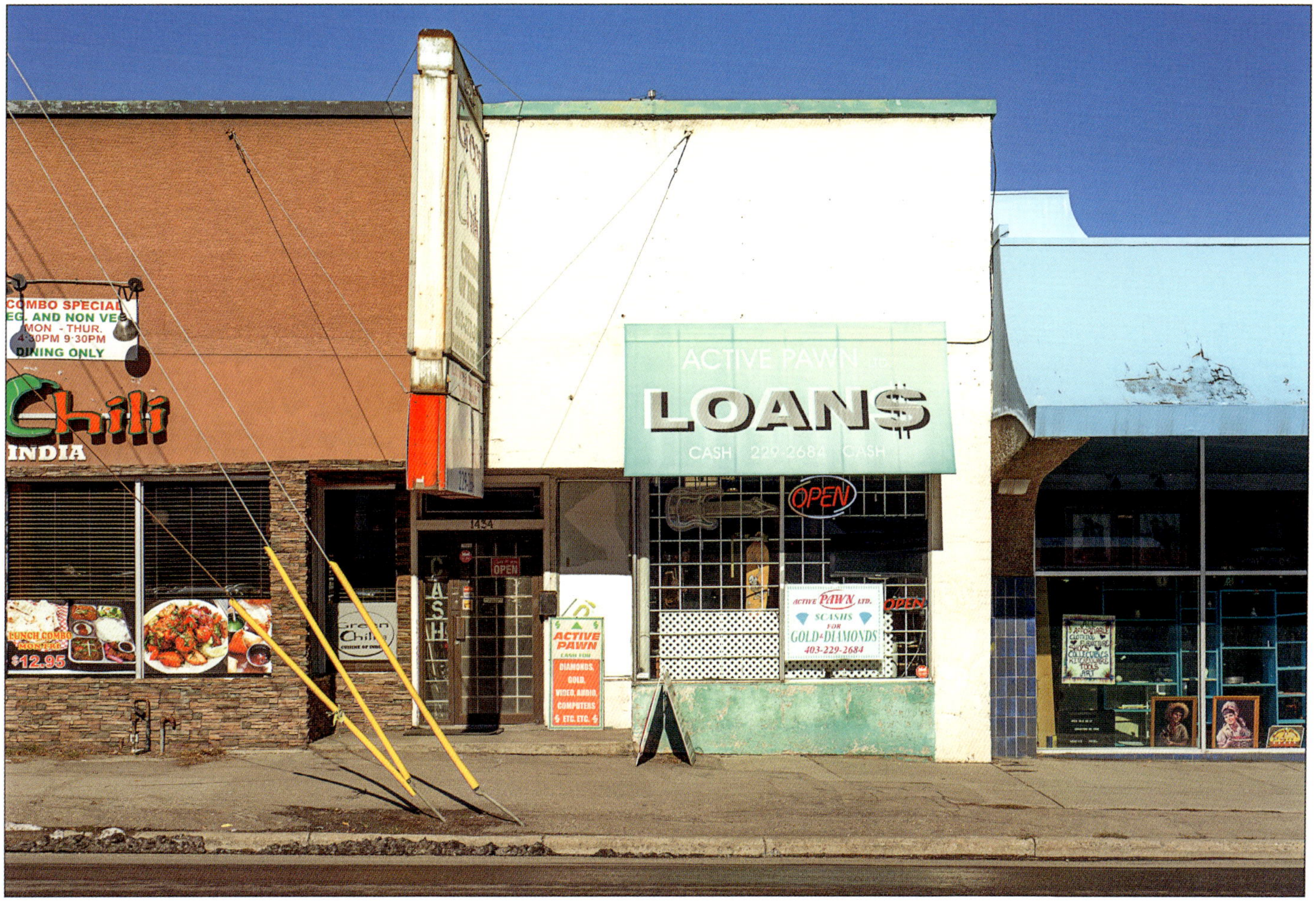

Active Pawn, 2018

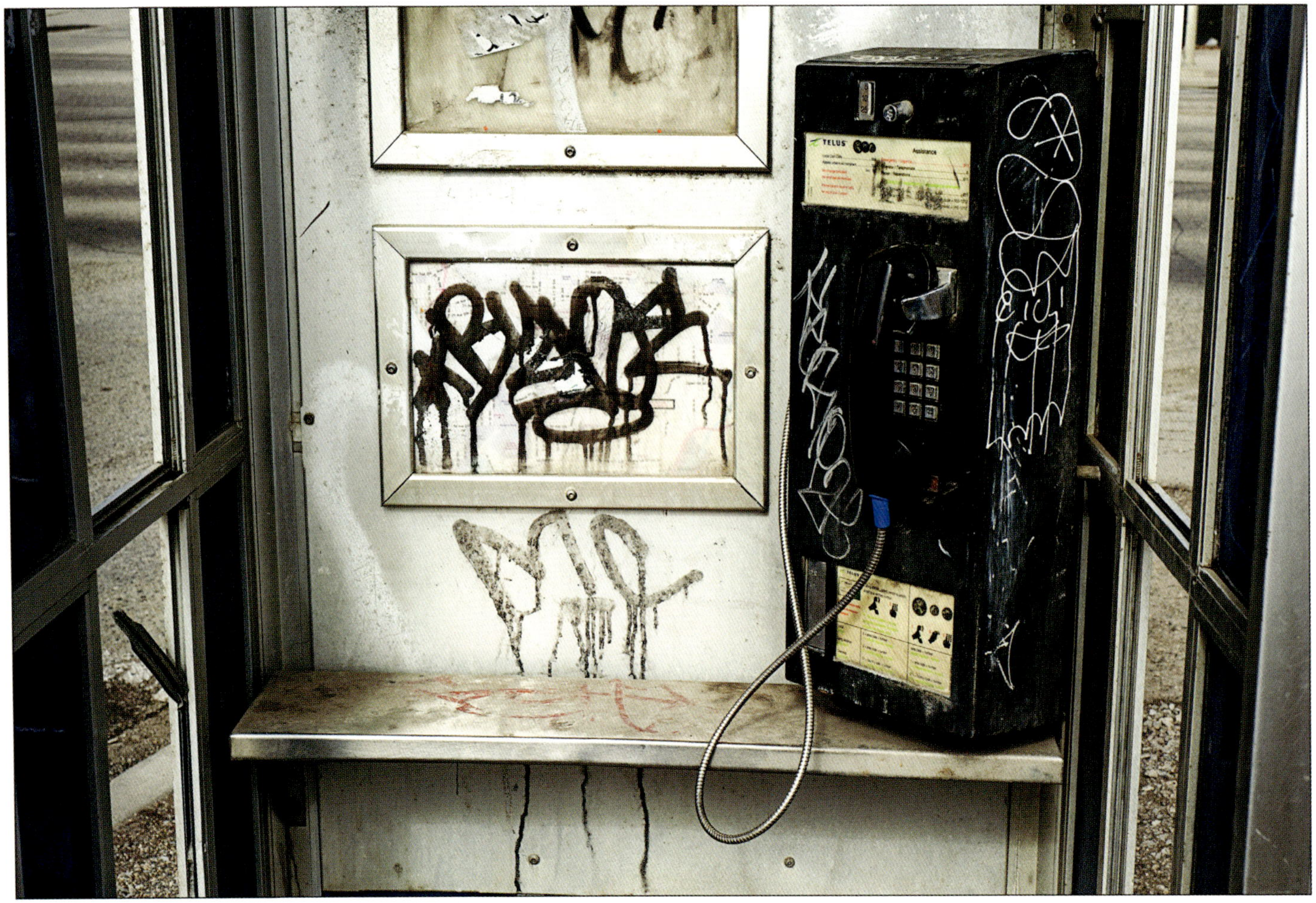

Near 39 Ave + Macleod Trail, 2014

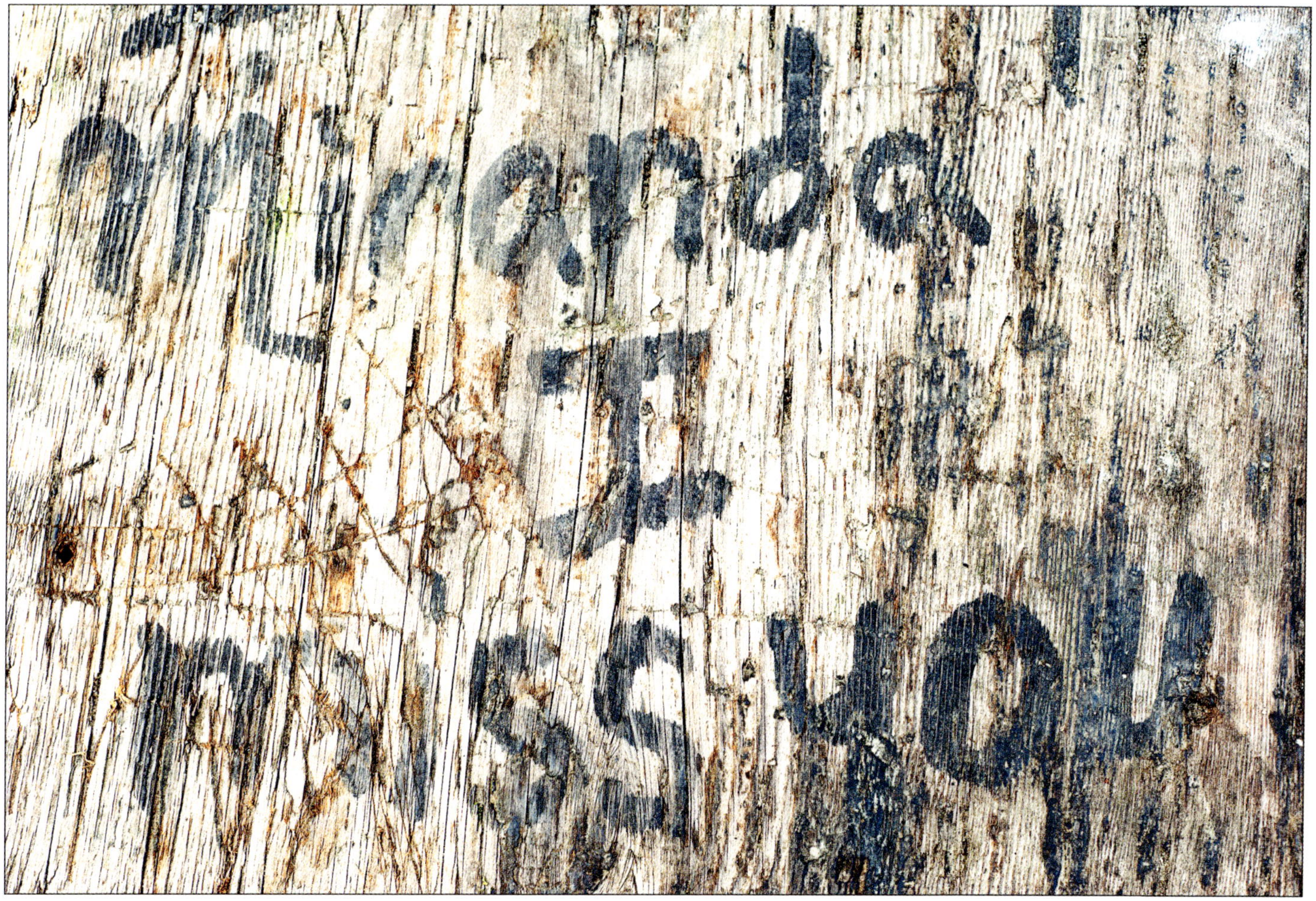

Near 19 Ave + 1 St SE, 2018

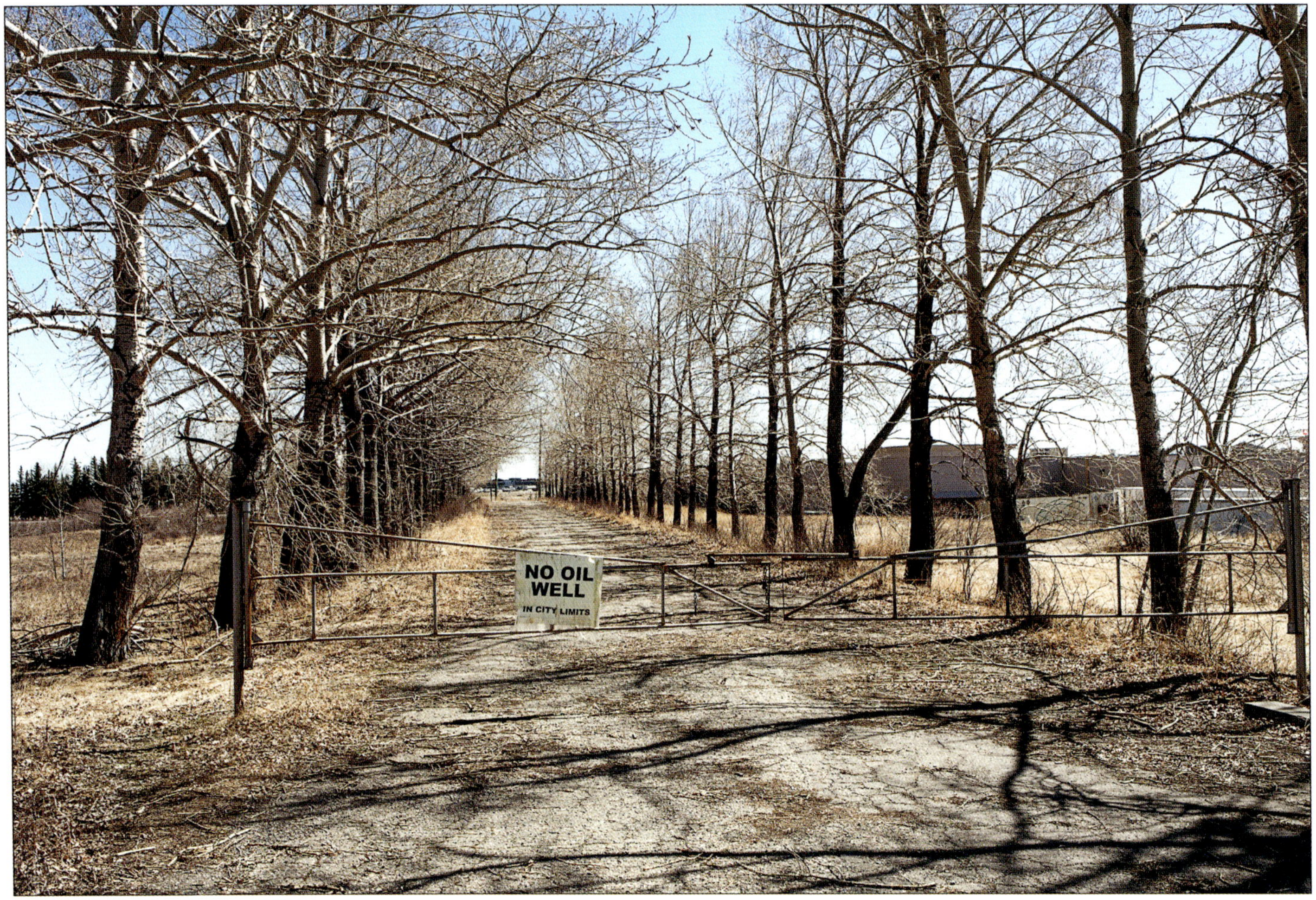

Near Southern Alberta Forensic Psychiatry Centre, 2013

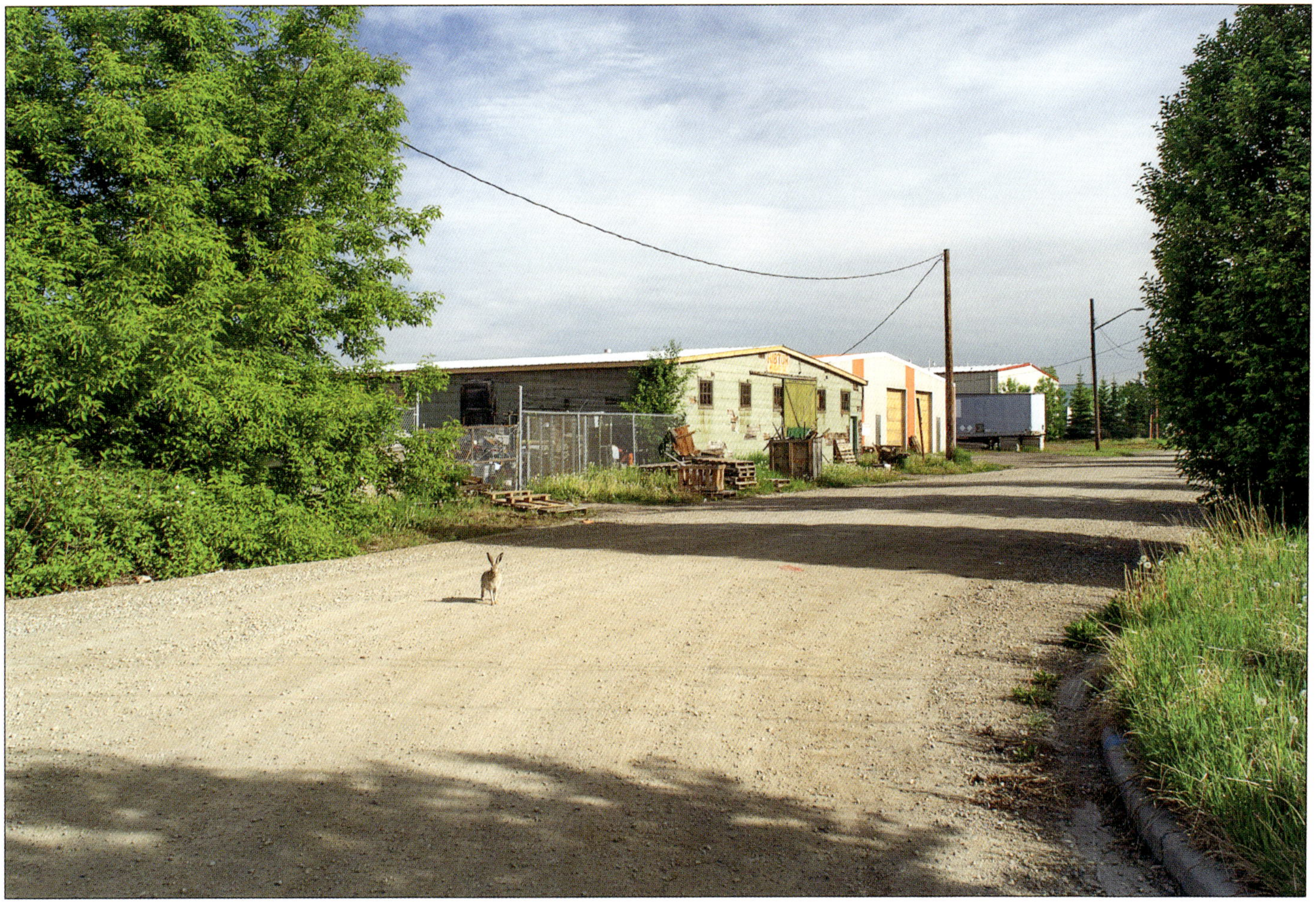

Ribtor Hardware, 2006

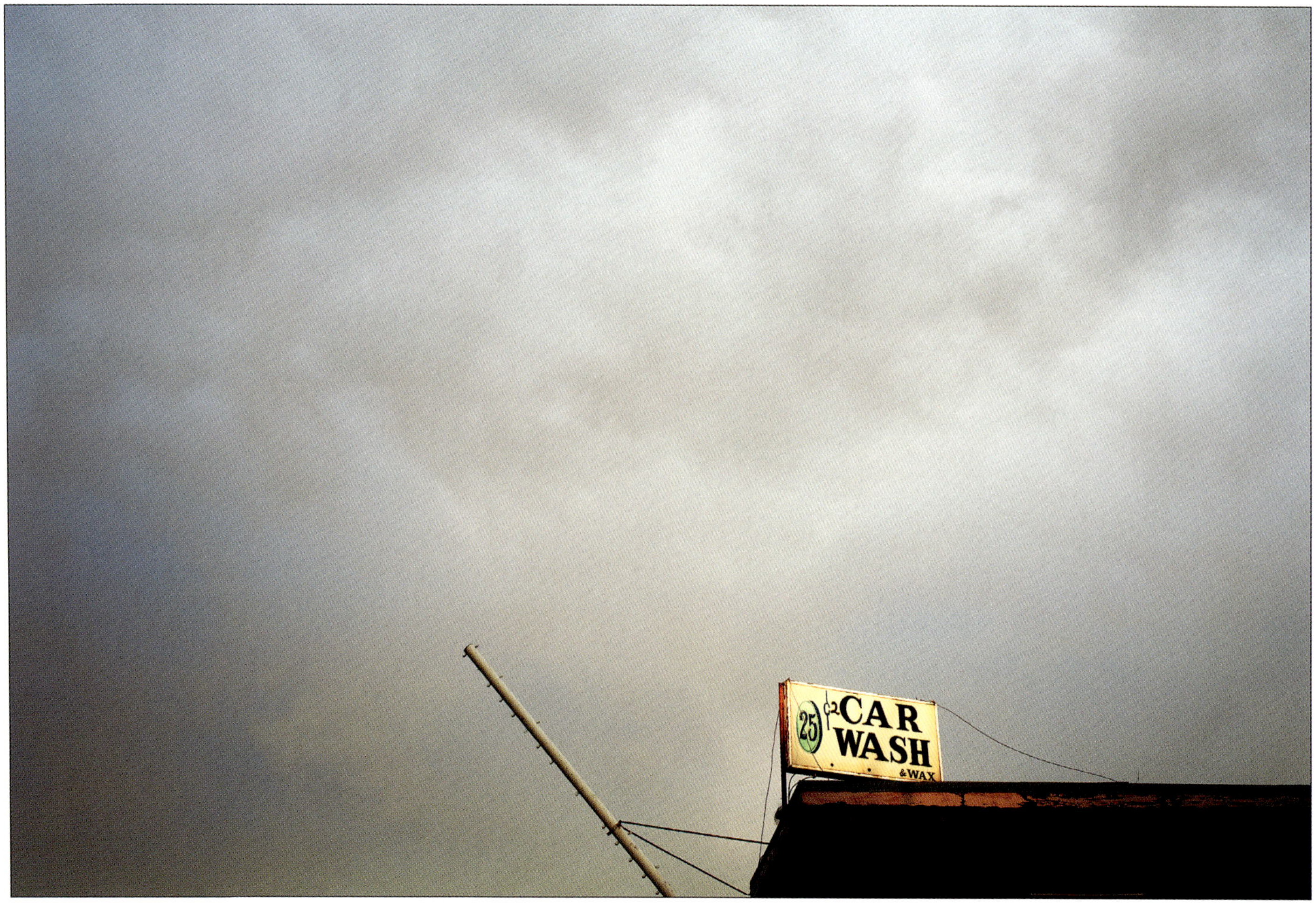

Near 41 Ave + 1 St NE, 2012

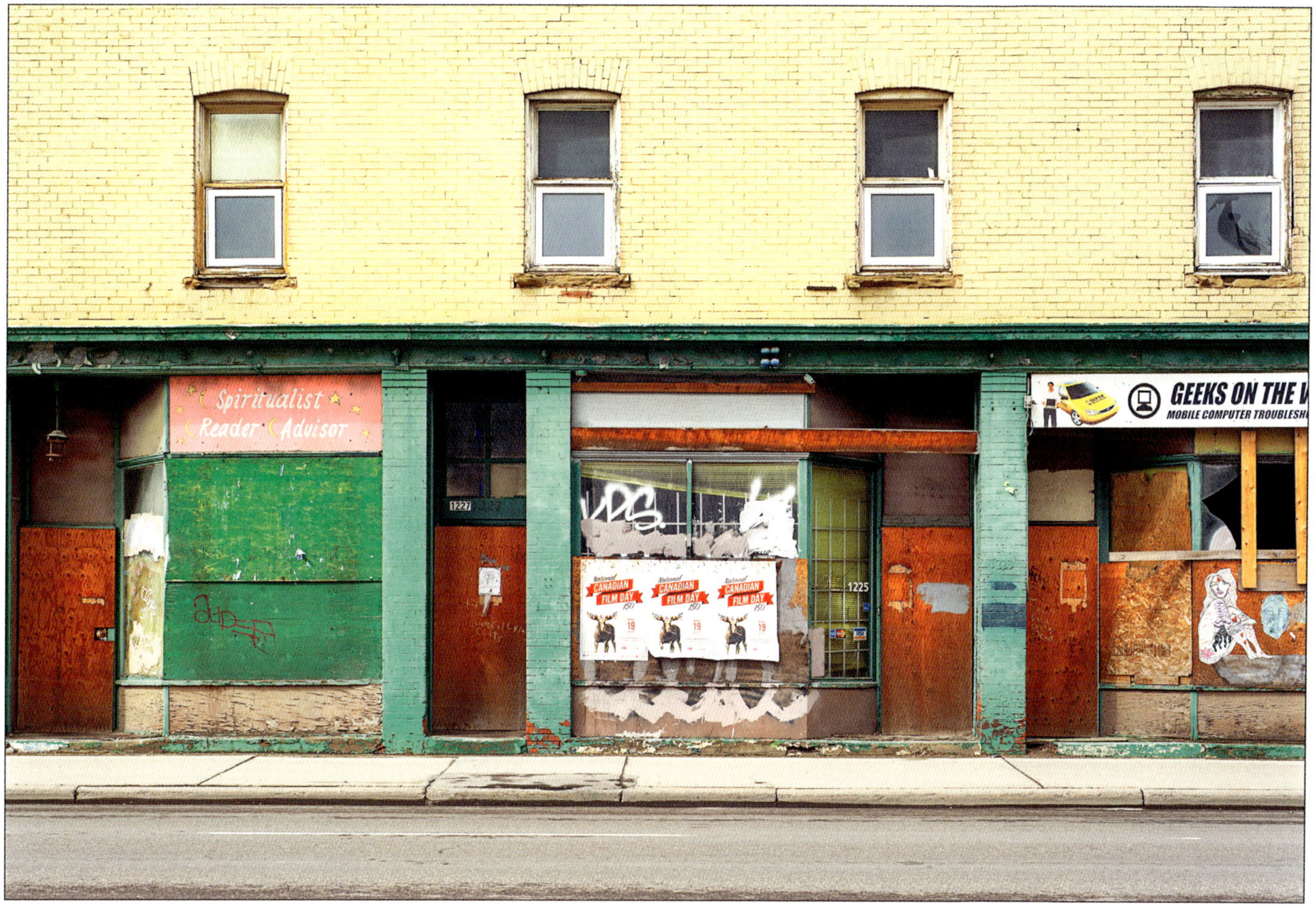

1225 Macleod Trail SE, 2017

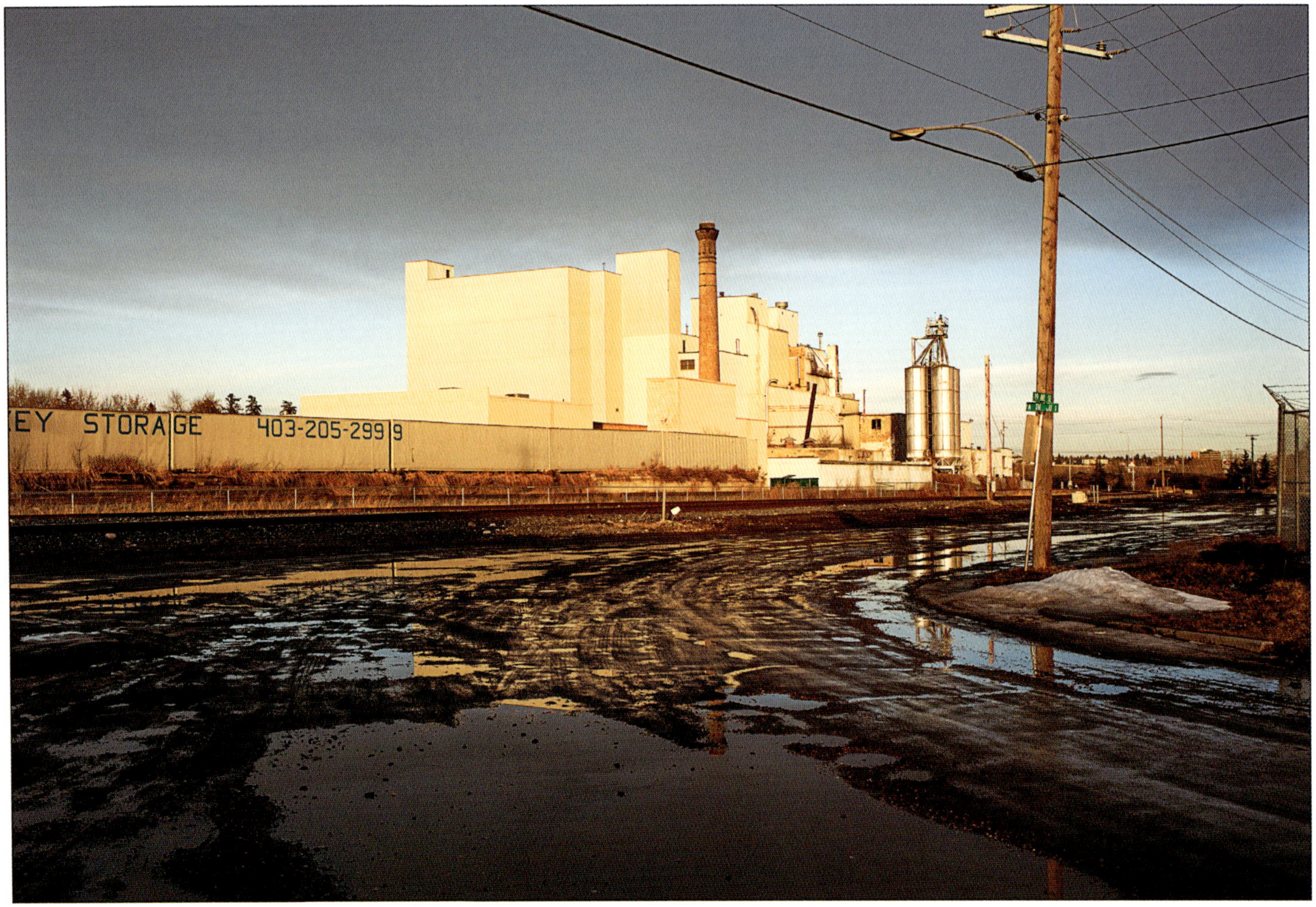

Abandoned brewery, 2015

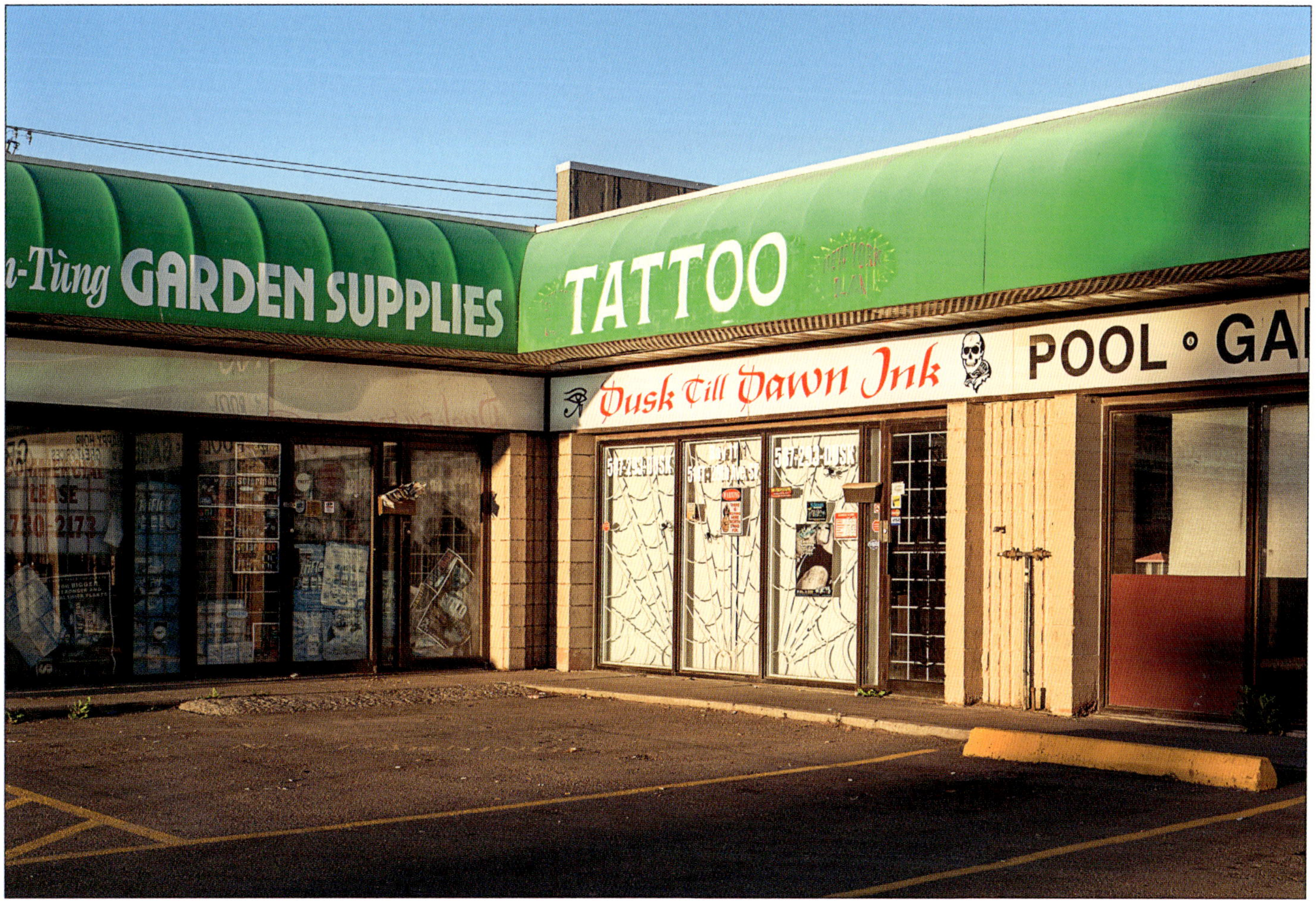

Dusk till Dawn Ink, 2014

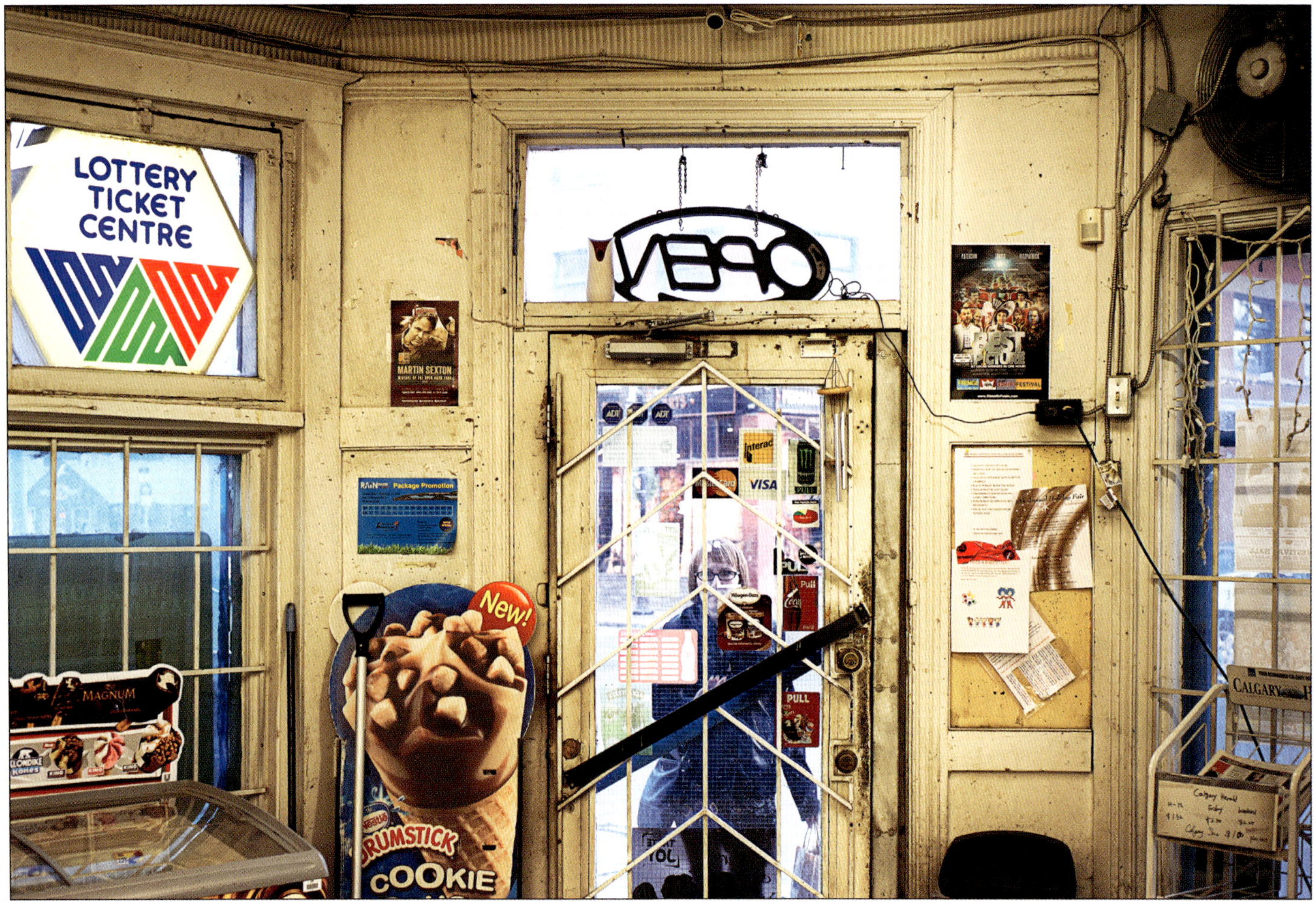

Near 9 Ave + 13 St SE 2015

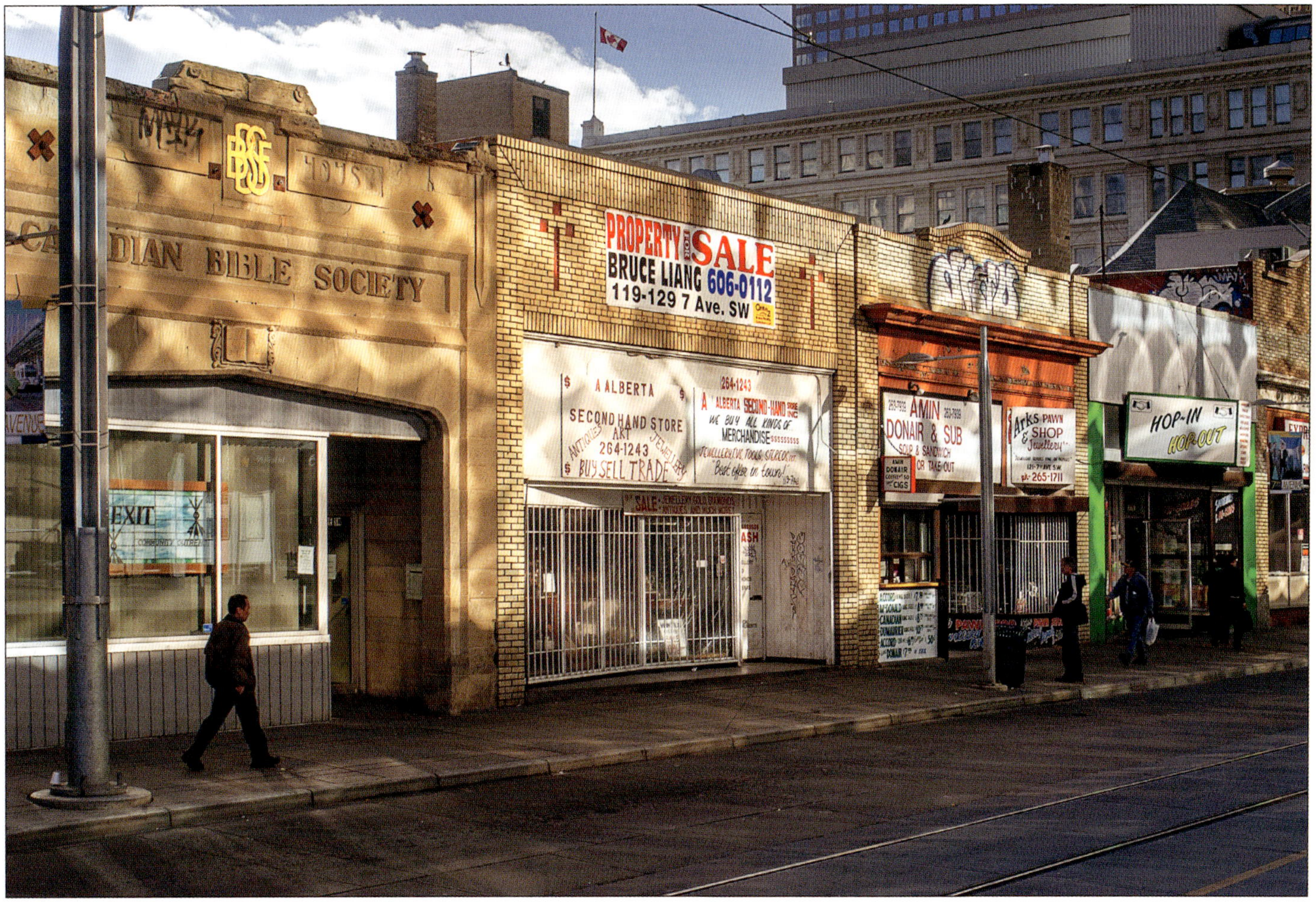
DIAN BIBLE SOCIETY
PROPERTY SALE
BRUCE LIANG 606-0112
119-129 7 Ave. SW
A ALBERTA
SECOND HAND STORE
ART
264-1243
BUY SELL TRADE
WE BUY ALL KINDS OF
MERCHANDISE
AMIN
DONAIR & SUB
HOP-IN
HOP-OUT
EXIT

7 Ave SW, 2007

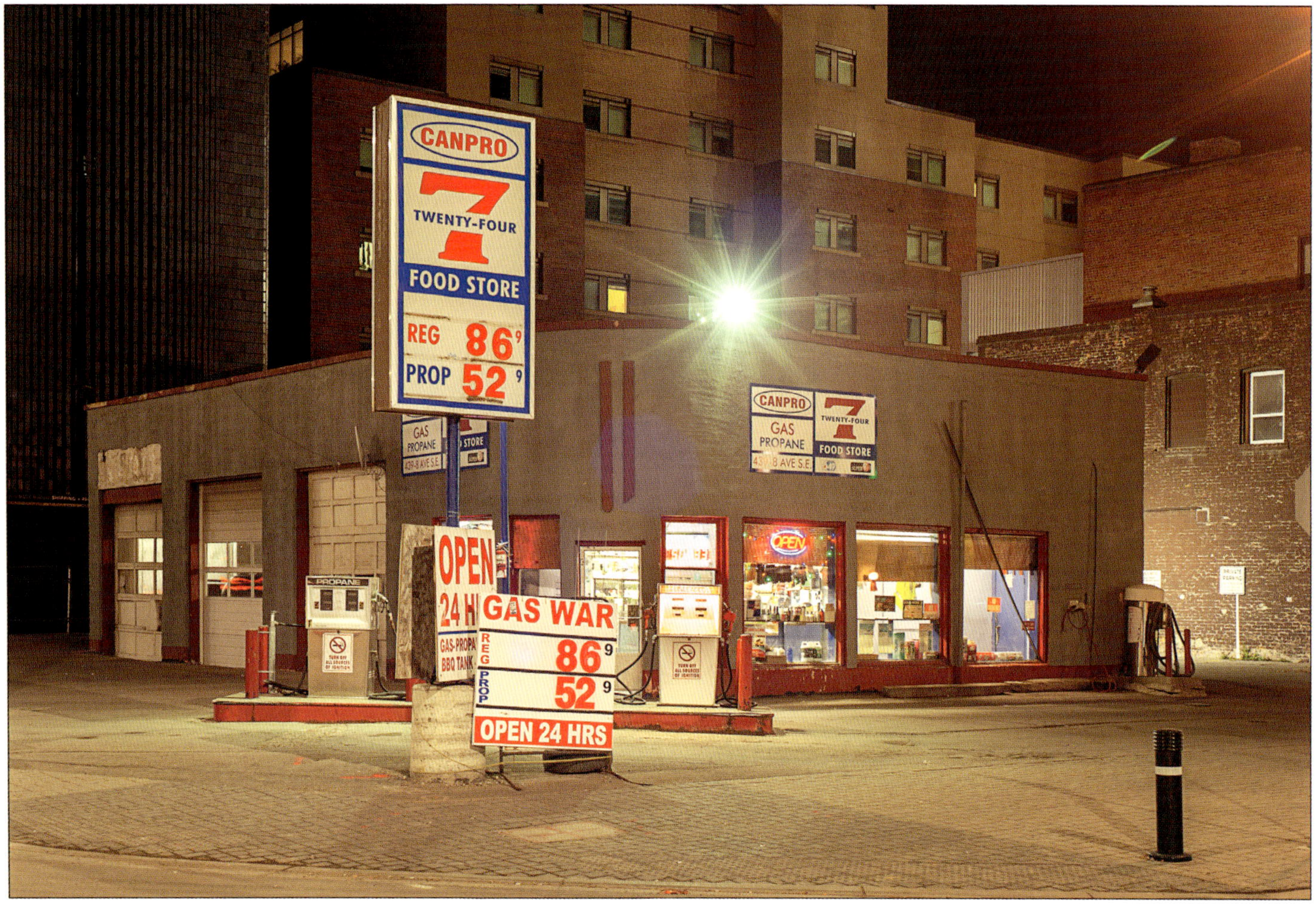
CANPRO
7
TWENTY-FOUR
FOOD STORE
REG 86 9
PROP 52 9
GAS WAR
REG 86 9
PROP 52 9
OPEN 24 HRS

Canpro, 2016

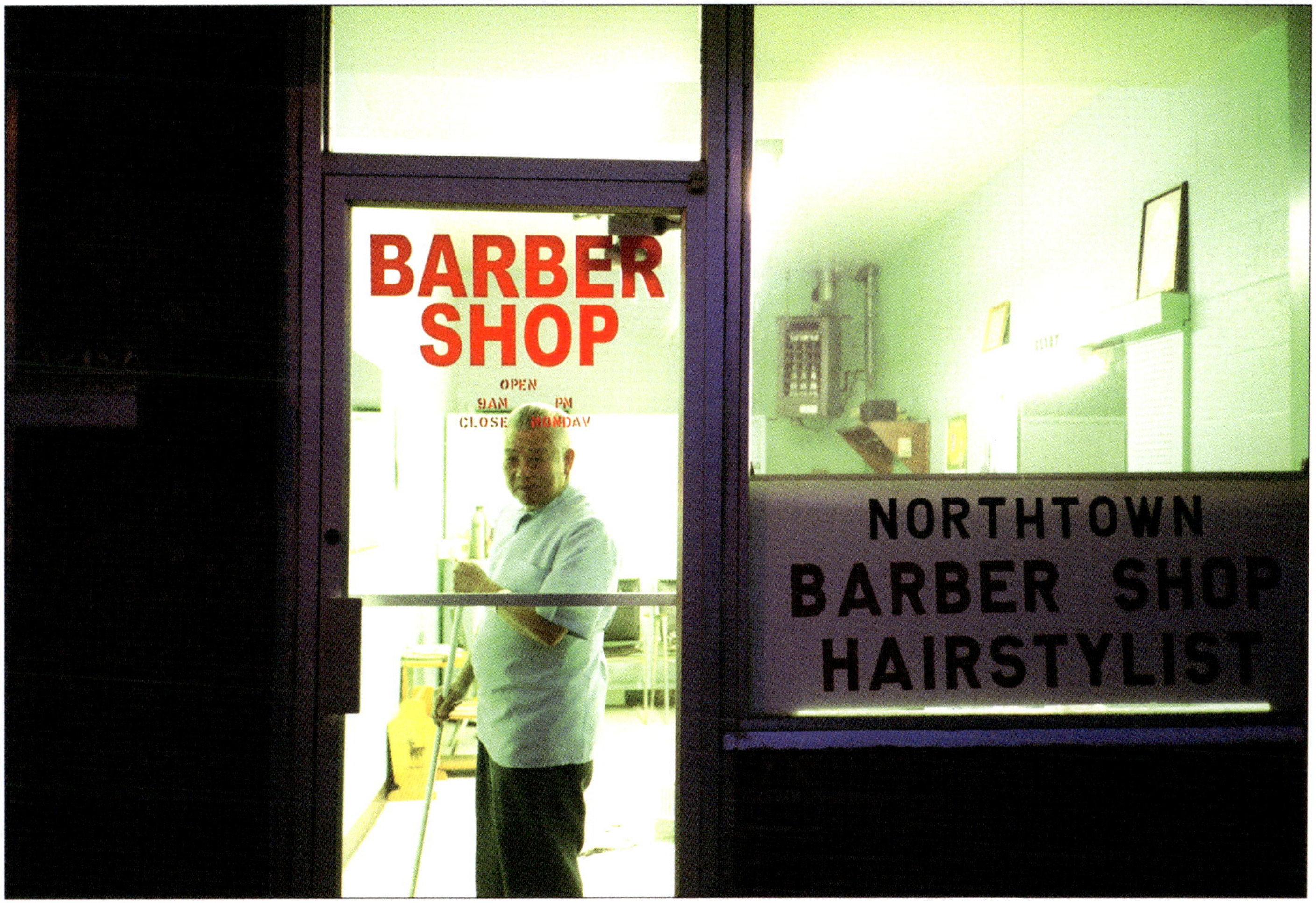

Gerry Young, Northtown Barbershop, 2002

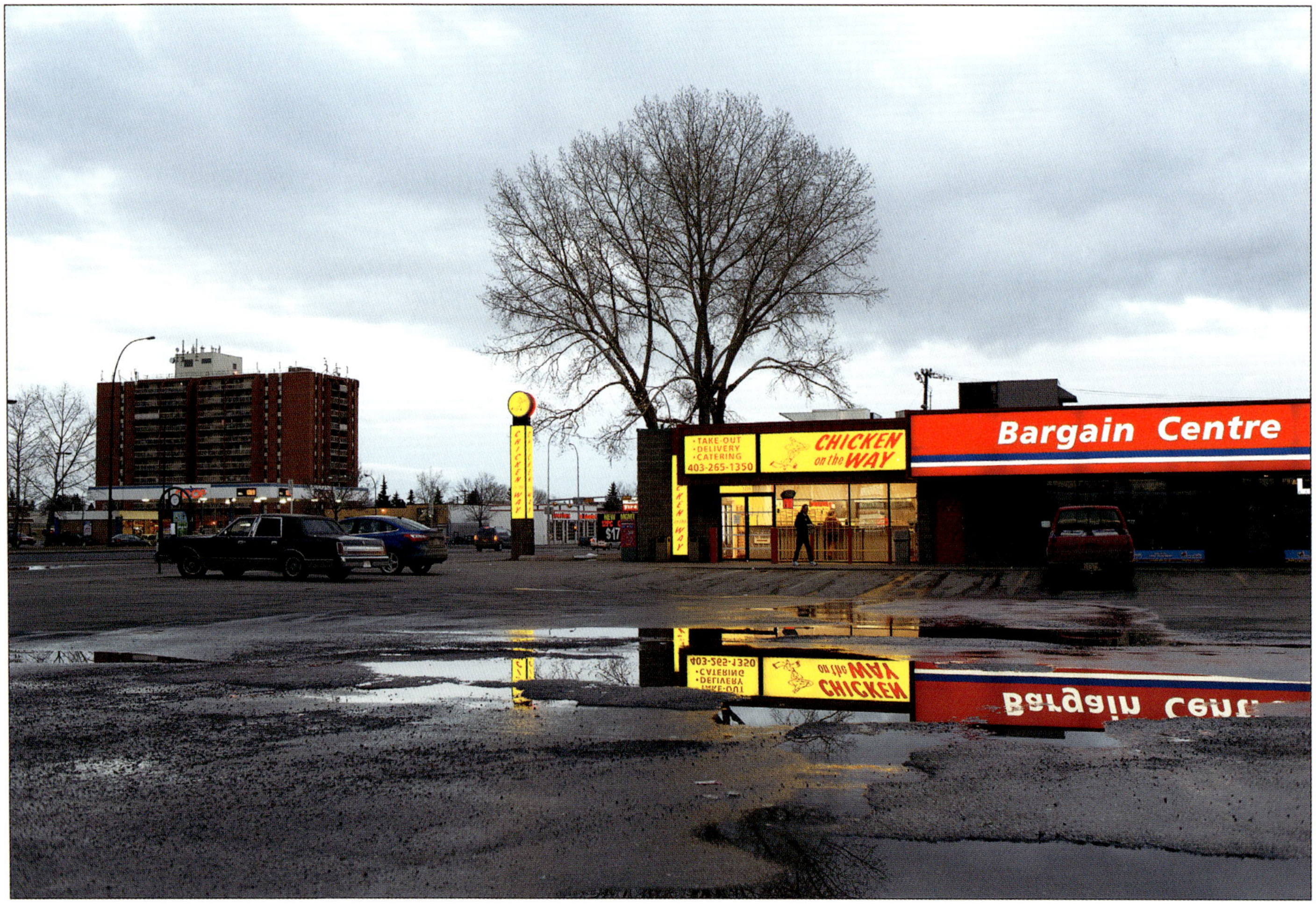

Chicken on the Way, 2012

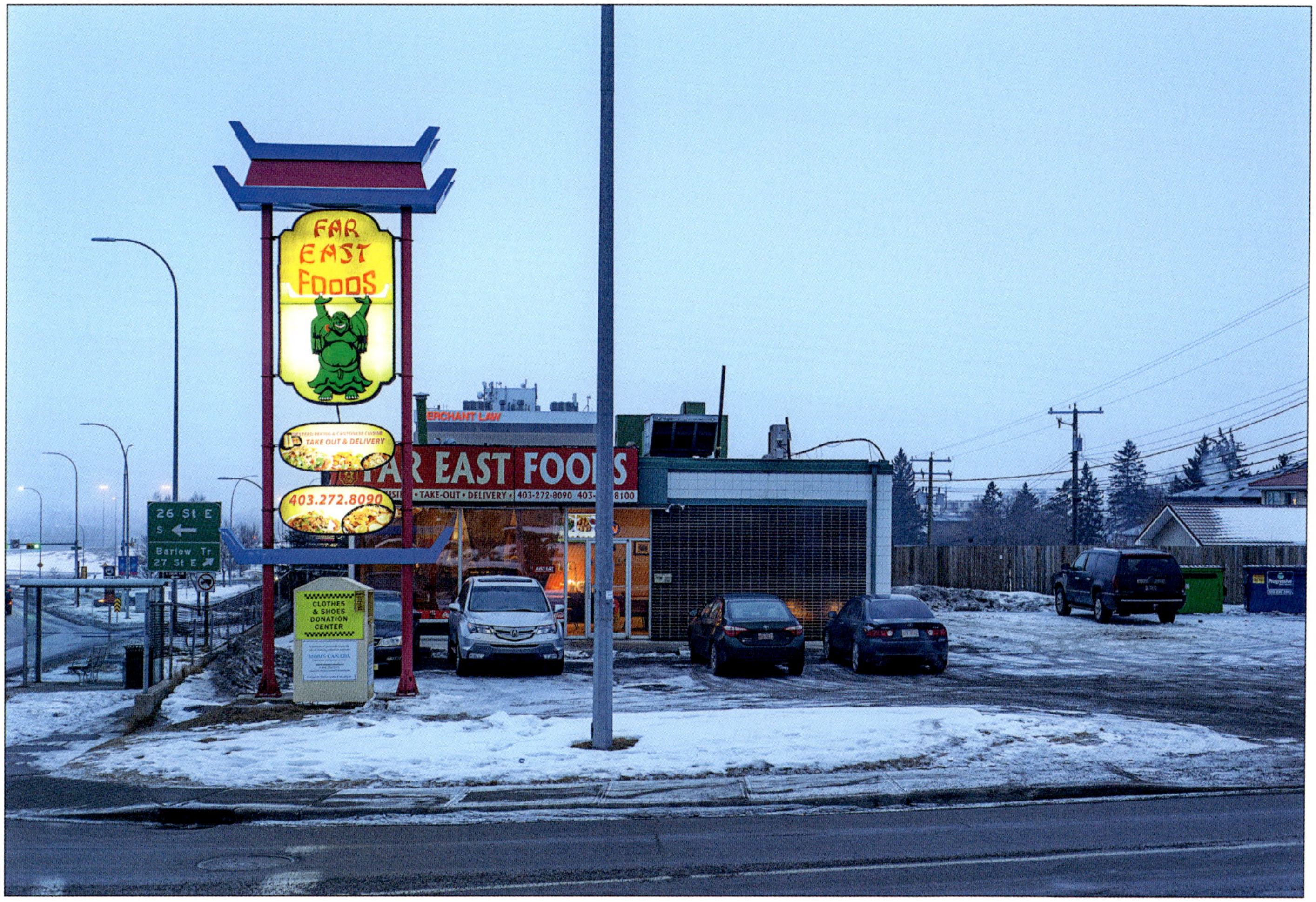

Far East Foods, 2017

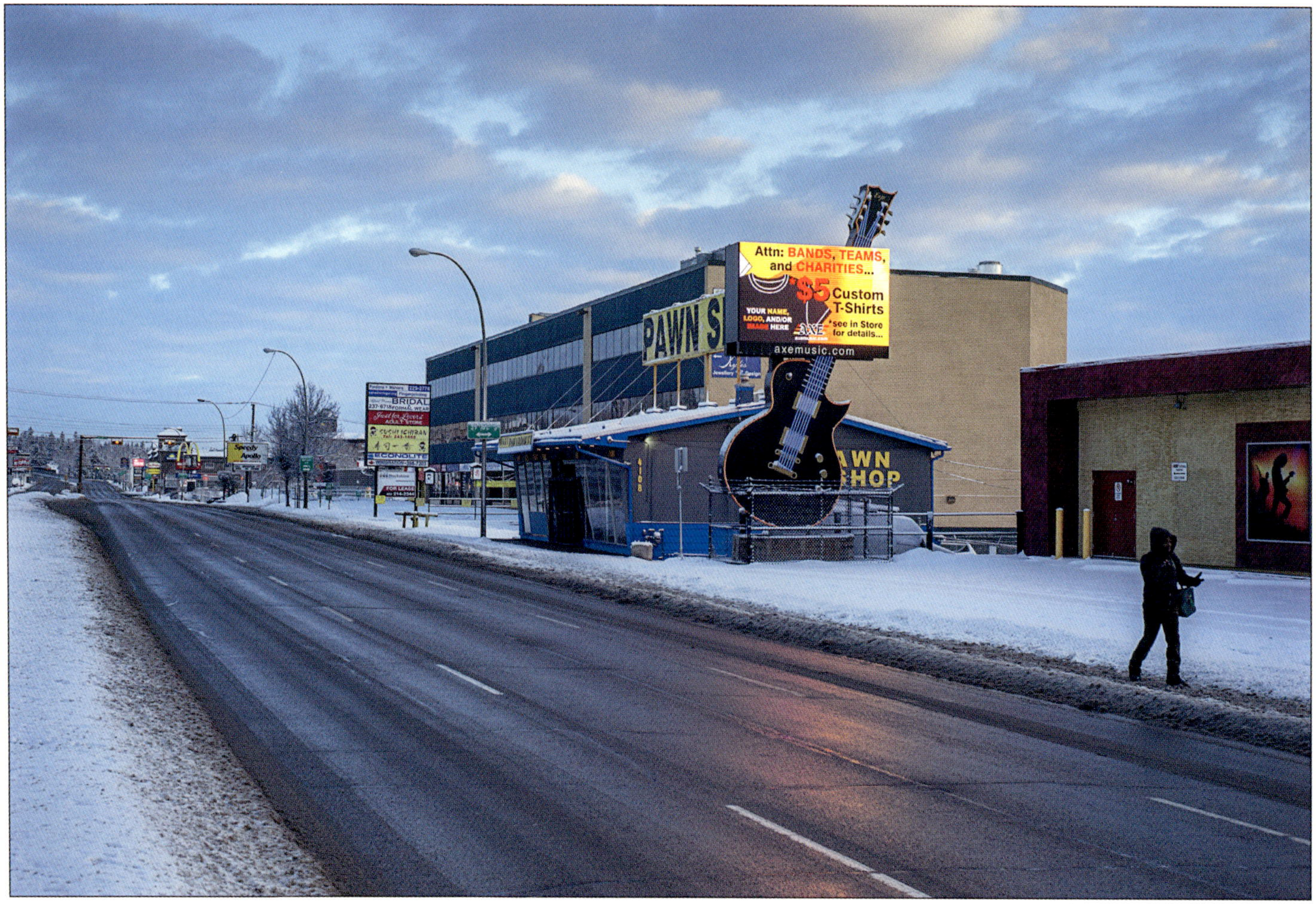

Macleod Trail, 2014

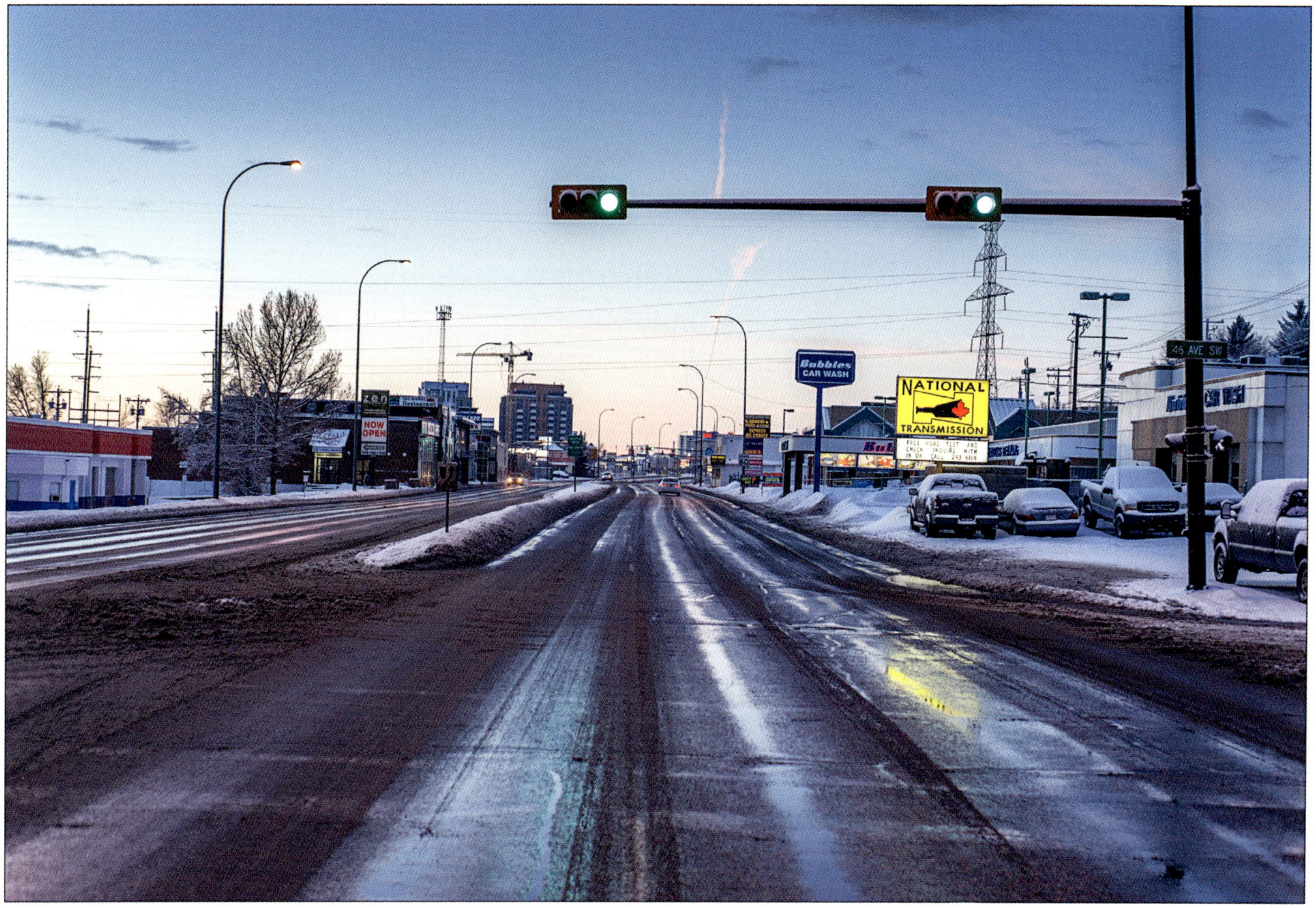

Macleod Trail, 2014

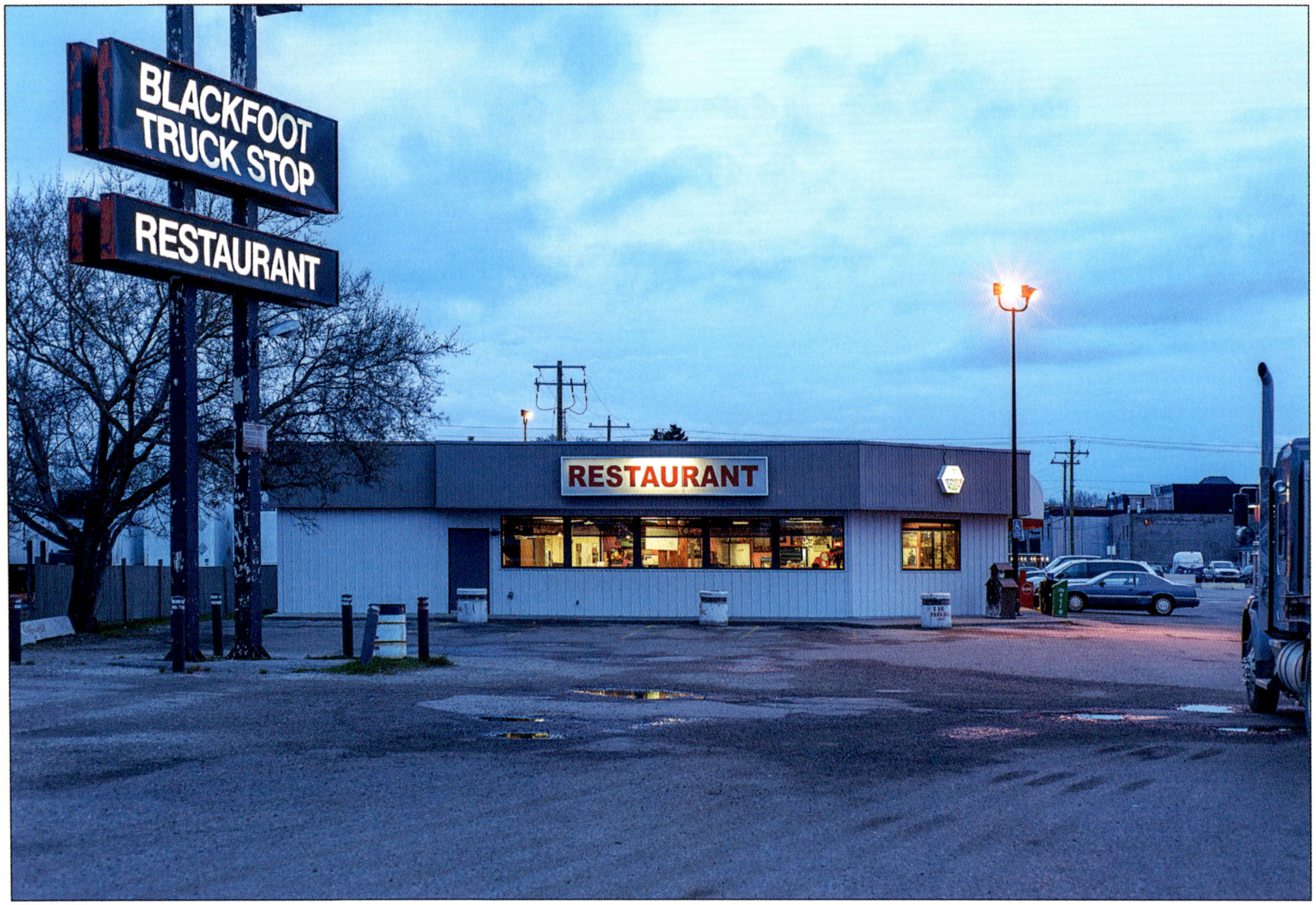

Blackfoot Truck Stop, 2014

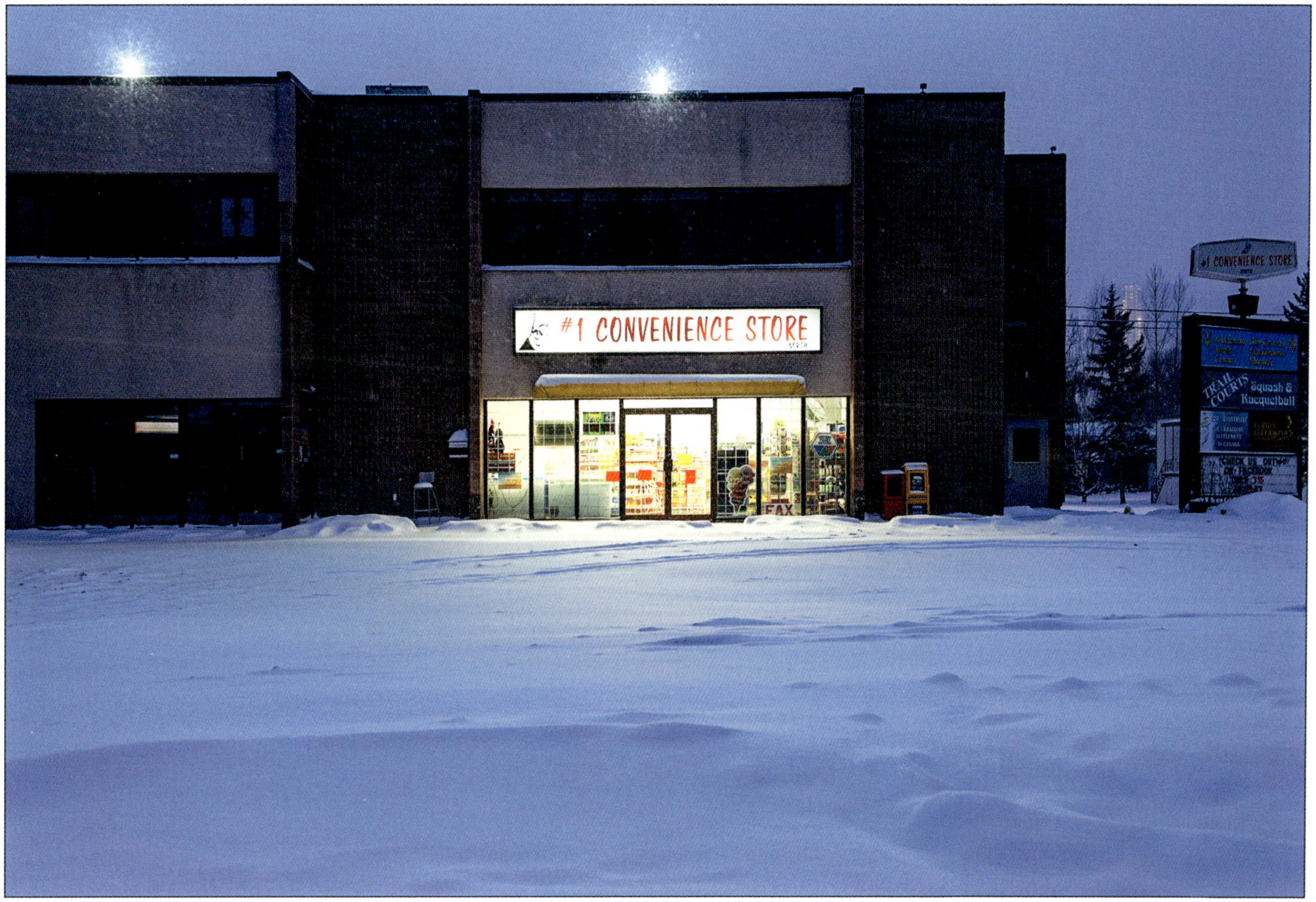

#1 Convenience Store, 2017

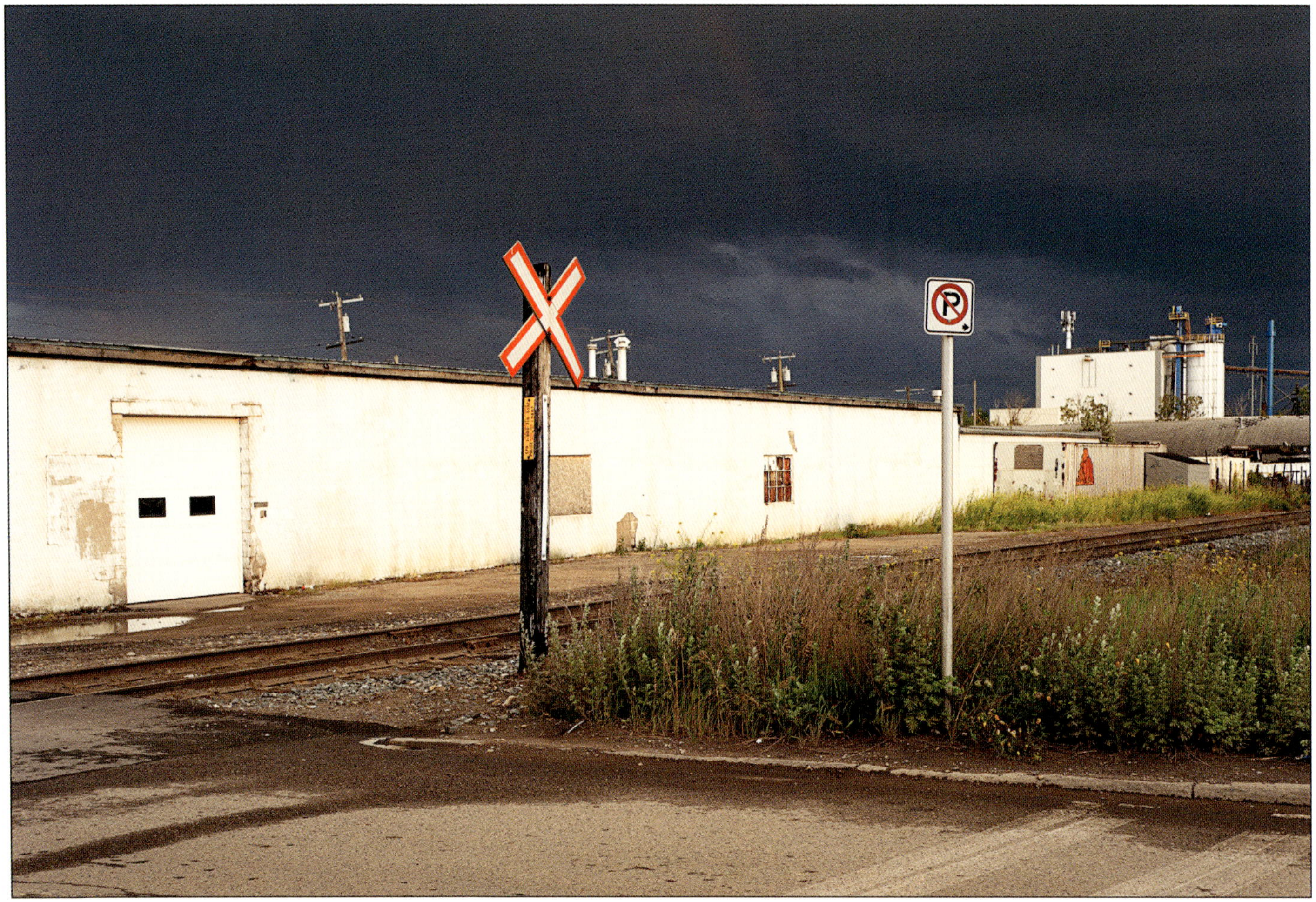

Near 1603 38 Ave SE, 2019

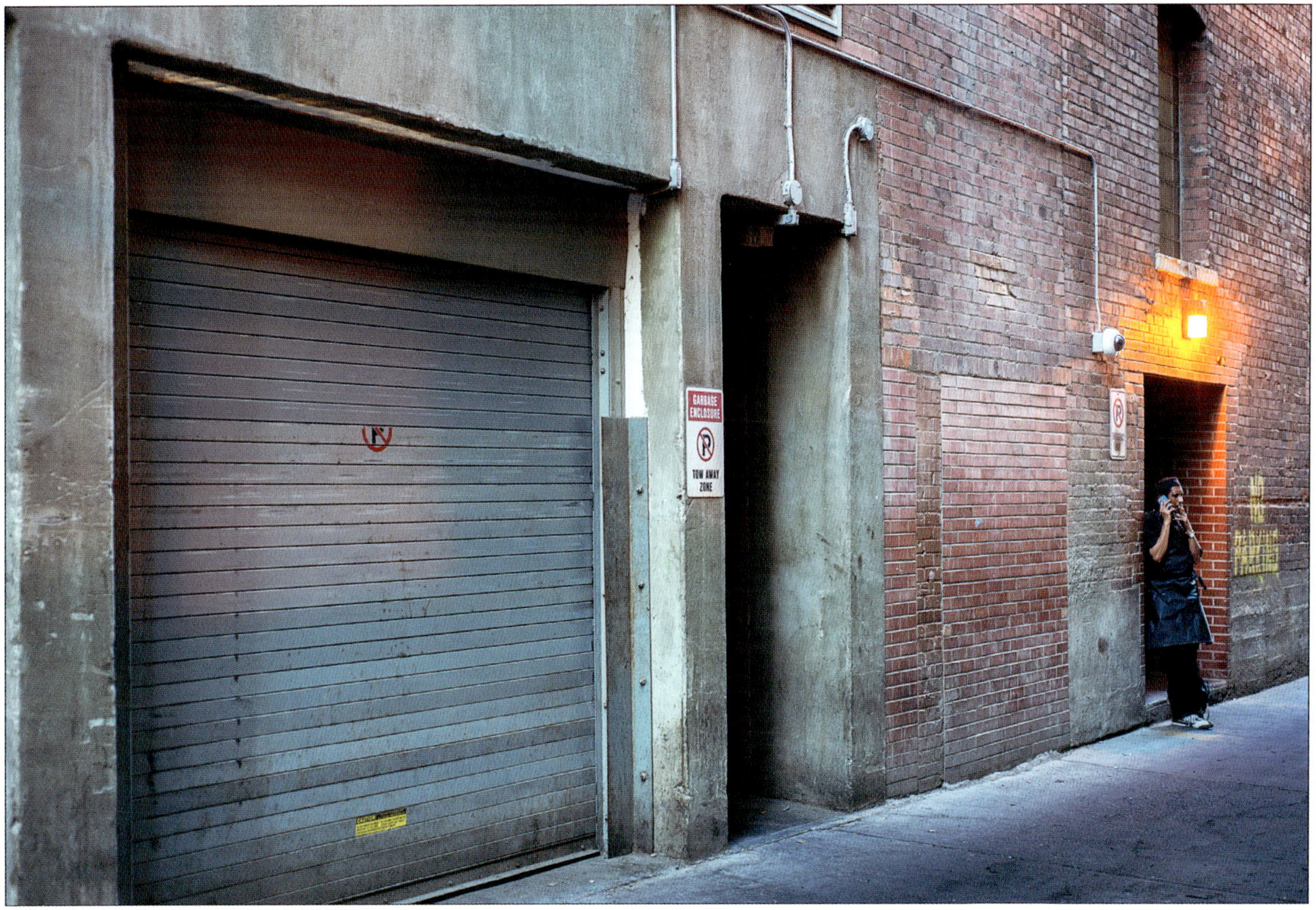

Near 7 Ave + 1 St SW, 2015

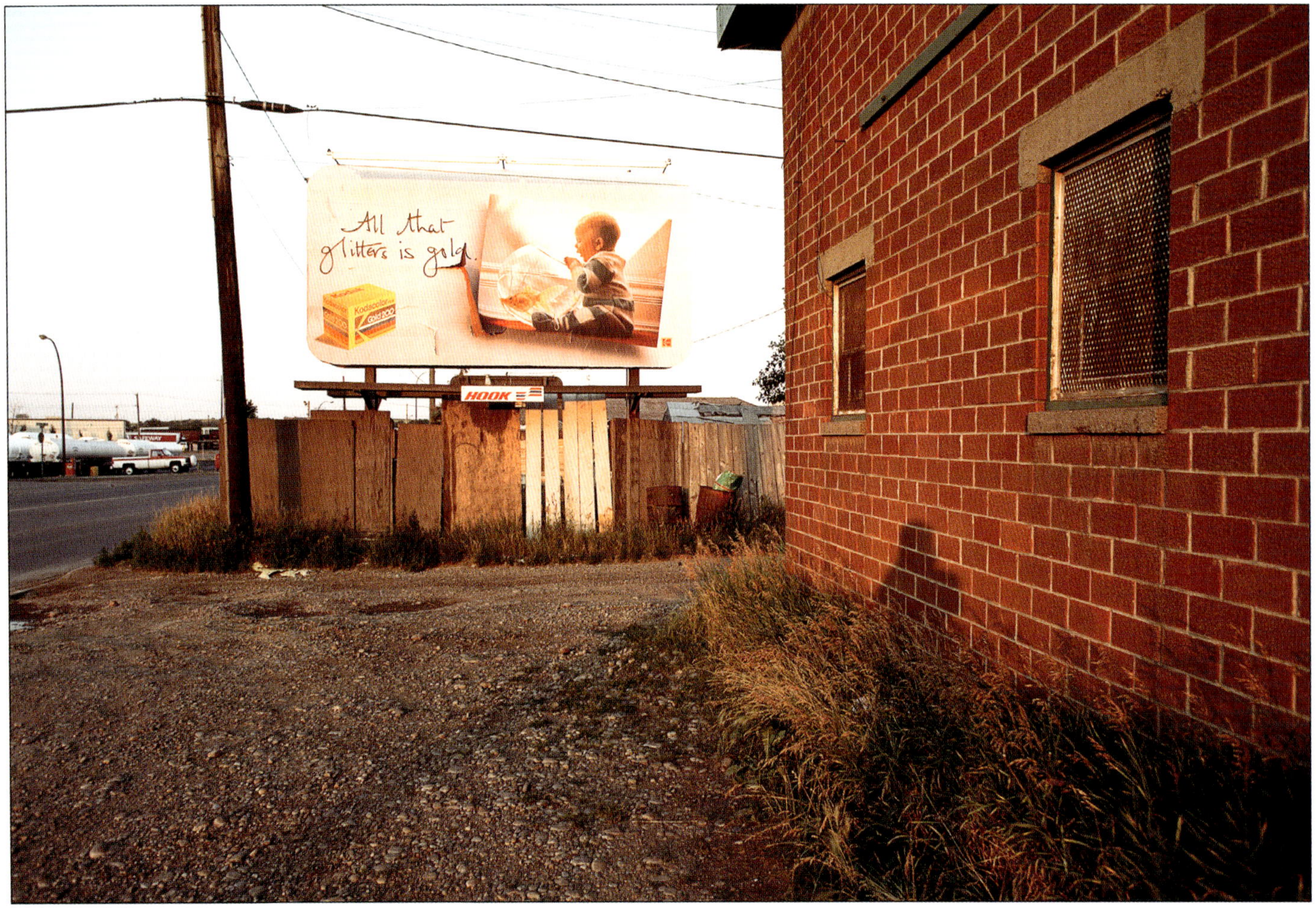

Southeast Calgary, 1989

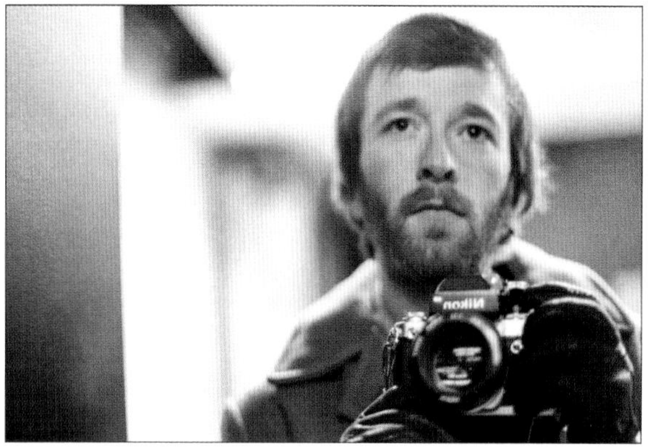

CAMERAS

Nikon, Leica and Hasselblad

GEORGE WEBBER BOOKS

Requiem, 1995, Folio Gallery
A World Within, 2005, Fifth House
People of the Blood, 2006, Fifth House
Last Call, 2010, RMB
In This Place, 2011, Frontenac House
Prairie Gothic, 2012, RMB
Badlands, 2015, RMB
Alberta Book, 2018, RMB
Saskatchewan Book, 2020, RMB
Borrowed Time, 2021, RMB

First Edition

For information on purchasing bulk quantities of this book, or to obtain media excerpts or invite the author to speak at an event, please visit rmbooks.com and select the "Contact" tab.

RMB | Rocky Mountain Books Ltd.
rmbooks.com
@rmbooks
facebook.com/rmbooks

Cataloguing data available from Library and Archives Canada
ISBN 9781771604420 (hardcover)
ISBN 9781771604437 (electronic)

Printed and bound in China

We would like to also take this opportunity to acknowledge the traditional territories upon which we live and work. In Calgary, Alberta, we acknowledge the Niitsítapi (Blackfoot) and the people of the Treaty 7 region in Southern Alberta, which includes the Siksika, the Piikuni, the Kainai, the Tsuut'ina, and the Stoney Nakoda First Nations, including Chiniki, Bearpaw, and Wesley First Nations. The City of Calgary is also home to Métis Nation of Alberta, Region III. In Victoria, British Columbia, we acknowledge the traditional territories of the Lkwungen (Esquimalt and Songhees), Malahat, Pacheedaht, Scia'new, T'Sou-ke, and W̱SÁNEĆ (Pauquachin, Tsartlip, Tsawout, Tseycum) peoples.

We acknowledge the financial support of the Government of Canada through the Canada Book Fund and the Canada Council for the Arts, and of the province of British Columbia through the British Columbia Arts Council and the Book Publishing Tax Credit.

Canada

Canada Council for the Arts | Conseil des arts du Canada

British Columbia | British Columbia Arts Council